Advance Praise for *Decolonizing Religion and Peacebuilding*

"In this brilliant, multilayered exploration of religious peacebuilding ventures in Kenya and the Philippines, Omer employs decolonial, queer, and feminist theories to expose and critique the religious peacebuilding industry that often reifies colonial legacies that undermine just peacebuilding efforts. She skillfully challenges facile and uncritical acceptance of 'purity' tendencies within decolonial theory and what she calls the 'harmony business' of religious peacebuilding, both of which hinder rather than enhance just peacebuilding efforts. Readers are left with a fresh understanding of how embracing complexity and contradiction can inspire creative and generative possibilities for just futures that are otherwise unimaginable when trapped within hermetically sealed epistemologies. Decolonial theorists and religious peacebuilders alike will be transformed and inspired by Omer's astute, timely, and innovative contribution."
—**Diane L. Moore**, Harvard Divinity School

"*Decolonizing Religion and Peacebuilding* offers an irreplaceable gift to the scholarship and practice of building peace, and to people motivated by faith who seek the transformation of harm and violence. The gift is this: to understand that lasting change starts with honest, critical reflection. This type of engaged scholarship requires the courage to unravel the paradoxical challenge of how to appreciate the deep commitment of the faith-inspired practitioner navigating difficult settings of violence while unveiling the ubiquitous overlay of historic and contemporary patterns of religious colonial patterns that perpetuate dehumanization. With extensive interviews and extraordinary mastery of interdisciplinary literature, Atalia Omer has surfaced the deep conversation our fields of peacebuilding and religious studies have long needed."
—**John Paul Lederach**, Professor Emeritus, University of Notre Dame

STUDIES IN STRATEGIC PEACEBUILDING

Series Editors
R. Scott Appleby, John Paul Lederach, and Daniel Philpott
The Joan B. Kroc Institute for International Peace Studies
University of Notre Dame

STRATEGIES OF PEACE
Edited by Daniel Philpott and Gerard F. Powers

UNIONISTS, LOYALISTS, AND CONFLICT TRANSFORMATION IN NORTHERN IRELAND
Lee A. Smithey

JUST AND UNJUST PEACE
An Ethic of Political Reconciliation
Daniel Philpott

COUNTING CIVILIAN CASUALTIES
An Introduction to Recording and Estimating Nonmilitary Deaths in Conflict
Edited by Taylor B. Seybolt, Jay D. Aronson, and Baruch Fischhoff

RESTORATIVE JUSTICE, RECONCILIATION, AND PEACEBUILDING
Edited by Jennifer J. Llewellyn and Daniel Philpott

QUALITY PEACE
Peacebuilding, Victory and World Order
Peter Wallensteen

THE PEACE CONTINUUM
What It Is and How to Study It
Christian Davenport, Erik Melander, and Patrick M. Regan

WHEN POLITICAL TRANSITIONS WORK
Reconciliation as Interdependence
Fanie Du Toit

EVERYDAY PEACE
How So-called Ordinary People Can Disrupt Violent Conflict
Roger Mac Ginty

WHERE THE EVIDENCE LEADS
A Realistic Strategy for Peace and Human Security
Robert C. Johansen

DECOLONIZING RELIGION AND PEACEBUILDING
Atalia Omer

Decolonizing Religion and Peacebuilding

ATALIA OMER

OXFORD
UNIVERSITY PRESS

Oxford University Press is a department of the University of Oxford. It furthers the University's objective of excellence in research, scholarship, and education by publishing worldwide. Oxford is a registered trade mark of Oxford University Press in the UK and certain other countries.

Published in the United States of America by Oxford University Press
198 Madison Avenue, New York, NY 10016, United States of America.

© Oxford University Press 2023

All rights reserved. No part of this publication may be reproduced, stored in a retrieval system, or transmitted, in any form or by any means, without the prior permission in writing of Oxford University Press, or as expressly permitted by law, by license, or under terms agreed with the appropriate reproduction rights organization. Inquiries concerning reproduction outside the scope of the above should be sent to the Rights Department, Oxford University Press, at the address above.

You must not circulate this work in any other form
and you must impose this same condition on any acquirer.

CIP data is on file at the Library of Congress

ISBN 978-0-19-768302-6 (pbk.)
ISBN 978-0-19-768301-9 (hbk.)

DOI: 10.1093/oso/9780197683019.001.0001

Paperback printed by Marquis Book Printing, Canada
Hardback printed by Bridgeport National Bindery, Inc., United States of America

For Jason

Contents

Acknowledgments	ix
Abbreviations and Frequently Used Non-English Words	xi

"What Works?" Is Not A Good Enough Question	1
Asking Other Questions	1
"We Cannot Eat Peace"	7
Methodology	12
Outline	17
1. Historical Background and Colonial Afterlives	21
Multiple Conflict Narratives	21
Slicing Up the Land	26
Soul Searching	30
Land and Insurgency	39
New Mindanaoan Scripts?	45
Who Are the Scribes of Peace?	50
2. "Sisyphean" Governance	53
What Is Neoliberalism?	53
"Governance" from the Neoliberal Textbook	55
Interreligious Peace Governance	58
Benchmarking	70
Double Closure	73
Fitting into "Harmony"	76
Sisyphean Persistence	79
Colonized Moral Imagination	80
Hopelessness	82
"The Rationality through Which Capitalism Finally Swallows Humanity"	84
3. Doing Religion	87
An Integrated Approach to Religion, Peace, and Development	87
Harnessing Religion Better	94
"Religiocrats"	98
Vocational Virtuosos	111
Local Access Actors	119

4. Survival Piety: A Preferential Option for the Poor? — 129
- Poverty Isn't an Excuse — 129
- Religion within the Neoliberal Frame — 134
- Interfaith Income-Generating Activities — 137
- Surviving around the Tana River — 149
- A Multidirectional Street — 152
- The Limits of "Partnership" — 153

5. Religion and "Soft" Security: Countermessaging and Surveillance — 163
- Containing "Bad" Religion — 163
- "Go Back to Mogadishu" — 165
- Peacebuilding Co-opted — 171
- Let Me Teach You to Be My Eyes and Ears — 173
- Countermessengers on the Battleground — 178

6. Religious Resiliency and "Soft" Security — 193
- Sheikh Google — 193
- Offline/Online Youths Renarrating Peace — 195
- Experiential Humanization — 202
- Interfaith Modeling/Performance of Peace — 210

7. Unrevolutionary Decolonial Love: The Spirituality of Just "Getting Along" — 221
- Peace Islands — 221
- Spiritualized Practice — 225
- Opening from the Underside — 233
- Nonrevolutionary Love — 241

8. Does Justice Have Anything to Do with Religion and the Practice of Peace? — 245
- Cohering the Peace — 245
- Disrupting the Peace — 251
- Decolonial Demystification — 254
- Decolonial Paralysis? — 261
- Existence, Not Resistance — 265
- Resistance as Cultural Lifelines — 269
- Thin, Not Queer, Religion — 278

Index — 283

Acknowledgments

Decolonizing Religion and Peacebuilding could not have come into being without the Andrew Carnegie Fellowship I was awarded in 2017. I am also thankful for Dean R. Scott Appleby, Ebrahim Moosa, Ann Mische, and the Keough School's Goal 16 Grant, which launched my pilot research in Mindanao, and to the Kroc Institute for International Peace Studies for always providing institutional support and for Dr. Emily Gravett's careful and patient editing assistance. The generosity of spirit and time of my many interlocutors in the Philippines and Kenya, however, made this book a reality. I am in debt especially to Myla Leguro, Deng Giguiento (aka Ate Deng), Edwin Antipuesto, Ibrahim Magara, Orson Sargado, John Ashworth, Alexandra Medina, Angel Calvo, Shamsia Ramadhan, Lakan Sumulong, Aaron Chasey, Nell Bolton, Rhea Silvosa, Abelardo 'Abel' A. Moya, Christine Vertucci, Jeanette Birondo-Goddard, Frederick Goddard, and Grace Nono. I published partial aspects and early versions of the research in a few other venues. They include "Religion and the Study of Peace: Practice without Reflection," *Religions* 12, no. 12 (2021): 1069, https://doi.org/10.3390/rel12121069; "Decolonizing Religion and the Practice of Peace: Two Case Studies from the Postcolonial World," *Critical Research on Religion* 30, no. 3 (2020): 273–96; "The Intersectional Turn: Theories and Practices for Understanding Religion and Peace," *Blackwell Companion to Religion and Peace*, edited by Jolyon Mitchell, Suzanna R. Millar, Francesca Po, and Martyn Percy (Oxford: Wiley Blackwell, 2022), 49–62; "Domestic Religion: Why Interreligious Dialogue of Action for the Reduction of Child Marriage in the Coast of Kenya Conserves Rather Than Disrupts Power," in *A Requiem for Peacebuilding?*, edited by Tom Sauer, Jorg Kustermans, and Barbara Segaert, Rethinking Peace and Conflict Studies (London: Palgrave, 2020), 59–94; and "Interreligious Action as a Driver for Social Cohesion and Development" (Baltimore, MD: Catholic Relief Services Press, 2017), 1–20.

Decolonizing Religion and Peacebuilding intervenes in multiple disciplinary and practitioner conversations. It highlights the need to reassess and reimagine what religion and peace praxis means for studying religion (at the decolonial turn) and vice versa. I therefore am particularly thankful to David

McBride, senior editor at Oxford University Press, for knowing precisely how to navigate my manuscript across disciplinary silos and other gatekeepers. The brilliant and constructive feedback I received from the anonymous readers has also been a special gift. Likewise, I cherish the enthusiastic and affirming reactions I received from John Paul Lederach, who pushed me to clarify some essential themes that surface in the book. I am also in debt to the profound challenges Professor Cecelia Lynch offered throughout the writing process. Throughout the research and writing process, my friendship and intellectual work with Diane L. Moore, Hilary Rantisi, and Reem Atassi have sustained me. Finally, I would not have been able to write this book without the support of my life partner, Jason A. Springs, who took care of our babies during my repeated trips to the Philippines and Kenya. Beyond that, of course, Jason offered his intellectual contributions to sharpen my argument further. I am thankful to him and our beautiful children, Yonatan (Yoni) and (Pneiʼel) Alois Omer-Springs, for their patience and love.

Abbreviations and Frequently Used Non-English Words

ARMM	Autonomous Region in Muslim Mindanao
BARMM	Bangsamoro Autonomous Region in Muslim Mindanao
BOL	Bangsamoro Organic Law
BRAVE	Building Resilience Against Violent Extremism
CBCP	Catholic Bishops' Conference of the Philippines
CICC	Coast Interfaith Council of Clerics, Kenya
CPP-NPA	Communist Party of the Philippines and New People's Army
CRAVE	Community Resilience Against Violent Extremism
CRS	Catholic Relief Services
EAI	Equal Access International
IMAN	Integrated Mindanao Association of Natives
IPs	Indigenous peoples
IRC	Interreligious Council, Kenya
IRD	interreligious dialogue
IRD/A	interreligious dialogue for action
KAICIID	King Abdullah bin Abdulaziz International Center for Interreligious and Intercultural Dialogue
MILF	Moro Islamic Liberation Front
MNLF	Moro National Liberation Front
MTYC	Mindanao Tri-People Youth Core
NGO	nongovernmental organization
PaRD	International Partnership in Religion and Sustainable Development
PAZ	Peace Advocates of Zamboanga
P/CVE	Preventing and Countering Violent Extremism
PTVE	preventing and transforming violent extremism
RfP	Religions for Peace
SDGs	UN's Sustainable Development Goals
3Bs	Binding, Bonding, and Bridging
TRL	traditional religious leader
UNDP	UN Development Program
UNYPAD	United Youth for Peace and Development in the Philippines
URI	United Religions Initiative
USAID	U.S. Agency for International Development

"What Works?" Is Not A Good Enough Question

Asking Other Questions

The conversations among scholars intersecting with policy circles and networks around the topic of the global engagement with religion celebrate the plurality of religious and cultural traditions to the extent that they prove useful for the promotion of peace and development. But if this is all that scholarship on religion and peace can do, there is a problem. When scholarship only responds to the question "What works?," it simply surrenders itself to the present. Delimiting the scholarly horizons to the demands and constraints of the present prevents a criticality without which new horizons cannot be imagined. Religion's occasional usefulness in peacebuilding does not necessarily mean justice-oriented outcomes. The praxis of religion and peace does not entail decolonial justice. It certainly does not disrupt global hegemonic constellations. On the contrary, a thin discourse concerning pluralism, or what I call "the harmony business," has been integral to western colonial discourse since the late nineteenth century. Rather than a prophetic irruption, religion and the practice of peace constitute a bureaucratic tool. Thus, a decolonial critique is a necessary step in demystifying the scaffolding of the harmony business that posits interreligious understanding as an instrument of peace and security and exposing it as the latest iteration of religion's long colonial history.[1] An intersectionality that challenges the extraction of religion from the histories of racialization and its construction as a bounded and distinct sector is what I bring to the analysis of religion and the practices of peace. I build here on the field-shaping work of Cecelia

---

[1] For a now-classic articulation of the consolidation of religious pluralism as a colonial discourse, see Tomoko Masuzawa, *The Invention of World Religions: Or, How European Universalism Was Preserved in the Language of Pluralism* (Chicago: University of Chicago Press, 2005). For an account that illuminates the ethical precarity and internal struggles shaping decisions in the context of western Christian empire, see Cecelia Lynch, *Wrestling with God: Ethical Precarity in Christianity and International Relations* (Cambridge: Cambridge University Press, 2020).

Lynch, whose scholarship traced how the "discovery" of religion in international relations entailed religion's neoliberalization and securitization in the service of the neocolonial agenda.[2]

However, I am also interested in why such an abyss exists between people's efforts to transform their lives on the ground through interreligious and intercommunal peacebuilding and development activities and the strong critique of religion's supporting role to empire that animates decolonial theory and the critical genealogical study of religion. During my fieldwork, I met people whose experiences of violence and marginality relate, historically, to colonial legacies and who understood their promotion of peace in terms of religious motivations and their peace agency as a form of spiritual practice. But these people are absent from decolonial theory, including decolonial feminist liberation theology. Sometimes it seems that only those on board with feminist, intersectional, and decolonial scholarship and who are thus "woke" enough to populate the halls of the World Social Forum (first convened in Porto Alegre, Brazil, in 2001, an annual global gathering of civil society and grassroots organizations) can, in effect, count as transformational and perhaps prophetic religious actors, while everyone else is somehow suspended in a "colonial stupor." Accordingly, only the "enlightened" possessors of critical political consciousness are counted as "transformational" or prophetic in articulating their theology or religiosity in emancipatory, polydoxic, feminist, anticapitalist, intercultural, and antiracist indigenous registers.

"Unwoke" religiosity can also be agentic and transformational in people's lived realities, for their survival and for their ability to rescript conflict narratives. Hence, a contrast between woke religiosity and the empirical realities of unwoke but transformative practice is one of the points I will be highlighting in this book, together with my interlocutors in the Philippines and Kenya. Religion (and culture) enters the resilience discourse as a "resource" to enhance its effectiveness by infusing resiliency with spiritual strength.[3] Doing so reduces such strength to utilitarian objectives and forecloses hermeneutical horizons. Here, critics are right on target with their

---

[2] See Cecelia Lynch, "Religious Communities and Possibilities for Justpeace" in *The Oxford Handbook of Religion, Conflict, and Peacebuilding*, ed. Atalia Omer, R. Scott Appleby, and David Little (New York: Oxford University Press, 2015), 597–612.

[3] For an effective analysis of the implications of the deployment of resiliency, see John Patrick Leary, "Keywords for the Age of Austerity 19: Resilience," Keywords: The New Language of Capitalism, June 23, 2015, https://keywordsforcapitalism.com/2015/06/23/keywords-for-the-age-of-austerity-19-resilience/; see also Siobhan McDonnell, "Other Dark Sides of Resilience: Politics and Power in Community-Based Efforts to Strengthen Resilience," *Anthropological Forum* 30, nos. 1–2 (2020): 55–72, https://doi.org/10.1080/00664677.2019.1647828.

analysis of religion's enduring participation in hegemony and coloniality, which decolonial theory traces back to 1492. But the decolonial critique also occludes other ways of comprehending the spiritualization of survival and the practices of ethical and social plurality as people experience them on the ground.

This is a book about interrelated paradoxes and contradictions. The first is that organic (from the grassroots) intercommunal dialogue efforts, institutionalized (from the top down) programming, and funded international and national NGO initiatives aimed at shaping interreligious peacebuilding projects and futures are **both empowering and disempowering**. They are empirically empowering as a pathway for negotiating plurality or the possibility of coexistence amid or in the aftermath of violent intercommunal divisions, conditions of marginalization, and fatalistic despair. Such intercommunal and interreligious projects are demonstrably effective in improving scores on quality-of-life metrics, which refer to enhancing people's capacity (or their "resilience," as this capacity is often termed) to survive materially and to be able to feed their families. Interreligious peacebuilding practices and intercommunal and interfaith dialoguing are spiritually nourishing and generative of new scripts of the "common good" as a space of intercommunal cooperation, shaped through ethics of plurality. This ethics, constituted through the meaningful relationships that form among the people, exceeds the gaze of decolonial critique. My point is grappling with the places where the "critical gaze" collapses under the burden of its privilege. A purist critique of (neo)colonial dynamics often obscures people's agency in rewriting hate into neighborliness and intercommunal peace and how this rewriting also constitutes a spiritual reclaiming of a religious and communal sense of authenticity.

One of the stories I capture in this book is how the paradigm of the prophetic exemplar is no longer a function of religious virtuosity or religious *knowing* in the sense of a deep and layered mastery of traditions of interpretations over historical epochs. Instead, it has transformed into generic trainings and workshops that rely on easy-to-digest packaging of religious traditions to enhance the *doing* of religion, by which I mean putting religion to work to promote various objectives, such as reducing the rate of child marriages in Kenya. As a result, the prophetic has turned into what I call the "prophetic lite," now embodied by an actor who is neither iconoclastic nor disruptive but rather useful and conforming (sometimes to survive) to a sphere of NGO-ized deployment of religion as a peacebuilding technology.

This book exposes, therefore, another contradiction: the seed of peace's theory of change carries within it an undoing of its pretenses to blossom and yield entire fields or, in more technocratic language, to scale up its horizontal relationship-building to a broad sociopolitical transformation. This is where empowerment translates into disempowerment.

Rather than a small-scale version or a seed, intercommunal and interreligious peacebuilding praxis elides visions of democracy as a set of values, virtues, and practices. The latter connotes something different than merely the depoliticizing task of navigating plurality as a form of conflict management. The "seed of peace" logic is, therefore, segregationist as it pivots on building networks of cross-communal cooperation (capital, including religious, to be moved around) for shared problem-solving among bounded communities. A focus on enhancing cooperation through investment in intercommunal mechanisms for conflict management is *not* the same as a democratic and pluralistic politics. Hence, the more a focus on religion and the practices of peace reinscribes and reifies religious and communal boundaries, the less religion can function prophetically to disrupt communal scripts and promote justice over entrenching the status quo. This constitutes an ironic finding that emerges from my study: **the more religion is integrated into peace and development policymaking, the less politically emancipatory it becomes.**

This irony leads me to yet another contradiction I wrestle with in these pages. Integrating more religion into peace and development practices, or *doing religion,* **is not necessarily indicative of** *knowing religion* as a discursive tradition or as a living form of historical arguments and interpretations. *Doing* religion thrives on hermeneutical or interpretive closures (discourses of authenticity) and on the assumption that religious traditions can be manualized. Indeed, the "discovery" of religion as a political force shuttered the secularist myopias undergirding reigning paradigms in international relations. Consequently, policy designs integrated "more religion," often framed through the language of enhancing religious literacy. This *doing* does not necessarily denote more substantive *knowing*. Instead, it signals a facility with what presents itself as useful knowledge and actors/partners: how to harness and mobilize such (implementing) actors/partners while containing and downplaying other, less favorable expressions. Hence, *doing* religion is ironically not indicative of *knowing* religion; likewise, *being* religious can merely be a function of communal belonging. Therefore, communal belonging is defined by religious belonging and vice versa; "being Muslim" or "being Christian" is a communal marker and, thus, a predetermined script into which all individual narratives must be assimilated. This closure in a predetermined script disenfranchises individuals' agency in writing their own stories and expanding the political imagination of peace beyond a segregationist approach to managing plurality. This diminishment of political horizons denotes a narrowing of the religious imagination. Here is another irony: **the more there is a programmatic investment in religion as a peace mechanism for managing divided societies, the more the capacity of each communal actor to disrupt their ascribed religious and communal scripts diminishes.** Likewise, a greater top-level interest in the religious dimensions of all facets of global policy and the consolidation of institutions, research centers, and interfaith bodies produced new forms of religious authority, speaking in the name of religion in general but actually in none at all. Such a generic investment in religion also produced an international class of religion experts, or "religiocrats," whose expertise or religious literacy is functionalist. Accordingly, religiocrats are more concerned with what religion does and can do in the world than with what it could do, its histories of interpretations, and its horizons of innovation.

However, the deployment of interreligious peace technologies that I trace in this book is not only utilitarian. It is also spiritual, depending on one's positionality. Therefore, my book is also finally one about the tension between the critique of ongoing colonial legacies and the people for whom partaking in interreligious and intercommunal efforts for survival and for overcoming hate of the "other" is both a spiritual practice and a path for material nourishment and survival. Even if more religion, once again, denotes less critical religious hermeneutics, fewer interpretive openings, and less disruptive or prophetic or feminist and/or intersectional political rescripting, these practices nevertheless exceed the critical gaze and its self-reflexive narrative of hegemony and emancipatory imaginations. I navigated these many tensions, contradictions, and paradoxes during my research for this book on interreligious peacebuilding praxis in the Global South, and specifically in Kenya and the Philippines.

Critically, the concept of the "Global South" is one I deploy heuristically, but with an understanding that, in the words of Leon Moosavi, it "is a drastically simplified notion which mimics the crude geographical categorization that colonialism was built upon."[4] Indeed, my analysis of religion and the practices of peace illuminates what Boaventura de Sousa Santos identifies as

---

[4] Leon Moosavi, "The Decolonial Bandwagon and the Dangers of Intellectual Decolonisation," *International Review of Sociology* (2020) 30, no. 2: 332–54 (344), https://doi.org/10.1080/03906701.2020.1776919.

a persistent, albeit shifting, "abyssal cartography."[5] With this phrase he refers to an abyssal thinking, a hallmark of modernity, which differentiates between the colonial and normative zones, or what Frantz Fanon influentially termed the "zones of being/nonbeing."[6] The abyssal cartography denotes "a system of visible and invisible distinctions, the invisible ones being the foundations of the visible ones. The invisible distinctions are established through radical lines that divide social reality into two realms, the realm of 'this side of the line' and the realm of 'the other side of the line.'"[7] In the postcolonial moment, however, "a neat divide between the Old and New World, between the metropolitan and the colonial is over."[8] Nevertheless, abyssal lines still operate and dehumanize, echoing the old amity lines drawn in the mid-sixteenth century, which had permitted lawlessness, dispossession, liquidation, and slavery in the colonial zone.[9] A much more "messy cartography,"[10] characterized by "social apartheid"[11] within the metropolitan centers, results in "pluralistic fascism," by which Santos means a condition in which "societies are politically democratic and socially fascistic."[12] I show in this book that the consolidation of religion as a technology of peace in the Global South constitutes a pivotal mechanism that reconfigures abyssal thinking through social apartheid. I also show that this is not the whole story.

Religion, and specifically Christianity, has functioned as a colonial and postcolonial tool of domination and abyssal division. Western Christian colonialism also relied on foundational gendered metaphors of domination, which gained status as divine authority through appeals to Christianity's universalizing cosmology and gendered ontology.[13]

---

[5] Boaventura de Sousa Santos, "Beyond Abyssal Thinking: From Global Lines to Ecologies of Knowledges," *Review* (Fernand Braudel Center) 30, no. 1 (2007): 45–89 (51), https://www.jstor.org/stable/40241677.

[6] Frantz Fanon, *Black Skin, White Masks* (1952), trans. Richard Philcox (New York: Grove Press, 2008), xii. See also Lewis R. Gordon, "Through the Zone of Nonbeing: A Reading of *Black Skin, White Masks* in Celebration of Fanon's Eightieth Birthday," *C. L. R. James Journal* 11, no. 1 (2005): 1–43, http://dx.doi.org/10.5840/clrjames20051111; Sylvia Wynter, "Unsettling the Coloniality of Being/Power/Truth/Freedom: Towards the Human, after Man, Its Overrepresentation—An Argument," *CR: The New Centennial Review* 3, no. 3 (2003): 257–337, https://www.jstor.org/stable/41949874.

[7] Santos, "Beyond Abyssal Thinking," 45.

[8] Ibid., 56.

[9] Ibid., 49n10.

[10] Ibid., 57.

[11] Ibid., 59.

[12] Ibid, 61.

[13] For example, see Anne McClintock, *Imperial Leather: Race, Gender and Sexuality in the Colonial Contest* (New York: Routledge, 1995); Mayra Rivera, "En-Gendered Territory: U.S. Missionaries' Discourse in Puerto Rico (1898–1920)," in *New Horizons in Hispanic/Latino(a) Theology*, ed. Benjamín Valentín (Cleveland, OH: Pilgrim Press, 2003), 79–97.

Suspicion of the neoliberal framing of its good intentions and global care is a hallmark of the study of coloniality. Coloniality is a technical concept signifying that modernity and the ongoing colonial conditions are symbiotic with one another.[14] Accordingly, the decolonial is distinct from the postcolonial in that it recognizes that the condition of coloniality does/did not end with postcolonial political independence but rather persists in ever-changing ideological frameworks and patterns of global exploitation, violence, and co-optation. Decolonial praxis rectifies, as Santos notes, the postcolonial afterlives of dispossession, enslavement, genocide, and modernity's epistemic violence. By "epistemic violence," he, along with many other scholars seeking to decolonize research methodologies, means the ways in which knowledge production is determined by, naturalizes, and universalizes Eurocentric perspectives and experiences, drawing upon the Global South extractively for raw material. The overall upshot of epistemic violence constitutes histories of erasures, including of Indigenous knowledges.[15]

"We Cannot Eat Peace"

I approached this research curious about the operation of the religion and peace business and its real impact on the daily experiences of the people touched by interreligious and intercommunal peacebuilding practices. Often, I heard people say "We cannot eat peace." They were referring to the need to link economic incentives to peacebuilding initiatives. Deploying religion in the service of livelihood has proved effective for the agendas of such groups, and this apparent effectiveness reinforces the fact that the harmony and security business is an expression of a transmogrified colonial dynamic. Consequently, in *Decolonizing Religion and Peacebuilding*, I bring decolonial theoretical insights to interrogate religion and the practice of peace. But I also interrogate decolonial theory's distance from the empirical evidence of interreligious peacebuilding, the practitioners of which have the capacity to feed, alleviate suffering, overcome hate, transform hopelessness into hope, and imagine peaceful (even if subdued and depoliticized) scripts

[14] The concept of "coloniality" was first articulated by Aníbal Quijano in "Coloniality of Power, Eurocentrism, and Latin America," *Nepantla: Views from South* 1, no. 3 (2000): 533–80, http://muse.jhu.edu/journals/nep/summary/v001/1.3quijano.html.
[15] For a classic articulation of this point, see Linda Tuhiwai-Smith, *Decolonizing Methodologies: Research and Indigenous Peoples* (London: Zed Books, 1999).

of coexistence in multiple sites in the Global South. Therefore, deploying a decolonial lens dispels myopia through a critique of the long centuries of "accumulation by dispossession,"[16] but it also brings with it decolonial imageries and emancipatory visions.

This book thus moves beyond this critique by analyzing the disconnect between decoloniality and religious peacebuilding on the ground. I focus on peace practices that often rely on the labor of people absent from the decolonial theoretical scope. Nevertheless, they rescript their social worlds and focus on survival within enduring cultural and particular forms of violence (such as heteronormativity, patriarchy, and cultural erasures), as well as global structural forms of violence and exploitation rooted in entrenched forms of coloniality. By focusing on what is happening on the ground, I expose decolonial critics' problematic approach to religion. Embracing this dialectical challenge facilitates the development of a theoretical lens that is at once informed by on-the-ground contexts and initiatives in religious peacebuilding and also critically reflective about them because it considers how they consolidate the harmony and security business. *Decolonizing Religion and Peacebuilding* traces the horizontalization and bureaucratization of religious virtuosity as a mechanism of neoliberalism that seeks to activate people's buy-in to their own pacification through resilience. The neoliberalization of religious virtuosity leads to the consolidation of "the harmony business."

For over two years of frequent trips, I researched religion and peacebuilding practices in two locations in the Global South, the Philippines and Kenya. Both locations carry deep scars from multiple centuries of colonialism.[17] Their histories reveal religion (mainly Christianity) as imperial, hegemonic, and enduring. From one side, a decolonial approach to religion and the practice of peace demonstrates that the bureaucratization of religion, through the consolidation of extensive utilitarian global networks of engagement with religion, is merely a postsecular phase of coloniality in its neoliberal variety. The "postsecular" denotes a departure from a secularist paradigm that views religion as of little public and political relevance even if this does not also mean unsettling modernist

---

[16] David Harvey, "The 'New' Imperialism: Accumulation by Dispossession," *Socialist Register* 40 (2004): 63–87; Ramón Grosfoguel, "Decolonizing Post-colonial Studies and Paradigms of Political Economy: Transmodernity, Decolonial Thinking, and Global Coloniality," *Transmodernity: Journal of Peripheral Cultural Production of the Luso-Hispanic World* 1 (2011): 1–38, https://doi.org/10.5070/T411000004.

[17] See chapter 1 for a historical overview.

assumptions.[18] From the other side, decolonial religion and theology seem to have little to do with the task of survival for many people who inhabit the Global South. For these people, religion, in its androcentric registers, operates as motivation for agentic, transformative peacebuilding actions and for the creation of an ethics of plurality from the margins. I highlight androcentricity or the centering of (or, rather, the refrain from interrogating) patriarchal norms to signify the double closures upon which religion and the harmony business rely—hermeneutical and communal—along with their mutual validation and reification, which contribute to depoliticized nonintersectional resiliency.

My focus on communities directly affected by neoliberal programming of religion and peacebuilding exposes the limits of a critique of ideology through the very stories that affected individuals articulate and their own narration of how their religiosity can help them to resist hate, fragmentation, and hopelessness, all of which are an outcome of colonial and state violence. The postsecular turn in liberal discourse reinscribes, in other words, a temporal and spatial colonial difference.[19] This postsecular shift explains the emergence of an interest in religious literacy for the purpose of enhancing the public understanding of religion and more effectively formulating policies for the global engagement with religion.

The consolidation of programmatic efforts to overcome religious illiteracy in the North coalesced with the apparent emergence of religion purportedly as a security threat and people's recognition that they needed to know something about it in order to contain it. Shapers of such literacy programs recognized the need to frame an interest in promoting religious literacy as a pathway for more capacious public engagements that acknowledge that "religion and belief are not 'something else somewhere else,' despite many of the assumptions that exoticise it."[20]

But what does "religious literacy" mean? Initial investments in religious literary projects were directed toward institutions of higher learning with an understanding that substantial conversations about religion needed to

---

[18] The "postsecular" as conceptualized by Jürgen Habermas—who is often credited with coining this concept. Jürgen Habermas, *An Awareness of What Is Missing: Faith and Reason in a Post-secular Age* (Cambridge, UK: Polity, 2010). For a critique of the "postsecular" in religion and the formation of American foreign policy, see Elizabeth Shakman Hurd, *Beyond Religious Freedom: The New Global Politics of Religion* (Princeton, NJ: Princeton University Press, 2015), 22–36.

[19] Achille Mbembe, *Necropolitics* (2016; Durham, NC: Duke University Press, 2019).

[20] Adam Dinham and Matthew Francis, "Religious Literacy: Contesting an Idea and Practice," in *Religious Literacy in Policy and Practice*, ed. Adam Dinham and Matthew Francis (Bristol: Polity Press), 3–25 (7).

be informed by actual facility with religious traditions. At its heart, this approach sees itself as promoting civic engagement. Some of the methodologies employed have involved scriptural reasoning, which requires extensive interactions with religious texts. In its most robust articulation, such a methodology opens up space for intergroup intimacy, one that follows from practitioners' facility with a textual and hermeneutical praxis.[21] Regardless of the best intentions of religious literacy programming, its practitioners have interpreted it as a form of extracurricular enrichment that has aimed to expand beyond the sphere of higher education, where it can equip not only religious studies scholars and religious professionals, but also other professional sectors and publics within society. Religion was no longer only the newly "discovered" "missing dimension of state craft"[22] but also a critically overlooked dimension of social and cultural institutions and policymaking. The programmatic advancement of "religious literacy" may brand itself as a tool for enriching postsecular and/or complexly secular civic engagement, but, in practice, it equips policymakers with skills to more effectively implement their own policies and agendas. In the field of journalism, for example, the focus for this programming was on nuancing questions around representation and thus on de-escalating potential conflicts and tensions. "Religious literacy" became a site for intentional investment by a variety of foundations dedicated to the public understanding of religion.[23] Even while journalists can tell more nuanced and less inflammatory stories about religion and religious people, such programmatic efforts still participate in the drawing of abyssal lines.

I have found one of the most critically grounded definitions of religious literacy in Diane L. Moore's work. According to her definition, which is informed by Donna Haraway's concept of "situated knowledges," religious literacy "entails the ability to discern and analyze the fundamental intersections of religion and social/political/cultural life through multiple lenses."[24] This means that "a religiously literate person" will have a command

---

[21] See Peter Ochs, "The Possibilities and Limits of Inter-religious Dialogue," in *Oxford Handbook of Religion, Conflict, and Peacebuilding*, ed. Atalia Omer, R. Scott Appleby, and David Little (Oxford: Oxford University Press, 2015), 488–515.

[22] A reference to the title of Johnston's book, *The Missing Dimension of Statecraft* (see n34), which captures the postsecular interest in religion.

[23] For example, see Henry Luce Foundation, "Religion, Journalism & International Affairs," n.d., https://www.hluce.org/fellowships/religion-journalism-international-affairs/ (accessed August 27, 2020).

[24] Diane L. Moore, "Overcoming Religious Illiteracy: A Cultural Studies Approach," *Religious Education* 109, no. 4 (2014): 379–89 (379). Moore is also one of the main authors of the definition of "religious literacy" adopted by the American Academy of Religion, which is almost verbatim of

of, or some fluency with, "a basic understanding of the history, central texts (where applicable), beliefs, practices and contemporary manifestations of several of the world's religious traditions as they arose out of and continue to be shaped by particular social, historical and cultural contexts."[25] This form of knowledge also cross-fertilizes with "the ability to discern and explore the religious dimensions of political, social and cultural expressions across time and space."[26] Clarifying that this approach to religious literacy is "non-denominational," Moore also argues that the most critical hermeneutical depth is not necessarily beholden to devotional practice or presumed devotion. She thus challenges that "sincerely held beliefs" or claims to authenticity by virtue of *being religious* justify certain practices and trump others and ought not be subject to historically located, intersectional, and ethically broad critical scrutiny.[27] Moore's articulation of a critical hermeneutical depth connects with decolonial theoretical accounts of interculturality, oriented to an analysis of power that crisscrosses experiences in ways that resist assigning cultural difference as the cause of violence and marginalization.[28] Operating on a segregationist peace formula grounded in practices of double closure of communal and religious boundaries, the interreligious peacebuilding/development practices I encountered did not present such critical hermeneutical depth.

My empirical findings show that "literacy" means one of two things. It means either a survivalist overcoming intergroup prejudices through activities that depend upon an abstract, rather than historical or situated, articulation of what it means to be a practitioner/member of this or that tradition, or it means the extracurricular capacity of new religiously literate professionals to deploy religion to solve a spectrum of problems. Both extracurricular and survivalist facets of the religious literacy discourse have

---

her earlier articulations in this essay. See American Academy of Religion, "AAR Religious Literacy Guidelines: What U.S. College Graduates Need to Understand about Religion," n.d., https://www.aarweb.org/AARMBR/Publications-and-News-/Guides-and-Best-Practices-/Teaching-and-Learning-/AAR-Religious-Literacy-Guidelines.aspx?WebsiteKey=61d76dfc-e7fe-4820-a0ca-1f792d24c06e#summary (accessed June 15, 2020).

[25] Moore, "Overcoming Religious Illiteracy," 380.
[26] Ibid.
[27] The argument that claims to sincerely held beliefs can consolidate legal cases through the rubric of religious freedoms in the United States has come under scrutiny by a variety of interlocutors from multiple disciplines. See Winnifred Fallers Sullivan, *The Impossibility of Religious Freedom* (Princeton, NJ: Princeton University Press, 2005).
[28] Moore engages explicitly with the question of peace and violence in its multiple forms in her "Methodological Assumptions and Analytical Frameworks regarding Religion," 2017, https://rlp.hds.harvard.edu/files/hds-rlp/files/method-moore.pdf.

no use for hermeneutical or intersectional depth. Hence, the neoliberal and securitizing logic of peacebuilding/development, in their postsecular (i.e., religiously literate) turn, works against a complex, intersectional, and substantively critical hermeneutical depth. In doing so, neoliberal rationality also diminishes the capacity of religious literacy programs to shift from emic expressions and self-representations to an etic, intersectional, and critical analysis of religion and ideology, including subjecting religious claims to critical scrutiny.

I consequently draw upon the academic study of religion's analysis of modernity, power, and historical and hermeneutical complexity (including the deployment of feminist lenses) to expand the discussion of religion and the practice of peacebuilding beyond the limitations of instrumentalism and what may present itself as the realm of the possible. Exclusive reliance on what is practical—rather than on a discursive understanding of tradition as contested, historically embedded, and fluid—may privilege rigidly traditionalist accounts of religion, religious agency, and leadership and render religion vulnerable to the utilitarian logic of neoliberalism. Conversations surrounding religious communities and the COVID-19 pandemic have exemplified this utilitarian logic. Policymakers have examined where and how religious actors can challenge and advance a public health agenda; in doing so, they have reverted to a utilitarian logic and relied on conventional authority figures within faith communities. This problem-solving logic seeks cohesive, rather than disruptive, religious partners. Thus, "the global engagement with religion" is beholden to the present rather than to future alternatives imagined through a constructive hermeneutic criticality. This is the case even if, as the COVID-19 pandemic has exposed, global inequalities, local structural forms of violence, and racialized nationalist discourses intersect violently with religion as a category of exclusion. Anything less than an intersectional account of religion will fall short of offering adequate resources to grapple with structural, symbolic, cultural, and direct forms of violence.

Methodology

First, a word about my positionality: I am from neither the Philippines nor Kenya. I came to the cases with fluency in the theoretical literature on religion and peacebuilding/development. Indeed, regardless of my Israeli accent, my affiliation with an American university and my appearance immediately associated me with whiteness in the eyes of my interlocutors. This association was relayed to me "with all due respect" by a Kenyan cleric who then proceeded to discuss the exploitation of children via "White sexual tourism" in the Kenyan coastal region. I brought a history of engagement with whiteness, colonialism, and modernity to the focus groups and interviews. I also had years of experience codirecting the Contending Modernities research initiative at the University of Notre Dame, which has a global focus on Catholic, Muslim, and secular understandings of modernity. Modernity's impact on theology, ideology, and the practices of empire and colonialism is pivotal to my interpretive work in this book.

As previously noted, many examples I provide in this book are from my engagement with interreligious peacebuilding work. I was able to gain familiarity with the two contexts of Kenya and the Philippines through Catholic Relief Services (CRS), a transnational, faith-inspired NGO whose model is to work with local partners on humanitarian, peacebuilding, and development efforts. I selected CRS as an initial entry point because it exemplifies efforts to systematize interreligious action. As an international organization, CRS began to shift from an exclusive focus on humanitarian and development work to a broader focus on structural violence, especially as it interrogated its thirty-year presence in Rwanda prior to the devastating genocide in 1994. When CRS's Peace and Reconciliation Program in the Philippines was put in place in 1996 to help with the implementation of the peace agreement between the government of the Philippines and the Moro National Liberation Front, this new focus was operative.[29] As one key shaper of this shift explained, "We wanted to work more at the grassroots level to provide accompaniment and create spaces for dialogue and Muslim-Christian engagement." This involved working closely with the Office of the Presidential Adviser on the Peace Process and UNICEF to develop a manual known as the Culture of Peace. This manual constitutes "the entry point for community-level engagement and dialogue" and outlines many workshops that were to take place over several days. These focused on "the self, the history of Mindanao, and the history of conflict in particular." In addition, the Culture of Peace involves modules devoted to resolving conflict nonviolently and imagining peace intercommunally.[30] The ubiquitous

---

[29] Berkley Center for Religion, Peace & World Affairs, "A Discussion with Myla Leguro, Director of the Interreligious Peacebuilding Program at Catholic Relief Services (CRS)," June 15, 2020, https://berkleycenter.georgetown.edu/interviews/a-discussion-with-myla-leguro-director-of-the-interreligious-peacebuilding-program-at-catholic-relief-services-crs.
[30] Ibid.

medium of communal and intercommunal workshops, which are designed to cultivate self-awareness and alleviate "othering," has generated reductive "sticky notes" accounts of people's traditions. This is done by literal sticky notes that capture participants' sincere responses to the question of "who we are" and what our values, cultural resources, conflicts, aspirations, and (mis)perceptions of other communities are. Therefore, the Culture of Peace seminar's interpretations of religiosity rely on hermeneutically closed accounts of communal and religious identities and their indexing to one another. They preclude intercultural hermeneutical openings that could potentially illuminate post-abyssal emancipatory horizons. Nevertheless, their outcomes are measurable as successful in terms of peace and development indices. This is where a segregationist peace logic is both empowering and disempowering.

By the time I began fieldwork in Mindanao, the Culture of Peace approach (translated into multiple manuals), which now also included a next step known as the "zone of peace," had become ubiquitous, and the "theory of change" underpinning it permeated the international peacebuilding terrains. For Myla Leguro, in a genuine and survivalist sense, the Culture of Peace generates peace islands in the midst of violence, or, in her words, "safe spaces for dialogue and interaction" in a context where such interactions are rare.[31] To this extent, interrupting violence and hate by creating "peace islands" or forming friendships empowers and helps write an alternative intra- and intercommunal script. This interruption occurs even if the concept of the Culture of Peace translated into a replicable copy-and-paste neoliberal manual. Indeed, it also exceeds its neoliberal underpinnings. This is what I uncover in my analysis as I oscillate between exposing the technocratic and persistently colonial dimensions of religion and practices of peace and the bottom-up, agentic, transformative processes that move beyond the master narrative of neoliberal coloniality.

As a transnational faith-inspired actor, it is within the Catholic Integral Human Development (IHD) framework that CRS has integrated an elicitive approach to grassroots peacebuilding. It essentially sees itself as empowering local communities to generate their own conflict mapping and to recover, discover, and cultivate their own ways to redress communal problems (see Figure I.1).[32] This elicitive method is often deployed to counter any criticism

---

[31] Ibid.

[32] John Paul Lederach is often credited with articulating the elicitive approach. Indeed, his approach has concretely influenced peacebuilding programming in Mindanao. See, for example, his *Little Book of Conflict Transformation: Clear Articulation of the Guiding Principles by a Pioneer in*

Figure I.1 Conflict mapping exercise in Mindanao. Reproduced with permission from CRS.

that these grassroots efforts are simply colonialism in disguise. People involved in facilitating elicitive methodologies would immediately underscore that they do not come to the communities with prescriptions. The elicitive mode, however, means that CRS has no way to critique a religion that perpetuates violence against women, for example, if that religion is also useful for advancing a peace and development agenda. This limitation shows that elicitive methods are not necessarily decolonial nor necessarily emancipatory for marginal and invisibilized members of the communities. My findings show that an elicitive approach, without hermeneutical criticality, is beholden to the present and to the utilitarian question of what works. It is undeniable that elicitive methodologies thrive on practices and notions of empowerment from the ground up, yet empowerment within a neoliberal frame also thrives on what I identify as a paradoxical process of depoliticization,

---

the Field (New York: Good Books, 2003) and his *Preparing for Peace: Conflict Transformation across Cultures* (Syracuse, NY: Syracuse University Press, 1995), especially 55–62.

solidified through the mechanisms of interreligious and intercommunal engagement.

CRS's focus on interreligious peacebuilding was developed through the peacebuilding/development synergetic prism that interprets peace that one cannot eat as no peace at all and thus the enhancement of people's productivity as intricately related to peacebuilding. CRS developed its approach most extensively in Mindanao, in the Philippines, with the intention to follow an elicitive method within an IHD framework. To reiterate, the IHD lens interprets itself as pushing beyond technocratic paradigms and as integrating insights from the ethics of the development field, most notably associated with Martha Nussbaum and Amartya Sen.[33] IHD, which sees itself as advancing a holistic conception of the person, frames CRS's focus on Indigenous nonviolent methodologies for conflict transformation and reconciliation. This framing allows CRS to interpret its work as potentially redressing structural root causes.[34] However, this often comes with blinders. Questions pertaining to gender are pushed outside the scope of religion and the practice of peace as either irrelevant or luxurious. Scrutinizing this bracketing of gender justice becomes important for my analysis of the limits of religion and peace praxis as thoroughly non-intersectional.

I selected CRS as the entry point for my research because of its long-term embeddedness in development/peacebuilding spaces in both Kenya and the Philippines. However, *Decolonizing Religion and Peacebuilding* is not a book about CRS. I also interfaced with other actors in the broader peacebuilding sphere in these countries through interviews and focus groups.[35] I met with 250 people in Mindanao. These meetings included twenty focus groups with key participants in various programs, encompassing religious leaders and professionals in civil society spaces of intra- and interreligious dialogue and peace education. In Kenya, I interviewed 150 people. I conducted six focus groups with women, youth, and religious leaders or clerics (they varied in numbers of participants from five to twenty-seven). The interviews focused on multiple actors in the religious field, including Preventing and Countering

---

[33] See Amartya Sen, "Development as Capability Expansion," *Journal of Development Planning* 19 (1989): 41–58; Amartya Sen, *Development as Freedom* (Oxford: Oxford University Press, 1999); Martha Nussbaum, *Women and Human Development* (Cambridge: Cambridge University Press, 2001); Martha Nussbaum, *Creating Capabilities: The Human Development Approach* (Cambridge, MA: Harvard University Press, 2011).

[34] See Aaron Chassy and Nell Bolton, "Putting Human Dignity at the Center: An Alternative Perspective on 'Countering Violent Extremism,'" in *The Ecology of Violent Extremism: Perspectives on Peacebuilding*, ed. Lisa Schirch (Lanham, MD: Rowman & Littlefield, 2018), ch. 35.

[35] All names of peacebuilding actors (unless based on published material) are pseudonymous.

Violent Extremism (P/CVE) spaces and interreligious dialogue. I also engaged civil society actors working on questions of corruption, devolution, gender justice, poverty, marginalization, and other key areas of concern.

Further, I had access to additional focus groups with key participants in interreligious dialogues of action—that is, dialogues for implementing "common good" projects. Such projects include reducing instances of child marriage, projects conducted by colleagues who followed up with some of the same communities in Malindi on the coast of Kenya. These resulted in a fruitful expansion of my empirical research. Their focus specifically concerned the problems of child marriage and acute poverty. I also triangulated this empirical research with the extensive interviews with religious actors in peacebuilding and development curated by Katherine Marshall of the Berkley Center at Georgetown University and with CRS's evidence-based evaluations of their programs. These invaluable resources offer a critical mass of testimonies that attest to the global relevance of religion to peacebuilding/development.

The empirical findings I gathered, the interview database, and the multidimensional, evidence-based research conducted by organizations that *do* religion have all contributed to my effort to shape a decolonial prism. Through this prism, I refract an analysis of religion and peacebuilding praxis, while also illuminating what and whom such a prism invisibilizes. The many stories of transformation and survival that emerged from my fieldwork speak back to decolonial scholarship and theory, exposing their limited traction and, often, their irrelevance to people's survival struggles. Hence, two paradoxical tensions frame my discussion here: first, religious peacebuilding practices are both empowering and depoliticizing, and second, more *doing* of religion does not necessarily denote deeper or more *knowing* or critical hermeneutical literacy.

Outline

Chapter 1, "Historical Background and Colonial Afterlives," sketches the relevant conflict and peace narratives in Kenya and the Philippines to contextualize my analysis of religion and the practices of peace. I foreground two themes in particular. The first relates to the integration of both Kenya and the Philippines into the global "war on terror." This opportunistic integration abstracted Muslims from their specific historical grievances in the postcolonial contexts of each country. This orientalist articulation diffuses anti-Muslim racialization, manifesting in profiling and securitizing by other means, including through the standardization of madrasa education. The second theme relates to an exposition of each case's colonial legacies and their afterlives in various conflict narratives and experiences of marginalization.

Chapter 2, "'Sisyphean' Governance," traces the operative logic of neoliberalism and how it shapes what I call "Sisyphean peacebuilding agency." Programmatic peace/development practices become sites of spiritual and vocational formation. Sisyphean persistence coalesces with religious commitments, which are incorporated into neoliberal peace governance. The analysis of interreligious peace governance draws on multiple examples from Kenya and Mindanao.

Chapter 3, "Doing Religion," examines the growth of the religion industry worldwide. I articulate a typology of religious actors and broadly analyze the convergences between peacebuilding and development. I then look more specifically at how such conjunctions pertain to the mobilization of religion in advancing various global agendas. I argue that an increased emphasis on *doing* rather than *knowing* religion, even if appearing as democratizing and expanding the scope of actors, denotes a utilitarian rather than a normative turn in the practice of religion and peace/development.

Chapter 4, "Survival Piety: A Preferential Option for the Poor?," unpacks the neoliberal underpinnings that inform interreligious peacebuilding's linking religious piety with a survivalist paradigm. Juxtaposing a partnership peacebuilding/developmentalist approach with a social justice, feminist, and liberationist outlook, I trace how individualist and culturalist explanations are deployed by a host of actors to locate the agency of change in intrasubjective transformation, which is fueled by an individual's capacity to be both productive and pious. On this account, economic resilience reinforces religious piety and vice versa. This interlinking of economic survival and piety consolidates survivalist piety. Triangulating this analysis with a broader theoretical discussion of religion and neoliberalism clarifies how the synergetic approach to peacebuilding/development (a hallmark of neoliberalism) mobilizes religion as social capital.

Chapter 5, "Religion and 'Soft' Security: Countermessaging and Surveillance," examines the securitization of religion that is carried out through development/peacebuilding practice, involving capitalizing on mothers, caregivers, and teachers as part of an ever-devolving security infrastructure. These actors function as the ears and eyes of the state's effort to identify warning signs of radicalization and recruitment among (mostly) young men to violent movements that deploy religion. Religion as a "soft power" thus becomes a site of security work. The focus of this chapter is mainly on the "first-aid" hermeneutics deployed by various social actors trained through workshops and manuals to counter 'bad' religious messaging, which also denotes the consolidation of "social influencers," or the "Twitter prophets," as useful religious authorities. These authorities, however, merely invert violent appeals to religious authenticity and "true" identity.

Chapter 6, "'Religious' Resiliency and 'Soft' Security," focuses on the securitizing discourse and its offline operations, complementing the online "first-aid" hermeneutical battles. This chapter examines the infrastructure for the formation of children and youth through immersive experiences across cultural and religious divides. I highlight how religious leaders' long-term presence and credibility enable them to de-escalate violence or reduce volatility by showing up in violence-prone contexts. Often, this happens also through trickle-down interfaith performativity, where the space of interfaith relies on some generic allusions to the peace and love kernels of all religions. The long-term investment in hermeneutical resiliency does not depend on critical hermeneutical horizons, but rather builds upon and interweaves with the people-to-people, bottom-up dialoguing and bridging approach designed to foster self-transformation through intergroup immersion or a programmatic focus on connector "public good" projects. The "public," as noted, is presumed to be self-evident and unitary. Youth, of course, present themselves as especially worthy of long-term investment in love and friendship, which translate into the refusal of hate and division. Indeed, this immersive focus consolidates and spiritualizes but also exceeds and transgresses the confines of a neoliberal peace discourse because the relationships do not necessarily end with the drying up of funds or the conclusion of strict neoliberal timeframes.

Chapter 7, "Unrevolutionary Decolonial Love: The Spirituality of Just 'Getting Along,'" focuses on two interrelated themes, namely, the promise and difficulty of moving from "peace zones" (including relational ones) to broader sociopolitical transformations, and the spiritualization of peace practices as mechanisms that contribute to depoliticization and work against systemic change. The concept of the "peace zone" is taken directly from the creation, through negotiations, of "peace islands" in the midst of violence in Mindanao. I also extend the concept to denote friendships and relationships produced through interreligious and intercommunal engagement. I show that the construction of peace islands, whether an upshot of intra- and intersubjective interfacing or through the consecration of the city, carves out a moment in time and space of harmony and friendship. This "peace island" construct is a variation of the planting-a-seed (of peace) metaphor, which I highlight in earlier chapters as co-opted by neoliberal forces that burden the individual as an engine of change, as if people's predicaments of marginality, poverty, and discrimination were merely expressions of their own cultural baggage. Still, I underscore here the decolonial openings that such peacebuilding practices create in ways that exceed the critical gaze.

Chapter 8, "Does Justice Have Anything to Do with Religion and the Practice of Peace?," reengages the limits of decolonial demystification and calls for epistemic and theological disobedience to congeal with empirical realities of suffering where hermeneutically closed religion more often than not enacts and illuminates decolonial openings. This assessment requires a recognition of the forces of resiliency without relinquishing a critique of these forces as they underpin religion's neoliberal instrumentalization in entrenching the status quo. Here, the decolonial lens exposes the religion and peace discourse's embeddedness in western hegemony. At the same time, the constructive role of religion and cultural empowerment and reclamation (especially relevant for Indigenous communities) in influencing communal and personal lives complicates decolonial critiques because of the latter's abstracts from actual experiences of survival on the ground.

Therefore, this book puts insights from the field of religion and peacebuilding into conversation with a decolonial scholarship to identify constructive sites of religion and peace praxis and asks those who engage in decolonial efforts to grapple with the empirical realities and struggles for survival that are unfolding on the ground. In sum, I wrestle generatively with the fact that the actors and institutions most able to curb violence or mitigate poverty frequently have neoliberal, patriarchal, and even colonialist outlooks. I also suggest that, despite these areas of compromise and complicity, something in their efforts to promote peace exceeds those ideologies. I contend that this "something" deserves analysis.

1
Historical Background and Colonial Afterlives

Multiple Conflict Narratives

> Before 1986, only a minority of religious congregations had members standing tall at public denunciations of martial rule. In Davao, among the more than a dozen women religious congregations, only the RGSs [Good Shepherd Sisters], the FMAs [Daughters of Mary of the Assumption], and the Maryknoll Sisters were willing to stick their necks out.... The rest followed the example of the Archbishop who played it safe and stayed within the safety of their convent walls, which is why, our generation of church people and activists engaged in the resistance to martial rule will forever hold these nuns in deep affection.[1]

This quotation captures the tension between the prophetic force of religious leaders and their priestly quietism. It was written by Karl Gaspar, a Redemptionist Brother and anthropologist who was a political prisoner from 1983 to 1985 and an activist, throughout his career, for Indigenous peoples (IPs), especially Lumad in the lowland communities of Mindanao. Gaspar refers to the intense time during martial law in the Philippines (declared in 1972 and lifted in 1981) when the Catholic Church, through its various institutional arms, chose to affirm martial law, even as it cautioned against human rights violations. It was only after the assassination of President Ferdinand Marcos's political opponent Benigno "Ninoy" Aquino in 1983 that a more explicit anti-authoritarianism was expressed by various spokespersons of

---

[1] Karl M. Gaspar, "Shepherding a Stalked, Stressed, but Struggling Flock," in *O Susana! Untold Stories of Martial Law in Davao*, ed. Macario D. Tiu (Davao: Ateneo de Davao University Publication Office, 2016), 55–62 (60–61).

the Church who later took on active roles in the revolutionary effort. The year 1986 is underscored here because it marks the fall of the authoritarian government of Marcos (1965–86), ousted after the People Power Revolution of February 22–25, 1986.[2] This historical moment of civil disobedience and resistance was actively endorsed by the archbishop of Manila, the Catholic Bishops' Conference of the Philippines president Cardinal Ricardo Vidal, and the archbishop of Cebu.

Another activist, Joaquin Y. Cadorna, who served as a relief and rehabilitation coordinator for the Mindanao-Sulu Secretariat for Social Action (a social work aspect of the Catholic Church's infrastructure in the Philippines, as I show below) during the height of the conflict between the Muslim Moro[3] insurgent groups and the government of the Philippines, wrote:

> One experience forever sketched in my mind was when I went to Jolo [located in the southwest Philippines] to deliver cash assistance . . . within a few days of the infamous 1974 burning of Jolo. The Marcos army threw its full weight in what was probably one of the fiercest battles of the Moro rebellion. . . . When I arrived, all I could see were the charred remains of what used to be the fabulous capital of the Sulu sultanate. Seeing so much devastation, I imagined the muted grief, suspicion, rage, fear, and uncertainty written on the faces of the local people.[4]

This experience captures the horrors of the Moro conflict and the devastating days of martial law, a central chapter of the conflict that provides the setting for my analysis of the harmony business in Mindanao.

Traveling from Marcos's Philippines to Kenya to the contemporary "war on terror," we find ourselves in a Nairobi marginalized district where a young Muslim man who has mobilized to fight against the appeal of violent ideological movements told me the reasons for his activism: "We are tired of burying

---

[2] For an analysis that complicates an overly simplistic attribution of the role of people power in toppling the Marcos regime, see Yuki Fukuoka, "Who Brought Down the Dictator? A Critical Reassessment of So-Called 'People Power' Revolutions in the Philippines and Indonesia," *Pacific Review* 28, no. 3 (2015): 411–33, 10.1080/09512748.2015.1011212. For a similar engagement with entrenched patronage legacies in the Philippines, see James Putzel, "Survival of an Imperfect Democracy in the Philippines," *Democratization* 6, no. 1 (1999): 198–223, https://doi.org/10.1080/13510349908403603.

[3] As I explain later in the chapter, this label "Moro" traces back to the encounter with the Spaniards in the fifteenth century.

[4] Joaquin Y. Cadorna, "Relief and Rehabilitation Work during Martial Law," in *O Susana! Untold Stories of Martial Law in Davao*, ed. Macario D. Tiu (Davao: Ateneo de Davao University Publication Office, 2016), 137–42 (140).

people, we are tired of being traumatized, we want to be resources for peace. We want to make a difference; we want to reduce some of these challenges we are experiencing as a community."[5] Another Kenyan researcher and practitioner of religion and peacebuilding acknowledged that the long-term ramifications of British colonialism need to be more closely investigated because they are "being swept under the carpet."[6] People blame marginalized communities, primarily Muslim, for their marginality, listing their supposed character flaws as the causes of their poverty. Even though these two men were far away from one another, the pain and urgency that the young man from Nairobi experienced and the researcher's informed analysis sounded eerily similar to what I heard from people in Mindanao about their struggles with marginalization dating back to colonial infrastructures, but mediated in complex ways through the postindependence era and the supposedly postcolonial governments in Nairobi and Manila.

I contextualize these case studies with an understanding that both sites are infinitely more variegated and complex than I can represent here. Each exhibits multiple loci of conflict and violence, and each involves different dynamics, even if overlapping, of minoritizing Muslims—a process that extends and connects to the racializing of Muslim subjects in the former metropolis of the colonial world.[7] Even if Muslims have long imperial histories, the modern colonial moment and its reliance on racializing communities, through their indexing to religious and cultural taxonomies, has reshaped Muslim experiences as subaltern subjects of colonies and postcolonies. I return to this point throughout the book. For now, it suffices to acknowledge the minoritization of Muslims within the context of Western Christian colonial engagements as well as during the colonial afterlives in the Philippines and Kenya, where such processes intersected with other conflict narratives, including those with anticolonial underpinnings.

For example, while my analysis regarding the Philippines revolves around the axis of the Moro conflict in the island of Mindanao (one of the three main islands of the archipelagic country), other axes interrelate and diverge.

---

[5] Participant in a focus group, Nairobi marginalized neighborhood, July 2019.
[6] Interview, Nairobi, November 2018.
[7] It is notable that both countries are majority Christian, and in both countries a sizable portion of the Christian demographics is associated with indigenously grown churches. For more on the demographic maps of each country, see the Berkley Center for Religion, Peace & World Affairs, "Faith and Development in Focus: Kenya," March 28, 2017, https://berkleycenter.georgetown.edu/publications/faith-and-development-in-focus-kenya and the Berkley Center for Religion, Peace & World Affairs, "Faith and Development in Focus: Philippines," October 2019, https://jliflc.com/wp-content/uploads/2020/03/faith-and-development-in-focus-philippines.pdf, 29–58.

These include the conflict between the government and the Communist Party of the Philippines, which converged with the New People's Army (referred to as CPP-NPA)—a conflict that spanned over half a century (since 1968) and killed over thirty thousand people around the CPP-NPA's objective of seeking to overthrow the government, exorcise U.S. influence, and create the foundations for the leadership of the peasant class. While this particular conflict was at its height during the 1970s and 1980s, the rebels continue to operate and exert influence on disenfranchised populations in the vast archipelago, drawing on deep reservoirs of anticolonial and anticapitalist struggles.[8]

The CPP-NPA reflected a revolutionary outlook led initially from Luzon through confrontational nonviolent tactics in 1970 against then-President Marcos, who met the protests with brutality that only reinforced CPP-NPA recruitment. Ongoing confrontations ultimately led to Marcos's declaration of martial law in 1972, which gave cover to repression while the left opposition consolidated (in 1973) under the umbrella of the National Democratic Front of the Philippines. Over many years, but especially in the 1990s and 2000s, this revolutionary coalition negotiated sporadically with Presidents Fidel Ramos and Gloria Macapagal-Arroyo (with a high level of conflict resuming during the presidency of Joseph Estrada). During the presidency of Macapagal-Arroyo, a short-lived effort to negotiate a cessation of hostilities ended with the labeling in 2002, upon her request, of CPP-NPA as a terrorist organization by the United States under the cover of the "war on terror."[9] Fast-forward to the regime of Rodrigo Duterte, who assumed power in 2016 and who initially attempted to advance a peace process on this front. Human rights defenders working with peasants on the island of Negros in the central part of the Philippines, an area rich with resources but monopolized by a few oligarchs, became subject to systematic extrajudicial killings (a familiar practice of this regime, initially as a key to the "war on drugs"). This targeting

---

[8] Paz Verdades M. Santos, "The Communist Front: Protracted People's War and Counterinsurgency in the Philippines (Overview)," in *Primed and Purposeful: Armed Groups and Human Security Efforts in the Philippines*, ed. Soliman M. Santos Jr. and Paz Verdades M. Santos, with Octavio A. Dinampo, Herman Joseph S. Kraft, Artha Kira R. Paredes, Raymund Jose G. Quilop, and Daina Rodriguez (Geneva: South-South Network for Non-State Armed Group Engagement and Small Arms Survey, 2010), 17–42.

[9] For an effective overview of the history of the CPP-NPA, see Center for International Security and Cooperation at Stanford University, "Group Narrative," https://cisac.fsi.stanford.edu/mappingmilitants/profiles/communist-party-philippines-new-peoples-army#text_block_19435 (accessed May 20, 2020). See also "The Communist Insurgency in the Philippines: Tactics and Talks," *International Crisis Group*, February 14, 2011.

was further consolidated under the cover of an antiterrorism law and the moment of opportunity for an attack on freedoms afforded by emergency declarations related to the COVID-19 pandemic.[10]

What I refer to as the "CPP-NPA conflict axis" is especially relevant in its pivotal anticolonial and anticapitalist consciousness because the harmony industry I portray through this study of religion and the practices of peacebuilding decidedly laments the pain of the colonial past without being anticolonial.[11] Not only that, but the "global engagement with religion" industry relies fundamentally on the logic of racial capitalism. As a depoliticizing force, authoritarian leaders are not antagonistic to religion and peace praxis, nor do they seek to eliminate religious actors through extrajudicial killings. On the contrary, they domesticate rhetorical and practitioners' appeals to religion and peacebuilding. They co-opt such appeals often through grandiose celebrations of peace and harmony, like the mandatory Mindanao Week of Peace (since Macapagal-Arroyo's Presidential Proclamation No. 127 in 2001). Indeed, sometimes they even invest in the religion and peace or harmony business, as does the Kingdom of Saudi Arabia, in an effort to veil and excuse otherwise authoritarian and violent practices.[12]

The Kenyan landscape is also complex and varied. Yet both case studies—especially because of the interlinking of poverty, marginalization, and violence that erupts along identity lines—reveal a narrative about the ongoing afterlives of colonial violence by other means, including through the registers of peace and development as not only the "new name for peace," as in the oft-cited papal quotation,[13] but also as a new name of enduring global structures

---

[10] Ted Regencia, "Human Rights Leader Killed in Philippine 'War against Dissent,'" *Al-Jazeera*, August 19, 2020, https://www.aljazeera.com/news/2020/08/human-rights-leader-killed-philippine-war-dissent-200818052014188.html. Duterte had declared the CPP-NPA a terrorist group already in 2017; see "Duterte Declares CPP-NPA a Terrorist Group," Presidential Communications Operations Office, December 5, 2017, https://pcoo.gov.ph/news_releases/duterte-declares-cpp-npa-terrorist-group/. The post-Duterte regime of Sara Duterte as vice president and Ferdinand "Bongbong" Romualdez Marcos Jr. as president (assumed office in June 2022) signals an entrenchment of antidemocratic trends.

[11] The Philippines has a long history of anticolonial and anti-imperial struggles. Notable figures in this chronology include José Rizal (1861–96), who was pivotal in the independence struggle and was subsequently executed by the Spanish authorities, and Isabelo de los Reyes (1864–1938), who was a prominent labor organizer among Manila's poor communities, focused on rejecting American corporations. The anticolonialism and anti-imperialism also feed into more contemporary anarchist outlooks. See, for this discussion, Bas Umali, *Pangayaw and Decolonizing Resistance: Anarchism in the Philippines* (Oakland, CA: PM Press, 2020).

[12] See chapter 3.

[13] This refers to Pope Paul VI's encyclical letter *Populorum Progression* (originally published on March 26, 1967), http://www.vatican.va/content/paul-vi/en/encyclicals/documents/hf_p-vi_enc_26031967_populorum.html.

of domination reaching back centuries. Highlighting that peace cannot be attained if the people do not also have the capacity to survive entails believing that poverty and food insecurity are not a natural condition but rather an upshot of policies and unjust systems. Offering opportunities for people's enhanced capacity to survive may de-escalate violence, but it does not necessarily reveal, or address, peace's violent legacy and how religion is implicated in it.

Slicing Up the Land

In the early years of the twentieth century, with the encouragement of the British colonial administration in Kenya, Christian missions expanded geographically, following an agreement among themselves regarding delineated spheres of influence.[14] This initial slicing of the land remains relevant to the contemporary mapping of religious demographics and topographies, sometimes synonymous with tribal affiliations. The earlier expansion of Islam to East Africa also yielded long-term ramifications for communal concentrations along the coast of Kenya, where one can find mostly Swahilis who intermarried with Arab traders. Additionally, ethnic Somali Kenyans constitute a distinct Muslim community that mostly inhabits the northeastern region, although some concentrations can be found in Mombasa and Nairobi (especially in the Eastleigh neighborhood).[15] Fast-forward a century, and both regions are marked by high levels of poverty and limited access to infrastructure and services, all of which is compounded by the devastating effects of climate change.[16]

The British clearly treated Muslim regions not accessible for Christian missionizing differently, as they competed for regional influence with the German colonists. The British colonial administration signed an agreement, initially involving the German Empire, with the sultan of Zanzibar in 1888

---

[14] Robert W. Strayer, "The Dynamics of Mission Expansion: A Case Study from Kenya, 1875–1914," *International Journal of African Historical Studies* 6, no. 2 (1973): 229–48, https://doi.org/10.2307/216776.

[15] See Arye Oded, *Islam and Politics in Kenya* (Boulder, CO: Lynne Rienner, 2000); Paul Gifford, *Christianity, Politics, and Public Life in Kenya* (New York: Oxford University Press, 2009).

[16] For a complex analysis of changing conflict dynamics in Kenya, especially on the coast and in the Northeast, related to global warming and climate change as well as other regional and international forces, see Roz Price, "Climate Change, Vulnerability to Violent Extremism and Conflict in Kenya," Institute of Development Studies, August 13, 2019, https://assets.publishing.service.gov.uk/media/5d9b4db740f0b607f3e67941/639_Climate_Change_and_Violence_in_Kenya.pdf.

(renewed in 1895), which resulted in the German and British overtaking the coastal trading station, which was previously under the control of the sultanate. Local resistance (such as the Abushiri Revolt)[17] notwithstanding, the encroachment completely diminished Zanzibar when, in 1890, it became a British protectorate, meaning its inhabitants were "protected" by the empire rather than being its "subjects." The Coast Province's different status under British rule meant that Muslims were allowed to continue to practice Islam and to be regulated according to Muslim law and the antecedent administrative structures.[18] It also meant that they had no access to the British educational system, which often coincided with a Christian (missionary) monopoly of educational and health institutions. This eventually put the Coast's population at a disadvantage in the postindependence era, exposing one critical site of the colonial afterlife in Kenya.

Notably, internal divisions between Arab Muslims and Africans who converted to Islam, as well as Swahilis who traced their ancestry back to Arab and African roots, were exploited by the British who, characteristically, displayed favoritism toward the Swahilis, denying land rights to converts. As the colonial era was coming to its official close, some Swahilis and Arabs called for the coast to become a separate political entity, creating the Coastal People's Party. However, in 1963, the sultan of Zanzibar and the British sealed the annexation of the coast to Kenya. In 1999, the separatist Mombasa Republican Council emerged, precisely to rectify the marginalization that its leaders attributed to the transfer of the ten-mile strip of land along the Coast Province first to the British and then to the government of Kenya. The Mombasa Republican Council's slogan, *Pwani Si Kenya*, "The Coast is not Kenya," captures the sense of alienation that people of the Coast Province have endured.[19] In Kenya, clearly, tribal or ethnic tensions intersect with religion in complex and recurring ways. These include the Mau Mau movement

---

[17] This insurrection (1888–89) was instigated by Arab and Swahili communities and was crushed by German forces.

[18] For an important intervention regarding the colonial and postcolonial dimensions of Islamic law in African contexts, including Kenya, see Shamil Jeppie, Ebrahim Moosa, and Richard Roberts, eds., *Muslim Family Law in Sub-Saharan Africa: Colonial Legacies and Post-colonial Challenges* (Amsterdam: Amsterdam University Press, 2010).

[19] For an analysis that contextualizes the unfolding of public articulations of Islam and Christianity on the coast of Kenya and that illuminates how, within a Christian-dominated framework, Islam became a language and a site of opposition and how the tensions between Muslims and Christians on the coast and in Kenya broadly need to be interpreted through this specificity rather than through allusions to some essential claims regarding each tradition, see Gregory Deacon, George Gona, Hasan Mwakimako, and Justin Willis, "Preaching Politics: Islam and Christianity on the Kenya Coast," *Journal of Contemporary African Studies* 35, no. 2 (2017): 148–67.

of the Kikuyu in the 1940s and 1950s, the ongoing manipulation of ethnic lines for political expediency during Daniel arap Moi's presidency (1978–2002), the 2007–8 postelection violence, which resulted in deaths and waves of displacement, to the mixed results of the devolutionary system articulated in the 2010 Constitution.[20] Finally, the weaponization of religion also manifests in the incorporation of Kenya, as is the case with the Philippines, into the global "war on terror" and its racialized anti-Muslim narrative.[21]

I now move back in time momentarily to some of the aforementioned examples in order to contextualize my fieldwork. The Mau Mau movement launched an anticolonial resistance against the British, who retaliated with a massive military assault spanning 1953 to 1956; this retaliation resulted, officially, in eleven thousand Kikuyu insurgents killed as well as more than twenty thousand Kikuyus put in detention centers designed to "cure" them of their political views. According to the Kenyan Human Rights Commission, however, the numbers were significantly higher.[22] This massive repression aside, the Mau Mau paved the way for a successful anticolonial national movement, which resulted in independence in 1963. The main engine propelling the Mau Mau was the theft of the most fertile lands, previously inhabited by the Kikuyus, by the British colonists who had claimed the lands were vacant. While the rebellion was initiated by the Kikuyus, it quickly spread to other ethnic groups and is still a major chapter in Kenyan national mythology.[23] However, the postcolonial moment has remained riddled with

---

[20] For the problematic issue of accountability for the violence and incitement, see Stephen Brown and Chandra Lekha Sriram, "The Big Fish Won't Fry Themselves: Criminal Accountability for Postelection Violence in Kenya," *African Affairs* 111, no. 443 (2012): 244–60, https://doi.org/10.1093/afraf/ads018.

[21] For an analysis of the risks and detrimental misunderstandings from the perspective of counterterrorism to assimilating groups such as the Mombasa Republican Council into broader Islamist networks and very distinct and different ideological framing, see Anneli Botha, "Radicalisation in Kenya: Recruitment to al-Shabaab and the Mombasa Republican Council," Institute for Security Studies Papers no. 265 (2014). The paper can be accessed at https://issafrica.s3.amazonaws.com/site/uploads/Paper265.pdf.

[22] See Atsango Chesoni, "The Mau Mau Settlement: Setting the Record Straight," Kenya Human Rights Commission, June 21, 2013, https://www.khrc.or.ke/2015-03-04-10-37-01/press-releases/404-the-mau-mau-settlement-setting-the-record-straight.html; Kenya Human Rights Commission, "Mau Mau Case: Dealing with Past Colonial Injustices," July 23, 2012, https://www.khrc.or.ke/2015-03-04-10-37-01/press-releases/454-mau-mau-case-dealing-with-past-colonial-injustices.html. See also David Anderson, *Histories of the Hanged: Britain's Dirty War in Kenya and the End of Empire* (New York: W. W. Norton, 2005); Caroline Elkins, *Imperial Reckoning: The Untold Story of Britain's Gulag in Kenya* (New York: Henry Holt/Jonathan Cape, 2005).

[23] It is also important to highlight the critical roles that Kikuyu women played in the rebellion. For this analysis, see Cora Ann Presley, *Kikuyu Women, the Mau Mau Rebellion, and Social Change in Kenya* (New York: Routledge, 1992). For a detailed engagement with incarceration of "hardcore" Kikuyu women and the gendered forms of engagement by the British colonial authority with their "containment," see Katherine Bruce-Lockhart, "'Unsound' Minds and Broken Bodies: The Detention

divisions and patterns of marginalization that have proven costly in terms of violent and secessionist mobilizations of disaffected groups.

Patterns of postelection violence have persisted. Violence erupts around ethnic tensions and perceptions of Kikuyu favoritism.[24] The 2007 eruption was primed by fierce opposition to President Mwai Kibaki's reelection, which was deemed illegitimate and quickly exacerbated ethnic and tribal animosities.[25] The violence eventually subsided as the result of a UN-brokered power-sharing agreement, but not before 1,200 were killed and 300,000 were displaced.[26] Religious leaders were often themselves implicated for their failure to offer moral appeals to calm such postelection violence, on the cusp of a civil war, as well as for being active participants in the symbolic politics and the photo ops of ever-campaigning politicians. Their embroilment in this corruption and violence diminished their potential as representatives of the religious sector to serve as constructive forces.[27]

The soul searching that resulted from the postelection violence led religious organizations and leaders to commit explicitly to reconciliation efforts as well as to reinforcing their ability (also through the recovery of their lost credibility) to prevent future violent eruptions.[28] Attempts to redress the issues involved the Kenya National Dialogue and Reconciliation and the

---

of 'Hardcore' Mau Mau Women at Kamiti and Gitamayu Detention Camps in Kenya, 1954–1960," *Journal of Eastern African Studies* 8, no. 4 (2014): 590–608, https://doi.org/10.1080/17531055.2014.948148.

[24] Still, there are many conventionally overlooked variables to such narratives of violence and conflict. For example, the digital revolution uniquely influenced the particular 2007 violent eruption as well as attempts of traditional elites to silence and contain social movement mobilization online. See Nanjala Nyabola, *Digital Democracy, Analogue Politics: How the Internet Era Is Transforming Kenya* (London: Zed, 2018).

[25] The postviolence reckoning then enabled the elections of 2013 to have a more peaceful outcome through de-escalating mechanisms, but without necessarily redressing historical grievances. See Nic Cheeseman, Gabrielle Lynch, and Justin Willis, "Democracy and Its Discontents: Understanding Kenya's 2013 Elections," *Journal of Eastern African Studies* 8, no. 1 (2014): 2–24, https://doi.org/10.1080/17531055.2013.874105.

[26] Berkley Center, "Faith and Development in Focus: Kenya," 23. For the scope of the violence and a human rights–focused analysis, see Kenya National Commission on Human Rights, "On the Brink of the Precipice: A Human Rights Account of Kenya's Post-2007 Election Violence," August 2008, http://www.knchr.org/portals/0/reports/knchr_report_on_the_brink_of_the_precipe.pdf.

[27] Berkley Center, "Faith and Development in Focus: Kenya," 18. See also the report on the postelection violence by the Kenya National Commission on Human Rights, "On the Brink." See also Huma Haider, "Religious Leaders and the Prevention of Electoral Violence," GSDRC, May 19, 2016, http://www.gsdrc.org/wp-content/uploads/2016/07/HDQ1366.pdf.

[28] Berkley Center, "Faith and Development in Focus: Kenya," 23. See also Philomena Njeri Mwaura and Constansia Mumma Martinon, "Political Violence in Kenya and Local Churches' Responses: The Case of the 2007 Post-election Crisis," *Review of Faith & International Affairs* 8, no. 1 (2010): 39–46, http://dx.doi.org/10.1080/15570271003707812.

National Cohesion and Integration Commission, both of which aimed to grapple with the realities of neglect and marginalization in the coastal and northeastern regions, which were deemed explosive in a context otherwise sliced up by ethnic and other lines of division. The above overview offers a glimpse of the subtext of various programmatic efforts to mitigate the intersection between religion and violence and to devise ways to mobilize religion for peace.

Soul Searching

This soul searching in Kenya also connects with the earlier mobilization of an ecumenical effort called the Ufungamano Initiative to generate, in its authors' understanding, multisectoral input from human rights organizations, religious groups, women's rights activists, and so forth to contribute to the constitutional review process undertaken in 1999. By June 2000, this initiative had led to the inclusion of ten members of what was dubbed the "People's Commission" in the official Constitution of Kenya Review Commission.[29] This ecumenical and interreligious collaboration, however, erupted in 2003 over the Muslim request to reform and expand the jurisdiction of the Qadhi courts first recognized under the British. It finally dissolved by 2005.[30] The Muslim request led to reactionary Christian rhetoric decrying a supposed Muslim takeover, a narrative only reinforced by the escalation of recruitment of Muslims into violent movements that boasted their Islamic identity and often deployed the tactic of separating Muslims from Christians during terrorist attacks. This tactic only enforced the narrative of a religious-based war that various Muslim religious actors, institutions, and organizations sought to combat. These efforts to de-escalate religious rhetoric then led to highly advertised moments of solidarity, when Muslims refused to be separated from Christians in crises, such as in the bus attack by al-Shabaab in December 2015.[31] The mobilization of "good" religion then responds to the

---

[29] Berkley Center, "Faith and Development in Focus: Kenya," 48. For an analysis of the Ufungamano Initiative and its implications, see Jacob Mwathi Mati, "Social Movements and Socio-political Change in Africa: The Ufungamano Initiative and Kenyan Constitutional Reform Struggles (1999–2005)," *Voluntas: International Journal of Voluntary and Nonprofit Organizations* 23 (2012): 63–84, http://dx.doi.org/10.1007%2Fs11266-011-9241-1.

[30] See Jeppie, Moosa, and Roberts, *Muslim Family Law*.

[31] Elahe Izadi and Sarah Kaplan, "Muslims Protect Christians from Extremists in Kenya Bus Attack," *Washington Post*, December 22, 2015, https://www.washingtonpost.com/news/acts-of-faith/wp/2015/12/22/muslims-protected-christians-from-extremists-in-kenya-bus-attack-reports-say/.

mobilization of the global "war on terror" and the internalization of its rhetorical force by "bad" religious actors.

The Kenyan landscapes are saturated with such religious forces and practices. These include established churches and Muslim communities as well as ecumenical and cross-denominational organizations. The latter, such as the Supreme Council of Kenya Muslims or the National Council of Churches of Kenya, are not democratically elected. Yet they assume representational power as civil society actors providing input in political and societal consultations. Indeed, they were key participants in the Ufungamano Initiative. Other "faith-inspired" organizations also gained political power by way of investing in health, education, and other dimensions often subsumed under the rubric of "development." The Aga Khan Development Network, associated with the Kenyan Ismaili community, is one example. Churches have a mixed legacy, some lending their theological support to authoritarianism and others fighting, for example, in the early 1990s, to reinstate a multiparty system against Moi's repressive government, which also clashed with the incipient Islamic Party of Kenya, established in 1992 with the intention of representing Muslim interests but denied registration for its alleged exclusionary character.[32] At the same time, and due to the dominance of Christianity and Christian interests in Kenya, Islam has become a language of alternative politics.[33]

Despite multiple attempts to redress violent episodes (including a Truth, Justice, and Reconciliation Commission created in 2009) and a formal apology by the National Council of Churches of Kenya in 2008, such efforts' rather narrow scope and limited effectiveness have left intact the underlying condition of land disputes, which are rooted in colonial patterns of dispossession, ongoing corruption, patronage politics, and disregard of historical injustices. Coastal populations and Somali Kenyans remain particularly marginalized, even with the reforms and devolutionary policies outlined in the 2010 Constitution. Their marginalization goes back to patterns of colonial investment, or lack thereof, in their respective regions and continues to manifest in unequal access to political power, public-sector jobs, and resources and infrastructure, including land, electricity, and water. In conversations, my interlocutors repeatedly underscored that tribal and ethnic divisions are

---

[32] See Deacon et al., "Preaching Politics."
[33] See Hasan Juma Ndzovu, "Kenya's Jihadi Clerics: Formulation of a 'Liberation Theology' and the Challenge to Secular Power," *Journal of Muslim Minority Affairs* 38, no. 3 (2018): 360–71.

most prominent. Yet the overlap between tribal and religious identities born out of the British colonial administration's close collaboration and coordination with Christian missionaries (who divided up the land) and their tribal targets emerges increasingly as fault lines along Muslim-Christian tensions, influenced clearly by global trends and efforts to capitalize on such fault lines both by movements such as al-Shabaab and by U.S. and European expansion of their security apparatuses and anti-Muslim rhetoric.[34]

The realities of the marginalization of Muslim populations have become fertile ground for recruitment by the Somalia-based al-Shabaab and thus reveal the correlation, but not causality, between poverty and security, which leads many actors I profile in this book to programmatically connect development and Preventing and Countering Violent Extremism (P/CVE) initiatives. The 2010 constitutional reform and its devolutionary aspects (implemented in 2013) were heralded as a systemic effort to redress historical marginalization and to de-escalate the potential explosiveness of presidential elections by bolstering a decentralized approach to political power and socioeconomic allocation of resources. However, persistent corruption,[35] together with high levels of urban violence and crime, as well as the massive number of refugees from Somalia, explain Kenya's high score on the Fragile State Index[36] as well as the propensity of marginalized people, in particular, to be attracted to apocalyptic narratives about a Christian-Muslim ongoing clash. Routine violation of the human rights of marginalized communities and their unaddressed legal grievances, including around land and citizenship rights, further contribute to their precarity and their susceptibility to grand narratives, though a process of radicalization into violence affects not only the poor but also professionals whose socioeconomic position reveals

---

[34] For an analysis that also incorporates Ethiopian interventionist policies in Somalia as contributing factors to the consolidation of al-Shabaab, see Mohamed Haji Ingiriis, "From Al-Itihaad to Al-Shabaab: How the Ethiopian Intervention and the 'War on Terror' Exacerbated the Conflict in Somalia," *Third World Quarterly* 39, no. 11 (2018): 2033–52, https://doi.org/10.1080/01436 597.2018.1479186.

[35] Kenya is ranked 137th out of 198, with a score of 28 out of 100, according to Transparency International, "Corruption Perceptions Index: Kenya," 2019, https://www.transparency.org/en/cpi/2019/results/ken. For a case study featuring a Kenyan effort to mitigate corruption through multisectoral efforts, see Alex Gruenewald, "Effective Anti-corruption Advocacy through Multi-stakeholder Engagement: Lessons from Kenya," *Transparency International*, July 1, 2020, https://www.transparency.org/en/blog/effective-anti-corruption-advocacy-through-multi-stakeholder-engagement-lessons-from-kenya.

[36] According to the metrics of fragility, there was recorded improvement in Kenya, but the country still scores high. See Cyrus Ombati and Roselyne Obala, "Kenya Improves in List of Fragile States," *The Standard*, August 30, 2019, https://www.standardmedia.co.ke/kenya/article/2001340030/kenya-improves-in-list-of-fragile-states.

that, while neither hungry nor uneducated, they too experience alienation.[37] However, beyond a Band-Aid approach in the form of programmatically focusing on minimal livelihood options (offering "at-risk" populations the ability to eat at the end of the day),[38] what the assimilation of Kenya into the global P/CVE discourse does is gloss over the complicity of the government, as well as the colonial administration, in the intergenerational marginalization of, on the coast, Somali Kenyans whose profiling for "de-radicalization" only enhances their sense of alienation.[39]

The Somalis in Kenya have been an ethnic "other" and a target of state violence and neglect since Kenyan independence, but their grievances reach back even further, to the colonial powers' portioning of Somali-inhabited territories among the British, French, Italians, and Ethiopians.[40] This colonial move fragmented not only the political units but also the grazing areas of the primarily pastoralist Somalis. A major moment was when the British administration granted the Somali-dominated Ogaden and Haws regions in 1948 and 1954, respectively, to Ethiopia. This enhanced the Somali resistance already in place and was most clearly articulated by the Somaliland National League, which sought to unify the fragmented Somali people and territories.[41] Hence, the appeal of al-Shabaab needs to be analyzed through

---

[37] For a scoping analysis of various factors underlying attraction to violent ideologies, see Matteo Vergani, Muhammad Iqbal, Ekin Ilbahar, and Greg Barton, "The Three Ps of Radicalization: Push, Pull and Personal: A Systematic Scoping Review of the Scientific Evidence about Radicalization into Violent Extremism," *Studies in Conflict & Terrorism* 43, no. 10 (2018): 854–85, https://doi.org/10.1080/1057610X.2018.1505686.

[38] Chapters 5 and 6 of this book focus on these issues through a critical engagement with the securitizing religion discourse.

[39] Anneli Botha, "Assessing the Vulnerability of Kenyan Youth to Radicalisation and Extremism," *Institute for Security Studies Papers*, no. 245 (2013): 1–28. One alienating mechanism is through Usalama Watch of 2014, an operation intended to identify and deport noncitizens but which was widely viewed as a form of profiling and targeting of Somalis, reminiscent of a 1989 screening exercise. See Human Rights Watch, "Kenya: Counterterrorism Operations Undermine Rights: No Justice for Security Force Abuses," January 29, 2015, https://www.hrw.org/news/2015/01/29/kenya-counterterrorism-operations-undermine-rights. See also Jeremy Lind, Patrick Mutahi, and Marjoke Oosterom, "'Killing a Mosquito with a Hammer': Al-Shabaab Violence and State Security Responses in Kenya," *Peacebuilding* 5, no. 2 (2017): 118–35, https://doi.org/10.1080/21647259.2016.1277010.

[40] Jeremy Lind, Patrick Mutahi, and Marjoke Oosterom, "Tangled Ties: Al-Shabaab and Political Volatility in Kenya," Institute of Development Studies Evidence Report no. 130, 2015, https://opendocs.ids.ac.uk/opendocs/bitstream/handle/20.500.12413/6018/ER130_TangledTiesAlShabaabandPoliticalVolatilityinKenya.pdf?sequence=5; Hussein A. Mahmoud, "Seeking Citizenship on the Border: Kenya Somalis, the Uncertainty of Belonging, and Public Sphere Interactions," *Codesria*, 12th General Assembly: Governing the African Public Sphere, 2008, https://codesria.org/IMG/pdf/Hussein_A-_Mahmoud.pdf. See also Ogenga Otunnu, "Factors Affecting the Treatment of Kenyan-Somalis and Somali Refugees in Kenya: A Historical Overview," *Refugee* 12, no. 5 (1992): 21–26, https://www.jstor.org/stable/45412094.

[41] Mahmoud, "Seeking Citizenship on the Border." For efforts for pan-Somali activism, see Cedric Barnes, "The Somali Youth League, Ethiopian Somalis and the Greater Somalia Idea, c. 1946–48,"

this historical prism rather than through the presentist logic of a global clash between Muslims and Christians, even if the rhetoric of this movement internalizes and echoes such a civilizational and historically decontextualized metanarrative.[42] I observe variations on this theme below, in recasting the Moro conflict in the Philippines in civilizational terms.

The appeal to pan-Somali identity initially thrived because of the colonial administration's failure to invest in and extend rights to the Somali regions. It also garnered momentum due to the colonial forces' dismissal of the results of a 1962 referendum in the North Eastern Province, where a majority of Kenyan Somalis expressed their desire to join the Somali Republic.[43] This pattern continued in postindependence Kenya, through the transformation of the Somali-Kenyan border into a conflict zone and through the deepening of colonial alienation of the Somalis and other ethnic minorities still struggling, against forms of bureaucratic torture, to obtain identification cards, without which any movement is constrained.[44] Portions of the North Eastern Province were later incorporated into the coastal region and eastern provinces and further subdivided within the 2010 Constitution, but, as one observer argues, they "continue to coalesce around a shared history of trauma and marginalization."[45]

The Somali resistance further garnered the support of other Muslim and pastoralist ethnic groups who sought a more inclusive Kenya. Key chapters in

Journal of Eastern African Studies 1, no. 2 (2007): 277–91, http://dx.doi.org/10.1080/1753105070 1452564.

[42] For a challenge to any trace of a civilizational abstract narrative, see Brendon J. Cannon, "Why al-Shabaab Attacks Kenya: Questioning the Narrative Paradigm," *Terrorism and Political Violence* 31, no. 4 (2017): 836–52, https://doi.org/10.1080/09546553.2017.1290607. For an analysis of al-Shabaab's pragmatic adaptability and elastic manipulation of clan and religious identities and long-lasting grievances in Kenya's marginalized Muslim communities, see David M. Anderson and Jacob McKnight, "Understanding al-Shabaab: Clan, Islam and Insurgency in Kenya," *Journal of Eastern African Studies* 9, no. 3 (2015): 536–57, http://www.tandfonline.com/action/showCitFormats?doi= 10.1080/17531055.2015.1082254.

[43] G. Günther Schlee, *Identities on the Move: Clanship and Pastoralism in Northern Kenya*, vol. 5 (Manchester: Manchester University Press), 51.

[44] Abdi Shamsa Birik, "Accidental Citizens: Etherealizing Securitized Identities of Somalis in Kenya: Contesting Representation, Identity and Belonging," *Lune University Student Papers* (2016), 1–70 (26); Otunnu, "Factors Affecting the Treatment," 21. On the issue of identification cards, see Hannah Whittaker, "Legacies of Empire: State Violence and Collective Punishment in Kenya's Northeastern Province, c. 1963–present," *Journal of Imperial and Commonwealth History* 43, no. 4 (2015): 641–57, https://doi.org/10.1080/03086534.2015.1083232. See also Kenya Human Rights Commission, "Foreigners at Home: The Dilemma of Citizenship in Northern Kenya," 2010, http://www.khrc.or.ke/publications/66-foreigners-at-home-the-dilemma-of-citizenship-in-northern-kenya/file.html.

[45] Ibrahim Magara, "Contestation of the Somali Identity and Its Implication on Countering Violent Extremism in Kenya," unpublished manuscript, 2017, 19.

this history are the Shifta War (1963–67) and the massacres of Wagalla (1984) and Garissa (1980), which the Kenyan Truth, Justice, and Reconciliation Commission of 2013 attributed to failures of the government, though it did not deliver reparations or affirmative action policies to victims and their families.[46] The Shifta War refers to the name of armed Somali Kenyans who mobilized for secession in the aftermath of the dismissal of the referendum and clashed violently with Kenyan security forces. The Wagalla massacre refers to the forced detention of five thousand ethnic Somalis in Wagalla near Wajir, where the Kenyan army subjected them to torture before three hundred were eventually executed.[47] The Garissa massacre occurred when the government forces retaliated brutally in the form of collective punishment against ethnic Somalis for an attack by a local gang against a Defense Forces camp in the Northeast; three thousand Somalis died as a result. Only when Somalia threatened retaliation did the Kenyan forces release the remaining detainees.

Another critical chapter in this violent history is the Kenyan invasion of Somalia as part of its crackdown on al-Shabaab and its incorporation, together with the African Union Mission in Somalia, into the U.S. global "war on terror." The invasion lacked an exit strategy and inflamed civilizational Islamist narratives while enhancing the traction of recruitment efforts among Kenya's Somali communities.[48] The globalization of the terrorism issue, in turn, has facilitated the Kenyan government's othering of Muslim communities that have become targets of antiterrorism measures in ways that elide their long history of marginalization. Incidentally, the official definition of terrorism as "anti-state violent activities undertaken by non-state entities which are motivated by religious (Islamic) goals"[49] highlights this elision, especially considering that Somalis are majority Muslim; the

---

[46] For an analysis of the potential ramifications of the Truth, Justice, and Reconciliation Commission, see Christopher Gitari Ndungú, "Lessons to Be Learned: An Analysis of the Final Report of Kenya's Truth, Justice and Reconciliation Commission," *ICTJ Briefing*, May 2014, https://www.ictj.org/sites/default/files/ICTJ-Briefing-Kenya-TJRC-2014.pdf.

[47] See, for an analysis of this massacre, David M. Anderson, "Remembering Wagalla: State Violence in Northern Kenya, 1962–1991," *Journal of Eastern African Studies* 8 (2014): 658–76. See also Donovan C. Chau, "The Fourth Point: An Examination of the Influence of Kenyan Somalism," *Journal of Contemporary African Studies* 28 (2010): 297–312, http://dx.doi.org/10.1080/02589001.2010.497347.

[48] E. O. Odhiambo, T. L. Maito, J. Kassilly, S. Chelumo, K. Onkware, and W. A. Oboka, "Al-Shabaab Terrorists Propaganda and the Kenya Government Response," *Journal of Humanities and Social Science* 3, no. 7 (2013): 125–31; Lind, Mutahi, and Oosterom, "Tangled Ties."

[49] Edward Mogire and Kennedy Mkutu Agade, "Counterterrorism in Kenya," *Journal of Contemporary African Studies* 29, no. 4 (2011): 473–91 (473), https://www.tandfonline.com/doi/abs/10.1080/02589001.2011.600849.

divide-and-conquer colonial logic was now reconfigured into a new conflict framing in a context that historically was not originally divided along "religious" boundaries. This exposition raises a question regarding whether investing in the religion, harmony, and development business further extends this divisive colonial logic, reframed through the incorporation of Kenya into antiterrorism discourse targeting Muslims.[50]

Another notable development in the Kenyan landscape was the emergence, in the 1930s, of the African Instituted Churches, an Indigenous effort that rejected modernist and capitalist European worldviews. Instead, these churches focused on a community empowerment that rejects colonial utilitarian and individualistic logic. This indigenizing of Christianity, the midwife of colonial expansion and control, surely enabled the later consolidation of the postindependence practice of *harambee*, or community self-help, advocated by Jomo Kenyatta, the first postcolonial president. *Harambee* is not the same as neoliberal "resiliency" discourse, but the two fertilize each other. It is compounded by the postcolonial Christian currents of Pentecostal, charismatic, and prosperity gospels, which infiltrated Kenya. It is likewise rearticulated through the localized peacebuilding/development efforts, which raise the expectation that more and more Kenyans should take care of themselves—and more effectively and piously at that. This is where embodying richness and prosperity signals supposed faithfulness; such faithfulness then becomes a resource for survival.[51] The repackaging of *harambee* as a Kenyan brand resonates with a similar repackaging of the Tagalog concept of *kapwa* (literally, "fellow being"), which conveys the significance of helping others and loosely informs the consolidation of extensive charity and development-focused organizations.

This kind of co-optation of people's agency and resilient survival is precisely what the radical genealogy of the praxis of mutual aid resists when its articulators link material survival with critical pedagogy and revolutionary politics.[52] Instead, the neoliberal domestication of the mutual-aid ethos

---

[50] Under the urgency of the war on terrorism, the Kenyan state self-authorized in accordance with its security laws of 2014, article 42, section (1) of the National Intelligence Service to undertake covert operations with no need for compliance with the constitution: "measures, efforts and activities aimed at neutralizing threats against national security" (Security Laws Amendment Act, 2014, 343).

[51] See, especially, chapter 4 for this discussion of neoliberal piety.

[52] The genealogy of mutual aid goes back to the philosophy of anarchism and to anarchist Peter Kropotkin's 1902 publication *Mutual Aid*. See Ruth Kinna, "Kropotkin's Theory of Mutual Aid in Historical Context," *International Review of Social History* 40, no. 2 (1995): 259–83, https://www.jstor.org/stable/44583751. Not all manifestations of mutual aid praxis are anarchist, as in their refusal to put demands on the state's failures to care for marginalized populations. See, for example, Thomas

means that relationship building happens through various efforts to connect communities by way of engaging them in projects for the "common good" and "social cohesion," which link mutually ensured peace to mutually ensured economic survival. This co-optation into a neoliberal frame is different from the revolutionary connection between mutual aid societies and the social and political change that such prefigurative communities envision through their acts of nonreliance on White supremacist and bourgeois societies for their material survival. The co-optation of mutual aid practices, as well as the neighborly and survivalist impulses underlying them, unfolds precisely through what I refer to as the "double closures" and "mutual indexing" to one another of communal and religiocultural boundaries. Hence, it is not only the case that engaging religion to reduce violence or enhance development praxis is expedient. Such utilitarianism, I show throughout, is also conducive to diminishing the horizons of the political imagination. Such closures reinforce the neoliberal resiliency discourse by spiritualizing people's capacity to peacefully ensure one another's mutual material survival. The double closures of communal lines and hermeneutical or interpretive spaces constitute a colonial afterlife; I explain and trace this operation and its push for peace without accompanying historical or affirmative justice throughout the book.

Religion's institutional capacity to feed people and deliver other life-sustaining services, and even religious communities' anticolonial efforts, can never be simplistically posited as a direct or innocent conduit of peace and justice. Like all other actors and institutions, religion is always mediated through historical and sociological mechanisms. Accounts that posit religion as potentially over and against such social mechanisms are simplistic in interpreting religion's causality in the world. This is not to argue that religion is not causal or potentially an independent, rather than merely a dependent, variable in sociopolitical analyses. It is instead to render it as always implicated in and bounded by human interpretive fallibility and mediating historical and sociological contexts. Hence, the convergence with and the co-optation of preexisting Christian-Muslim localized conflict narratives into the global "war on terror" entailed the differentiated assimilation of Muslim communities into global colonial/modernist grammars of racialization and the scaffolding of the contemporary orientalist security discourse.

Hummel, "Mutual Aid Networks: Toward a Constructive Critique," *Left Voice*, July 6, 2020, https://www.leftvoice.org/mutual-aid-networks-toward-a-constructive-critique.

By "racialization," I refer to race as a dehumanization category intrinsic to modernity's political and economic projects of displacement, exploitation, and nation-building. Related to the underlying role of orientalism as a discourse authorizing the colonial project and the construction of the West as a political and intellectual project juxtaposed with the Orient or its ideal other, Muslim communities have become racialized as postcolonial subjects in the West through their continuous othering and marginalization. The racialization of Muslims in the postcolonial moment assimilates Muslim communities into other "people of color" who collectively embody the other of enduring White supremacist (Christian) nationalist/civilizationist discourses. These processes illuminate the complex relations among nation, religion, and race in modernity. Accordingly, disentangling "religion" from such patterns is insufficiently attentive to the ways in which religion is mediated sociologically, politically, and, in my case studies, through a global discourse of counterterrorism. Political elites, in both Kenya and the Philippines, abstracted "their" Muslim communities and assimilated them into the counterterrorism discourse, thereby extrapolating expediently the "religion" variable from an interrogation of historical injustices and how colonial policies of divide and conquer cast long shadows on contemporary sites of violence.

Therefore, the ideological diffusion of the war on terror constitutes an afterlife of coloniality. So does the transnational diffusion of Wahhabism and its purist comfort with secularist abstractions that work to depoliticize Islam and, at the same time, mobilize it as an anticolonial currency and police its boundaries, especially pertaining to gender and race.[53] Both Kenya and the Philippines, therefore, reveal complex religious landscapes that resist easy categorization of either the colonial or the anticolonial legacies of religion and ethnocultural identifications. I now turn to examine the Moro conflict narrative in Mindanao, which exemplifies the assimilation of particular postcolonial dynamics of minoritization and dispossession into the hegemonic, securitizing, anti-Muslim, racializing discourse—a dynamic both of my case studies share, despite their many differences.

---

[53] For this critical engagement with Wahhabism for its failure to perform decoloniality, see Piro Rexhepi, Samira Musleh, and Romana Mirza, "Bandung before and after: Islam, the Islamicate and the De/Colonial," *Reorient*, n.d., https://www.criticalmuslimstudies.co.uk/bandung-before-and-after/ (accessed November 2, 2020).

Land and Insurgency

The Philippines, like Kenya, epitomizes the enduring centrality of land thefts and disputes as well as the marginalization of IPs (in this case, the Lumad people) and Muslim populations to contemporary conflict and violence.[54] Indeed, going back to the seventeenth century, revolts of Chinese Filipinos coalesced with the Moro struggles and with a host of Indigenous resistance efforts all revolving around property rights, tax collection, and Catholic conversion practices.[55] Religious and communal identities themselves do not constitute the source of the conflict in Mindanao; rather, enduring systemic inequalities and discrimination against Muslim and Lumad Mindanaoans, combined with Manila's settlement policies of channeling Christians to the southern island (known as "domestic colonization"), transformed the island's demographics. The socioeconomic hierarchization dates back, however, to the long centuries of Spanish colonialism and to its evangelizing (and "civilizing") legacy.

The valuation and devaluation of humans relied initially, in the sixteenth century, on a proto-race category already in play at the early historical moments of European colonial expansion, concurring with the proto-nationalist construction of Spain through the formal exclusion of Jews and Muslims and subjecting them to the mechanisms of the Inquisition and expulsions. The racializing and nationalizing of religion (consecrating the "nation" as a people with a specific destiny and pure boundaries) are part and parcel of abstracting "religion" as a taxonomic instrument of empire.[56] Tracing pedagogical history, Jeffrey Ayala Milligan underscores that the American policy of "imperial pedagogy" explains the contemporary dynamics of Muslim-Christian relations in the Philippines, a country still "enmeshed in a more or less neocolonial relationship with the United States."[57] Accordingly,

---

[54] For an analysis of the centrality of land-related grievances and how the global war on terror functions to distract from these grievances as it relates to colonial afterlives as well as ongoing legacies of marginalization, see, for example, Astrid S. Tuminez, "This Land Is Our Land: Moro Ancestral Domain and Its Implications for Peace and Development in the Southern Philippines," *SAIS Review* 27, no. 2 (2007): 77–91, https://www.jstor.org/stable/27000092.

[55] Berkley Center, "Faith and Development in Focus: Philippines," 8.

[56] For example, David Chidester, *Empire of Religion: Imperialism and Comparative Religion* (Chicago: Chicago University Press, 2014). See also Masuzawa, *The Invention of World Religions*; Tisa Wenger, *Religious Freedom: The Contested History of an American Ideal* (Chapel Hill: University of North Carolina Press, 2017); Tisa Wenger, *We Have a Religion: The 1920s Pueblo Indian Dance Controversy and American Religious Freedom* (Chapel Hill: University of North Carolina Press, 2009).

[57] Jeffrey Ayala Milligan, *Islamic Identity, Postcoloniality and Educational Policy* (Singapore: Palgrave Macmillan, 2020), https://doi.org/10.1007/978-981-15-1228-5, 6.

the recasting of the Moro conflict as civilizational echoed deeper colonial developmentalist discourse that marked the American colonization of the southern Philippines and was extended through postindependence internal colonization. Imperial pedagogy constitutes an "intermediate step in the evolution of colonial relations from explicit economic exploitation and religious evangelization to a discourse of social development that masks the continued subordination of religious and cultural minorities behind the benevolent face of the teacher and the democratic ethos of the public school."[58] Hence, to the degree that religion and the practices of peace/development continue to operate with a double closure that delimits the communal boundaries to religious lines and vice versa, the peace discourse persists as an extension of the colonial frames by other means. Only an intersectional lens would unsettle such closures.[59] Mindanao manifests such colonial afterlives. Although the Spanish colonial administration was never able to conquer the Moro in the southern part of the Philippines, the modern/colonial logic of racialization has been operative and evident in the era of postcolonial domestic colonization that has resulted in the minoritization of the Muslims in Mindanao. In ways similar to the long-term outcomes emerging from British colonialism in Kenya, the poorest areas are also majority or traditionally Muslim and/or Indigenous.

Through the tool of land titles or the Regalian Doctrine that the Spaniards (whose rule lasted from 1565 to 1898) brought with them in the sixteenth century, together with the Spaniards' labeling of the internally plural and diverse Muslim tribes as "Moros" (i.e., Moors), Muslims and Lumads became dispossessed.[60] Because the Spaniards never attained total control of Moro lands, this process, which undermined the Moro tradition of communal

---

[58] Ibid., 56.

[59] For the conceptual underpinnings of this argument regarding the proto-race category and the role of the Inquisition, see Nelson Maldonado-Torres, "AAR Centennial Roundtable: Religion, Conquest, and Race in the Foundations of the Modern/Colonial World," *Journal of the American Academy of Religion* 82, no. 3 (2014): 636–65, https://www.jstor.org/stable/24487991; Gil Anidjar, *Blood: A Critique of Christianity* (New York: Columbia University Press, 2014); Anthony Marx, *Faith in Nation* (Oxford: Oxford University Press, 2003).

[60] The Moros, a political category of identification denoting Muslim resistance to the forces of Catholic conversion and Spanish colonization, include many ethnic groups: Iranun (in northern Maguindanao and especially in the districts of Matanog, Barira, Buldon, and Parang, as well as Lanao del Sur and Cotabato); the Kagan in the Coastal Davao Gulf; the Kalibugan in the Zamboanga Peninsula; the Maguindanao in Maguindanao and Cotabato; the Maranao in Lake Lanao in Lanao del Sur and Lanao del Norte; the Molbog in Balabac Island and Bataraza; the Palewanon in Palawan; the Sama-Baju in Tawi Tawi; the Sulu Archipelago, and all across the coastal southern Mindanao; Sangil in Sarangani Islands; the Coastal South Cotabato, and Davao del Sur; the Tausuk in Sulu, Basilan, Taw-Tawi, and Palawan; and the Yakan in Basilan and Zamboanga City. For this breakdown, see Berkley Center, "Faith and Development in Focus: Philippines," 53.

landownership, accelerated under the U.S. administration (1898–1946), whose laws voided previous claims to Moro lands by their inhabitants as well as their traditional and political associations with regional sultanates.[61] This dispossession and land grab also involved the disestablishment of Catholicism (1901) and the preferential treatment of Protestant denominations, which, as in the practice of the British, were given, by way of the First Comity Agreement of 1898, designated spheres for their evangelizing efforts. Prior to American colonization and Manila's domestic colonization, Muslims of multiple tribal affiliations enjoyed a clear majority. With domestic colonization, first through the Americans and then by Manila, they became, as noted, minoritized.[62] This is the background to the eventual emergence of separatist Muslim insurgent movements in the late 1960s and to the unfolding of bloodshed and massive displacement of populations throughout Mindanao over decades.[63]

As in Kenya, numerous tragic moments populate the Mindanaoan chronology. The Jabidah Massacre on March 18, 1968, is often cited as the starting point of the Moro conflict, but, of course, this periodization, as is often the case, glosses over deeper causes rooted in colonial encroachment, economic exploitation, and erosion. Also known as the Corregidor Massacre, denoting its location, the Jabidah Massacre refers to the murder by the Armed Forces of the Philippines of sixty Moro army recruits undergoing a military operation to reclaim Sabah from Malaysia, citing an earlier (since 1658) agreement that granted territorial control to the sultanate of Sulu. The massacre primed University of the Philippines professor Nur Misuari to launch an armed insurgency, the Moro National Liberation Front (MNLF), which sought secession and independence. Eventually, the MNLF splintered into various groups, including the Moro Islamic Liberation Front (MILF), which focused

---

[61] The legal maneuvers included the Land Registration Act of 1902, designed to exclude Moros and IPs still operating with ancestral and communal ownership concepts. The Land Registration Act also depended on legal and other forms of literacy not available to Moros and IPs at the time. The 1902 law was followed by the Philippine Commission Act No. 718 in 1903; it eliminated the ability to obtain land grants by Datus, non-Christian tribes, and Moro sultans. This paved the way for the Public Act of 1905, which declared that unregistered land would immediately be under the possession of the government. See Tuminez, "This Land Is Our Land," 79.

[62] See Tuminez, "This Land Is Our Land," 80.

[63] "The Moro conflict" usually refers to the postcolonial era, but an insurgency had also taken place between 1899 and 1913, known as the Moro Rebellion, as well as the Spanish-Moro conflict. For a historically nuanced account of the mythology of a transcendent Moro identity and how it reflects a European imposition directly related to the long presence of Spanish colonialism in the region, see Thomas M. McKenna, *Everyday Politics and Armed Separatism in the Southern Philippines* (Los Angeles: University of California Press, 1998), especially ch. 4.

on establishing an Islamic state. As in Kenya, countering the insurgency gradually became folded into the global war on nonstate terror(ism), as did the repression of the communist insurgence and eventually human rights defenders of peasants' rights. The war on terror's orientalist securitizing frame enabled the glossing over of the long, layered histories of colonial dispossession and the particularities of regional dynamics in favor of grand metanarratives about transnational threats and civilizational claims.

Such opportunism notwithstanding, the insurgency's roots go back to Bangsomoro's long resistance to colonial intrusions. In addition to the Jabidah and other massacres (e.g., the Manili Massacre of 1971) under Marcos's watch, another important point of reference in the Moro resistance narrative is the Treaty of Paris of 1898, which established the American military government over the Philippines and shortly thereafter replaced the Spanish government. After guaranteeing Moro neutrality during the American-Philippine War by way of an agreement with the sultan of Sulu (Jamalul Kiram II), the American occupation of the Philippines resulted not in Moro sovereignty but in an American invasion in 1904.[64] Another key event was the bilateral ceasefire, the Tripoli Agreement signed in 1976 between the Philippines government and the MNLF, which also stipulated that Mindanao should remain within the jurisdiction of the Philippines, but with thirteen provinces designated as an autonomous government of the Bangsamoro people. However, Marcos soon violated the terms of the Tripoli framework and subsequently reignited violence.

Sheikh Salamat Hashim established the MILF in 1978 as a splinter movement alienated by the MNLF's willingness to negotiate with the government on the government's own terms. During the late 1980s and the final decade of the twentieth century (essentially during the tenure of Presidents Aquino and Ramos), a series of negotiations ensued, resulting in the establishment of the Autonomous Region in Muslim Mindanao (ARMM) in 1989 under Republic Act No. 6734, also known as the ARMM Organic Act, which encompassed the five provinces of Basilan, Lanao del Sur, Maguindanao, Sulu, and Tawi Tawi, with the city of Cotabato as its governance center. However, the tensions escalated with the establishment of the Abu Sayyaf Group in 1991 as a result of cross-fertilization initially with Jemaah Islamiyah from Indonesia, then with Osama bin Laden and al-Qaeda, and then with the

---

[64] Notably, the leaders of Moro communities in Mindanao petitioned the U.S. administration in 1921, 1924, and 1935 to grant Moros an autonomous sphere to separate these communities from Hispanized and Christianized Filipinos. Of course, such petitions were rejected.

all-out war against the MILF declared by President Estrada in 2000.[65] This war destroyed much of the MILF's insurgent infrastructure in Mindanao. Still, the government's assault fueled terrorist actions, including kidnappings and bombings in Manila and other regions. The terrorist actions also sowed a reign of insurgent terror in Mindanao, as many villages were seized by the insurgency in the North Cotabato Province in the 2000s to exert pressure on the government to include the province in the ARMM. The Supreme Court rejected this demand, due to concerns of the Christian inhabitants in the region. Eventually and after a plebiscite in February 2019, sixty-three *barangays*[66] in six different towns of North Cotabato became integrated into the Bangsamoro region.

The contours of the Moro conflict were reframed as Operation Enduring Freedom–Philippines (2002–15) with the co-optation of the Philippines into the American war on terror, absorbing, as noted, opportunistic versions of its underlying anti-Muslim racism, which suggests why Muslims within the context of modernity/coloniality are colonized subjects, regardless of and in distinction from Muslim imperial histories, including their own traces in both the Kenyan and Filipino contexts.[67] Hence, the opportune assimilation of fault lines within both countries into the orientalist discourse of the "war on terror" itself extended the colonial logic into the postcolonial space through the importation of ahistorical conflict narratives and convenient culturalist reductionism. Indeed, to gloss over the ongoing logic of the Regalian Doctrine, the "war on terror" reductively shifted the analysis of conflict from the realm of historical accounting for injustice and colonial plunder to a civilizational plane trapped in ahistorical and essentializing explanatory frames. Efforts for peace need to be read within and through this global lens and amid ongoing realities of extractive economic plunder.[68]

During the presidency of Benigno Aquino (2010–16), some efforts to reopen peace talks between the MNLF and the government as well as

---

[65] For an analysis of the genesis and consolidation of the Abu Sayyaf Group, see Rommel C. Banlaoi, "The Abu Sayyaf Group: From Mere Banditry to Genuine Terrorism," *Southeast Asian Affairs* (2006): 247–62, https://doi.org/10.1080/10576100701812902.

[66] *Barangay* is the native word for "village" and constitutes a small administrative unit.

[67] Salman Sayyid, "Empire, Islam and the Postcolonial," in University of South Australia's International Centre for Muslim and Non-Muslim Understanding Working Paper no. 9, 2012, https://apo.org.au/sites/default/files/resource-files/2012-07/apo-nid57054.pdf.

[68] The extractive dynamics are still in play in Mindanao, implemented with the help of local politicians and informal miners as well as other relevant actors. See, for example, Boris Verbrugge, "Undermining the State? Informal Mining and Trajectories of State Formation in Eastern Mindanao, Philippines," *Critical Asian Studies* 45, no. 2 (2015): 177–99, https://doi.org/10.1080/14672715.2015.997973.

representatives from the MILF joined with Norway to monitor the implementation of a ceasefire between the MILF and the government in 2011. However, violence ensued nonetheless. Then in January 2014, a peace agreement was signed in Kuala Lumpur between the Philippine government and the MILF, which finally paved the way for the establishment of a new Muslim autonomous entity, the Bangsamoro, with an intention to bring it, together with the disarming of the MILF resurgent forces, into fruition by 2016.[69] In March 2014, negotiations resulted in the Comprehensive Agreement on the Bangsamoro between the government of the Philippines and the MILF,[70] but more confrontations with splinter insurgent groups continued from 2015 through the present time of writing, especially in Northern Cotabato and Maguindanao,[71] with the particularly shocking siege on Marawi (in Lanao del Sur) in 2017, which led Duterte to declare martial law in Mindanao, reigniting for many people the specter of past nightmares.[72] Most of my interlocutors in the intra- and interreligious spaces in Mindanaoan civil society participated in various ways in managing the frustrations and fears of communities affected by these events and the possibility of Bangsamoro autonomous governance, including an interreligious peacebuilding focus on negotiating and settling different types of land disputes, which was interpreted as a critical dynamic in working toward the broader implementation of a peace framework.[73]

---

[69] The term *Bangsamoro* derives originally from Malay, the word *bansa* referring to descent groups or castes. *Moro*, of course, derives from the Spanish label, but denotes people who identify as Muslims and who inhabit southern Mindanao and Palawan provinces as well as the Sulu archipelago.

[70] See Paul D. Hutchcroft, ed., *Mindanao: The Long Journey to Peace and Prosperity* (Mandaluyong City: Anvil, 2016), especially chs. 4 and 5.

[71] Maguindanao or, more specifically, the town of Ampatuan (in the Maguindanao Province) was the site of the Amptuan or Maguindanao massacre in 2009. The massacre of fifty-eight people, including thirty journalists, was politically motivated to crush the candidacy of Esmael Mangudadatu, whose convoy was on its way to file formal candidacy papers. The Amptual massacre also became part of a narrative of trauma and oppression, and it led the Committee to Protect Journalists to declare the Philippines one of the most dangerous places for journalists and free media.

[72] See Rohan Gunaratna, "The Siege of Marawi: A Game Changer in Terrorism in Asia," *Counter Terrorist Trends and Analyses* 9, no. 7 (2017), https://www.jstor.org/stable/pdf/26351533.pdf?refreqid=excelsior%3Ad097d9e8cb210db534e8b36ec8fa8976.

[73] Land disputes in Mindanao include boundary conflicts, mortgage and transactional conflicts, and competing land claims, the resolution of which required devising ways to strengthen the Lupong Tagapamayapa (communal barangay-based pacification mechanism), traditional leaders, and multisectoral cooperation with municipalities and legal authorities. This is the rationale behind the kind of interreligious peacebuilding work that CRS engaged in and that I study in this book as an exemplar of religion and the practice of peacebuilding. For a description of the typology of land disputes and a self-assessment of CRS's efforts through its "Applying the 3Bs" between 2012 and 2015 focusing on twenty barangays, see Nell Bolton and Myla Leguro, "Local Solutions to Land Conflict in Mindanao: Policy Lessons from Catholic Relief Services Applying the 3Bs (Binding, Bonding, Bridging) to Land Conflict Project," CRS, October 2015, https://www.crs.org/sites/default/files/

New Mindanaoan Scripts?

The Siege or Battle of Marawi lasted from May 23 to October 23, 2017. It involved the killing of Christians by Muslim militants as well as severe clashes with the forces of the government deployed to the city to fight the instigators of the violence. They included the Maute Group, or the Islamic State of Lanao,[74] and Abu Sayyaf, along with a few other self-defined Muslim forces[75] allegedly linked to Daʻesh in ways that shift the contours of the Moro conflict and escalate its religious rhetoric. Over a thousand people were killed over the course of the siege, and over 100,000 were displaced. Many of the peacebuilding actors I met in Mindanao were redirected to Marawi and to efforts to work with the communities there to facilitate receptiveness to the implementation of the peace process and the Bangsamoro Organic Law (BOL, signed into law by Duterte in July 2018) and to de-escalate frustrations and fears.[76] The siege was shocking because Marawi had long been a site of interreligious peacebuilding and efforts to strengthen intercommunal relationships in anticipation of peace.[77]

In June 2019, in Cagayan de Oro, I met a Catholic priest named Teresito "Chito" Soganub Chito who had been sent to Marawi to promote interreligious peace decades before the siege, 117 days of which he had spent as a hostage, together with a hundred others, in the basement of the Bato mosque, which served as the headquarters of the insurgent operation.[78] Throughout his captivity, Father Chito found himself in a complicated relationship with his captors, as he dined with and prayed for them. To survive, he even helped make bombs, as they all—captors and hostages—endured aerial bombardment by the U.S.-assisted governmental forces. When I met

---

tools-research/local-solutions-to-land-conflict-in-mindanao.pdf. I address the logic of the A3Bs in my analysis of interreligious peace governance in chapter 2.

[74] The Maute was named after two brothers who returned to the region after exposure to Daʻesh.
[75] Additional active armed insurgent groups include the Bangsamoro Islamic Freedom Fighters, established in 2014, and the Ansar Khalifa Philippines, established in 2008.
[76] If implemented correctly, the BOL essentially is designed to devolve powers to the Bangsamoro government. For an analysis of the BOL, see Malcolm Cook, "Three Challenges Facing the Bangsamoro Organic Law," *Yusof Ishak Institute*, no. 82 (2018), https://www.iseas.edu.sg/images/pdf/ISEAS_Perspective_2018_82@50.pdf.
[77] Rory MacNeil, "Marawi: Behind the Headlines," *The Diplomat*, August 31, 2017, https://thediplomat.com/2017/08/marawi-behind-the-headlines/.
[78] See, for example, Josephine Casserly and Howard Johnson, "The Priest Who Survived the Siege of Marawi," *BBC News*, September 5, 2019, https://www.bbc.com/news/stories-49584150.

Father Chito, in what turned out to be the last year of his life, he served as the chairman of the Board of Interfaith Leaders of Pakigdait.

Pakigdait (Tagalog for "peace"), to which I will return throughout the book, defines itself as an interfaith grassroots peacebuilding organization. It focuses on conflict transformation, peace advocacy, interfaith dialogue, cultural sensitivity, and peace-anchored community development in northern Mindanao.[79] Father Chito prominently featured in the work of Pakigdait as he made his way, in the months following his captivity, through violence-affected spots in Mindanao, bringing together the military and MILF and embodying the meaning of forgiveness and the overcoming of divisions for the sake of peace. Such efforts to shuttle interfaith actors across Mindanao are often sponsored by larger intergovernmental or global organizations focused on religion as "the missing dimension" in peacebuilding and development praxis.[80] Of course, familiarity with the story of Father Chito and many others challenges any attempts to reduce their religious peace agency to a global design. Nevertheless, the rhetorical and performative emphasis on peace as interreligious harmony, which defines interreligious and intercultural praxis in Mindanao, has functioned both as a survival mechanism with authentic openings toward new Mindanaoan scripts and as an instrument of the harmony business that relies on people's capacity to survive and, through relationship building, ensure one another's security and livelihood, as a mechanism to maintain the status quo.

This is where a different narrative of conflict between the New People's Army and other communist strands diverges with its critique of colonialism, imperialism, and exploitative capitalism from the orientalist abstraction and assimilation that the Moro conflict axis lends itself to. The same explanatory frame that glosses over colonial and historical underpinnings and assimilates this conflict into the "war on terror" also informs the work of religion and peace. An emphasis on engineering interreligious harmony muffles through its mechanisms of double closures the indexing of communal interests to religious boundaries, and the delineation of these boundaries according to conservative and hermeneutically closed horizons.[81] Structural inequalities and

---

[79] Pakigdait pamphlet description, shared with me ahead of my focus group with the board in June 2019 in Cagayan de Oro.

[80] This is an allusion to a book often credited as a point of departure for the literature on religion and international relations: Douglas Johnson and Cynthia Sampson, eds., *Religion: The Missing Dimension of Statecraft* (Oxford: Oxford University Press, 1994).

[81] For an important intervention tracing the corruption of Filipino efforts to decolonize due to continuous American shaping of the postcolony, see Charlie Samuya Veric, *Children of the*

identity-based discrimination, grounded in familiar patterns of racialization or social hierarchization, remain key issues that reflect an enduring history of privileging property rights for (Christian) settlers and ranchers from the mainland and commercial interests of logging companies at the expense of protecting Indigenous rights and ancestral domains.[82]

The issue of ancestral domains became pivotal for cultivating conditions for a peace agreement and for the consolidation of the Bangsamoro Autonomous Region in Muslim Mindanao (BARMM) after the ratification of the BOL in the 2019 plebiscite (designed to redress Muslim grievances).[83] The IPs' Rights Act passed in 1997 constitutes a key point of reference for its recognition of self-determination, ancestral domain, and other rights for the over 110 Indigenous ethnolinguistic groups, all of which embody cultural traditions and practices that need protection.[84]

The BARMM replaces the earlier ARMM and focuses on parliamentary-democratic forms of governance intended to include representation of IPs. In terms of legal systems, exclusively Muslim cases fall under the jurisdiction of Shari'a courts, a point that generated, as in the Kenyan case of Qadhi courts, fears in Christian residents that promoters of the BARMM attempted to dispel, often through the mechanisms of intra- and interfaith engagements.[85]

Postcolony: Filipino Intellectuals and Decolonization, 1946–1972 (Quezon City: Ateneo de Manila University Press, 2020).

[82] For a genealogy of the concept of "ancestral domain" as central to the promotion of and claiming of the rights of IPs in the Philippines as well as for the complicated legacy of the Indigenous Peoples Rights Act of 1997 as yet another mechanism for economic exploitation by outside investors and opportunists (including those related to the mining agenda) and conflicting claims of Islamized IPs in the "Bangsamoro homeland" and other IPs, see Dennis S. Erasga, "Ancestral Domain Claim: The Case of the Indigenous People in Muslim Mindanao (ARMM)," *Asia-Pacific Social Science Review* 8, no. 1 (2008): 33–44, http://dx.doi.org/10.3860/apssr.v8i1.704.

[83] The BOL was heralded by women's rights activists as a welcome development; see UN Women, "Passage of the Bangsomoro Organic Law Promises New Hope for Women in Southern Philippines," March 4, 2019, https://www.unwomen.org/en/news/stories/2019/3/news-bangsamoro-organic-law-promises-hope-for-women-in-southern-philippines. However, non-Islamized IPs (Lumads) were often excluded from the peace negotiations, which led to yet another layer of marginality and inaccessibility to land claims. Initially referred to as the Bangsamoro Basic Law, or BBL, the bill was understood as the future legal framework of the ARMM, and its ratification was directly linked to the implementation of the Comprehensive Agreement on the Bangsamoro entered into between the government of the Philippines and the MILF. The aim of the BBL was to establish the new political entity of the Bangsamoro. See Office of the Presidential Adviser on the Peace Process, "Bangsamoro Basic Law (BBL): Myths vs. Facts," a pamphlet given to me during my visit to the autonomous Muslim region in June 2018.

[84] However, the mere passing of the Indigenous Peoples Rights Act and awarding of Ancestral Domains Claims do not solve the environmental threat posed by loggers and other economic exploiters. See June Prill-Brett, "Contested Domains: The Indigenous Peoples Rights Act (IPRA) and Legal Pluralism in the Northern Philippines," *Journal of Legal Pluralism and Unofficial Law* 39, no. 55 (2007): 11–36.

[85] See also chapter 7.

Of course, insistence on Shari'a jurisdiction also assumes that all Muslims are interested in being subject to Shari'a-based rulings. Such an assumption exemplifies the double closures underlying religion and peace praxis. In addition to Shari'a courts, tribal laws are designated to adjudicate disputes within and between IPs, with the same assumptions. As I indicated, in Kenya, along with the other "hot button" issues regarding reproductive rights, the inclusion of Qadhi's courts system—the operation of which is a highly familiar feature of the British colonial legacy of divide and rule—in the 2010 Constitution regulating personal status issues among the minority-Muslim communities also generated much rhetoric and fear.

In both locations of my fieldwork, anti-Muslim fearmongering was nourished by the global "war on terror." Consequently, in both cases, a narrative about the marginalization of Muslim communities is inverted into an amnesic narrative of fear about a Muslim takeover. Accordingly, we see how foregrounding religion in the analysis of conflict and the practices of peace risks the erasure of questions about historical injustices and their long-term implications for affected communities. This narrative inversion certainly feeds into a harmony discourse that locates the sources of violent conflict in interreligious misinterpretations, misperceptions, and perverse understandings of the "true" message of faith/religion/culture and thus focuses peacebuilding efforts on alleviating fears through "getting to know one another." Religion and the practices of peace, in other words, reinforce culturalist and ahistorical explanatory frames regarding the causes of violent eruptions and the conditions of poverty and marginalization. Such practices also enhance the modernist dynamics of double closure of communal and hermeneutical boundaries and their mutual indexing.

As in the Kenyan case, religious institutions in the Philippines are central players in the harmony and development discourse, both helping people eat (cultivating resilience to repeated and increasing environmental disasters and violent eruptions) as well as promoting peace. Such institutional organs include the Catholic Bishops' Conference of the Philippines (CBCP), originally the Catholic Welfare Organization, which was established in 1945 in response to the humanitarian devastation in the aftermath of the Japanese occupation during World War II, but which shifted its focus to doctrine and evangelization in 1967 and was thus renamed. Its social work was reinstated through the National Secretariat for Social Action in 1969, which aspired to more than just targeted charity and effected a broader social transformation.[86] As noted, this institution eventually (but not immediately) sided with the revolutionary effort to oust the authoritarian regime of Marcos and occasionally played a role defending democratic practices moving forward, including issuing a pastoral letter in 2019 that examined the moral implications of Duterte's practice of extrajudicial killing. The CBCP also partook in interfaith engagement to secure readiness for the implementation of the Bangsamoro peace agreement and to resist escalation in the aftermath of the Jolo Cathedral bombing.[87]

The CBCP's sphere of work is augmented by a massive phenomenon of lay Catholic organizations, mostly populated by charismatic Catholics[88] and various faith-inspired organizations, such as CRS, World Vision, and Iglesia Ni Cristo.[89] On the Muslim side, the National Commission on Muslim Filipinos coordinates development in Muslim communities that concentrate in the Sulu Archipelago, southern Palawan, and western Mindanao—an effort further enhanced by assistance from Islamic Relief, among other such transnational faith-inspired organizations, as well as intergovernmental, governmental, and transnational development agencies more broadly. In the chapters that follow, I highlight the immense effort devoted to interreligious and intercultural peacebuilding in Mindanao as the people who populate that organizational space aspire to implement the Bangsamoro peace vision, as Father Chito did, in the midst of the co-optation of the Moro struggle into

---

[86] Berkley Center, "Faith and Development in Focus: Philippines," 33. For an analysis of the underlying conditions leading to the shift in the CBCP's approach to martial law from a global perspective examining structural imperialism, see Robert L. Youngblood, "Structural Imperialism: An Analysis of the Catholic Bishops' Conference of the Philippines," *Comparative Political Studies* 15, no. 1 (1982): 29–56, https://doi.org/10.1177%2F0010414082015001002. For an analysis of the CBCP's ambivalent maneuvering in the postauthoritarian period, see Antonio D. Moreno, "Engaged Citizenship: The Catholic Bishops' Conference of the Philippines (CBCP) in the Post-Authoritarian Philippines," in *Development, Civil Society and Faith-Based Organizations*, ed. G. Clarke and M. Jennings, International Political Economy Series (London: Palgrave Macmillan, 2008), 117–44. For the long-term ramifications of the colonization of the Philippines on the contours of involvement of the local Catholic church in intervening and shaping public discourse, see Roberto Rivera, "Philippine Catholicism as Disruptive Public Religion: A Sociological Analysis of Philippine Catholic Bishops' Statements, 1946 to 2000," *Philippine Sociological Review* 58 (2010): 75–96, https://www.jstor.org/stable/i40138245.

[87] Berkley Center, "Faith and Development in Focus: Philippines," 34. For a statement of the CBCP in support of the BOL, see "The Bangsamoro Organic Law and Beyond," *CBCPNews*, January 23, 2019, https://cbcpnews.net/cbcpnews/the-bangsamoro-organic-law-and-beyond/. Bishops also mobilized in advance to the plebiscite on the BOL (2019) in peaceful support; see Mark Joy G. Basallajes, "Kidapawan Bishop Calls for Peace amid BOL Vote," *CBCPNews*, January 23, 2019, https://cbcpnews.net/cbcpnews/kidapawan-bishop-calls-for-peace-amid-bol-vote/.

[88] Berkley Center, "Faith and Development in Focus: Philippines," 38.

[89] Ibid., 60.

global apocalyptic and/or anti-Muslim racialized narratives, both of which contribute to erasures of concrete Moro grievances and political objectives. Even with the assimilation of the Philippines and Kenya into the abstraction of the global war on terror, inverting its logic by stressing the role of religion and peace cannot reside in similar abstractions.

Who Are the Scribes of Peace?

The brief sketches of these two sites in Kenya and the Philippines, both deeply religious societies and both reflective of regional disparities and variations in terms of poverty and other vulnerabilities, gesture toward the colonial afterlives in the postcolonial moment and the complex ways in which religious and ethnic/tribal identifications intersect with structural and historical injustices as well as conflict and peace narratives.[90] Both contexts divulge an enhanced collaboration between the government and private sectors and signal an acquiescence to the logic of neoliberal developmentalism rather than a social justice approach.[91]

In addition to its robust civil society, of which religious actors are an integral part, the Filipino private sector has long participated in poverty reduction efforts through charity and philanthropy, performing their "corporate responsibility"[92] but actually further entrenching the systemic and historical injustices. I found an analogous dynamic in Kenya, where, as I noted, the revolutionary potentialities of the mutual aid praxis of *harambee* (like *kapwa*) are depoliticized through their co-optation into charity and developmentalist logics. However, a key player in the Kenyan private sector resisted any such implication. Sitting in a Nairobi café, he told me in a regretful tone that human rights defenders' "noisiness and confrontational style"[93] accomplish nothing except the "media coverage they need for their donors."[94] In contrast, he stressed, he and other actors in the private sector

---

[90] For an examination of the patterns of religiosity and secularity in the postcolonial Philippines, see David T. Buckley, *Faithful to Secularism: The Religious Politics of Democracy in Ireland, Senegal, and the Philippines* (New York: Columbia University Press, 2017), chs. 6–7.

[91] See National Economic and Development Authority, "Philippines Development Plan, 2017–2022: Abridged Version" (Pasig City: National Economic and Development Authority, 2017), http://www.neda.gov.ph/wp-content/uploads/2017/12/Abridged-PDP-2017-2022_Final.pdf.

[92] Berkley Center, "Faith and Development in Focus: Philippines," 23.

[93] Interview, Nairobi, November 2018.

[94] Ibid.

can achieve much more in terms of peacebuilding and other dividends by methodically exerting pressure and convening forums of pertinent players whose inclusion is the result of invitation rather than agitation.

He further underscored that, to label the "business community" as concerned only with "profit" amounts to "a demeaning generalization." In reality, he said, "there are wonderful people within my work, within the private sector who actually want to see a great Kenya very much, a Kenya of shared prosperity."[95] He also repeatedly stressed that the private sector constitutes the "scribe" of a new script for Kenya. It has foresight and the know-how to implement progress. It was this same private-sector actor who lamented the "underdevelopment" in the Coast Province as a direct result of its inhabitants' personal failings. Positing the "business community" as key, through partnership and/or philanthropic relations, to development and peace, therefore, comes in the flavor of reductive culturalist assumptions and capitalist amnesic triumphalism, myopic of the extractive and dehumanizing racialization and historical structural forms of violence underpinnings of contemporary wealth and other disparities. Partnership with the private sector is likewise heralded as one of the keys to economic growth in the Philippines' likely transition from its status as a middle- to an upper-middle-income country.[96] The same Duterte who engages in extrajudicial killings is likewise celebrated as creating favorable conditions for multilateral aid coordination,[97] often by introducing devastating outcomes to IPs' sacred lands.[98]

Both the Philippines and Kenya, therefore, are subject to neoliberal developmentalist frames without redressing grievances, the underlying root causes, the long-term implications of extractive capitalism, or the afterlives of colonial inheritances. Additionally, both contexts relatedly confront local and global movements that utilize violent tactics, exclusionary interpretations of identity, and apocalyptic/utopian imaginations sanctioned by appeals to religious traditions.

---

[95] Ibid.

[96] Berkley Center, "Faith and Development in Focus: Philippines," 21–22. Poverty at 21.6% in 2015 was uneven, with the ARMM region suffering the highest regional rate of 70%.

[97] Ibid., 23–27. The international development partners include the Asian Development Bank and the World Bank Group, and the bilateral partners include the China International Development Cooperation Agency (signaling a growing Chinese influence through aid regionally); the German Society for International Cooperation; the Japan International Cooperation Agency; and the U.S. Agency for International Development.

[98] For example, a Chico River Pump Irrigation Project financed by China's International Development Cooperation Agency encroached on the land of the Kalinga and Bontoc peoples, echoing earlier mobilization against a dam that resulted in violence and land defenders' casualties.

Like the global war on terror's own erasures, mobilization and recruitment into violence in both contexts capitalize also on the respective governments' collaboration with Euro-American geopolitical agendas and counterterrorism schemes. Violent insurgent ideologues interpret such collaborative work in a Manichaean manner as a continuation of Christian colonialism/the Crusades. Targeting Christians and churches thus signifies an apocalyptic act against domination and a recovery of a "Golden Age."[99] This intersection of religion and discursive, structural, and terrorist violence also illuminates why peacebuilding and conflict transformation practices similarly intersect with religion. The question, to reiterate, is to what degree interreligious peacebuilding practices enhance (neo)colonial legacies, and to what extent such practices expose decolonial religiocultural peacebuilding agency nevertheless.

---

[99] A manual for internal use by Building Resilience against Violent Extremism was shared with me during a visit in Nairobi in November 2018. The manual is authored by Mustafa Yusuf Ali and Othman Mujahid Bwana, *Peace-Building and Conflict Prevention Training Manual and Resource Guide for Building Resilience against Violent Extremism* (Nairobi: Center for Sustainable Conflict Resolution, 2015).

2
"Sisyphean" Governance

What Is Neoliberalism?

In Kenya and the Philippines, I saw the overlaying of the neoliberal moment upon the long colonial legacy of extraction, dispossession, and displacement.[1] Hence, at the outset, it is essential to clarify the concept of neoliberalism. Neoliberalism is associated with the ascendance of the economic theory of Austrian British economist Friedrich Hayek (1899–1992). One of the ways it differs from classical economic liberalism is in its focus on the necessity of proponents of neoliberalism to control the state apparatus so that they can actively ensure the operation of the free market. The neoliberal lens submits all aspects of human society to an economic calculus.[2]

Wendy Brown's critique of neoliberalism in *Undoing the Demos* highlights the implications of the neoliberal turn and market fundamentalism for democratic conceptions and practices. Extending Michel Foucault's analysis in *The Birth of Biopolitics* of the transmogrification of liberalism since the 1950s into neoliberal governmentality,[3] Brown analyzes neoliberalism not as a set of policies favoring capital (which it certainly is), but as a "political rationality" that constitutes a governing discourse that shapes human subjectivity.

In *Undoing the Demos*, therefore, Brown demonstrates the economization and devaluation of democracy.[4] This results, as Brown argues in her later book *In the Ruins of Neoliberalism*,[5] in the emergence of authoritarianism in Euro-America (accelerated in the second decade of the twenty-first century),

---

[1] For an analysis of the "green capitalism" informing the purchases and managing of "natural reserves" in Kenya (and elsewhere), see Wario Malicha, "Why Conservancies Are Clashing with Villagers," *The Standard*, January 9, 2020, https://www.standardmedia.co.ke/commentary/article/2001355766/why-conservancies-are-clashing-with-villagers.

[2] Naomi Klein, *The Shock Doctrine: The Rise of Disaster Capitalism* (New York: Picador, 2008).

[3] Michel Foucault, *The Birth of Biopolitics: Lectures at the Collège de France, 1978–79*, ed. Michel Senellart, trans. Graham Burchell (New York: Palgrave Macmillan, 2008).

[4] Wendy Brown, *Undoing the Demos: Neoliberalism's Stealth Revolution* (Princeton, NJ: Princeton University Press, 2015), 31.

[5] Wendy Brown, *In the Ruins of Neoliberalism: The Rise of Antidemocratic Politics in the West* (New York: Columbia University Press, 2019).

which is highly consistent with neoliberalism's assault on democratic values and institutions. Nonetheless, the demolition of the democratic space, an outcome of the convergences between neoliberalism and neoconservatism,[6] takes place in the name of, or under the guise of, democracy. This is evident in how proponents of neoliberalism use the language of "freedom" and "patriotism," mobilizing women's and LGBTQI rights. The neoliberal moment is filled with rhetorical contradictions that channel both progressive and conservative arguments regarding sexuality and gender, among other issues, subsequently generating unlikely coalitions.[7] Indeed, according to Brown, neoliberal policies often rely upon the state's regulation and buttressing of "traditional morality" and the "traditional family."[8]

Brown convincingly argues that "Hayekian neoliberalism is a moral-political project that aims to protect traditional hierarchies by negating the very idea of the social and radically restricting the reach of democratic political power in nation-states."[9] Hence, as is the case with religion and the practices of peace in the Global South—where hermeneutically closed religious and cultural traditions, as well as expedient traditional hierarchies and gendered scripts, prove effective from the perspective of *realpolitik*—traditional and heteropatriarchal norms enhance the neoliberal shift from equality and democracy to authoritarianism and intergroup management. Here, appeals to hermeneutically uncritical accounts of religious traditions are integral. In Brown's analysis, Hayek prescribed "reformatting traditionalism as freedom,"[10] which entails the weaponization of "tradition" through the language of liberty and through policies designed to enlarge the sphere of personal freedom, the aim of which is to eventually "recolonize" formerly democratic spaces and virtues.[11]

While Brown is preoccupied with the diminishment of democratic virtues and practices in Euro-American contexts, her critique of neoliberal technologies of the self and mechanisms for their dissemination can also apply to the Global South. There, neoliberalism is channeled toward engineering peace-as-harmony discourse grounded in reclaimed "authentic"

---

[6] Ibid., 91–92.
[7] Sara R. Farris, *In the Name of Women's Rights: The Rise of Femonationalism* (Durham, NC: Duke University Press, 2017); Jasbir Puar, *Terrorist Assemblages: Homonationalism in Queer Times* (Durham, NC: Duke University Press, 2007).
[8] See Brown, *In the Ruins*, 11–12, 91–3, for example.
[9] Ibid., 13.
[10] Ibid., 104.
[11] Ibid., 105.

traditions, including their scripted hierarchies. Programmatic efforts to build intergroup peace rely on indexing communities to their religious and cultural affiliations and highlighting their capacity to thinly overlap ethically to create a cooperative "public" space for market rationale. Hayekianism, as Brown correctly identifies, is a moral as much as an economic project. Religion, too, becomes a technocratic instrument within the neoliberal framework, even if its effectiveness occasionally relies on something that exceeds neoliberal rationality. Indeed, religion becomes a tool of governance.

"Governance" from the Neoliberal Textbook

"Governance" is a term distinct from government. Governance denotes the diminishment of robust conceptions and practices of democracy that may be associated with a representative government in favor of "best practices" and "benchmarking" as normative frames that masquerade as governance techniques. Hence, the promotion of governance is not the same as the promotion of democratic virtues. Neoliberalism as a political rationality depends upon the concept of "governance," which amounts to "neoliberalism's primary administrative form, the political modality through which it creates environments, structures constraints and incentives, and hence conducts subjects. Contemporary neoliberalism is unthinkable without governance."[12]

Governance also constitutes a central focus of peacebuilding with theorists such as Oliver Richmond articulating "peace-as-governance."[13] With this concept, Richmond attempts to incorporate a critique of the liberal discourse of peace faced with the failures of peacemaking forces in the 1990s, but also qualifies the vogue within peacebuilding known as the "local turn," whereby policymakers discover ways in which people may be tasked with solving their own conflicts. Richmond thus may be labeled a "critical localist" or someone carefully threading the local turn while still presuming that his own location is the construct known as "the international community." However, even in this purportedly emancipatory variety of peace—with its ethics centered on integrative human needs, which also cross-fertilizes with the subfield of development ethics[14]—we find neoliberal ideas such as

---

[12] Brown, *Undoing the Demos*, 122.
[13] Oliver Richmond, *A Post-Liberal Peace* (London: Routledge, 2011), 6.
[14] See chapter 3 for a discussion of development ethics that nuances this field's complicity with hegemony and neocolonial trends.

governance, devolution, benchmarks, best practices, and the redistribution of wealth through the mechanisms of charity.

Governance, accordingly, saturates the development and peacebuilding fields and features centrally in the United Nation's Sustainable Development Goals (SDGs), ratified in 2015 as the UN 2030 Agenda. In particular, Goal 16, "Peace, Justice, and Strong Institutions," and Goal 17, "Partnerships for the Goals," convey the importance of good governance. The targets of Goal 16, for instance, include cultivating "effective, accountable, participatory and representative decision-making at all levels" and "broaden[ing] and strengthen[ing] the participation of developing countries in the institutions of global governance."[15] Goal 17 foregrounds that the "sustainability" of the development agenda depends upon "partnerships between governments, the private sector and civil society," suggesting that such partnerships will entail foreign direct investment and "*unlock[ing] the transformative power of trillions of dollars of private resources*."[16] This cultivation of partnership, in turn, will be subject to oversight, evaluation, and monitoring.[17] Indeed, the SDGs reflect years of global deliberations and multiple debates with internationally diverse sectors[18] as well as the expansion of an introspective subfield of development ethics with its hallmark of the capabilities approach;[19] "sustainability," "accountability," "monitoring and evaluation," and "capacity building for participatory decision-making" are keywords from the neoliberalism *qua* governance textbook.

The turn to religion and the so-called religious actor is not a departure from but rather integral to the local turn and to neoliberalism's collusion with and appeals to "traditional morality." Indeed, the ubiquitous language of "local ownership" foregrounds the difficulty of escaping neoliberal rationality and the metaphorical force of the market. Hence, even if often presenting itself as an alternative to the neoliberal/technocratic frame, interreligious

---

[15] UN Sustainable Development Goals, "Goal 16: Peace, Justice, and Strong Institutions," (2015) https://www.un.org/sustainabledevelopment/peace-justice/.

[16] U.N. Sustainable Development Goals, "Goal 17: Partnerships for the Goals," March 27, 2020, https://www.un.org/sustainabledevelopment/globalpartnerships/, italics mine.

[17] I illuminate a critique of the concept of partnership in greater detail in chapter 3. See also Lynch, *Wrestling with God*, 202–3; Janice Gross Stein, "Humanitarian Organizations Accountable—Why, to Whom, for What, and How?," in *Humanitarianism in Question: Power, Politics, Ethics*, ed. Michael Barnett and Thomas G. Weiss (New York: Cornell University Press, 2008), 124–42.

[18] Oliver Fox and Peter Stoett, "Citizen Participation in the U.N. Sustainable Development Goals Consultation Process: Toward Global Democratic Governance?," *Global Governance* 22 (2016): 555–74.

[19] See chapter 3 for an overview of the field of development ethics as it relates to the subfield of religion and development.

peacebuilding practices are generally consistent with the operative force of neoliberal rationality. Through this prism, people who "benefit" from development/peacebuilding initiatives are "beneficiaries," divided into "sectors," each of which becomes a "stakeholder" in governance and in the implementation of initiatives through collective "buy-in."

The clerics of the Kenyan Coast Interfaith Council of Clerics (CICC) echo this neoliberal rationality. They agree that their locations in mosques, temples, churches, and comparable institutions provide them with privileged "local" access to shaping the social norms taught to children. Further, their relative credibility within their communities allows them to intervene in conflict resolution. This is occasionally done by employing local mechanisms to settle conflicts. One cleric I spoke to noted, "When there was trouble among the people at the Tana River, I think that even the government was unable to resolve the conflict. But when the religious leaders came together, Muslims and Christians and others, they went there and sat with the Pokomos and Ormas, they managed to talk with them and listen."[20] Another participant in the focus group affirmed that their location as religious and traditional leaders and their coming together under an interfaith framework for action positioned them as especially credible: "CICC has a unique way of actually approaching conflict among the community and that is why you find that it is something that is making people have more trust in the CICC, because it is interreligious and different faiths come together and when they see our faces, it becomes very easy to sort out that problem."[21] They are local actors who are sought after by interveners lacking "local access" through the framework of multisectoral partnerships (see Figure 2.1).

The partnership model tends to reify and abstract religious traditions from their hermeneutical complexities and turn religious interventions into a technology of peace governance.[22] Even if critical localism challenges the neoliberal frame, this postsecular turn relies on conservative, textual, and androcentric interpretations of normative traditions because more subversive interpretations would not easily comport with the instrumental value of religious actors and institutions. In the next section, I examine interreligious

---

[20] One participant's response during a focus group with CICC in Mombasa, January 2018, referring to two tribes that have experienced growing tensions primarily concerning issues of food scarcity and droughts.
[21] Participant in a focus group with CICC, Mombasa, January 2018.
[22] See especially chapter 3.

Figure 2.1 CICC's intercommunal prayer as part of conflict resolution activities in the Malindi area with community members. Reproduced with permission from Catholic Relief Services.

peace governance to underscore its dependence on hermeneutically closed accounts of religion and culture.

Interreligious Peace Governance

CRS, a transnational faith-inspired organization, has developed a sensitivity to the roles of religious actors and communities in implementing a variety of humanitarian and development/peacebuilding agendas. The organization's focus on religious actors in peacebuilding has become a hallmark of its work in the Philippines. Their approach there has been disseminated to other contexts where the organization identifies similar conditions conducive to intra- and interreligious peacebuilding. Interreligious peacebuilding practices involve "Binding, Bonding, and Bridging" activities, or what the organization, in an NGO-inflected acronymic packaging, has dubbed the "3Bs approach." "Binding" refers to intrapersonal change processes often involving the healing of trauma and overcoming hatred. "Bonding" moves from the intrapersonal to the intragroup level. "Bridging" activities involve cultivating intergroup trust and relationships that may result in positive outcomes for the "common good" and thus might cohere with the demands of work toward "social cohesion," which is a crucial concept animating international frameworks such as the SDGs.[23]

In Mindanao, CRS applied the 3Bs methodology mainly to facilitate the reduction of land disputes, one of the main drivers of conflict.[24] For example, implementing the 3Bs often resulted (by design) in "solidarity" or connector projects that tangibly improved communal life. These "dialogues of action" included devising safer methods for waste disposal and other public health and safety projects. Another activity included the creation of Zones of Peace, or *Ginapalad Taka*. These were created amid violence and through the leadership and initiative of local communal leaders. As I note throughout this book, the creation and maintenance of peace islands relies on the convergence and synonymizing of peacebuilding as a religious vocation and spiritual self-formation (and vice versa).

This 3B methodology entails a theory of change, according to which personal healing processes, reconnections with peace-promoting resources within traditions, and the identification of commonalities among traditions will lead, through context-sensitive analyses and intergroup engagements, to communal healing, reconciliation, joint decision-making, and action for the common good. However, in assessing the implementation of Advancing Interreligious Peacebuilding, as the CRS program is called in multiple sites, the designers and implementers concurred that change does not unfold linearly, from the individual to the community, but is instead cyclically reinforced on all levels of Binding, Bonding, and Bridging.[25]

Nevertheless, intrasubjective transformation remains pivotal for pursuing new scripts of social cohesion. This individualistic focus sheds light on the operative force of neoliberal rationality in interreligious peacebuilding,

---

[23] For an effort to trace the consolidation of "social cohesion" as a policy agenda, see Joseph Chan, Ho-Pong To, and Elaine Chan, "Reconsidering Social Cohesion: Developing a Definition and Analytical Framework for Empirical Research," *Social Indicators Research* 75, no. 2 (2006): 273–302, https://doi.org/10.1007/s11205-005-2118-1.

[24] See chapter 1 for a discussion of the historical background. See also Myla Leguro and the A3Bs Project Team, "Mindanao: Binding, Bonding and Bridging," in *Interreligious Action for Peace: Studies in Muslim-Christian Cooperation*, ed. Tom Bamat, Myla Leguro, Nell Bolton, and Atalia Omer (Baltimore, MD: Catholic Relief Services, 2017), 71–82.

[25] This is according to an unpublished internal evaluation document authored by Myla Leguro and Nell Bolton in 2018 at the conclusion of the program.

"capacitating" (a word I heard for the first time in the context of the project-driven NGO universe) individuals to adjust to and navigate their predicaments better, whether through "generating" and "augmenting income" (other phrases I heard only in this context) or through locally resolving conflicts. Accounts of religious and cultural traditions within the programmatic spaces of 3Bs may be elicitive, and, to this extent, they may lead to peace and conflict resolution. However, their claims to rewrite social scripts depend on hermeneutical closures and thus realist surrender to the present and to the questions of "what works" or "what is possible" rather than hermeneutical and historical criticality that generates openings for alternative future horizons.

The theory of change underpinning the 3Bs and multiple other programmatic foci on intergroup engagement or dialogue of action has been informed by an extensive body of social scientific literature loosely subsumed under the logic of the "contact hypothesis." This theory states that positive contact and relationship building across communities constitutes a preventive mechanism for intergroup violent eruption.[26] Such research spans cases from the United States to India and likewise informs the massive industry of people-to-people peacebuilding dialogue initiatives. These initiatives are consolidated through and in conjunction with the aforementioned common critique of top-down approaches. However, such practices have been co-opted and turned into another kind of top-down approach by psychologizing the causes of violent conflict. In doing so, scholars and practitioners used depoliticized, natural metaphors such as "critical yeast" and "planting a seed," which denote a change from a "culture of violence" to a "culture of peace."[27]

Robert D. Putnam offers one theoretical affirmation of this industry, but it is squarely grounded in the Global North. His is a discourse of privilege in which he laments the erosion of civic engagement as signaling American decline.[28] His key concepts, such as "bridging," traveled to the Global South

---

[26] For an oft-cited work that articulates this logic, see Ashutosh Varshney, *Ethnic Conflict and Civic Life: Hindus and Muslims in India* (New Haven, CT: Yale University Press, 2002).

[27] For a critique of the co-optation of "bottom-up" approaches to peacebuilding, see, for example, Sandrice Lefranc, "A Critique of 'Bottom-Up' Peacebuilding: Do Peaceful Individuals Make Peaceful Societies?," in *Peacebuilding, Memory, and Reconciliation: Bridging Top-Down and Bottom-Up Approaches*, ed. Bruno Charbonneau and Geneviève Parent (New York: Routledge, 2013), 34–52.

[28] Robert D. Putnam, *Bowling Alone: The Collapse and Revival of American Community* (New York: Simon & Schuster, 2000). Putnam's thesis has generated much discussion. See, for example, Richard Florida, *The Rise of the Creative Class* (New York: Basic Books, 2002). For the deployment of the "critical yeast" metaphor, see John Paul Lederach, *The Moral Imagination: The Art and Soul of Building Peace* (Oxford: Oxford University Press, 2005).

together with an expanding neoliberal logic seeking to capitalize on networks and institutions that can further entrench the status quo, which constitutes a different understanding of "keeping the peace." In particular, the 3Bs framework in Mindanao resonates with Putnam's analysis. The 3Bs echo a neoliberal rationality that bonds and bridges communal interests as forms of social capital that can leverage intergroup relationships and consolidate conditions for economic prosperity. In particular, the 3Bs method reveals a network analysis approach to social capital. Accordingly, Bonding refers to intracommunity reinforcement of identities and objectives, while Bridging highlights intercommunal commitments to problem-solving cooperatively. Such a problem-solving approach is different from democratic virtues and practices, a point to which I will return.

A change from simply "getting by" to "getting ahead" accordingly depends on a shift from Bonding to Bridging.[29] Bonding and Bridging dynamics are complex and depend upon principles of reciprocity and trust, as well as the perception of shared social norms and values. The repackaging of social capital theory to local and horizontal peacebuilding in the Global South reveals not a focus on improving economic prosperity or the ability to bridge vertically across status and power differentials but a focus on enhancing people's capacity to "get by" and "get along" and to transform this getting by, which enhances resiliency as "peace," into pious governance.[30] What is at stake is economic and social survival based on activating identity-bridging social capital where Bonding (i.e., intragroup consolidation of the "we") and Binding (i.e., intrapersonal transformation) rely on reifying religion as a dominant definitional index of one's identity, a source from which one can draw and (re)write the script of the "common good." The logic underpinning such efforts posits the public space as a site of intergroup cooperation where individual identities are stabilized in ahistorical and hermeneutically closed claims to traditions. In contrast, democratic praxis would promote an intercultural hermeneutical elasticity and equitable democratic norms, a political "we" resistant to the segregationist logic of neoliberal postsecular peacebuilding and its reliance on the double closures of communal and religiocultural hermeneutics. Because interreligious peacebuilding operates within the pragmatic

---

[29] Mary Foster, Agnes Meinhard, and Ida Berger, "The Role of Social Capital: Bridging, Bonding or Both?," *Centre for Voluntary Sector Studies, Ryerson University* no. 1 (2003): 3, https://pdfs.semanticscholar.org/0d58/6678490686aaf63fd3b7cd2a2f63332dfcdb.pdf.
[30] For the distinction between vertical (or status) and identity-based bridging, see Robert Wuthnow, "Religious Involvement and Status-Bridging Social Capital," *Journal for the Scientific Study of Religion* 41, no. 4 (2002): 669–84, https://doi.org/10.2307/3712334.

constraints of the present and the question "What works?" it blocks elicitive writing of an alternative future script that imagines the world as it should be. In contrast, an intersectional approach would expose how imagining a different script requires openings rather than closures.

However, one cannot deny the measurable effectiveness as an instrument for conflict management of the reductive approach to social and hermeneutical scripts that construe religion as a form of social capital. For example, implementing the 3Bs methodology in twenty barangays in Mindanao between 2012 and 2015 resolved thirty-five land disputes by enhancing local capacities as well as establishing connections among municipal and governmental authorities, a network of traditional religious leaders, and the Lupong Tagapamayaoa, or village pacification committees. Concurrently, eighteen community-based reconciliation projects, such as the improvement of health facilities and bridge building, benefited more than twenty-one thousand people.[31]

Since the locus of change is in the sites of interpersonal relationships, substantive accounts of religiocultural traditions are unnecessary. Instead, what is needed is an understanding of how religion can facilitate people's resilience in the face of their present conditions. While much of the debate around people-to-people peacebuilding interrogates ways of linking vertically from people on the ground up to policies (scaling from the "bottom" to the "top"), scrutiny of the resiliency discourse illuminates that the enhancement of people's capacity to resolve their problems, rather than the elusive scaling itself, entrenches neoliberal rationality under the pretense of elicitive peacebuilding processes. Accordingly, peace or coexistence, in effect, repackages structural, cultural, and historical violence. It does so through the deployment of "bottom-up" or elicitive methodologies, whose effectiveness becomes ever more potent because these methodologies are then imbued with religious and spiritual meanings that thrive on people's intrasubjective "conversion" from hate to friendship, love, and cooperation. This spiritualization of bottom-up, horizontal peace exposes religion's role in sustaining peace governance through a focus on problem-solving.[32]

The problem-solving approach, a distinctly neoliberal concept, is profoundly different from the problem-posing approach that is central to the world-transforming imperative Paolo Freire articulated in *Pedagogy of the*

---

[31] For a discussion of the A3Bs as applied to land conflict in Mindanao, see Leguro, "Mindanao: Binding, Bonding and Bridging," 75–78.

[32] I will return in chapter 7 to offer further analysis of the scaling logic.

Oppressed.[33] Operating within the tradition of critical theory, Freire's critical pedagogy exposes the delimiting structures and dehumanizing frameworks that contribute to what he understands as the "submersion" of people within a historical context they deem inevitable and natural. Cultivating such a critical consciousness does not cohere with an approach that simply focuses on localized problem-solving. This, for Freire, would amount to action without reflection[34] and would fall short of a praxis that facilitates the potential for radical futurity. Indeed, such a problem-solving approach shapes the harmony and peace business and informs the training of its influencers and practitioners. This is the case even if the elicitive approach that John Paul Lederach envisions draws centrally on Freire's critical reflexive praxis;[35] its operationalization resists its world-transforming potential and its antiprescriptive impulses.[36] Instead, an elicitive harmony discourse depoliticizes and obscures people's problem-posing horizons. The persistent focus on individuals and their self-transformation *qua* spiritual formation and their adaptability/resilience conveys how religion and peacebuilding/development infrastructures, in their neoliberal and devolutionary registers, work against the possibility of achieving social justice via coalition building and the systemic dismantling of matrices of oppression. Locating the change engine within individuals (trained in the prophetic "lite") works against an intersectional political consciousness. Hence, in these cases, the deployment of religion constitutes an action that reinforces neoliberalism's de-democratizing and depoliticizing rationality.

Indeed, employing the mechanism of interreligious dialogue, often framed as interreligious dialogue for action (IRD/A), conveys an explicit intention to produce an action (or problem-solve) for a conception of the public good, the implementation of which is measured in terms of progress toward social cohesion. IRD/A is distinct from interfaith dialogue, which focuses on examining one another's faith commitments, texts, and ritualistic

---

[33] Paolo Freire, *Pedagogy of the Oppressed*, 4th ed. (New York: Bloomsbury, 2017), 79–84.
[34] Ibid., 125. See also Atalia Omer, "Religion and the Study of Peace: Practice without Reflection," *Religions* 12, no. 12 (2021): 1069, https://doi.org/10.3390/rel12121069.
[35] See John Paul Lederach, *Preparing for Peace: Conflict Transformation across Cultures* (Syracuse, NY: Syracuse University Press, 1995), especially 25–33.
[36] Especially within the framework of the Innsbruck School of elicitive conflict mapping, efforts to articulate a map for elicitive conflict workers tried to navigate the nonprescriptive approach to peace, articulating concepts such as "many peaces" as an expression of transrational peace philosophy. See, for example, Wolfgang Dietrich, *Elicitive Conflict Mapping*, trans. Hannah Ilka Kuske and Jennifer Marie Murphie (London: Palgrave Macmillan, 2018); Wolfgang Dietrich, *Elicitive Conflict Transformation and the Transrational Shift in Peace Politics* (London: Palgrave Macmillan, 2013).

contexts. IRD/A sees itself as a departure from such apparently "unmeasurable" practices and seeks to provide evidence of success through its work. It is only such evidence that can justify further investment.[37] The ubiquity of IRD/A in peacebuilding and development efforts conveys the sectoralization of religion as a central dimension of the postsecular neoliberal turn. Through this turn, the peacebuilding industry seeks to "partner" with religion as a sector with special access to "local" communities and (in some cases) robust global networks and institutions. I surround "local" with scare quotes to signal the aforementioned critique that the binary local-global/international often assumes the latter term as constituting universal (and so-called secular) norms and institutions. Critics scrutinize the persistently Eurocentric presumptions underlying such a binary and who counts or does not count as a part of the "international" or "global" frame.[38] Regardless, the "local" is often posited, by scholars such as Richmond, as the site where religious actors are found with special access to relevant demographics and stakeholders in promoting social cohesion and managing conflicts.

Within the framework of IRD/A for social cohesion, religious traditions are flattened (often through proof-texting and boiling the tradition down to a supposed essence) into a set of operationalizable principles, ritual practices, and institutional networks. Because such a hermeneutical closure means a "literal" reading of religious traditions as contained in texts, androcentric modes of interpretation, that is, "traditional morality," in Brown's words, dominate. The global engagement with religion as part of the convergence of the postsecular and local turns, therefore, does not promote substantive and hermeneutically critical religious literacy but rather utilitarian understandings of religion that allow for religion to more effectively partner with neoliberal peacebuilding and to effect development objectives.

---

[37] CRS shared with me internal studies that use cutting-edge methodologies for evidence-based research for monitoring and evaluation for the organization's own processes of self-assessment as well as resources to seek further grants from agencies such as USAID and, in the UK, the Department For International Development. CRS is not unique in its reliance on and mastery of such research mechanisms that attempt to develop and produce measurements for success, which then also ensure their own organizational sustainability. Indeed, they often partner and collaborate with academic institutions to produce the research necessary to determine their programming. I partook in such a collaboration between the University of Notre Dame and CRS on a study designed to offer relevant evaluative findings but in no way to question the underlying premises.

[38] For a penetrating relevant analysis focusing on the global and international claims of Islamists, see Darryl Li, *The Universal Enemy: Jihad, Empire, and the Challenge of Solidarity* (Palo Alto, CA: Stanford University Press, 2019).

Indeed, in the case of religious interventions into the multisectoral effort to reduce child marriage, the clerics of CICC employ the delegitimized practice of proof-texting from scriptures to establish their consistency with human rights approaches to the rights of children.[39] The clerics situate themselves as key interlocutors in discussions about whether their religious and cultural traditions condone or condemn harmful practices, such as female genital mutilation. At stake is not only the neoliberal (and orientalist) positing of "culture" as an obstacle for "progress" and "peace," but also whether said "culture" or "religion" can offer a countermessage that is more "real" and more conducive to peace as a technology of social cohesion and economic survival.

In this case, the clerics produced a manual,[40] which they employ in peace and justice club meetings in the schools where, according to teachers I met, almost all children have experienced sexual abuse of one kind or another.[41] The manual exposes the multiple ways in which the textual traditions support a fundamental commitment to human rights and are consistent with internationally ratified declarations and conventions pertaining to the rights of children, which include the right of young girls to an education.[42] For example, a general rule is said to derive from Shari'a and is based on the Prophet having said that "there should be neither harming nor reciprocating harm" to establish a prohibition against violence against children, including of the sexual variety, but also including the neglect of their moral formation. Similarly, to bolster Christianity's consistency with the legal framework for child protection, my Christian interlocutors cited a variety of verses from the Bible, including Luke 18:16, to stress that the "care of children was central to the work of Jesus";[43] Genesis 1:27, to affirm the dignity of the child as a human made in the divine image; Deuteronomy 6:4–9, to highlight the

---

[39] For a profound feminist intervention on this question of literalism as well as hermeneutical and contextual expansions, see Aysha A. Hidayatullah, *Feminist Edges of the Quran* (Oxford: Oxford University Press, 2014).

[40] CICC, "They Need Your Care: An Interfaith Approach to Child Protection," n.d. This is an unpublished internal document shared with me in February 2018 during a visit to Malindi.

[41] I conducted interviews and focus groups in three elementary schools in the Malindi area in February 2018.

[42] They cite the UN's Convention on the Rights of the Child and the African Charter on the Rights and Welfare of the Child, which specify that a child is any human under the age of eighteen. They also refer to the specific Kenyan legal framework, stressing the Children's Act (2001), the Sexual Offense Act (2006), the Gender Policy in Education (2007), the Disability Act, the Kenyan Constitution of 2010, and the Penal Code as relevant for the defense and articulation of the rights of children.

[43] CICC, "They Need Your Care."

communal responsibility for the spiritual development of the child; and other carefully selected verses.

Shifting from this discussion of a general commitment to the education and formation of children, the Christianity-focused segment of the clerical manual turns to the problem of child marriage specifically. It identifies this practice as one that "disrupt[s] education, limit[s] girls' economic potential, and correlate[s] with high levels of sexual abuse and violence ... [and] is also associated with increased rates of maternal and infant mortality."[44] These ramifications, in turn, "[perpetuate] the cycle of poverty, reinforcing it, and making it hard to escape, and ultimately contributing to regional instability."[45] The clerics affirm their rejection of child marriage as harmful both to the child and the community. To support this claim, they cite the Genesis creation story and other verses suggesting that women, like men, are created in the image of God, which implies that girls and boys must be treated equally. This manual's African Kaya traditionalist section conveys an oral narrative from the Mijkenda society, related by an elder from the Malindi District Cultural Association. It states that child marriage was allowed only during famines, and even then, the girl "would not be given to the 'husband' until she reaches maturity age.... The man entitled for that girl was warned to wait until he got permission from the older women."[46] This and the other quotations exemplify how the deployment of generic human rights language ("equality") does not result in a feminist reading of the textual and oral traditions.

These examples of proof-texting underscore that the practice of child marriage is a matter of cultural norms and not necessarily condoned by the tradition. Intended to facilitate "interfaith child protection,"[47] which involves multiple "stakeholders," including members of the Parent Teacher Association and community-based child protection groups, this approach to hermeneutics reflects the link between changing cultural norms as a means for attaining regional stability and religious or tradition-specific literacies. Connecting child insecurity with political insecurity, the manual and the multisectoral efforts intend to redress deeper issues related to intergenerational poverty, marginalization, and the breakdown of the social fabric, about

[44] Ibid.
[45] Ibid.
[46] Ibid.
[47] Ibid.

which the clerics talked with great pain. They related the devaluing and "selling off" of girls and their lack of education to the perpetuation of cycles of poverty and marginalization, which in turn contribute to harmful practices and violent conflicts, as well as to an environment ripe for recruitment to violent groups such as al-Shabaab and Da'esh.[48] Reclaiming an "authentic" religion thus constitutes a mechanism for tackling "harmful cultural practices," insecurity, and poverty. This reflects a broader approach to engaging "faith actors" in ways that cross-reference public health education and scriptural/theological approaches with a structural analysis of poverty. This approach intends to both recruit/educate "faith actors" and refrain from colonial undertones that attribute the sources of "underdevelopment" to culture or religion. Hence, various studies[49] designed to measure the effectiveness of faith-based interventions conclude that it is best to refrain from using the construct of "harmful cultural practices." Nevertheless, as I show throughout the book, a scriptural/theological tactic requires an essentializing of faith as good and consistent with international norms.

The clerics of the CICC comprise one sector of society that is attempting to solve the problem of child marriage in Malindi. The gravity of the predicament authorizes a hermeneutically closed approach to cultural and religious traditions, which exerts a responsibility on religious leaders to convey to children and caregivers that employment of cultural and religious warrants harmful to children amounts to an inaccurate reading of traditional norms. The CICC instantiates the institutionalization of and the capitalization on the religious sector. The clerics participate in bureaucratized efforts to tackle specific social, economic, and cultural problems plaguing the communities. Here, rather than a prophetic function, their specialized religious knowledge and positionality are channeled as a "partner" in a broader, multisectoral, responsibilizing effort to facilitate governance. Nevertheless, governance focused on problem-solving rather than on democratic praxis illuminates the utilitarian deployment of the religious sector.

A similar logic of governance is also operative in Mindanao. Here, certain bodies are selected by the government and/or intergovernmental and international actors to promote acquiescence to the ongoing implementation of peace programs. A prime example is Pakigdait, which I described in the

---

[48] Focus group with CICC in Mombasa, February 2018.
[49] See, for example, Elisabeth Le Roux and Brenda Bartelink, "No More 'Harmful Traditional Practices': Working Effectively with Faith Leaders," research report, Tearfund, 2017, https://jliflc.com/wp-content/uploads/2017/11/HTP-report-final-draft.pdf.

previous chapter as an interfaith grassroots organization. An affirmation of the multisectoral framing and its sectoralization as an interfaith actor enables this organization to incorporate itself into peace governance, working with multiple investing partners, including the Asia Foundation and U.S. Agency for International Development (USAID). Together, they work on an interfaith peacebuilding program called the PeaceConnect Project. This project is implemented in six municipalities of Lanao Del Norte. In describing the target communities (religious and traditional leaders, local government units, civil society organizations, security sector and nonstate actors, and women and youth sectors) and the kind of peace work that Pakigdait enacts, especially in anticipation of the implementation of the BOL and the consolidation of the BARMM,[50] this interfaith organization encapsulates the meaning of "interreligious peace governance." This is because the postsecular turn subsidizes capitalizing on religion by the global centers of economic and political power. This "global engagement with religion" requires religious actors to enact hermeneutical closures or to bracket any substantive intra- or intertheological discourse—a point to which I will return in later chapters, but which is nevertheless telegraphed in the repeated underscoring of members of the interfaith council that "all religions are about peace."[51]

For this chapter it suffices to highlight how instrumentalizing religious actors with local access cultivates the conditions for peace, partly by facilitating intentional spaces for people to process their fears, prejudices, and hopes for a peaceful future and by helping them grasp what the BARMM's framework is all about, thus dispelling any misunderstandings. Pakigdait's approach is elicitive. Its members participated in what they call "listening sessions" with people associated with MILF and MNLF in advance of the ratification of the BARMM as part of their effort to ensure peace, regardless of the outcome of the elections. This intentionality reveals the link between resilience and securitization that underpins the social capital network approach. Pakigdait chose the listening session when, for example, conducting peacebuilding sessions in regions especially affected by tensions between the military and other stakeholders. As one interlocutor told me, "[We do this] because we never assume that we know everything. On the contrary, the people on the ground know better in terms of identifying the conflict and the solutions."[52]

---

[50] See chapter 1 for an overview and historical background of this development in the Moro conflict narrative.
[51] A consensus I gleaned from my focus group with the entire board in Cagayan de Oro, July 2019.
[52] Participant in the focus group with Pakigdait, Cagayan de Oro, June 2019.

The facilitators who exemplify interfaith cooperation invited the participants to identify a range of seven emotions (represented as emoticons such as smiley or frowny faces) that they associate with the BOL. The facilitators then use the results to explain specific dimensions of the peace framework. They deem this approach much more effective than, for example, a PowerPoint presentation about the BOL. Such interventions allow them to understand more directly people's misunderstandings and fears. Further, the interfaith composition of the facilitators assuages those same fears through the very performativity of their composition as an interfaith delegation. Emoticons and trickle-down interfaith performativity hence exemplify the meaning of interreligious peace governance and convey that it does not depend on critical and layered religious knowledge. Here, learned accounts of people's religious and cultural traditions are almost irrelevant to the performance of interfaith peace (or the practice of "getting along"). Ironically, the more religious literacy the postsecular and local turn demands within its neoliberal framework, the less hermeneutically open religions and the practices of peace become (see Figures 2.2 and 2.3).

Figure 2.2 Members of Pakigdait's board in a listening session in a violence-affected region. Reproduced with permission from Pakigdait.

Figure 2.3 Youth gather for a celebratory photo during a listening session. Reproduced with permission from Pakigdait.

Benchmarking

The neoliberal language of governance is operative in my case studies, where technocratic problem-solving orients and shapes multisectoral efforts. For example, a conference cosponsored by the Tanenbaum Center for Interreligious Understanding—a center exemplifying the postsecular turn to enhancing religious literacy in the Global North, established in New York City in 1992—and CRS took place in Davao City, Philippines, in August 2017. Participants presented it as an opportunity to compare and streamline lessons from efforts to advance interreligious action for peace in Mindanao, Indonesia, and Nigeria. Examining the proceedings of this conference is worthwhile because of its efforts to develop benchmarks, standards, and mechanisms for deploying religion in peacebuilding. These efforts show how a religious peacebuilding agency can become bureaucratized. In other words, benchmarking, when it comes to religion and the practice of peace, turns peacebuilding into a skill in which everyone can be trained. Such training occurs through "professional development" seminars rather than a rigorous and lengthy credentialing process as authoritative and lifelong interpreters of traditions. The individuals populating religion and peace practice programmatic spaces may be unique. Still, their methodologies can travel, especially since they think of manualized religion as a source and a tool for establishing a common denominator (generic) ethics of peace and love.

To offer a platform for cultivating best practices and benchmarks, the Mindanao-based conference's organizers gathered dialogue practitioners and peacebuilders from across Mindanao and two Tanenbaum Peacemaker awardees. These awardees, Pastor James Wuye from Nigeria and Pastor Jacky Manuputty from Indonesia, are poster children for interreligious peacebuilding. That the Tanenbaum Center was a co-organizer is significant because, as a nonprofit dedicated to combating discrimination based on religion in various U.S. settings (such as the workplace), it is also engaged globally with efforts to identify religiously influenced and motivated actors who work for peace. Tanenbaum identifies such actors for prestigious awards, creating a growing global network of religious peacebuilders. The awardees can share lessons learned as "religious peacebuilders" who should "cultivate friendship with one another."[53]

Again, we can identify neoliberal motifs. Rather than focusing on social movement mobilization, which would disrupt communal closures that index apparent group interest to their hermeneutically closed ethnoreligious and cultural identity and homogenizing storyline, the emphasis is on individual exemplars (or social influencers who are not necessarily also religious virtuosi). Accordingly, the engine of change is located in the emotional labor associated with cultivating interpersonal friendship, trust, and partnership. These foci are what ignite the peacebuilding engine. This form of peacebuilding is oriented toward stabilization and securitization. It delegates responsibility for achieving those goals to the people whose mere survival (or resiliency) is now rearticulated as expressions of their spirituality. The location of the conference in Davao was not accidental. Indeed, it reflected how the peacebuilding practices in Mindanao had framed the discourse of interreligious dialogue for action. It conveys neoliberal rationality even if the organizers did not articulate it as such.

---

[53] CRS, "A Synthesis of Learning from the Conference on Advancing Interreligious Action for Peace: Learning Lessons from Mindanao, Indonesia, and Nigeria," August 21–23, 2017, Apo View Hotel, Davao City, unpublished internal paper, 2. As part of its operation and effort to enhance "lessons learned" across its network of religious peacebuilders, the center produced a series of publications, including the Tanenbaum Center for Interreligious Understanding's *Peacemakers in Action: Profiles of Religion in Conflict Resolution*, ed. David Little (Cambridge: Cambridge University Press, 2007), and *Peacemakers in Action Volume II: Profiles in Religious Peacebuilding*, ed. Joyce S. Dubensky (Cambridge: Cambridge University Press, 2016).

However, comparative benchmarking and best practices did not erase the urgency and specificity of the Mindanao context. The conference convened shortly after the siege on the Muslim-majority city of Marawi. The outcome of this siege was devastating in terms of displacement, death, the destruction of homes and religious and historical structures, and the declaration of martial law over the island of Mindanao by President Duterte.[54] Therefore, the conference's timing allowed local civil society actors to think of ways to prevent the Marawi siege from deepening intercommunal divides among Muslims and Christians. The fear was that such a deepening would "cause irreparable damage to the peacebuilding efforts of civil society organizations and the government."[55] Against this backdrop of religiously framed violence, grappling with the siege likewise rekindled "the momentum to reclaim religion as a resource for peace, not war."[56] Indeed, foregrounding IRD/A as a mechanism for violence reduction implies that interreligious and intercommunal tensions are the root cause of disharmony, violence, and "underdevelopment." Such a framing conceals what a deeper historical approach could illuminate: the afterlives of colonial violence and its ongoing legacies. This concealment also occurs when appeals are made to hermeneutically closed accounts of tradition. To reiterate, these accounts treat religion as being authentically about "peace." This discourse of authenticity thus presents religion as a form of resistance to the forces of violence, as if they simply were the upshot of "inauthentic" cultural/religious interpretation. The analysis I provide here shows IRD/A's service to the neoliberal frame, which allows other forms of violence to escape unnoticed.

However, listening to the success stories in Nigeria and Indonesia did not merely provide a mechanism for disseminating neoliberal rationality through "best practices." The stories told about peacebuilding in these locations, together with the stories from Mindanao of "personal change, community actions, and human relationships," imbued this conference with sacredness. Inspired participants from regions affected by violence[57] marveled at the spiritual force that gathering all those civil society actors in one space generated, as it affirmed their commitment to peacebuilding as

---

[54] See chapter 1 for an overview of this critical event.
[55] CRS, "A Synthesis of Learning," 4.
[56] Ibid.
[57] These areas included Basilan, Zamboanga City, Pikit, North Cotabato, Cotabato City, Iligan City, Malaybalay, Bukidnon, Bacolod, Lanao del Norte, Valancia, Bukidnon, Aleosan, Magpet, Tugaya, Lanao del Sur, Dumalinao, Zamboanga del Sur, Datu Odin Sinsuat, Maguindanao, Davao City, Pagalongan, Tacurong City, and Marawi City.

a sacred vocation that also injected sacredness into the act of conferencing itself. Indeed, this sentiment substantiates my argument that the spiritualization of the peacebuilding space is what makes the local and postsecular turns such effective frameworks for promoting neoliberal rationality. And this is also what unmasks peacebuilding as an enduring repackaging of violence.

Double Closure

The film *The Imam and the Pastor* (2012) was shown at the conference and set the tone for IRD/A sharing and its spiritual force. It tells the story of how Imam Muhammad Ashafa and Pastor Wuye transformed from enemies and leaders of opposing militant groups clashing in Kaduna in northern Nigeria to partners in promoting interfaith peacebuilding efforts. In a plenary session with Pastor Wuye, co-executive director (with Imam Ashafa) of the Interfaith Mediation Centre in Kaduna, one topic that was discussed was the need to reclaim religion's "goodness and peace."[58] His reflection conveyed key motifs: personally transforming, despite trauma and deep-seated hatred; reapproaching scripture through proof-texting to show that religions are authentically about "peace"; reaching out across identity lines and de-othering; and turning this relationship (in this case, the imam and pastor's) into an NGO that foregrounds "faith" or "interfaith" as its defining framework for peacebuilding and conflict transformation. This NGO-ization of faith locates the engine of change in intrapersonal transformation, as in the CRS's 3Bs paradigm. It also generates hermeneutically closed accounts of religions as concerned primarily with peace but indexed to closures of communal narratives into unitary homogenizing stories and bounded identities. These operate to depoliticize and obscure an intersectional analysis of power and imagining alternative futures and scripts not from within the constraints of the present but rather through critical hermeneutics.

For an example of the operation of hermeneutical closures, one typical breakout session at the conference involved a discussion between identity groups about "key principles of religious peacebuilding based on their faith and spirituality."[59] Such intercommunal sharing of "who we are" typically entails using large sheets of paper with sticky notes. This kind of practice

[58] CRS, "A Synthesis of Learning," 15–16.
[59] Ibid., 17.

Figure 2.4 A bridging trust-building exercise with yarn and sticky notes, Mindanao. Reproduced with permission from Catholic Relief Services.

again reflects an elicitive principle that guides the process of self-reflection and conflict mapping (Figure 2.4). "Sticky notes" sharing is hermeneutically closed, albeit elicitive. This is the case even though it involves overcoming apparent misunderstandings about others' cultural and religious practices. Indeed, the practices of religion and peace homogenize communities, reduce their complexity into a reified account of tradition *qua* group identity, and prioritize emic and devotional expressions of religion and cultural traditions in which practitioners of faith or cultural traditions, by default, constitute authorities: their *knowing* religion is in their *being* religious as a matter of communal belonging. This prioritization serves neoliberal peace discourse's devolutionary logic, which works more effectively with unitary accounts of traditions and communities.

This double closure is enhanced through interreligious peace governance. Even if interreligious work appeals to the language of liberation, is this depoliticizing bridging aimed at emancipation or liberation? My findings suggest that it is not. Instead, I discovered that this form of "peacebuilding" promotes religious illiteracy and a closed sociopolitical and religiocultural hermeneutics that ensures, rather than disrupts, the status quo. My analysis of the mechanisms of religion and peace practices exposes that *being* religious and *doing* religion and peacebuilding diminishes and forecloses the horizons of *knowing* religion and critical religious hermeneutics. Indeed, *doing* religion, as I show in later chapters, solidifies and reduces the scope of communal belonging to religious markers, which prevents a political discourse that would transcend a segregationist logic of multiculturalism.

In a discussion, locals from Mindanao had the chance to respond to the imam, the pastor, and other NGO-ized exemplars. On the level of leadership, Professor Abhoud Syed M. Lingga, executive director of the Institute of Bangsamoro Studies in Cotabato City, commented that the requirement for intrapersonal transformation was good, but also suggested that there was a need for the "contextualization of programs on the ground" since, "unlike the cases of Indonesia and Nigeria, the Mindanaoan conflict is not religious. . . . The real enemy of the Bangsamoro is injustice, not the government and certainly not the Christians."[60] Undoubtedly, challenging any interpretation of violence and the conflict as "religious" is a common refrain of the religion and peace industry. This industry seeks to unlock and reclaim religion *qua* peace. Another respondent, Easter Luna S. Canoy, executive director of Kitanglad Integrated NGOs in Bukidnon, spoke about the necessity of learning how to coexist in diversity, telegraphing the inverse side of the neoliberal peace discourse, which interprets conflict as an outcome of a "culture of violence" and of the supposed inability of persons to live in diversity, as if diversity itself is at the root of suffering.

Canoy also spoke about the long-term struggle of IPs to overcome the legacies of "bloodshed and violations to the ancestral lands" and pressed the point that this "violated the spirit of the land."[61] Her interjection about the IPs' historical and cultural perspectives unfolded, however, in a space already shaped by the depoliticizing harmony discourse of the peacebuilding industry and thus precludes critical indigeneity.[62]

Without a doubt, participants affirmed Canoy's articulation of Indigenous perspectives and spiritual practices.[63] It reflects how often this

[60] Ibid.
[61] Ibid., 9.
[62] I address this approach in chapter 8.
[63] This point was echoed later by Timuay-Labi Sannie Bello, supreme chieftain of the Teduray-Lambangian in Maguindanao. He unpacked the concept of peace among the IPs, with a particular emphasis on the Teduray-Lambangian in Maguindanao and their organic relationship to nature and their land as the source of all knowledge. Emphasizing collective leadership and consultation, a practice consistent with a sense of communal ownership and tribal restorative justice practices led by

kind of inclusion involves reshaping their worldviews to conform to the Mindanaoan-wide vision of tripartite harmony—a concept essential (for its logic of double closure) for the deployment of interreligious action for peace governance. Interreligious hostility and ignorance, rather than histories of injustice and extraction, are imagined as the purported issues to be addressed in order for peace to be achieved.

Fitting into "Harmony"

Another plenary session at a different conference focused on shifts from enmity to friendship and identified "lessons learned" from three Mindanaoan peacebuilders. The summary of the proceeding gestures toward the scope of people's peacebuilding agency. One reflection came from Miriam "Deddette" Suacito, executive director of Nagdilaab Foundation, in Basilan, Philippines. Basilan, where the Abu Sayyaf Group has employed the tactic of kidnap-for-ransom and has also carried out killings, is where Deddette has worked for four decades as a "peaceweaver."[64] She has engaged in development and interreligious peacebuilding work among the Indigenous Yakan people, Muslims, and Christians. Deddette overcame her anger, resentment, and frustration through trauma-healing practices and psychosocial interventions. In 2003 she founded Nagdilaab, which means "burning," in reference to the biblical burning bush, as a metaphor that captures her mission as a Christian peacebuilder.[65]

Kafedewan (tribal justice officers), he also spoke of progressive pluralism, or *lemer linanga*, denoting a balance between rootedness and openness to others (CRS, "A Synthesis of Learning," 13).

[64] Mindanao Peaceweavers (MPW) is an effort conceived in 2003 during a MindaNow Conference to synergize peace advocates in Mindanao and to make their individual organization work reinforce one another through the creation of a solidarity network in Manila and Visayas. The MPW reflects an effort by seven peace groups to develop a common peace platform. It represents the largest peace constituency in Mindanao and encompasses NGOs, academics, human rights groups, religious organizations, and grassroots organizations that seek a peaceful outcome to conflict. This network reflects the intricate tapestry of on-the-ground peacebuilding in Mindanao. All of these organizations play crucial roles in the de-escalation of conflict, case-by-case conflict resolution, and relationship building. They function to strengthen intergroup ties and friendships, but, as I found in my overall analysis of interreligious and intergroup peacebuilding efforts, they do not necessarily disrupt the underpinning power structures, and they rely on individuals to overcome their identity base to build peace and to cultivate a moral imagination of cohabitation. For more information regarding the work of MPW, see its Facebook page: https://www.facebook.com/Mindanao-Peaceweavers-MPW-125811777429868/ (accessed June 15, 2020).

[65] CRS, *From Enmity to Friendship: Interreligious Dialogue and Action for Peace* (a synthesis of learning from a conference held August 21–23, 2017, in Davao City), 11.

Deddette's overcoming of pain and anger echoes that of many other religious peacebuilders (and nonexplicitly religious peacebuilders as well) for whom a story of personal transformation (the "seed of peace" theory) is an impetus for broader societal and intercommunal dialogue. This narrative of personal transformation is exemplified in the duo of the imam and the pastor. Still, its motifs permeate the religion and peacebuilding field, regardless of people's degree of spiritual and religious virtuosity and earned authority. This democratization of peacebuilding as a spiritual practice and vocation also denotes the operative force of devolutionary neoliberal rationality.

If "interfaith" means "getting along" across communal divides, others, such as Archbishop Capalla and Aleem Mahmod Mala Adilao, critical participants in the Bishops-Ulama Conference, stressed the need for intrafaith dialogue involving religious communities' institutional channels. In all of these examples, the leaders of IRD/A confirm the need for intrafaith dialogue. They see it as a requirement and an instrument to ensure a shift to intergroup cooperation, problem-solving, and the cultivation of tripartite harmony. They envision Mindanao as a harmonious space for Muslims, Christians, and IPs to cohabit. This is precisely the form of harmony that conceals peace's violent legacy through a dependence on double closures. Despite this legacy, the harmony discourse dominates Mindanaoan discussions about peace and drives investment in intercommunal dialogue and performances of peace. One example of such a performance is the mandatory Mindanao Week of Peace. It has been in place since 1997[66] due to the work of the Peace Weaver Network and involves marches, the painting of hopeful murals, the singing of peace songs, and other enthusiastic endorsements of the aspiration to overcome divisions.[67] The benchmarking conferences in Davao reinforced this harmony narrative, one that requires isolating "religion" or "culture" as a source from which to retrieve a commitment to plurality, which itself relies on a unitary approach to communal narratives. Hence, deploying religion as a source of "harmony" in Mindanao overlooks the violent legacy of peace and the domestication of the discourse of religious plurality itself as a colonial and depoliticizing tool. Indeed, the harmony business codifies cultural boundaries while it also erases and elides historical memories.

---

[66] It was codified in Gloria Macapagal-Arroyo's Presidential Proclamation No. 127, 2001.
[67] For a description of the history of this celebration on its twentieth anniversary in 2017, see Zabida, "Mindanao Week of Peace on its 20th Year," n.d., https://zabida.org/2017/11/30/mindanao-week-of-peace-on-its-20th-year/ (accessed September 10, 2020).

Karl Gaspar, whom I cited in chapter 1, was also present at the conference. Since the 1970s, he has been involved in the Arakan Manobo's struggle to reclaim and protect their ancestral lands. In his writing on the Lumad's struggle, he describes a Matigsalug friend, Isidro Indao, a leader of the Kulamanon Manobo Lumadnong Panaghiusa (Kelamanon Manobo Indigenous People's Unity). The latter aspired to write down Lumad beliefs and thus create Lumad scriptures. "He believed," Gaspar writes, "that a sacred book about their beliefs would be very useful for their own struggle to retain their identity."[68] Indao knew Lumad cultural practices and knowledges depended on securing ownership of what remained of their ancestral domain: "These are dreams of peace, of food on the table every day, of their children going to school so that the settlers would not look down on them, dreams that their culture, traditions, and their beliefs would not vanish."[69]

Gaspar has been involved with the Kaliwat Theatre Collective and the Mindanao Theatre Movement since 1994. He has worked with them to perform Indigenous rituals and stories to convey to a broader public why land exploitation and theft constitute cultural violations. Like Indao, his activism has focused on the link between "having a religion and culture" and having rights. In the case of IPs, their cultural survival is intertwined with their presence in their ancestral lands. Hence, shaping Lumad traditions into a "religion" (by creating "scriptures," for example) constitutes a political act of cultural survival and vice versa. Cultivating an "identity," in other words, is a vital tool for promoting IP rights to their ancestral domains. But this cultural reclamation also constitutes an act of reification of their practices in terms familiar to the dominant discourse. Such reification delimits the dynamic horizons of cultural and religious traditions as historically embedded, embodied, and elastically contested. Indeed, the IPs' "hold on their ancestral domain rested on how strongly they have retained the memory of their ancestors from their folklore to their belief in the spirit world ... from their approaches in dealing with conflict to their kinship system."[70]

However, shifting from this agentic storytelling and cultural reclamation to subordination into a neoliberal tripartite harmony discourse is problematic. Many of my interlocutors critically reflected on how this harmony narrative introduces erasures through a push for homogenizing storylines.

---

[68] Karl M. Gaspar, *Manobo Dreams in Arakan: A People's Struggle to Keep Their Homeland* (Quezon City: Ateneo de Manila University Press, 2011), 2.
[69] Ibid., 2–3.
[70] Ibid., 198. This argument resonates with Wenger, *We Have a Religion*.

One interlocutor spoke about the erasures of Lumad and Muslim histories in conventional accounts of Filipino history that celebrate the tri-people narrative. Another agreed, adding that "there is no holiday marking the Jabidah Massacre," a fact that contributes to the ignorance of the younger generations.[71] The youth, accordingly, are drawn into an amnesic celebration of diversity that does not force them to grapple with historical injustices, but does force everyone into closed communal and religious containers that are indexed to one another. An intentional emphasis on "the identity of one Mindanao, peaceful coexistence among tri-people" is pushed by the government in Luzon. Because of these erasures, it is unsurprising that some of those actors populating peacebuilding in Mindanao strive to move toward a new narrative: "our Mindanao." This phrase is less formulaic and more open-ended. Further, because it emphasizes "our" rather than "tri," it is more conducive to plurality and to the acknowledgment of painful historical memories.[72] This nuance, however, is difficult to maintain within a neoliberal discourse of interreligious governance that, as I have shown repeatedly, relies on double closures and leads to erasures. It does so through the domestication and co-optation of a Sisyphean persistence and the spiritualization of peacebuilding.

Sisyphean Persistence

What does this critique of neoliberal peacebuilding mean concerning religious practices? It affirms my exposition of how best practices and benchmarking diffuse techniques of grassroots actions involving religion. Let me return to Malindi and the case of the CICC. The clerics' instrumentalization as agents equipped with local access to tackle "cultural/individual failings" contributes to the flattening of discourse about what counts as "authentic" religiosity. On the one hand, multisectoral problem-solving subordinates theological engagement to neoliberal rationality that posits cultural practices as obstacles to overcoming conditions and cycles of poverty. On the other hand, the religious actors here are not mere instruments of a neoliberal leviathan; their peacebuilding agency cannot be discounted. Every day they resist the forces of despair resulting from marginalization and

---

[71] Focus group #15 in Mindanao, June 2019. I also discuss this massacre and others in chapter 1.
[72] Focus group #15 in Mindanao.

poverty. Their daily interactions with people in the community from which they come involve a Sisyphean modality of peacebuilding—one that, unlike Albert Camus's reading of the myth of Sisyphus, does not persist in resigning to the struggle. This modality, rather, seeks to transform the conditions for the persistence of suffering, but does so with a recognition that this transformation entails an everyday struggle against despair. Whether this struggle requires resolving conflicts between pastoralists and farmers that erupt along ethnic and tribal lines in Kenya or concentrated efforts to reduce child abuse by working with schools, teachers' networks, and municipalities in the Kenyan coast, Sisyphean peacebuilders creatively navigate the neoliberal landscape with both its epistemic and donor parameters. Critically, the Sisyphean path cannot simply be interpreted as a reaction to and mastery of rules beholden to a narrative shaped by actors in the Global North. Sisyphean peacebuilding becomes incredibly robust when it constitutes a form of spiritual formation and practice that both sustains coloniality while also gesturing toward decolonial survivalist piety and love that exceeds the colonial clutches.[73]

In Mindanao, but also broadly within the religion and harmony discourse, the depoliticization of religion and its relocation into the space of civil society creates a neoliberal variation of a much longer history of instrumentalizing religion in the service of power and domination. Yet the actual people who inhabit the civil society spaces in Mindanao, and whose activism often coalesces around intercommunal interfacing, challenge this decolonial dismissal of harmony talk with their dreams, aspirations, and shaping of this vision of tripartite harmony, or "our Mindanao." There is nothing cynical about this. The need to identify where empirical realities exceed ideological frames is a challenge I take up in this book.

Colonized Moral Imagination

The conference From Enmity to Friendship concluded with a dreaming session, which was framed by the language of tripartite harmony. During the session, participants imagined how they wanted the future to look. This exercise explicitly operationalized Lederach's concept of the "moral imagination," which entails a creative embrace of possibilities that present themselves

---

[73] This paradoxical tension is a point to which I return to throughout the book.

within contexts otherwise defined by protracted violence. Challenging technocratic paradigms, he interprets social transformation as akin to artistic creation. Such creation is grounded in a complex analysis of webs of relations that include enemies and friends. It calls for people to unlock their curiosity and capacity for interaction so they can imagine future paths that transcend their divisions.[74]

Based on this future-oriented imagination (but already predetermined by the harmony framing of IRD/A), participants were asked to devise actionable plans for moving in the direction of their imagined peaceful futures. For example, the representatives from the region of Zamboanga, Basilan, and Pagadian identified three priorities: intrafaith challenge, discrimination, and radicalization (religious violent extremism). These action plans, however, reflect a process of neoliberal colonization of the imagination. They centralize individual responsibility in intra- and interreligious peacebuilding and dialogue and confine, because of the operation of the hermeneutical closures, the elicitive imagination of the future to the constraints of the present. Such work depoliticizes. It facilitates devolution and marginalization through mechanisms that enable relative stability and effective local conflict resolution. The devolutionary logic of responsibilization also applies to the IRD/A practices themselves.

Speaking at the Interreligious Solidarity Conference, Guiamel Alim—who is chairperson of the Consortium of Bangsamoro Civil Society, a counterpart of Cappalla from the Muslim community—concluded, "Ultimately, IRD practitioners must determine if religion will remain a source of conflict or become a resource for peace."[75] It is important to reflect for a moment on the framing of this sentence. "Religion" is described in a way that is in line with much of the literature on religion, conflict, and peacebuilding—as a currency for *either* violence *or* peacebuilding. Those working in this area fixate on the emergence and cultivation of religious entrepreneurs (whose own religious virtuosity is beside the point) who can move capital around effectively.

What does it mean to frame religion as a resource/currency/capital? As I have already indicated, such notions of religion are often light on prophetic critique and serve to reinforce traditional hierarchies and social

---

[74] Lederach, *The Moral Imagination*.
[75] CRS, "A Common World among Us in Mindanao: Love of God, Love of Neighbor, Love of Earth: A Synthesis of Learnings from the 2016 Mindanao-wide Interreligious Solidarity Conference," Royal Mandaya Hotel, Davao City, September 21–22, 2016, 12. This conference was cosponsored by CRS, the Episcopal Commission on Interreligious Dialogue, and the Tanenbaum Center for Interreligious Understanding. This synthesis is an internal document shared with me by CRS actors.

scripts. In this chapter's examination of conversations between Mindanaoan civil society's local actors, I have highlighted postsecular sectoralization, the responsibilization of religious actors, and the unique moralizing and spiritualizing properties that accompany such processes. Here and elsewhere in the book, I press against the boundaries of the colonial gaze to discuss religion's role in perpetuating grassroots and Astroturf (referring to nonorganically engineered "locals")[76] interreligious action as a form of hope, even while recognizing that it is precisely this capacity to sacralize mere survival and "getting by" and "getting along" that facilitates the capitalization of religion and the entrenchment of a neoliberalism that perpetuates hopeless situations.

Hopelessness

Father Bert Layson's peacebuilding work in the violence-prone town of Pikit, Cotabato, is an example of a Sisyphean practice that is world-weary and born out of recurring struggle. A process of introspection and awakening to the suffering and humanity of Muslims and IPs led him to embrace peacebuilding as the main vocation of the Church. This means persisting to write a different script for Mindanao based on teaching a "culture of peace" through seminars, tangible relationship building, and humanitarian work. His struggle is not against "liberal peace" or neoliberal peacebuilding. From the perspective of Father Bert and many others who are immersed in grassroots interfaith and intergroup peacebuilding work, what should be resisted is hopelessness, hatred, and division. Their personal and interpersonal capacity to overcome divisiveness itself constitutes a spiritual praxis. While this resistance is occasionally motivated by theological introspection about what it means to be Christian or Muslim, especially as a leader within those communities, their agency as religious actors often echoes and reinforces the assumptions undergirding the 3Bs methodology, its theory of change, and the burden it places on individual self-transformation and responsibilization. This neoliberal burdening becomes particularly effective when paired with religion because of the latter's capacity to spiritualize the

---

[76] This metaphor is apt as a challenge to the mislabeling of some actors as "grassroots" while they most fittingly would be labeled as "artificial turf" underwritten by global neoliberal dynamics and patterns of investment in "the local turn."

very praxis of self-transformation (from hate to love or "getting along"). It is also effective in spiritualizing Sisyphean persistence against hopelessness and investing daily survival tasks with religious piety. I return to this point in subsequent chapters.

Capacity building, leadership training, and human rights advocacy are mainstreamed in Mindanao's grassroots peacebuilding context. But their embrace does not amount to a total co-optation by the neoliberal peacebuilding agenda and its ideological formations. Instead, when one asks about their motivations, as I did during my fieldwork, such actors share their aspiration to problem-solve, to redress the conditions of human insecurity, and to find a way to live together with other communities. But even as they articulate these motivations, they convey their embeddedness within a neoliberal rationality. This rationality depoliticizes religion and focuses on responsibility and the reshaping of subjectivities from the ground up rather than structural change and reparation for historical harms. This is the case, I contend, even if people's aspirations to "scale up" their bridges and friendships are authentic and generative. The trickle-down interfaith performativity of Pakigdait (Figure 2.5) and similar organizations also enables a harmony discourse of "unity in diversity" whose reliance on

Figure 2.5 Members of Pakigdait's interfaith board celebrating Interfaith Harmony Week. Reproduced with permission from Pakigdait.

sociopolitical and religiocultural hermeneutical closures may be generative of peace but preventative of the actual materialization of the scaling-up rhetoric that the "planting a seed" metaphor denotes. Rather than analyzing the matrices and webs of power and the ongoing legacies of colonialism, the depoliticizing maneuver here posits the supposed "culture of violence" as the cause of people's predicaments of poverty, marginalization, and insecurity. Conversely, the "culture of peace" mechanisms become an amnesic antidote whose spiritualizing properties render it effective.

"The Rationality through Which Capitalism Finally Swallows Humanity"

The focus on self-transformation (or self-transcendence) as the engine of change captures how the postsecular turn entrenches rather than disrupts neoliberal rationality. Peace practice becomes a form of spiritual formation and vice versa. This feedback loop depends on closing the hermeneutical horizons of religious and cultural traditions, holding them in place as a set of prescriptive principles and values constitutive of corresponding unitary conceptions of social identities. They are imagined as a utilitarian building block for "keeping the peace."

Hence, when I invoke "democracy," in this and subsequent chapters, I mean something very different from the neoliberal "social cohesion." I mean a political praxis of hermeneutical openness that neoliberal interreligious peace governance diminishes through its technocratic regime's reliance on hermeneutical closures. Brown laments the depoliticization and de-democratization generated by neoliberalism, declaring neoliberal rationality "the rationality through which capitalism finally swallows humanity"[77] and turns people into "implementing partners." Indeed, this lament comes from a place of privilege in the Global North, on one side of the "abyssal line" or in the "zone of being," as Fanon and those working within his intellectual tradition underscore.

Brown's declension narrative relies on the presumption of the humanity of citizens. This presumption invisibilizes long histories of dehumanization, racialization, exploitation, and slavery on the backs of which both liberal and Marxist political theoretical traditions have constituted themselves.

---

[77] Brown, *Undoing the Demos*, 44.

To put it another way: to those in the zone of nonbeing, to those on the margins, and to those whose bodies are marked with the scars of centuries of dehumanization—and with it depoliticization, commodification, and exploitation—the neoliberal turn is not a declension narrative but rather a new chapter in the same old dehumanizing story. A decolonial lens draws a direct line from the tradition of liberalism to neoliberalism. It illuminates how the neoliberal frame capitalizes on the religious sector to perpetuate itself. But this time it is perpetuated through the praxis of bridging and dialogue and by making religion a site of spiritual resilience dependent upon multiple hermeneutical closures.

Indeed, neoliberalism resists critical hermeneutical openness and historically located interculturality oriented toward emancipatory rescripting of futurity.[78] Hence, along with Brown, I see governance as a depoliticizing force that employs ideas like "social cohesion" and "promoting inclusive societies" as technologies intended to reduce democratic potentials to multisectoral "buy-in" and cohabitation to "problem-solving."

Still, the neoliberalization of peacebuilding does not degrade the agency of those acting on the ground who seek to build friendships across lines of difference—even if such friendships are not political—that, Danielle S. Allen renders, constitute the building blocks of democracy.[79] That the "bridging" mechanisms generate nonpolitical friendships (understood, in bridging activities, as "social capital") that are spiritually powerful and causal is not insignificant, even if not scalable, despite the ubiquity of the seed metaphor.

While policy actors—now that they inhabit this postsecular junction—may be "more religiously literate," the "religious actors" who they engage in the Global South through programmatic efforts reinforce, through feedback loops, the neoliberal convergence between the marketization of everything

---

[78] For examples of this line of argument within decolonial critical peace education designed to challenge this neoliberal logic, see Vanessa de Oliveira Andreotti, "Soft versus Critical Global Citizenship Education," in *Development Education in Policy and Practice*, ed. S. McCloskey (London: Palgrave Macmillan, 2014), 21–31. For an earlier critical engagement with the development discourse, see Gayatri Spivak, "Can the Subaltern Speak?," in *Marxism and the Interpretation of Culture*, ed. Cary Nelson and Lawrence Grossberg (Chicago: University of Illinois Press, 1988), 271–313. Decolonial and postcolonial critical peace education, therefore, seeks to disrupt assumptions that persist in positing a presumption of occupying the "center" of the world, which is a rearticulation of the old Eurocentric civilizational discourse. For this argument, see Basma Hajir and Kevin Kester, "Toward a Decolonial Praxis in Peace Education: Postcolonial Insights and Pedagogic Possibilities," *Studies in Philosophy and Education* 39, no. 6 (2020): 515–32.

[79] Danielle S. Allen, *Talking to Strangers: Anxieties of Citizenship since* Brown v. Board of Education (Chicago: University of Chicago Press, 2004). See also chapter 8.

and an unreconstructed reliance on "traditional morality." I now examine the religion industry and its construction of the "religious actor" as pivotal for the consolidation of an integrated approach to peacebuilding and development. In particular, I focus on consolidating "*doing* religion," a technocratic reshaping of religious authority and action.

3
Doing Religion

An Integrated Approach to Religion, Peace, and Development

The postsecular moment signaled the consolidation of a religious authority grounded, rather than in *knowing* (in a hermeneutically capacious way), in neoliberal and utilitarian imperatives, or *doing*. This focus on *doing* requires interrogation of the broader landscape of religion, development, and peacebuilding. The mainstreaming of religion was evident when, in 2015, the World Bank, together with the German Federal Ministry for Economic Cooperation and Development, USAID, the GHR Foundation, World Vision, and the Joint Learning Initiative on Faith & Local Communities,[1] convened a global meeting, "Religion and Sustainable Development," with an emphasis on the concept of "partnership." Indeed, the conference, which was cosponsored by a host of faith-inspired organizations, such as CRS, Islamic Relief USA, Tearfund, and American Jewish World Service, contained the telling subtitle "Strengthening Partnerships to End Extreme Poverty."[2] The explicit intention of the conference and numerous others like it—which have increased in the second decade of the twenty-first-century[3] and which often

---

[1] Formed in 2012 as a result of a collaboration among international development organizations, UN agencies, academic institutions, and religious bodies, the Joint Learning Initiative on Faith & Local Communities represents the consolidation of a discourse—which includes both knowledge and power—around the effectiveness of investing in religion for development and peace policies/practices. The initiative suggests an international effort to offer empirical evidence for the importance of engaging religious actors. Put simply, the more evidence that can be produced to justify investment in religion, the more sustainable the religion business is. The Initiative defines itself as a network "seeking to build the evidence on activities and contributions of faith groups to the achievement of the Sustainable Development Goals (SDGs) and the role of faith in community health and wellbeing." See Joint Learning Initiative on Faith & Local Communities, "Member Benefits," https://jliflc.com/member-benefits/ (accessed September 23, 2020). Of relevance are the UN Interagency Taskforce on Religion and Development and PaRD, the latter of which I discuss in this chapter.

[2] All these organizations became immersed and fluent in the ethos and jargon of development. See, for example, Dena Freeman, *Tearfund and the Quest for Faith-Based Development* (New York: Routledge, 2019); David P. King, *God's Internationalists: World Vision and the Age of Evangelical Humanitarianism* (Philadelphia: University of Pennsylvania Press, 2019).

[3] About this convening, see, for example, World Bank, "Global Conference on Religion and Sustainable Development: Strengthening Partnerships to End Extreme Poverty," July 12, 2015,

feature the same participants—was to enhance cooperation among "faith and development" actors so they could fulfill their goal of alleviating poverty and underdevelopment through peacebuilding initiatives.

Religion's utility needs to be demonstrated to attract investment for *doing religion*. The sustainability of the harmony business increasingly depends upon strengthening the religion and development subfield, and both depend upon hermeneutically uncritical manualized religiosity. This entails the horizontalization and bureaucratization of religious virtuosity and its packaging as a measurable variable. The NGO-ized prophetic lite form of religion is therefore both replaceable and reproducible. This is one of the upshots of interreligious peace governance I discussed earlier. It is misleading to suggest that increasing such "evidence-based" knowledge of religion's effectiveness, when it is "right-sized" (meaning when the precise role of religion, on a case-by-case basis, is determined),[4] provides a form of "religious literacy" that pertains only to the capacity of policy (and civil society) actors to know how to deal with (or engage) religion. It does not entail knowing the history of religious traditions.

When I asked my interlocutors about hermeneutical depth, they—even the most knowledgeable—repeatedly dismissed the question as irrelevant or as potentially detrimental to the task of survival and peace. But this dismissal makes sense only against a backdrop in which peace is configured through the lens of a harmony discourse that indexes the hermeneutical closure to the closure of the community as a unitary homogenized identity interest group rather than through a decolonial prism that challenges such double closures and analyses of conflict that posit culture and religion as the source of disharmony. The neoliberal frame of *doing religion* does not need to challenge such accounts as long as they function effectively to promote its agenda.[5] In other

---

https://www.worldbank.org/en/news/press-release/2015/07/12/global-conference-religion-sustainable-development.

[4] See Peter Mandaville and Melissa Nozell, "Engaging Religion and Religious Actors in Countering Violent Extremism," United States Institute of Peace, Special Report 413, August 30, 2017, https://www.jstor.org/stable/pdf/resrep12243.pdf?refreqid=excelsior%3A24912ffdd7612c696f7958ceb d0e33c3.

[5] For an example of the pragmatic approach, see the UN Interagency Task Force on Engaging Faith-Based Actors for Sustainable Development/UN Task Force on Religion and Development, "Engaging Religion and Faith-Based Actors on Agenda 2030: The SDGs 2017," 2018, https://www.partner-religion-development.org/fileadmin/Dateien/Resources/Knowledge_Center/2017_Annual_Report_UNIATF.pdf.

words, religion and peacebuilding practices paradoxically thrive on religious illiteracy.[6]

At this point, it is important to sketch the underlying scholarly and practitioner developments that led to the horizontalization and reduction of the prophetic function of religion. Consistent with the postsecular "discovery" of religion,[7] a scholarly niche of religion and development has gained momentum. This is due in no small part to financial investment by policy actors and agencies in the first two decades of the twenty-first century.[8] Indeed, the utilitarian focus on *how* religion can help promote global agendas highlights the discursive complicity of scholarship. Marie Juul Petersen and Ben Jones demonstrate that the impetus for creating a dialogue between religion and development emanated from donors and development practitioners rather than the academy.[9] Research came later and was funded initially and for the most part by governmental granting agencies, such as the United Kingdom's Department for International Development. This research sought to understand how values, beliefs, and religious institutional frameworks interacted with other actors and sectors in promoting development and aid goals.[10]

---

[6] This reliance on diminished (illiterate) accounts of tradition is highlighted, unusually for this genre of reports on the global engagement with religion, as part of a collaboration between Oxfam and Harvard Divinity School's Religious Literacy Project. The report helpfully exposes the blind spots and ignorance of so-called secular agencies and organizations and pushes back against neocolonial tendencies. Yet the ways in which neoliberal rationality operates to prop up local ownership do not necessarily constitute a departure from global structural and historical violence. See Tara R. Gingerich, Diane L. Moore, Robert Brodrick, and Carleigh Beriont, "Local Humanitarian Leadership and Religious Literacy: Engaging with Religion, Faith, and Faith Actors," Oxfam & Harvard Divinity School's Religious Literacy Program, March 30, 2017, https://www.oxfam.org/en/research/local-humanitarian-leadership-and-religious-literacy.

[7] Explicit deployment of the concept of postsecular as pertaining to engaging with religious actors can be found in Alastair Ager and Joey Ager, "Sustainable Development and Religion: Accommodating Diversity in a Post-secular Age," *Review of Faith and International Affairs* 14, no. 3 (2016): 101–5, https://doi.org/10.1080/15570274.2016.1215813.

[8] For examples of the growing bibliography, see Séverine Deneulin and Carole Rakodi, "Revisiting Religion: Development Studies Thirty Years On," *World Development* 39, no. 1 (2011): 45–54, https://doi.org/10.1016/j.worlddev.2010.05.007; Jeffrey Haynes, *Religion and Development: Conflict or Cooperation?* (Basingstoke: Palgrave Macmillan, 2007); Emma Tomalin, *Religion and Development* (London: Routledge, 2013).

[9] See Marie Juul Petersen and Ben Jones, "'Instrumental, Narrow, Normative?' Reviewing Recent Work on Religion and Development," *Third World Quarterly* 32, no. 7 (2011): 1291–306, https://www.jstor.org/stable/41300284.

[10] Examples include the British Development Agency's sponsoring of research on religion and development in Birmingham University; the American Henry R. Luce Foundation program's sponsoring of academic programs on religion and international affairs; the Netherlands Ministry of Foreign Affairs' Knowledge Forum on Religion and Development Policy; and the UN Family Planning Agency. See also note 1.

Some scholars grappled with the complexity of distinguishing "secular" from "religious" facets of development practice and approaches,[11] while others cultivated integrative approaches.[12] Notably, the postsecular interest in religion does not focus on religion's ethical impulses or content but rather on religion's form, function, credibility, and capacity. This is because the postsecular interest is in religion's usefulness.[13] The "teachings" or "content" of religious traditions become essential only to the extent that they can be subcontracted and selectively utilized as currency for attaining some security, development, or peace goals. This is what it means to "partner" with religion.[14]

However, development theory constitutes a highly complex landscape that defies simple caricatures. Indeed, a line of scholarship labeled "development ethics" sheds light on the field's complex ethical dimensions and thus also on its critical intersections with the practice and theory of peacebuilding. The roots of development ethics are found in the work of Denis Goulet. In the 1980s, he synthesized secular and religious ethical sources to reconceive development practices outside of a technocratic paradigm. Goulet famously criticized the development field as a "one-eyed giant" incapable of encompassing multiple rationalities and conceptions of the good.[15] The work of Nobel Laureate economist Amartya Sen encouraged the critique

---

[11] For example, Michael Barnett and Janice Gross Stein, eds., *Sacred Aid: Faith and Humanitarianism* (New York: Oxford University Press, 2012); Katherine Marshall, *Global Institutions of Religion: Ancient Movers, Modern Shakers* (Abingdon: Routledge, 2013); Tanya B. Schwarz, *Faith-Based Organizations in Transnational Peacebuilding* (New York: Rowman & Littlefield, 2018).

[12] Alastair Ager and Joey Ager, *Faith, Secularism, and Humanitarian Engagement: Finding the Place of Religion in the Support of Displaced Communities* (New York: Palgrave, 2015).

[13] This is also true in cases where authors seek to identify what is distinctly secular about secular humanitarianism. See Olivia Wilkinson, *Secular and Religious Dynamics in Humanitarian Response* (London: Routledge, 2020).

[14] One of the key scholar-practitioners who has worked in the space of religion, development, and peace (as well as gender justice) is Azza Karam. She warns against the increasing and highly problematic approach to religion in development that treats religion as a "transactional commodity." Such treatment risks a disconnect from the actual communities of faith and represents an opportunistic engagement on the part of faith-based organizations with policymakers and donor agencies. Such forms of engagement work against gender justice. See Azza Karam, "Religion and Development: An Enhanced Approach or a Transaction?," *Inter Press Service*, April 12, 2019, https://www.ipsnews.net/2019/04/religion-development-enhanced-approach-transaction/. Karam's may be a mediating intervention that operates within a bifurcated understanding of religious actors as either instruments of neoliberal international aid business or a postsecular embrace of "partnership with religion" that sees such "global engagement" uncritically and rejects accusations that this simply denotes a nefarious contemporary mechanism to reconfigure the balance of power.

[15] Denis Goulet, "Development Experts: The One-Eyed Giants," *World Development* 8, nos. 7–8 (1980): 481–89. For later engagements with Goulet's significant contributions, see, for example, Des Gasper, "Denis Goulet and the Project of Development Ethics: Choices in Methodology, Focus and Organization," *Journal of Human Development* 9, no. 3 (2008): 453–74.

of developmentalism by asking ethical questions about the ends, and not only the means, of development policy. This opened up a space for ethical reflections and participatory, agent-centric processes of articulating such ends. Sen was unequivocal about the importance of not predetermining the capabilities necessary for enabling socioeconomic justice, even if he developed his approach as a way of evaluating the justness of economic policies.[16]

An increased interest in development ethics in conjunction with the postsecular turn of development practice signals a more integrated approach to development and peacebuilding that the SDGs telegraph. Goals 16 and 17 especially pertain to this book's discussion in emphasizing (Goal 16) the relations among peace, justice, and strong institutions and development objectives and the importance of "partnerships" (Goal 17) across sectors necessary for achieving the SDGs.[17] R. Scott Appleby, whose early work launched the subfield of religion, conflict, and peace,[18] celebrates the concept and practice of "partnership" among development practitioners, peacebuilders, and religious communities for shifting the conversation away from compartmentalizing these three sets of actors and toward examining fruitful convergences.[19] The convergences are critical for ensuring that aid and development practitioners observe the fundamental principle "Do no harm" and cultivate integrated approaches to poverty reduction and social exclusion.

---

[16] Amartya Sen, *Development as Freedom* (Oxford: Oxford University Press, 1999). See also Amartya Sen, "Capabilities, Lists, and Public Reason: Continuing the Conversation," *Feminist Economics* 10, no. 3 (2004): 77–80, https://doi.org/10.1080/1354570042000315163. Sen's approach to capabilities is distinct from Martha Nussbaum's, even though they collaborated at one point. Nussbaum rejects Sen's approach for engaging in an instrumental logic while, in her own, underscoring philosophical coherence, a focus on human dignity, and the design of a theory of justice. Sen's focus is instead on articulating a framework to evaluate people's quality of life and enhance individual freedom. See Martha Nussbaum, *Women and Human Development* (Cambridge: Cambridge University Press, 2001).

[17] The SDGs, a part of the UN 2030 Agenda, reflect an extensive global process of consultation with civil society actors. Unlike the Millennium Development Goals, which had informed the UN agenda from 2000 to 2015, the SDGs (comprising 169 specific targets within the broad seventeen goals signed by 193 UN member states in 2016) came about through a more grassroots consultative process, which explicitly involved "faith-inspired" actors.

[18] In peacebuilding, as in the development field, religion has increasingly gained traction since the publication of R. Scott Appleby's *The Ambivalence of the Sacred: Religion, Violence, and Reconciliation* (Lanham, MD: Rowman & Littlefield, 2000) and a host of other works that tapped into the empirically evident erosion of a secularist myopia. For an account of the subfield of religion, conflict, and peace, see Atalia Omer, "Religion and the Study of Peace: Practice without Reflection," *Religions* 12, no. 12 (2021): 1069, https://doi.org/10.3390/rel12121069.

[19] R. Scott Appleby, "The New Name for Peace? Religion and Development as Partners in Strategic Peacebuilding," in *The Oxford Handbook of Religion, Conflict, and Peacebuilding*, ed. Atalia Omer, R. Scott Appleby, and David Little (Oxford: Oxford University Press, 2015), 183–211.

Just like the religion and development subfield, scholarship in religion and peacebuilding is generated chiefly through funding provided by governmental, intergovernmental, and other policy actors. It is thus constrained by the demands of *realpolitik* and confined to realist underpinning logic, which has fixated on the question of *doing* religion. Additionally, the more the subfield of religion and peacebuilding has expanded, the more its proponents have impressed upon scholars and practitioners the importance of broadening the parameters of its research from its specific focus on leadership. The latter is often patriarchal and gerontocratic. To counter this bias, the utilitarian religion industry has pushed for a broader account of religious actors, which includes the potential contributions of women and youth. However, this expansion is called for not because of scholars' (or donors') concern with epistemologies from the margins but rather because of the potential devolutionary usefulness of youth and women. This scholarship has also expanded to encompass analytic engagements with the role of the media, interfaith dialogue, and critiques of secularism. It has focused on metrics and designs (tools called "monitoring and evaluation," or M&E, within the NGO universe) in its aim to produce more "scientific" measurements or demonstrate religion's effectiveness in promoting peace/development.[20] The turn to the measurement of *doing religion*, in particular, exposes the neoliberal underpinnings of the postsecular turn.

What is overlooked in the literature on religion, development, and peace practice is how the understanding of religion with which development and policy practitioners operate leads them to categorize certain actors as useful "religious actors" (and others as useless).[21] The problem with the scholarly literature, often sponsored by the same agencies that seek to instrumentalize

---

[20] For an example of how the search for evidence-based research to sustain investment in religion (in addition to the Joint Learning Initiative examined above) is mostly driven by research centers and policy circles, see this report by the Collaborative Learning Projects: Jennie Vader, *Meta-review of Inter-religious Peacebuilding Program Evaluations*, Peacebuilding Evaluation Consortium for CDA Collaborative Learning Projects, June 2015, https://www.cdacollaborative.org/wp-content/uploads/2016/01/Meta-Review-of-Inter-Religious-Peacebuilding-Program-Evaluations.pdf. For examples of a scholarly effort to measure religion's effectiveness in conflict reduction, see Johannes Vüllers, Birte Pfeiffer, and Matthias Basedau, "Measuring the Ambivalence of Religion: Introducing the Religion and Conflict in Developing Countries (RCDC) Dataset," *International Interactions: Empirical and Theoretical Research in International Relations* 41, no. 5 (2015): 857–81, https://doi.org/10.1080/03050629.2015.1048855; Jonathan Fox, "A World Survey of Secular-Religious Competition: State Religious Policy from 1990 to 2014," *Religion, State, and Society* 47, no. 1 (2019): 10–21, https://doi.org/10.1080/09637494.2018.1532750.

[21] Emma Tomalin posits the postsecular partnership model and the critique of instrumentalizing as two distinct positions she seeks to mediate. See Emma Tomalin, "Global Aid and Faith Actors: The Case for an Actor-Oriented Approach to the 'Turn to Religion,'" *International Affairs* 96, no. 2 (2020): 323–42, https://doi.org/10.1093/ia/iiaa006.

religion better, is that, in its effort to release the "religious actor" from structural (and discursive) reductionism by highlighting her agency—or her *doing religion*—it assumes that the religion such actors do can be boiled down to some kind of essence.[22] In other words, the Jewish actor's Judaism is not a subject of analysis, only what she *does* in her capacity *as* a Jewish actor. The very diminishment of the vision of the prophetic grounded in deep knowledge of tradition, or the "truly prophetic," to the prophetic lite through NGO-ization and securitizing discourse reveals that the "religious actor" is both an instrument and an authentic normative actor.[23] On the one hand, the effectiveness of this actor depends on repackaging religion in ways that depoliticize and enhance a neoliberal resiliency discourse. On the other hand, it signals relational openings that convey where the practices exceed neoliberal ideology, a point to which I will return. In this chapter, I argue that an increased emphasis on *doing* rather than *knowing* religion, even if it expands the scope of actors, denotes a utilitarian rather than a normative turn in religion and peace/development.

However, gaining clarity on the scope, capacities, and fluctuations of the religious actors has bracketed "religious horizons" not directly relevant to the task of *doing* religion. This instrumentalist and neoliberal form of religious literacy seeks understanding to better capitalize on religious actors, networks, and institutions. Becoming religiously literate in the development/peacebuilding field depends on sociopolitical and religiocultural hermeneutical closures. Most critically, it relies on mobilizing religious institutions' communal traction, service provisions, institutional frameworks, and credibility. It relies on *doing*, not *knowing*.

In the moment of the proliferation of postsecular policy-oriented research centers, confusion emerges where literature (even in peer-reviewed publications) that describes, maps, and proposes actionable pathways for engaging "religious actors" is mislabeled as "scholarship on religion."[24]

---

[22] In "Global Aid and Faith Actors," Tomalin is precisely attempting to reclaim agency for the "religious actors" in such a way that nonetheless underscores their usefulness to the development frame, specifically the SDGs. In doing so, she pays no attention to the version of the "faith" such actors deploy. This account is challenged by Tomalin's own important earlier analysis of the relation between female ordination within Buddhist contexts and women's politicization and empowerment pathways. See Emma Tomalin, "Buddhist Feminist Transnational Networks, Female Ordination and Women's Empowerment," *Oxford Development Studies* 37, no. 2 (2009): 81–100, http://dx.doi.org/10.1080/13600810902859510.

[23] See also my discussion of the imam and the pastor in chapter 2.

[24] For examples that reflect on this growing bibliography and links to donors and policy patterns, see Alan Robinson, *Faith-Based Organizations and Government Funding: A Research Note* (Oxford: Tearfund, Oxford Centre for Mission Studies, 2011), http://faithindevelopment.org/doc/

This mislabeling exposes how the production of knowledge about religion perpetuates rather than decolonizes "common sense." Relying on hermeneutical closures, this subfield imagines "solutions" or a better future ("developed," peaceful) from within the constraints of the present. To this degree, it simply answers the questions of what works, why it works, and how we can make it work more effectively. This bureaucratization entails disciplining religious actors across multiple fields and consolidating the organizational, intergovernmental, and transnational frameworks that can act as religious authorities in and of themselves.

Some of the limitations of the field, which I have identified elsewhere,[25] involve an enduring reliance on secularist paradigms that differentiate the "religious" from the "political" to allow "religion" to influence political actions. Such a move is problematic because it assumes that religious persons act outside political formations and discourses. This, in turn, leads to the specialized integration of religion into neoliberal peace governance. If what counts as religion is not historicized, its employment remains susceptible to ahistorical claims of authenticity, whether "good" and thus peace-promoting, or "bad" and thus violence-condoning.[26] Such uncritical (and instrumentalist) approaches fail to demystify the interlacing of religion and ideology with structures of violence and other mechanisms of dehumanization.[27] I now turn to unpack further the operation of technocratic religious actors, authorities, networks, and hermeneutics.

Harnessing Religion Better

"It is increasingly recognized that faith-based actors both presently and historically have played a fundamental role in fostering resilience, preventing violent conflict, and sustaining peace. They do so both through theological

---

FBOs_and_government_funding_final.pdf; Gerard Clarke, "Agents of Transformation? Donors, Faith-Based Organizations and International Development," *Third World Quarterly* 28, no. 1 (2007): 77–99, https://doi.org/10.1080/01436590601081880.

[25] Atalia Omer, "The Intersectional Turn: Theories and Practices for Studying Religion and Peace," in *Religion and Peace*, ed. Jolyon Mitchell (Malden, MA: Blackwell, 2022), 49–62.
[26] See also Moore, "Methodological Assumptions and Analytical Frameworks regarding Religion."
[27] For an analysis of the limits of the subfield of religion and peace and how it overlooks cultural and structural violence, see Jason A. Springs, "Structural and Cultural Violence in Religion and Peacebuilding," in *The Oxford Handbook of Religion, Conflict, and Peacebuilding*, ed. Atalia Omer, R. Scott Appleby, and David Little (Oxford: Oxford University Press, 2015), 146–79.

interpretation and dialogue as well as by providing leadership in action, both in peacebuilding and in development." This is an opening reflection in a report on how to conceptualize and implement partnerships with religion in pursuit of achieving Goal 16 and Goal 17 of the SDGs.[28] "At the same time," the report continues, "challenges remain in establishing fruitful partnerships between international actors and LFAs [local faith actors]. Such challenges include a lack or inaccessibility of documented and disseminated evidence regarding the impact of LFAs, a lack of research synthesizing the disparate initiatives around the world, and the difficulty in navigating the diversity among LFAs." The report also highlights other challenges, which include "an overall lack of trust, knowledge, and capacity on the part of secular/nonreligious institutions" and "a lack of clear and coordinated efforts towards implementable actions to improve partnership between LFAs and international actors."[29] This is precisely what the religion business seeks to mitigate to better "harness" so-called local religious actors.

This form of *doing* religion relies on the consolidation of a new type of religious actor/authority, namely, the *religiocrat* who speaks in the name of all religions and none at all. This technocratic turn denotes the consolidation of a "religion sector" and religion experts within policy circles and development practitioners. The operative neoliberal concept of "partnership" depends upon a "generic" account of religion that is conducive to preserving traditional hierarchies and the status quo. The religious part or content that makes certain actors religious is irrelevant to the doing of religion, so long as the doing is useful for a humanitarian, development, and peacebuilding agenda. The *doing* is a function of *being* religious as communal belonging. The irrelevance of a more hermeneutically expansive account of religious traditions, and those who exist at the margins of those traditions, is especially pronounced in the religiocratic sphere.

Indeed, postsecular efforts to mainstream religion in the peacebuilding/development integrated agenda entail the shaping of generic and unelected religious authorities with various networks and actors. This is evident in the establishment of intergovernmental bodies, such as, in 2012, the

---

[28] I refer here to a paper produced by the Joint Learning Initiative on Faith & Local Communities and PaRD, with input from KAICIID Dialogue Center, the Network for Religious and Traditional Peacemakers, and CRS. See S. Trotta and Olivia Wilkinson, *Partnering with Local Faith Actors to Support Peaceful and Inclusive Societies* (Washington, DC: Joint Learning Initiative on Faith & Local Communities and International Partnership on Religion and Sustainable Development, 2019), 2, https://jliflc.com/resources/peace-sdg-16-pard/.

[29] Ibid.

King Abdullah bin Abdulaziz International Center for Interreligious and Intercultural Dialogue (KAICIID), formed by the Kingdom of Saudi Arabia, the Republic of Austria, and the Kingdom of Spain. It is also evident in the establishment of nongovernmental organizations, such as Religions for Peace (RfP), the United Religious Initiative, the World Council of Churches, and others. These organizations all explicitly focus on the role of religion in reducing violence and promoting peace/development, positioning themselves as interfaith, ecumenical religious actors and authorities. They rely on thin conceptions of common morality conducive to programmatic integrated peacebuilding/development initiatives like those I study in this book. They ultimately reinscribe, rather than disrupt, the secularist/modernist developmentalist paradigm and its taxonomies. These taxonomies map and divide up religions, which then, through spokespersons, communicate coherent instantiation of their essences back to the centers of global power. Such spokespersons and composite religious authorities representing a generic religion emerge at multiple levels. This allows religious actors' peacebuilding/development capacities to be harnessed more effectively. Such harnessing is then carried out in a way that reflects the partnership paradigms undergirding the SDGs.

Take, for example, the Building Bridges Initiative Taskforce, which, in 2018, was initiated in Kenya by President Uhuru Kenyatta and Prime Minister Raila Odinga (who served in that capacity from 2008 to 2013 and has been a leader of the opposition since 2013) in the aftermath of the tense 2017 elections. The purpose of this taskforce was "to evaluate the national challenges outlined in the Joint Communiqué of 'Building Bridges to a New Kenyan Nation'" and to produce practical recommendations for reform. The objective of such reforms was building a lasting unity. Religious leaders were brought in as a distinct sector that would be able to devise actionable plans for redressing multiple issues, including police corruption.[30] To have

---

[30] See the Presidential Taskforce on Building Bridges to Unity Advisory, "Building Bridges to a United Kenya: From a Nation of Blood Tie to a Nation of Ideals," October 2019, http://jadili.ictpolicy.org/docs/jadili-bbireport2019. For a reaction from the Kenya Conference of Catholic Bishops to the report, see Mercy Maina, "Bishops in Kenya Want 'a Dialogue Process' for Building Bridges Initiative (BBI)," Association for Catholic Information in Africa, December 19, 2019, https://www.aciafrica.org/news/570/bishops-in-kenya-want-a-dialogue-process-for-building-bridges-initiative-bbi. The bishops highlighted the need to redress the issues raised in earlier reports, including the Truth, Justice and Reconciliation Commission and the findings of the Commission of Inquiry, both of which reflect on the 2007–8 postelection violence that I discussed in chapter 1. The government's recognition of the religious sector as useful for problem-solving and assuaging social tensions is reflected in calls for their involvement in building bridges. See, for example, Presidential Communication Service, "Uhuru Urges Religious Leaders to Speak Boldly against Vices Holding Kenya Back," *Capital News*,

bargaining power as a sector, such religious leaders and nonelected representative bodies rely on generic accounts of the faith (community) about which they speak. This is the case even if individual representatives within national umbrella organizations, such as the Supreme Council of Kenya Muslims, articulate the specific needs of their respective communities.

The Building Bridges Initiative built upon earlier iterations of similar efforts. These include the Dialogue Reference Group, which replaced an even earlier interfaith effort in Kenya that the government implemented to ensure the Constitution reflected the values of religious communities.[31] The objective of the Dialogue Reference Group was to develop a national dialogue framework. In the words of a participant I interviewed, this meant "leading a process of national dialogue for peace and conflict transformation . . . working with faith communities and religious people to influence the reform process, governmental narratives, and methods to deal with conflict in the country and grievance. And to deal with the root causes of conflict, namely inequality and social exclusion."[32] Such language reflects the diffusion of the neoliberal sectoralization of religion, a sector that is curiously differentiated, by him, from the "women sector," the "youth," and so forth:

> I [was involved in the initiation of] the Dialogue because of our experience around 2013, where we didn't have a good enough framework to deal with the issues that arose under the toxic nature of our politics. So, we thought it is better to develop something which incorporates the leadership of the religious sector but incorporates other sectors, the business sector, the women sector, the youth sector, the disability sector, so we could have an inclusive dialogue and an inclusive mechanism of ensuring the elections in 2017 were conducted in a better way and they secured the country.[33]

September 26, 2020, https://www.capitalfm.co.ke/news/2020/09/uhuru-urges-religious-leaders-to-speak-boldly-against-vices-holding-kenya-back/. See also Agatha Ndonga, "Reforming Kenya's Security Sector: Policing Culture and Youth," *International Center for Transitional Justice*, November 26, 2019, https://www.ictj.org/publication/reforming-kenya's-security-sector-policing-culture-and-youth. The latter provides critical input on the communiqué and is articulated through engagement with marginalized youth in Kenya who were involved in postelection violence and were thus of central importance. However, the author of the report expresses concern regarding the youths' capacity to reform the security apparatus and their brutal policing.

[31] See chapter 1 for an overview of such efforts.
[32] Interview #54, Nairobi, November 2018.
[33] Ibid.

My concern is not the inclusion of religion in the national dialogue framework but rather that such an inclusion is non-intersectional by design. It separates religion from other sectors. Such separation contributes to reifying "good" religiosity, which does not require its spokesperson to historicize or grapple with, for example, the gendering and racializing of the accounts of tradition that they provide. Accounting for these factors seems irrelevant when responding to the immediate demands of *realpolitik*. To this extent, this partnering with religion is hermeneutically uncritical. It hermetically contains religion/culture within neoliberal boundaries, making it impossible to understand the political ramifications of these accounts of tradition. I now turn to sketch a typology of "religious actors."

"Religiocrats"

Global and international stages bestow prestige upon local conflict resolution efforts such as Pakigdait in Mindanao and the CICC in Kenya and vice versa: local success stories exemplify the relevance of the religion industry and top-level interfaith performances. A feedback loop operates here from bottom-up solicitation to top-down sanctioning. This feedback loop is further reinforced through the proliferation of commissioned studies that populate the field with self-reinforcing evidence-based research. Thus, the religious peacebuilding networks cannot be interpreted simplistically through binaries between the "local" and the "global," especially since this binary itself is flawed, presuming the "global" or "international community" as a site of "secular" and universal norms over and against "local" religious and cultural norms and communities.

This is where an analysis of the consolidation of the religiocratic class is pertinent. Take, for example, KAICIID, a member of this class. KAICIID sees its mandate as involving the "promot[ion of] the use of dialogue globally to prevent and resolve conflict to enhance understanding and cooperation."[34] Among other institutions and networks, KAICIID partners with the United Nations Development Program (UNDP); the United Nations Educational, Scientific, and Cultural Organization; RfP; the Network for Religious and Traditional Peacemakers; and the International Partnership in Religion

---

[34] See KAICIID, "About Us," https://www.kaiciid.org/who-we-are/about-us (accessed September 10, 2020).

and Sustainable Development (PaRD). KAICIID's declared intention is to "bring religious leaders and political decision-makers together to develop and implement multilateral social cohesion building and conflict resolution initiatives."[35] As a center for interfaith dialogue, KAICIID underscores the vital role of religious leaders and the need to enhance links between religious and political leaders. This enhancement unfolds through immersion in neoliberal rationality. The familiar language of "social cohesion" points to KAICIID's foregrounding of interfaith platforms as especially poised to "capacitate" religious actors through interreligious initiatives.[36]

The requirement to embolden the relationships between religious and political leadership structures is more explicit around the question of religiously motivated violence and the development of policies and practices to prevent such violence. In this space, religious leaders and experts appear to be most politically relevant beyond their traditional role as service providers. This is where bodies like KAICIID mobilize. Such mobilization is evident, for example, in its convening of a global conference (2018) on how religious communities can promote social cohesion and inclusive peaceful societies. Essentially, this conference was focused on how such communities can be integrated into governance efforts to harness "good" religion.[37] Another conference, United Against Violence in the Name of Religion (2014), which was supported by multiple Muslim and Christian religious leaders, promised to "capacitate" actors in the "religion space" with the skills to counter hateful speech as well as to "empower youth and women" so that they could function as positive agents in promoting "social cohesion and equal rights."[38]

KAICIID attempts to fight the perversion of religion and to counter violent interpretations using the exact mechanisms other religiocrats implement. First, they target women because women are potentially useful for their location in the social reproductive sphere. They likewise target (male) youth for being "at risk" of succumbing to violent interpretations of religion.[39] The

---

[35] KAICIID, "What We Do," https://www.kaiciid.org/what-we-do (accessed September 10, 2020).

[36] For example, KAICIID, "CAR [Central African Republic] Capacity Building Workshops," https://www.kaiciid.org/news-events/events/car-capacity-building-workshop (accessed October 12, 2020).

[37] By deploying the binary of "good" versus "bad" religion, I allude to the critique of culturalist explanations at the expense of geopolitical and historical accounts. See Mahmood Mamdani, *Good Muslim, Bad Muslim: America, the Cold War, and the Roots of Terror* (New York: Pantheon Books, 2004).

[38] KAICIID, "What We Do," https://www.kaiciid.org/what-we-do/promoting-coexistence-arab-region (accessed October 12, 2020).

[39] See also my discussion later in the book, particularly in chapters 5 and 6.

second way KAICIID fights against the perversion of religion is by using religious authorities' facility with the ("correct") resources of their respective religious traditions to promote an inclusive understanding of their religions. These authorities' local religious knowledge and sociopolitical and cultural stature operate as specialized forms of capital. The United Against Violence in the Name of Religion conference resulted in the Vienna Declaration (signed on November 19, 2014) and captured the moral unity of a diverse group of religious leaders who denounced the manipulation of religious traditions in the service of violent agendas, especially in the Middle East.[40] The declaration specifies the principles that underpin the moral unity of this diverse group of religious leaders. These include dialogue as a peacebuilding methodology for the promotion of coexistence and common citizenship, rejection of human rights violations regardless of people's religious identity, solidarity with the oppressed, repudiation of the manipulation of religion for political gains, repudiation of the perversion of religious symbols as instruments of exclusion, and respect for freedom of belief and religious practice.

The Vienna Declaration was followed by the Athens Declaration United Against Violence in the Name of Religion: Supporting the Citizenship Rights of Christians, Muslims, and Other Religious and Ethnic Groups in the Middle East. It was signed by high-level Christian and Muslim leaders on September 3, 2015, and echoed the same themes and appeals to diversity, human rights, and religious freedoms as the Vienna Declaration. Out of these formal symbolic declarations that, by default, reflected hermeneutical closures, multiple programming priorities have emerged at the local level, as funds moved from donor countries to receiving locations. Such foci reflect an emphasis on activating youth on social media to promote "counter-messaging" and to bring together interreligious educational networks that

---

[40] KACIID, "Vienna Declaration: United against Violence in the Name of Religion," November 19, 2014, https://www.kaiciid.org/vienna-declaration-united-against-violence-name-religion. The Vienna Declaration is just one in a series of such pronouncements with which KAICIID is associated at the highest levels of UN deliberations. For example, in 2017, KAICIID was a signatory to the UN's Office on Genocide Prevention and the Responsibility to Protect, "Plan of Action for Religious Leaders and Actors to Prevent Incitement to Violence That Could Lead to Atrocity Crimes." This plan dates back to another series of high-level consultations, dubbed the "Fez process," which took place between April 2015 and December 2016. These involved "religious leaders, faith-based and secular organizations, regional organizations and subject matter experts from all regions of the world." See UN Office on Genocide Prevention and the Responsibility to Protect, "Plan of Action for Religious Leaders and Actors to Prevent Incitement to Violence That Could Lead to Atrocity Crimes," https://www.un.org/en/genocideprevention/documents/Plan%20of%20Action%20Advanced%20Copy.pdf (accessed October 3, 2020).

can provide know-how or expertise for local practitioners of interreligious or intercultural dialogue. The work of the "local access" religious actors solidifies the importance of partnerships in global development/peacebuilding.

Additionally, in partnership with other global agencies, such as the Network of Religious and Traditional Peacemakers, the International Mediation Center, and UNDP, expressions of commitment by high-level leadership to sharing tools and relaying "lessons learned" provide an infrastructure and an ability to build capacity for local interreligious governance. Such support allows those working at the local levels to employ "dialogue as a tool to reach mutual understanding and to enhance social cohesion."[41] Yet engaging in these forms of dialogue, I have shown, depoliticizes peacebuilding. Rather than fostering sociopolitical power through coalition building and crosscutting structural analyses, "dialoguing" within a neoliberal frame pushes individuals to see the site of struggle as their own cultural and religious trappings and their misconceptions about others. Peace becomes the psychologized task of getting along. Moreover, the religion ingredient, turned into a sound bite, invests dialogue and bridge-building activities with spiritual qualities.

Likewise inhabiting the religiocratic space is the Network for Religious and Traditional Peacemakers (established in 2013). It reinforces an emphasis on partnership by design.[42] The Network's purportedly human rights approach entails references to increasing the inclusion of religious communities and women, following UN Security Council Resolution (UNSCR) 1325 and UNSCR 2242, and youth, per UNSCR 2250.[43] They do so through peacebuilding processes as well as by illuminating religious and tribal

---

[41] KACIID, "What We Do," https://www.kaiciid.org/what-we-do/united-against-violence-name-religion (accessed October 12, 2020).

[42] Network for Religious and Traditional Peacemakers, "About," https://www.peacemakersnetwork.org/about-us/ (accessed July 1, 2019). The focus on partnership is a matter of design. It is reflected explicitly in Goal 17, but also in international development policy's increased postsecular understanding of the need to engage so-called religious actors. A series of conversations in the UN and under the leadership of Azza Karam are especially relevant, as they produced multiple documents, statements, and action plans for more "synergetic" (a neoliberal buzzword) and effective work with religious or faith actors. See, for example, UN Inter-Agency Force on Engaging Faith-Based Actors for Sustainable Development/UN Task Force on Religion and Development, "Annual Report," 2018, https://www.partner-religion-development.org/fileadmin/Dateien/Resources/Knowledge_Center/2017_Annual_Report_UNIATF.pdf. For an introspective reflection on the consolidation of the partnership agenda in the UN, see a dialogue between Jose Casanova and Azza Karam at the Berkley Center, "Religious and Secular Global Dialogue: A Conversation with Azza Karam," September 24, 2020, https://berkleycenter.georgetown.edu/events/religious-and-secular-global-dialogue.

[43] These are key UN Security Council Resolutions pertaining to women and youth in peace and security.

traditions that reinforce the ideas of coexistence, dignity, and peace.[44] In its collaborations with an array of institutions and centers in the Global North,[45] the Network pursues its mission to facilitate multitrack peacebuilding activities. Here, linking elites with grassroots/Astroturf actors is the primary path for building "a sustainable peace" (a current vogue construct reflective of the peacebuilding/development nexus).

The Network for Religious and Traditional Peacemakers is not the only institution that aspires to develop best practices for global outreach and cross-fertilization with local communities. RfP—which was initially led by William Vendley and is currently led by Azza Karam—predates KAICIID and the network by several decades. It was established during the first World Conference of Religions for Peace, in Tokyo in 1970, and has devoted much of its work to establishing its UN consultative status. Through a structure of regional and country-specific interreligious councils (in five regions and ninety-two countries), RfP has played a role in many diverse peace processes and postviolence reconciliation processes. RfP has mobilized religious leaders around moral concerns such as nuclear disarmament and has also facilitated community efforts around appeals to pluralism, democracy, and governance.[46] To respond to the criticism that men dominated the councils,

---

[44] Network for Religious and Traditional Peacemakers, "About." See also Network for Religious and Traditional Peacemakers, "Mission," https://www.peacemakersnetwork.org/about-us/vision-mission-objectives/ (accessed July 1, 2019).

[45] They include the United Nations Peacemaker, United Nations Alliance of Civilizations, United Nations Development Programme, United Nations Population Fund, UN Office for Genocide Prevention and Responsibility to Protect, United Nations Women, Ministry of Foreign Affairs Finland, Finn Church Aid, KAICIID, Organization of Islamic Cooperation, Religions for Peace, Adyan Foundation, Aga Khan Development Network, Al Amana Centre, Archbishop of Canterbury's Office for Reconciliation, Berghof Foundation, Berkley Center for Religion, Peace & World Affairs, Crisis Management Initiative, Conciliation Resources, Danmission, Da'Wah Institute of Nigeria, Dialogue Advisory Group, Finn Church Aid Americas, Government of Kosovo, Inclusive Peace and Transition Initiative, International Center for Religion and Diplomacy, Islamic Relief Worldwide, Middle East Women's Leadership Network, Organization for Security and Co-operation in Europe, International Partnership on Religion and Sustainable Development, Salam Institute for Peace and Justice, the Ministry of Awqaf and Religious Affairs, Oman, and many others of similar caliber.

[46] In terms of engagement with violence, RfP has emphasized a toolkit approach for "deradicalization" involving multifaith actors, religious actors, and "strategic" aid. For RfP's approach to religion and violence, see Religions for Peace, "Religions for Peace: Rejecting Violent Religious Extremism and Advancing Share Well-Being," received by the Forum for Peace in Muslim Societies, Abu Dhabi, December 13, 2014, chrome-extension://efaidnbmnnnibpcajpcglclefindmkaj/https://www.unaoc.org/wp-content/uploads/Statement-of-Multi-Religious-Action-English-13-December.pdf; Religions for Peace, "Action Plan to Counter Violent Religious Extremism, 2015–2018," https://rfp.org/wp-content/uploads/2017/09/Action-Plan-for-Countering-Violent-Religious-Extremism.pdf; Religions for Peace, "Partnership among All to Overcome Terrorism," March 4, 2019, https://rfp.org/partnership-among-all-to-overcome-terrorism-religious-leaders-respond-to-terrorist-suicide-bombing-in-kashmir/.

RfP launched the Women of Peace network as well.[47] Nevertheless, the women's platform remains marginal to the "main" flagship body of RfP. This representational issue may change under the leadership of Karam, who became a key interlocutor/actor in the field of religion and peace/development in her capacity in UNDP and a whole spectrum of "religion and..." initiatives and programs.[48] These programs grappled with the problematic intersection of gender, development, and religion.[49] But a change in representation does not entail a substantive change in the kind of utilitarian religiosity and religious authority that religiocrats within such intergovernmental and transnational bodies promote. This is because these bodies remain subsumed under a functionalist/instrumentalist approach to partnership with religion. This is true regardless of the various faiths and cultural traditions that the officeholders within such organizations inhabit. Likewise irrelevant is the distance between the logic of partnership and the people who embody their faith but are now marked as "partners" for their utility.[50]

In Kenya, a prominent member of the Interreligious Council (IRC) and an active interlocutor in the national dialogue framework unpacked for me how the IRC solicits input from the grassroots, but also how the IRC authoritatively speaks more generally in the name of all religions and none at all:

---

[47] RfP, while global, is based in New York City and has a consultative status with the United Nations Economic and Social Council, UNESCO, and UNICEF.

[48] A conscious effort to mainstream women under Karam's leadership was the convening of the summit Women, Faith, and Diplomacy as part of a cosponsored event by RfP, the Foundation Peace Dialogue of the World Religions and Civil Society (Ring for Peace), and the German Ministry of Foreign Affairs in November 2020. See Ken Chitwood, "Religions for Peace Leader Azza Karam Shows the Role of Women in Faith and Diplomacy," *Religion Unplugged*, November 12, 2020, https://religionunplugged.com/news/2020/11/12/religions-for-peace-leader-azza-karam-shows-the-role-of-women-in-faith-and-diplomacy.

[49] Karam, a professor of religion and development at the Vrije Universiteit in Amsterdam, served as a senior adviser on culture at the United Nations Population Fund and as coordinator/chair of the United Nations Inter-Agency Task Force on Religion and Development. In this capacity, she coordinated the engagement of the Global Interfaith Network for Population and Development with over six hundred faith-based organizations from around the world. She is also the lead facilitator for the UN Strategic Learning Exchanges on Religion, Development, and Diplomacy. Karam's work in this religiocratic space is motivated by her own faith. This leads her to engage critically with instrumentalizing bureaucrats who are bereft of a deep understanding of the embodied and textured meanings of religiosity in people's individual and communal lives. She identifies such engagement as "a transactional commodity." See Azza Karam, "Religion and Sustainable Development: The Journey from Why to Engage to a Plea for Caution," inaugural lecture for her chair at the University of Amsterdam, June 13, 2019, 16, https://www.godgeleerdheid.vu.nl/en/Images/Inaugural_Lecture_Azza_Karam_tcm239-918580.pdf.

[50] For a critical engagement from within the technocratic space with this space's utilitarian drives, see Karam, "Religion and Development."

We did the national dialogue conference and we are now going to the county [level] to give an opportunity to the Kenyans at the grassroots level to say what they want. We are also involved in advocacy around key issues that we believe there should be dialogue. For example, advocacy around inclusive government—how do we make the government more inclusive so that people do not feel excluded, marginalized. We are collecting evidence around issues of postelection violence. We are creating partnerships with places where people are badly affected by this violence, trying to help the victims with counseling, trying to get the victims to access justice, trying to hold some of those people to account. We are involved in also trying to bring consolation in situations where consolation is possible, sometimes providing support for counseling and trauma healing.[51]

The IRC, therefore, becomes a conduit for processing grievances on the ground and for translating that processing into advocacy work that can then shape a framework for the Kenyan national dialogue. This "consultative" process is not dialogic but rather a mechanism to release, diffuse, and redirect grievances and prop up sectoral "representatives."

Further, in my interlocutor's view, the religious sector, as he understands it, has a particular mandate to intervene in matters concerning the radicalization of some citizens into participants in violent movements. He underscores the unique access to communities that the religious sector has and, therefore, on which it needs to capitalize: "Yes, [access] is much easier. . . . In fact, many accusations we've received from civil society is that 'you're not using your access to advocate most strongly for the rights of citizens and Kenyans, and to stop the extrajudicial killings and other human rights abuses.' The other thing is, the fact that you are interreligious means you cannot be pigeon-holed as being supportive of this or that. It gives also some measure of comfort."[52] This religious actor celebrates "some measure of comfort," underscoring that advocating for a generic composite of "religious interests" assuages donor worries about being associated with promoting a particular religious agenda: "It gives comfort to our partners and funders and donors that when they give resources to an interreligious group, they are not

---

[51] Interview #53, Nairobi, November 2018.
[52] Ibid.

advancing a specific religion and this money is not being used to evangelize. All those things come into play."[53]

Such religious actors derive their religious authority from technocratic practices and associations with global networks and epistemic communities firmly grounded in hegemonic sites. Unlike other forms, this variation of a religious authority does not depend on learned hermeneutics or mastery of the traditions across time and space. People populating the institutional spaces of RfP and the IRCs worldwide may, but do not necessarily, have such backgrounds. Regardless, what qualifies them for their positions is their fluency in the business of religion and peace. Within this framework, input from local faith actors is received through generic versions of "religion in general." Such versions are conducive to depoliticization, the horizontalization of virtuosity, and the NGO-ized prophetic lite approach to religious *doing*.

Like RfP, a similarly ambitious global (and localized) reach also animates the United Religions Initiative (URI), established in 2000 as a global interfaith organization headquartered in San Francisco. Under the leadership of Episcopal priest Victor H. Kazanjian, URI attends more to the systemic and structural conditions correlated with recruitment to violent religious movements than to the role of religious actors in correcting (mis)interpretations of religious traditions. Likewise, URI claims that it takes more of a grassroots, bottom-up approach—through engaging in autonomous Cooperation Circles—rather than a top-down approach, as RfP does. URI's Cooperation Circles encompass eighty-eight faith traditions in eighty-four countries and form the backbone of multiple interfaith peacebuilding and solidarity projects. The Cooperation Circles' link to URI is franchised through the minimal requirement to sign the charter (2000) that stresses the organization's commitment to promote "daily interfaith cooperation, to end religiously motivated violence and to create cultures of peace, justice and healing for the Earth and all living beings."[54] URI constitutes one of the religiocratic agencies with whom Pakigdait partners as it works on intercommunal receptivity to the BOL, which offers the peace framework in Mindanao's Moro conflict narrative.

---

[53] Ibid. It is interesting that "evangelization" operates through multiple channels and that the technocratic turn reveals what Cecelia Lynch and Tanya B. Schwarz call "humanitarianism's proselytism problem." See their "Humanitarianism's Proselytism Problem," *International Studies Quarterly* 60, no. 4 (2016): 636–46.

[54] United Religions Initiative, "URI Preamble, Purpose and Principles," https://uri.org/who-we-are/PPP (accessed October 8, 2020).

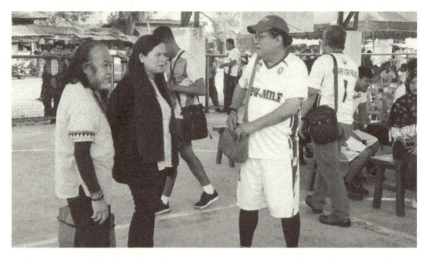

Figure 3.1 Father "Chito" (left) standing across from a player wearing a MILF team jersey. Reproduced with permission from Pakigdait Camp Bilal in Lanao del Norte, 2019.

Specifically, URI's investment has resulted in efforts to overcome disharmony through sports. This is seen as a fun way to build relationships among the Philippine military, the police, and militants affiliated with the MILF. "Sportspeace," as this immersive activity has been labeled, was implemented in six towns in Lanao del Norte affected by violence. By watching and participating in public basketball games played between former enemies, people have the chance to experience a trickle-down form of intercommunal healing (see Figure 3.1).[55] Here, URI channeled the interfaith capacity of Pakigdait to alleviate some of the tensions and triggers around elections and plebiscites regarding the BOL (February 2019). Interfaith listening sessions (see Figure 3.2), carried out by interfaith delegations, supplemented Sportspeace. Leading the interfaith delegation at the time was the late Father Teresito "Chito" Soganub, a survivor of captivity during the Marawi siege, whom I discussed earlier. Father Chito and Abdullah Macapaar ("Commander Bravo") managed frustration and potential escalation at listening sessions in the biggest MILF camp, Camp

---

[55] The initiative was described to me during the focus group with Pakigdait in June 2019 in Cagayan de Oro.

Figure 3.2 Listening session with women facilitated by Pakigdait prior to the plebicte in 2019. Reproduced with permission from Pakigdait.

Bilal in Lanao del Norte. These sessions were held immediately before the plebiscite, following a series of explosions and the subsequent spread of misinformation.

This interfaith work reveals that these leaders' effectiveness depends upon their rootedness in the contexts in which they operate, their positionality as visibly representing communal divides, and their ability to underscore a common aspiration to live together and overcome intercommunal discord. In this case, external religiocrats such as URI connect to the local access capacity of an organization such as Pakigdait to perform a trickle-down version of peace. This trickle-down interfaith performativity allows religiocrats to co-opt such local access groups to enhance interreligious peace governance. Pakigdait's capacity to enact intergroup peace performativity, facilitate frustration management, and de-escalate the potential for violence is only tangentially related to their gravitas as a group of religious leaders. This capacity also relates to the genuine relationships among the members of the organization's interfaith board. I observed how fondly they joked with one another in my focus group, just like old friends. Their capacity to manage frustrations could have nothing to do with their position as religious actors. The value-added to their ability to intervene relates to the easier access religious actors enjoy due to the conventional trust that community members have in them.

While underscoring the functionality of their roles as religious actors, the example of Sportspeace demonstrates the irrelevance of religious hermeneutical depth to such interreligious peacebuilding work and to the social script it tries to write. The source of religious authority, unlike the "truly prophetic," is not the sacred but the power and prestige of the religiocratic infrastructure and the embodiment of religion (the *being* religious). The religious actors' credibility is not necessarily an outcome of their *being* religious. Still, their positionality as religious leaders locates them as particularly effective for attaining local access and enacting the performance of "getting along." The emphasis is on *doing* religion, not *knowing* it. Regardless of what accounts of "religion" they espouse, the developmentalist frame defines them as "local religion/faith actors" with whom religiocratic actors pursue "partnership" to perform necessary tasks. It is the acting, not the actors, that matters. The hermeneutical content of their religiosity or cultural worldviews also do not matter. In this case, the possibility of one Mindanao is captured in a simple basketball game. The successful implementation of the Sportspeace events and the listening sessions' capacity to de-escalate frustrations and fears provide evidence for a feedback loop that returns to the religiocrats at the epistemic center. Religiocrats, in turn, reinforce, through their programmatic and monetary investments, the sustainability of such partners as Pakigdait. When members of Pakigdait internalize the neoliberal vocabularies animating interreligious governance, they complete the feedback loop.

More recent efforts, such as PaRD, shape the multidirectionality of neoliberal peacebuilding. To mainstream religion as an effective sector in development efforts, PaRD "synergizes" governmental and intergovernmental entities with civil society organizations, including those that are faith-based or faith-inspired.[56] The objective is "to engage the social capital and capacities vested in diverse faith communities for sustainable development and humanitarian assistance in the spirit of the 2030 Agenda for Sustainable Development."[57] In other words, PaRD represents a top-level governmental

---

[56] For an account of the key actors in the PaRD space and a conceptualization of its role as an intergovernmental mechanism—spearheaded by the Deutsche Gesellschaft für Internationale Zusammenarbeit—intended to enhance development policies, see Ulrich Nitschke and Bennet Gabriel, "The International Partnership on Religion and Sustainable Development/PaRD: A Global and Inclusive Partnership to Harness the Positive Impact of Religion in Development and Humanitarian Assistance," *Ecumenical Review* 68, no. 4 (2016): 378–86.

[57] PaRD, "Vision," http://www.partner-religion-development.org/about/vision-and-structure/ (accessed July 10, 2019).

and intergovernmental attempt to fully systematize and bureaucratize religion's interfacing with the promotion of the development agenda. PaRD is authorized by SDG 17, which stresses the centrality of partnerships. It is this focus on partnership that underlies the neoliberalization of religion in these spaces. Religion is a form of capital to mobilize. Further, religion is subordinated to a neoliberal logic that requires religious authority to be vested in technocratic religious actors. The insidious aspect of this partnership discourse is how the global engagement with religion cloaks itself with a veneer of taking faith seriously, often in displays of pomp and circumstance, in fancy convention hotels in global metropolitan centers. But "taking faith seriously" here unfolds a neoliberal utilitarian logic. More attention to religion under this paradigm leaves fewer substantive openings for critiques of religion.[58] For example, the religious leaders of Pakigdait may have a tangible impact in terms of conflict management while nevertheless failing to officially accept same-sex marriage.[59] The religiocratic logic of partnership subordinates marginal accounts of tradition to expediency.

As such a technocratic actor, PaRD's foci has been SDG 16 (sustainable peace), SDG 5 (gender equality and empowerment), and SDG 3 (health). Partners interact around these goals, measurable in terms of development indices. This focus on measuring religion's effectiveness is the rationality behind the joint learning initiative on faith and local communities with which I opened this section. It brought together PaRD, CRS, the Network for Religious and Traditional Peacemakers, and KAICIID to produce evidence-based research to measure the success of local faith actors in promoting peacebuilding and inclusive societies. They sought to use such measurements to recommend specific ways of investing and partnering with such local actors, many of whom I met in Kenya and the Philippines.

These examples of global institutional frameworks illuminate extractive efforts to unlock religious actors' ability to participate effectively in peacebuilding/development efforts. These efforts are pursued through the bridging mechanisms of interfaith dialogue of action, mobilizing (and co-opting) Indigenous conflict resolution tools, identifying common concerns, making ethical commitments to preserving human lives, and building capacity to mobilize toward social cohesion. Religious traditions, under this

---

[58] See also Karam, "Religion and Development."
[59] During my visit in June 2019, many religious leaders I met with in Mindanao shared with me their opposition to same-sex marriage.

schema, are understood as containers/vessels of ahistoric messages. Some are seen as conducive to promoting peace and stability, while others are not. Such reductionism constitutes a hermeneutical closure, whether the bottom line of the message is peace or violence. Ironically, these religious leaders/actors, the religiocrats, are the ones called to the highest proverbial tables to provide their expertise as representatives, in the aggregate, of the so-called religious sector. Hence, under the guise of more religion, the mechanisms of global engagement with religion actually contribute to less religious literacy, hermeneutically foreclosed accounts of religiosity, and the propping up of generic (and unelected) religious authorities.

Critical hermeneutics and *knowing* threatens religious engagement's sponsors such as Saudi Arabia and the United States. Foregrounding the utilitarian approach over and against critical hermeneutical depth prioritizes people's "sincerely held beliefs" as unreconstructed and ahistorical truths whose status as "belief systems" trumps any critical scrutiny.[60] Religiocratic knowledge also comes from scholars once removed from the field in research centers and think tanks constitutive of the global epistemic community. They ground their expertise in the evidence extracted from the field. At the same time, for scholars and practitioners in this religiocratic space, the pressure to offer operationalizable outcomes works against any possibility of hermeneutical depth.

Azza Karam's expert intervention regarding consolidating religion-focused technocratic spheres of influence is relevant here. Based on years of experience, she criticizes the technocratic field of religious peacebuilding for its cherry-picking of those aspects of religious traditions that appear expedient in utilitarian terms but may otherwise be implicated in human rights violations. For her, "thinly veiled conditionalities," such as those stipulated by various "western and Gulf-based donor governments and policymakers," may be "good" for "peacemaking, environmental stewardship, protection of children and minorities," but may carry also "the price . . . of foregoing—or silencing—of the human rights—and dignity—of others."[61] Therefore, the

---

[60] This is precisely where Diane L. Moore's intervention in the literature on religious literacy is important in deflating the prioritization of "sincerity." See her "Diminishing Religious Literacy: Methodological Assumptions and Analytical Frameworks for Promoting the Public Understanding of Religion," in *Religious Literacy in Policy and Practice*, ed. Adam Dinham and Matthew Francis (Bristol: Policy Press, 2017), 27–38.

[61] Azza Karam, "Religion and Sustainable Development: From Overlooking to Commodifying Faiths," Vrije Universiteit Amsterdam, June 13, 2019, 17, https://www.frt.vu.nl/en/Images/Inaugural_Lecture_Azza_Karam_tcm239-918580.pdf.

challenge for engagement with religion is not to be selective and to centralize a human rights framework. For Karam, authentic religiosity coheres with the objectives and spirit of the SDGs. Certainly, Karam takes aim at the utilitarianism of the technocratic space for its potential emboldening of harmful religious actors. But her critique remains beholden to a similarly reactive logic in framing human rights, especially those pertaining to gender and sexuality, as colonial impositions against which traditions supposedly external to modernity become sites of anticolonial resistance.

My point here is twofold. On the one hand, incorporating religious voices and attention to religious meanings signals an appreciation of religion's sociopolitical relevance. On the other, a concentrated effort to systemize, measure, and NGO-ize constructive religious forces and their effectiveness in peacebuilding shows how the rhetoric regarding their "prophetic" voice translates to "priestly" neoliberal problem-solving. Religion and peace, therefore, remain beholden to what I have referred to as "generic" or androcentric accounts of religion, as well as to generic understandings of interfaith religious authority. The latter speaks in the name of all religions and none at all. This is the case even though the neoliberalization of the field has resulted in more attention to promoting women's empowerment. This focus is driven by the neoliberal interest in activating the potential social capital of social influencers, not a concern for human rights. On my account, it can be best understood as part of a security discourse and a reliance on synergistic approaches to peacebuilding/development. Still, the language of human rights as a lowest common denominator permeates the religion industry.

Vocational Virtuosos

Within the technocratic schema, most of the people I met during my research exhibited a "prophetic lite" modus operandi. They do not operate with the traditional definition of the "truly prophetic," wherein a virtuoso inhabits an iconoclastic religiosity that questions and disrupts the status quo. Nor do they necessarily exhibit virtuosity when it comes to religious knowledge or methodologies of learning. An example is a young Catholic priest I met who worked in the city of Isabela, in the Basilan province of Mindanao. He primarily promoted and facilitated interreligious dialogue among Muslims and Christians, a practice that involved overcoming his own deeply held prejudices. He told me how he became "a religious actor" who collaborated with CRS because of the organization's humanitarian food assistance. This was carried out through a partner organization during times of "civil disturbance" in Mindanao: "I am a product of CRS. I ate all the bread that they gave."[62] This priest exemplifies a religious actor. He is a communal leader whose peace(building) vocation was shaped by his own experiences of hunger, hardship, and loss. His virtuosity manifests through his facility with bureaucratized mechanisms of interreligious peacebuilding. He fits the conventional view of religious actors and missionaries as "service providers" rather than charismatic, learned masters of their tradition or iconoclastic revolutionaries.

Sister Genevieve of St. Joseph of Tarbes is another example of a virtuous religious actor who embodies the archetype of the service provider by working with the poor and the marginalized. During my fieldwork in Kenya, I met her as we were traveling from Nairobi to Garissa, where she had initiated an intergroup co-op of women focused on generating income and bolstering intercommunal relationships. A Kenyan from a small village herself, Sister Genevieve belongs to a missionary order that originated in France. When I visited her convent in Nairobi, I was struck by the White Jesus staring at me from all corners. The sisters—all Black Kenyans—did not seem to be concerned with this iconic representation. Their lives are devoted to serving the poor.

Sister Genevieve is a religious virtuoso working within the institutional framework of the Church and within a long legacy of the Church's missionary activity, in Kenya and beyond. She embodies the traditional part of the religious actor as a service provider, a role that is ripe for engagement and collaboration with policymakers. She is also a virtuoso in her masterful navigation of the organizational and institutional fields within which she lives out her vocation. The female co-op was entirely her idea. She described to me the unbearable misery of the women she got to know in the region. She noted that they had resorted to prostitution and that they lived in poverty. She attained permission from the Catholic Church to invest a small amount as initial seed money for what would become an informal lending and borrowing community of women around the Tana River. It is also a site of intercommunal economic collaboration that will, at some point, become suitable for receiving

---

[62] He shared this with me during a focus group with other actors in the peacebuilding sphere, Zamboanga City, June 2018.

other kinds of investments from external agencies, such as CRS, wishing to partner with local initiatives.[63]

As a religious virtuoso and a "company person," Sister Genevieve's story relates to religion and empire in complex ways. Not only is she part of a European religious order whose iconography reflects centuries of dehumanization, but she is also an entrepreneurial Kenyan sister whose spiritual strength and calling can, under no circumstances, be considered "colonialist." She is touched by the misery of her people and understands that their suffering is not an inevitable outcome or a natural predicament, but rather the result of policy. On our ride back from Garissa to Nairobi, Sister Genevieve told me, "If the government only wanted, they could develop this land and make the lives of these people better. Yet they are just neglected."[64]

Her witnessing of neglect and marginalization called her to serve. It is her religious practice. She is not merely an instrument of a resiliency discourse, nor does she lack political awareness. She also recognizes the risks of working in the regions where she works. There are deaths, kidnappings, and other forms of hostility related to the history of Christian colonialism in the region and how colonialism plays into the violent ideological slogans and narratives of al-Shabaab and similar groups. But Sister Genevieve adds, "You have to value the ministry more than the problems and challenges and fears that may prevent you from answering the call to serve."[65] Here, Sister Genevieve treads familiar missionary discourse about perseverance amid difficulty. Her claim reflects the colonial baggage that many of the religious service providers, virtuosos and bureaucrats alike, cannot entirely shed, no matter how many times they underscore their disinterest in, and sometimes absolute rejection of, the conversion agenda.[66]

Back in Mindanao, I met Dan, another virtuoso and an employee of CRS who focuses specifically on interreligious peacebuilding in the violence-prone region of Cotabato. Like many people populating the peacebuilding space, he experienced loss and pain during his formative years. Subsequently, he was tempted to enlist in the military and to engage in combat in a quest for

---

[63] As I note in chapter 1, there is a long tradition in Kenya of mutual aid, or *harambee*, organizing, the nature of which has changed over the years but which nonetheless constitutes a familiar grassroots repertoire of social practices, not only a neoliberal prepackaged instrument.
[64] Interview #20, Kenya, January 2018.
[65] Ibid.
[66] For analyses of the complex histories of mission and its relation to conquest, colonialism, and developmentalism, see Peter Stamatov, *The Origins of Global Humanitarianism* (New York: Cambridge University Press, 2013); Lynch, *Wrestling with God*.

revenge: "In my elementary school age during the administration of martial law in the seventies, I already heard of so many killings between Christian settlers and Moro militias against each other victimizing innocent civilians. My parents evacuated us to safety with our relatives out of our province. I heard friends telling me that we must take revenge when my brother, the soldier, was killed among five others in an attack launched by Moro rebels to their highway detachment. It was then that I became interested in firing a gun."[67] However, Dan's self-understanding as a person of the Catholic faith propelled him toward the Church's peace and justice work,[68] along with international organizations such as CRS:

> My parents and siblings had always discouraged me from doing violent things. They brought me to church every Sunday. When I reached Notre Dame high school [in Cotabato], I put attention to church activities such as "knights of the altar" assisting priest during the mass in the barrio at weekends. I then . . . told myself, I should be a priest someday to serve the poor people especially in the countryside. The simple lifestyle of the priests I went along with had enticed me to finally join with other classmates to enter the Notre Dame seminary in college.[69]

Entering seminary finally made Dan realize that "violence is not an option as my immediate feeling and reaction to news of killings and gangsterism in the city. I developed an attitude, a behavior to advocate and defend human rights of the poor and the disadvantaged as a result of human rights violations during the martial rule."[70] But as suffering became pronounced all around him, Dan struggled with the path of nonviolence: "I almost joined with a rebel group out of desperation of the situation and the government. But I stepped back and reflected. Again, to me, violence is not an option. There was still so much to do as a committed justice and peace, human rights worker in the field assisting human rights victims to seek redress to their grievances in courts. As [a] paralegal, I also began to document, investigate,

---

[67] Interview #77, follow-up via Facebook Messenger, May 2020.

[68] For further clarity on the patterns of peace and justice work within the Catholic Church and Catholic modernity, see Scott Appleby, Robert J. Schreiter, and Gerard Powers, eds., *Peacebuilding: Catholic Theology, Ethics, and Praxis* (New York: Orbis, 2010).

[69] Interview #77. In a June 2018 focus group in Cotabato with teachers and administrators at the Notre Dame School, I learned that the school emphasizes interfaith engagement and appreciation, which it interprets as central to students' spiritual formation.

[70] Interview #77.

write affidavits and help the lawyer to file cases with the complainants/victims of human rights."[71]

Working for CRS is not just a job for Dan, though he does need to support a large family; it is his vocation. He is a virtuoso religious peacebuilder. Yet he is neither the archetypal religious service provider nor the charismatic "true prophet" conventionally highlighted in accounts of religion and peace. The latter is someone who can see outside the frames of war and violence because of her intimate and unmediated experiences of the sacred—what has been called "divine pathos"—and her layered knowledge of traditions across time and place.[72] Dan is not a virtuoso prophet. Yet neither is he a technocrat *doing* religion in the way that I illuminate in this book's critical engagement with the religion industry. Instead, he is a person deeply rooted in his landscape and in his religiosity. He expresses this deep-rootedness through his interreligious peacebuilding work in an international faith-inspired organization, the operation of which depends on hermeneutically closed, rather than critically open, horizons.

What immediately caught my attention was Dan's refusal to use the CRS van as his means of transportation from one barangay, or village (which is also an administrative unit), to another. "It is estranging," he told me. He travels primarily using the means of transportation that the people there use, which, in this case, is either a motorized rickshaw or a tricycle. The latter, in particular, stands in stark contrast with the air-conditioned and secured company vans, which are the vehicles used by international agencies and many of the locals employed by them. The grassroots intra- and interreligious peacebuilding work that Dan facilitates is more likely to be received well when it embeds itself in the local forms of life, which include local forms of travel.[73]

Dan is by no means the only genuinely religious and locally embedded employee of a technocratic faith-inspired actor such as CRS. I spent my time in Mindanao with many of these people. Myla Leguro is one such vocational religious peacebuilder who, like Dan, works within CRS's bureaucratized

---

[71] Ibid.

[72] The concept of "divine pathos" refers to Abraham Joshua Heschel's view of the prophet. See Abraham Joshua Heschel, *The Prophets* (New York: Harper and Row, 1962).

[73] Not all of my local hosts in Kenya and the Philippines exercised similar sensitivity to how their association with an international agency might come across and to what degree it could interfere with their work. One Kenyan employee of CRS, for example, did everything in her power to avoid using the non-Western toilets "in the field." Another told me about a frequent "evaluator" from the U.S.-based headquarters who hated looking outside the car's windows and did everything to disconnect from the environment there.

framework and thus the broader landscape of donor agencies and countries. In a published interview, she spoke about her self-understanding as a peacebuilder. This vocational call came, in a way similar to Dan's, through her experiences of Marcos's martial law and the violence she witnessed during that time (1972–81). As in Dan's case, Leguro's Christian commitments also animate her special interest in interreligious and intercommunal reconciliation processes. Before joining CRS, where she has been employed for decades, she worked for an ecumenical community education NGO focused on justice and peace issues in Davao City. She then worked on agrarian reform services under governmental auspices. During the time she held these positions, she "was first exposed to the unique issues facing the Muslim community... in South Cotabato." This work educated her about the challenges in central Mindanao of Maguindanao's Muslims.

"Fortunately," Leguro said, "unlike many or most Filipinos raised in Christian families, I did not carry a lot of bias that prevented me from engaging with Muslims. In the Philippines, Christians are often socialized to understand Muslims as traitors, as enemies. I feel lucky that I had little of such social conditioning."[74] Undergoing her own spiritual and educational formation during times of intense violence, her "university education was about the theology of service—how to encourage others to join the pursuit of social justice." This education led her to dedicate her life to "finding [her] role to help create peace and justice in Mindanao... [which she viewed as her] own humble way... towards the building of the kingdom of God."[75] She is an employee of a faith-inspired international organization (itself considered a faith actor), but, like Sister Genevieve, her view of service spiritualizes her commitment to peace work and vice versa. While neither is a prophet nor a hermeneutically critical and elastic interpreter of their tradition, both women are virtuosos and "company persons" navigating and excelling within organizational and institutional parameters. They represent the changing meanings of religious virtuosity from the truly prophetic to the "prophetic lite." They also embody the organizational or NGO-ized company person and the subcontracted service provider religious virtuoso. They *do* religion masterfully within a bureaucracy that is more conducive to "priestly" forms of religious actions that preserve the status quo.

---

[74] Berkley Center for Religion, Peace & World Affairs, "A Discussion with Myla Leguro."
[75] Ibid.

If for Leguro and Dan a peacebuilding vocation constitutes living out their faith centering Jesus as peacemaker, Fadi, a teacher in Cotabato dedicated to helping the Muslim community in Mindanao, likewise underscored that his calling to engage in interreligious dialogue for peace was grounded in the model provided by the Prophet Muhammad:

> Prophet Muhammad (peace be upon him) is our leader, our model.... This is what I want to tell to brothers in Islam: don't be extreme in Islam. Not even in the time of the Prophet did everybody accept Islam. There were some Jews and some Christians who did not accept Islam. But what did the Prophet do? He signed a treaty in Medina informing them how they can live together, because in the Qur'an it says also: "You have your religion and I have my religion." There is no compulsion. For me, for some of our Christian friends . . . sometimes we explain to them what Islam is so they can understand.[76]

For this learned teacher, the Prophet and the Medina Agreement offer a blueprint for peaceful coexistence and mutual respect.[77] Like many of the actors I met, Fadi's peacebuilding vocation is also his religious calling. His *imitatio* Muhammad is analogous to Dan's *imitatio* Jesus. For Dan, even as an employee of a technocratic faith-inspired international organization such as CRS, a commitment to peace and nonviolence exemplifies his *imitatio* Jesus:

> Jesus died on the cross violently. I believe that I must die for Jesus peacefully. Through following his simplest life, his humility in service is a grace. An example of leadership to liberate his own people in his time. His teaching of "Love your neighbor as yourself," "Love your enemies," is very mysterious to me. Despite how he was treated violently in his time, his love was so liberating. But I know it is not easy to follow his example. There are many thorns along the way to peace, but the perseverance and harmonious assertions that peace is the way are an option to me, no more, no less.[78]

---

[76] Interview #62, Cotabato region, June 2018.
[77] For a broader engagement with how early Muslim history and pluralistic motifs play out in contemporary Muslim practices of interfaith dialogue, see Muhammad Shafiq and Mohammed Abu-Nimer, *Interfaith Dialogue: A Guide for Muslims* (2007; Herndon, VA: International Institute of Islamic Thought, 2011).
[78] Interview #77.

For Dan, then, imitating Jesus orients his peace vocation. This expression of peacebuilding as a religious calling, and vice versa—even if such a calling unfolds within the neoliberal and technocratic landscapes—significantly challenges any analysis that would render religion and the practices of peace merely a contemporary constellation of a former colonial logic. Even if these forms of religious peacebuilding agency rely on hermeneutically closed and prophetic lite forms of religiosity, it is insufficient to subsume the actors' agency entirely within this paradigm.

Here I am reminded of my drive with two vocationally faith-inspired actors from Mindanao. They are long-term employees of CRS from Davao City who worked in the field where CRS and its partners engaged in interreligious peacebuilding projects. Initially, I could not understand why we stopped so frequently to buy small food items such as cookies and other baked goods, as well as mangos and pomelos, from vendors on the side of the road. It was only when we arrived at the office of the Integrated Mindanao Association of Natives (IMAN) to say hello to Mike, the Muslim founder of this local association, that I understood. The small food purchases provided time for the CRS actors to chat with Mike about issues that had emerged in the communities since the last time they had all spoken. It also provided time to listen to him discuss his ailments and personal challenges, all while sipping a hot cup of indigenous coffee. Nothing in these small acts of relationship building with a "partner" in the field cohered with the technocratic global designs within which peacebuilding and religious engagement for the common good unfolds. I use scare quotes around "partner" because, as I further examine in the next section, the concept of partnership betrays the neoliberal logic within which interreligious peacebuilding is implemented. Even if my vocationally faith-inspired Mindanaoan CRS's companions spoke of IMAN as a "partner," clearly the depth of their relationship with Mike and his family exceeds the neoliberal frame within which he functions as a subcontractor for *doing* religion. Indeed, despite the proliferation of technocratic actors, the institutional transnational religiocratic actor depends often on vocational/missionary commitments for its efficacy. These are measured through the implementation of "secular" objectives, such as land dispute resolution in Mindanao.[79] I now turn to examine further the landscape of local actors.

---

[79] Back in Davao City in June 2019 (Interview #64), in the main office of CRS, I spoke to the social scientists in charge of monitoring and evaluating the overall effectiveness of the interreligious peacebuilding work at the conclusion of the second iteration of the 3Bs in 2018. They shared with me their methodologies for measuring the success of programming and multiple brochures marked with the logos of CRS, but also USAID and other granting agencies, which highlighted carefully curated

Local Access Actors

The religiocratic feedback loop depends on the country-specific, faith-inspired or communal actor. Occasionally this actor will have links to global and transnational faith-inspired organizations that will enable her to mobilize keywords such as "income augmentation" and "social cohesion" that resonate within the donor and Eurocentric epistemic communities. Such actors, who often work within local access organizations, can become pivotal in efforts to implement a variety of policies, including peace agreements. This is because, as we saw with Pakigdait, they offer a readily available local infrastructure and networks with which international faith-based and faith-inspired—as well as other bodies seeking the buy-in of the religious sector—can work. As a result of partnership patterns, the religious actors working within this sphere—which I have also referred to as "local access" interfaith actors—are part of an institution that can transform in such a way that it resembles an NGO, with all of its monitoring and implementing of evaluation mechanisms that help turn grassroots mobilization into a brand. These institutions also resemble NGOs when actors within them create manuals based on lessons learned and benchmarking, as I described in chapter 2.

Another example of an organization that is grounded in a particular local community rather than in a more generalized interfaith community is United Youth for Peace and Development in the Philippines (UNYPAD). It was started in 1998 and now has chapters all across the country. In 2004, it begun to focus on Muslim youth. In the words of one key interlocutor in the Cotabato office, "We realized that if the youth are good, they can be very powerful; they will have the power to move mountains and cross oceans."[80] This focus is critical, especially since the discourse around securitizing Muslim youth has been perceived as necessary for ensuring peace and for generating the investment crucial for the sustainability of such local access organizations.

One of my interlocutors at UNYPAD explained the operationalizing of local access: "We are the largest Muslim peace organization in the country. Our chapters include almost twenty thousand people, as far as Manila.... In terms of immediate mobilizations, we can mobilize at least five thousand

---

success stories that reflected the objective of strengthening relationships in contexts (and here is the principle of selection) defined by interethnic/religious animosity and discord.

[80] Focus group with UNYPAD, Cotabato Province, Mindanao, June 2018.

immediately. In one province alone, we have more than three thousand members."[81] This sense of network and mobilization capacity relates directly to UNYPAD's recognition of the links between underdevelopment and violence. Conversely, it also relates to development and peace, as the organization's name captures. Another interlocutor remarked:

> Our position was very clear: passing the Bangsamoro Basic law is an antidote to violent extremism. . . . The [statement of] peace that we released was that failure to pass the Bangsamoro Basic Law would give a leeway to the rise of violent extremism because people from outside would capitalize on the frustrations of the Bangsamoro youths. They could use the failure of the peace process to gain more recruits. I was there, leading that position of the organization. . . . I was the one representing this concern. . . . Then one or two years later the Marawi siege and killings happened. We feel that, basically, it is the frustrations of those youths who are educated in secular universities where political discourse is very intense. They are then backed up by social media's misrepresentation of Islam.[82]

This quotation captures the local access religious actor who has institutional tools, political capital, and organizational identity and, as such, can be an active participant in promoting the peace and development agenda. Because of the long-established presence of UNYPAD in Mindanao and its inclusion in the Civilian Lead Ceasefire Watch organized by the Mindanao's People's Council, the MILF recognized UNYPAD as a third party to monitor the implementation of the peace agreement. Consequently, UNYPAD reports directly to the Bangsamoro Transition Commission. UNYPAD's support of the peace agreement also takes the form of what the organization calls "multisectoral" rather than "interreligious" dialogue, a word choice that reflects the organization's operationalization of religion in a way that focuses on its communal and cultural connotations rather than any "thick" theological understandings. Underwritten by PeaceConnect, a line of international programmatic investments in local access religious actors, UNYPAD seeks intergroup cooperation through various activities designed, if successful, to

---

[81] Ibid.
[82] Ibid. UNYPAD's work on de-escalation is ongoing. See Rahim M. Lasak, "UNYPAD Joins in Mindanao Multi-sectoral Peace Rally Calling for Justice for Kabacan Massacre Victims," UNYPAD, September 6, 2020, http://unypad.org/2020/09/06/unypad-joins-in-mindanao-multi-sectoral-peace-rally-calling-for-justice-for-kabacan-massacre-victims/.

enhance social cohesion. In the previous chapter, I discussed how USAID and the Asia Foundation enabled Pakigdait's PeaceConnect Program to conduct seventeen major activities and reach 633 persons over seven months. This was done in anticipation of political and legal changes around the plebiscite to determine the contours of the BARMM.[83] As in this case, the purpose of UNYPAD's PeaceConnect was to cultivate intercommunal receptivity, alleviate fears, and imagine ways of dignified cohabitation: "There are many Christians who are afraid. . . . That's why we have PeaceConnect; we want to reach out to these communities and we want to have this dialogue. . . . We are not talking about religion, that is why we stay away from the language of 'interfaith.' We call what we do an 'intercultural dialogue.' So, we are talking about our cultural differences, how we can work together despite our cultural differences, how these people become supportive of the peace process."[84] Still, the religious factor is not absent, but rather permeates the self-understanding of this local access organization. In the words of another interlocutor: "Faith is there as a guiding conscience to discuss our morals and above all it's known that both Christians and Muslims (and even the Indigenous peoples) believe in this life and the hereafter. So, the most important thing is what you are doing in preparation for what will happen to us in the hereafter."[85] Beyond this presumption that religion represents the lowest common denominator, in response to my question regarding what specifically makes the organization Muslim, one interlocutor replied, "In terms of belief, first that's who we are. Second, in our daily work, we are guided by how we interpret Islam. So, for example, if you look at us we will practice the pillars of Islam. And our president is an *ustadh* [a Muslim teacher]. And in our structure, we have the committee on *da'wa* [the 'call' to Islam]."[86] The answer,

---

[83] According to material shared with me, such activities spanned seven months and contributed to defusing the tension and fear on the plebiscite of February 6, 2019. On March 6, 2019, PeaceConnect convened seventy-eight Muslim religious leaders and community stakeholders in the Plaza Alemania Hotel in Illigan City, where they signed the Covenant for Peace, committing to peace regardless of the results of the plebiscite. PeaceConnect reportedly also improved relationships among religious leaders through, for example, a series of intra- and interfaith conversations and prayers that aspired to a peaceful and credible plebiscite. These took place on February 5, 2019, in Lapayan Kauswagan, and involved forty-seven religious leaders. Another activity was the Intra Dialogue Learning Conference of Faith and Peacebuilding on March 6, 2019. Yet another area of focus is enabling youth leaders to break the cycle of violence by reducing prejudices across communal lines, the boundaries of which are defined by faith. Activities designed for youth included a three-day immersion in April 2019 under the heading "Cultural and Faith Journey." During this activity, sixty-one youth leaders from the Higaunon tribe, Merano Muslims, and Christian Cebuano/Bisaya interacted with one another intensely.
[84] Focus group with UNYPAD.
[85] Ibid.
[86] Ibid.

in other words, is "We are Muslims as a matter of course," which confirms the seamless shift from *being* religious to *doing* religion, leaving the depth of religious *knowing* and hermeneutics as irrelevant to the tasks of *doing* religion. A response like the one I just quoted exemplifies the upshot of the process of double closures where social identities are indexed to religious identities, which are both hermeneutically closed and unitary.

Notably, their Muslim identity, as they understand it, is also manifest in the distinct (but complementary) work of women within the organization. UNYPAD's Women Affairs Committee participates in the organization through workshops, conferences, and other activities. These are intended to strengthen the capacity of women to assume leadership positions in the task of nation building, which is demanded by the peace framework and the BOL. Concepts such as "moral governance" saturate the women's gatherings designed to reinforce, through supporting roles, the other efforts of UNYPAD.[87]

Hence, UNYPAD exemplifies a communal, Muslim, organizational, local access institution that is broadly networked across Mindanao and guided by Muslim principles, which are translated into NGO-ized language. As another interlocutor succinctly put it, "Islam is who we are and it is also our brand."[88] Indeed, *being* religious and *doing* religion are one and the same. Neither depends on *knowing* in hermeneutically layered and prophetically robust ways. Yet another interlocutor linked *being* Muslim with Islamic organizational branding: "In our case the most important thing is being a Muslim, it's within us, how we move, how we run the affairs of the organization, it's in accordance with the balance and accepted order of Islam. When we engage with other groups or audiences, we see to it that we would behave in accordance with what Islam prescribes us to behave. But in that discussion, it is not necessary to say that 'We are Muslims,' it is not necessary to say that our group united youth for Islam and development."[89] Again, organizational and religious virtuosity converge and become interchangeable. We have seen

---

[87] For example, one key speaker at a Women Affairs Committee's peace conference is quoted as having said, "One good woman can be a great tool in nation building." See Northana Galmak Cosi, "UNYPAD-Women Affairs Committee Conducts Women Peace Summit," UNYPAD, March 12, 2020, http://unypad.org/2020/03/12/unypad-women-affairs-committee-conducts-women-peace-summit/. See also Rahim M. Lasak, "UNYPAD North Cotabato Cluster II—Women Affairs Committee (WAC) Holds Islamic Leadership and Management Training," UNYPAD, August 30, 2020, http://unypad.org/2020/08/30/unypad-north-cotabato-cluster-ii-women-affairs-committee-wac-holds-islamic-leadership-and-management-training/.

[88] Focus group with UNYPAD.

[89] Ibid.

this already in manifestations of *doing* religion. This neoliberal conversion erodes the need for a person to have actual religious knowledge to be able to intervene in the name of religion. It also signals the enhanced demand for a facility with the international development and peacebuilding discourse.[90]

In addition to these interfaith (e.g., Pakigdait) and singular faith-based (e.g., UNYPAD) local access communal actors, another type, the religious leader, is the formal or informal leader of a religious community who can mobilize the community's networks and institutions. For example, one prominent Kenyan Christian who is a professional practitioner of interreligious work and who is intricately associated with international and transnational nongovernmental entities such as the IRC echoes the global secularist configuration of the religious as a sector with potential for effective mobilizing capacities. This practitioner told me:

> Well, I believe the "religious" is a sector. But for me, what do the religious people bring? First of all, they bring the people. Because you know there is no conflict between trees. Primarily it's people's conflict of ideas of how we should deal with issues. Where you can find people? In markets, churches, etc. . . . But primarily people are organized around religion, so if you want to talk to people, to influence their thinking, you can reach to the people through religion. So, the one powerful thing that religion does is that it convenes, it brings them together in a way that, especially in Africa, no other agency is able to do.[91]

The clerics of the CICC exemplify another, more localized variation of this type. In the aggregate, the CICC is an interreligious, local access, communal organization, the actors within which exercise their agency as communal religious leaders. With a focus on informal spaces, the scope of religious leadership extends to women and youth and uncertified male leaders and others invested in offering countermessages against violent interpretations of religious and cultural identities. In other words, the concept of "leadership," as is the case with the different varieties of the local access religious actors, does not always (or at all) depend upon disciplined learning of the tradition's standard processes for granting certification to its leaders. In

---

[90] See also Jean-Pierre Olivier de Sardan, *Anthropology of Development: Understanding Contemporary Social Change* (London: Zed, 2005) for an argument regarding which actors get to be "partners" and how their mastery of the discursive formation plays into this process.

[91] Interview #55, Nairobi, November 2018.

fact, in addition to the NGO-ized organizational variety of UNYPAD, its leaders rely on sociocultural traction and personal charisma, as well as certification through workshops, which capacitate them with practical secular skills. The purpose is not for leaders to develop deep knowledge of a tradition but to mobilize religion for this organization's particular aims. This is what is meant by *doing* religion. Within the neoliberal framework, this emphasis on *doing* denotes a horizontalization of religious virtuosity, which also entails reducing traditions to sound bites. Doing so reifies ahistorical and hermeneutically closed forms of "authentic" religiocultural traditions as peaceful in their essence. This religious illiteracy is useful for the neoliberal rationality of peace, which, in turn, explains neoliberal investment in (the subcontracting of) the interreligious dialogue mechanisms and their harmony discourse.

Another type, the communal actor, operates in less apparent ways. This actor is the "beneficiary"—that neoliberal concept that reveals the persistent operation of a paternalistic colonial approach—of intercommunal or intracommunal engagements. This actor's participation in such engagements revolves around her communal belonging as a manifestation of the double closure and mutual indexing of religion and culture to the threshold of communal belonging and vice versa. Here, one's religious or cultural identity provides a communal boundary marker. However, the nature of the intergroup engagement in which this actor participates is not oriented toward a harmony discourse but rather toward concrete survival tasks. Supporting people's "livelihood"—another neoliberal euphemism—is the focus of such projects. For example, among the participants in the women's co-op in Garissa, intergroup peace is measured as a spillover outcome. To survive, the economic venture becomes not only a source of food but also a source of peace or a site for overcoming stereotypes likewise defined by religiocultural (and tribal) boundaries.[92]

Another type of religious actor is the member of grassroots or Astroturf local organizations that, along with communal actors, emerges from a complex community where problem-solving—whether concerning livelihood, public health, and/or other sites traditionally subsumed under development or intercommunal violence—involves negotiating religious boundaries. Yet this problem-solving does not necessarily involve robust engagement or even facility with tradition as a hermeneutically elastic and embodied discourse.

---

[92] I trace this process in chapter 4 in my detailed discussion of the women's co-op in Garissa.

This is the "local" that usually becomes ripe for partnership with some investing agency. Here, members of a group, such as IMAN, embody religious agency by virtue of their self-perception as grassroots agents emerging from within the Mindanaoan Muslim community.

Grassroots/Astroturf local actors' problem-solving foci work well with neoliberal interreligious governance. Still, they should not be defined reductively as such, especially if such "partners" existed before being co-opted into a framework of investment and (inter)religious governance. (See Figure 3.3 for a graphic representation.) The people I met who embody this type of religious actor had been immersed in their processes of self-transformation, intercommunal relationship-building, and problem-solving long before global and international agencies identified their work as useful. The grassroots/Astroturf problem-solving organizational actor may or may not focus on intra- and interreligious dialogue that involves self-examination or a deeper understanding of one's tradition across various communal boundaries. Facilitators would instrumentally pursue this self-examination to reduce estrangement, suspicion, and ignorance about the other's practices and beliefs. Often, donor agencies deem such psychologizing processes required for any measurable development indices to be implemented. I also introduce the concept of the Astroturf religious actor to denote that, occasionally, communal organizational actors emerge nonorganically in response to directives, objectives, and, of course, funds generated by the donor and epistemic communities where the "grassroots" label may be misleading. This is the case even if staff within those spaces are vocationally driven organizational employees like those I profile above.

To conclude the typology, interpreting the agency of the religious actor and how she does religion through a binary approach—which might be seen as focusing on either individual agency or on the structures that constrain that agency—remains beholden to the question of *doing* religion as "implementing partners" rather than the horizons of meanings that are constitutive of religious traditions. Religion is featured at the intersection of peacebuilding and development because of the aforementioned turn to more complex ethical evaluative accounts of development. These accounts illuminate structural obstacles for implementing an enhanced capabilities-focused approach. Religion is also featured in such accounts because violent interpretations of religious traditions often promote structural and direct violence. The integrated approach to development/peacebuilding therefore signals how religion is relevant to this integration; that is, religion's role in

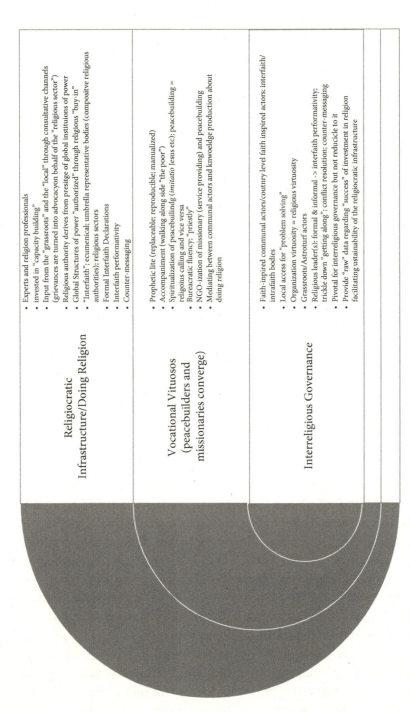

Figure 3.3 Religiocratic feedback loop.

providing healthcare, education, and other services correlates with the possibility of peace.

The utilitarian deployment of religion within a neoliberal frame may rhetorically offer an alternative to a technocratic discourse, purportedly promoting social justice through the currency of development ethics. However, it brands "religion" and "culture" as prepackaged currencies to cash out or mobilize/demobilize. Religious actors as "implementing partners" are the key to the utilitarian intersection of peacebuilding/development. Therefore, the emphasis on *doing* rather than *knowing* signals the horizontalization of virtuosity as a utilitarian rather than a normative turn in the practice of religion and peace/development. It is one that burdens the individual with the task of producing social transformation, and it often requires that individual to undergo a spiritual and religious formation.[93] The next chapter further clarifies the spiritualization of survival and the limits of the partnership logic.

---

[93] See, for example, World Vision, "Channels of Hope," https://www.wvi.org/faith-and-development/channels-hope (accessed October 3, 2020).

4
Survival Piety
A Preferential Option for the Poor?

Poverty Isn't an Excuse

Speaking to select community members and traditional religious leaders in Cotabato City, I was told "poverty isn't an excuse" for child marriage, a phenomenon all participants agreed is a growing problem in their communities, regardless of religious affiliation.[1] The emerging consensus in the focus group was that combating the child marriage epidemic had to begin with the family, especially with parents' hands-on involvement with their children. A similar understanding of women's (i.e., mothers') responsibility as "change agents" was echoed in what representatives of an association of approximately fifty Muslim women in Maguindanao, in the Autonomous Muslim region of Mindanao, told me. Established in 2015, the association, with the help of IMAN,[2] facilitates income-generating activities where women who previously only gardened and took care of children could now produce banana chips, dishwashing liquid, and soap. This "income augmentation" (as it is called in the development field's universe of terms) is conditional on the women's participation in monthly meetings where they discuss their peace-promotion contributions. They also attend Arabic lessons once a week with an *ustaz* (Muslim teacher) where, they shared with me, they are taught how to pray, read the Qur'an, and receive practical lessons about how to live their lives "correctly." By their accounts, this learning helps them with their daily challenges, such as caring for their children.

Echoing other sectors' stress on the responsibility of Muslims to focus on cleanliness and hygiene as a way of combating stereotyping of the Moro communities and living out what "Allah prescribed,"[3] one focus for the

---

[1] Focus group, Maguindanao, Mindanao, March 2017.
[2] See chapter 3 for a discussion of this organization.
[3] An intercommunal sharing in a multisectoral gathering in Maguindanao, March 2017.

women's education is sanitation. The intention is to "responsibilize" them to enhance the cleanliness of their surroundings, which usually lack infrastructure for clean and running water and often involve dealing with devastating flooding and storms. The lessons are designed for women, who are perceived as the engine of change within the community and as an optimal (or target) demographic for responsibilization.[4] Still, even if it lacks feminist hermeneutical elasticity, the fact that women can gain access to Arabic and the Qur'an departs from traditional practice that excludes them from Quranic studies.

Through a partnership with CRS, IMAN has also worked on integrating what it refers to as a "peace education framework" into all aspects of the curriculum of violence-affected communities in Maguindanao. One Muslim teacher spoke about the significant transformation of students in her region. She described how, before mainstreaming the peace curriculum, which she interprets as grounded in Islam, female students did not wear the hijab. Now, "the girls are wearing respectful clothes and the hijab as well as adopting more respectful gestures in their interactions with adults."[5] The teachers also echo the argument that the real onus for peace education is on the family—parents and mothers, in particular—but also that their students are often terribly poor and in need of food and basic school supplies. We can discern here that patterns of responsibilization, with a particular focus on women, involve religionization and vice versa. The women as communal religious actors mainly focus on their capacity to augment their livelihood (or economic survival). Yet, in the process, they also gain greater access to their tradition in ways that can be immediately concretized in their lives. To this extent, the conception of tradition emerging from these activities constitutes a "how to" guide for personal and communal engagements. It is thus consistent with neoliberal manifestations of religiosity as a prophetic-lite resource that can be mobilized for problem-solving. Still, this utilitarian survivalist approach is inhabited piously and thus paradoxically challenges an exclusively utilitarian interpretation of the dynamics of religiosity on the ground.

I met these women in Maguindanao during a multisectoral engagement facilitated by IMAN and underwritten by CRS. At the end of a meeting during which representatives shared success stories, but also enduring

[4] Focus group #2, Magindanao, March 2017.
[5] Participant in an intercommunal sharing in a multisectoral gathering that I participated/observed in Maguindanao, March 2017.

challenges, and after a delicious lunch with the community, they took me to see their "connector" or "solidarity" project. It was a green footbridge they built to ensure that the children crossing the river on their way to school would not drown, an occasional occurrence that had scarred the community (see Figure 4.1). How is religion relevant to this footbridge? It is relevant to the extent that "stakeholders" and "beneficiaries" are communally and organizationally defined (reductively) within and through the tri-people harmony formula, denoting Mindanao's aspirational ethos of Christian-Muslim-Lumad plurality. But it is also pertinent in how self-transformation and responsibilization entail people's religionization, or reclaiming specific, often hermeneutically closed interpretations of tradition and mutual recognition of other groups' accounts of their traditions. Interreligious dialogue for action (IRD/A) and the 3Bs methodology (of Binding, Bonding, and Bridging) rely on the neoliberalization of religion, placing the burden on

Figure 4.1 This footbridge in Maguindanao is the result of a solidarity project of intercommunal problem-solving. Reproduced with permission from CRS.

individual and communal actors to overcome their divisiveness, as if this divisiveness were the source of their poverty, marginalization, and experiences of violence.[6]

Even if many beneficiaries declared with confidence that "real" religion was not the source of their problems—some even recalled a golden age in Mindanao when Muslim women nursed Christian babies and Christian women nursed Muslim babies—their extrication of religion from the analysis of the causes of violence in itself reflects the pervasiveness of a postsecular neoliberal logic that is intent on harnessing "good" religion, the kind that can help keep the peace through depoliticized registers.[7] The theory of change animating interreligious peacebuilding practices anticipates measurable outcomes such as a bridge or a well and the reduction of child marriage and land-based conflicts. These underlying assumptions that render religious and cultural traditions as a set of prescriptions are ripe for neoliberal responsibilizing of individuals as their own agents of change. This time, it is through repackaging religion, as in the case of the women from Maguindanao, into a how-to manual for being a functional and economically self-sufficient adult. This mechanism disseminates neoliberal rationality, which targets marginalized sectors such as women who are already overburdened.[8] Now, the religionization of responsibilization is particularly effective as a spiritual praxis.

Rather than destabilizing gendered norms as root causes of structural, cultural, and direct violence against women, "devolution,"[9] in designing various peacebuilding/development interventions, thrives on the

---

[6] See chapter 2, in particular, for an analysis of this methodology and its attendant theory of change.

[7] Such an analysis resonates strongly with critiques of the neoliberal turn to social enterprise and entrepreneurship as a business logic that contradicts the logic of social movements seeking to transform systemic issues and forces. For an analysis of this point, see Marshall Ganz, Tamara Kay, and Jason Spicer, "Social Enterprise Is Not Social Change," *Stanford Social Innovation Review* (Spring 2018): 59–60, 10.48558/z8f0-3080.

[8] Brown, *Undoing the Demos*, 132. For the monitoring and evaluation team based in the CRS office in Davao City, the "women sector" is pivotal for the sustainability of peacebuilding/development projects. They constantly take on background labor and disseminate "learnings." This reflection was articulated during my interview session with the Monitoring Evaluation and Learning team in Davao City, June 2019.

[9] For an assessment of the devolutionary prospect in Kenya, see, for example, Institute of Economic Affairs, "Devolution in Kenya: Prospects, Challenges and the Future," Series No. 24, ed. Albert K. Mwenda (Nairobi: Institute for Economic Affairs, 2010). The point is not to devastate the concept of "devolution" and its proclaimed intent on strengthening institutions, accountability, and transparency, but rather to highlight how, when executed outside an affirmative action and decolonial lens, its engagement with religion (and other communal stakeholders) often assumes a subcontracting flavor.

gender imbalance of neoliberal responsibilization.[10] Indeed, neoliberalism exacerbates liberalism's old gender problem by distinctly disadvantaging women who share a disproportionate burden of responsibilization. Religion, religiosity, and spiritualization enhance this process. Responsibilization therefore "signals a *regime* in which the singular human capacity for responsibility is deployed to constitute and govern subjects and through which their conduct is organized and measured, remaking and reorienting them for a neoliberal order."[11] As one social worker nun in Garissa, a contested poor region of Kenya touching Somalia,[12] affirmed in her interview with me, mothers "should be responsibilized" because the potential for positive change rests on them:

> Mothers are God-created persons with a lot of passion, but since they can easily be moved, they are misused too. They are the ones who will be called to begin chaos and it will continue with the men. For that reason, we use the same women for positive growth of the community by telling them, "God had created you to be peace-makers." Most of the mothers in the world are the ones who build up their families. A strong family means a strong church, a strong nation, and a strong world. So the mothers continue to be the strong peace-builders in society.[13]

This burdening of mothers and the family unit as a building block for broader peace conveys the reliance of neoliberalism on traditional hierarchies and the "seed of peace" metaphor, with its rhetoric of scaling up and its concern with the empirical realities of the entrenched status quo.[14]

Other Catholic sisters I met in the Muslim-majority region of Garissa spoke about the challenges they faced as religious leaders in promoting livelihood projects. They linked those challenges to donor demands for local ownership and sustainability, local Muslim communities' distrust, and the long time it takes to build relationships.[15] One sister joked about needing to write a report even before the money was deposited in the bank, leaving little time for anything else. After a lengthy conversation about Muslims' fears

---

[10] See my discussion of the utilitarian rather than normative "targeting" of women for de-radicalization efforts, especially in chapters 6 through 8, as well as chapter 2.
[11] Brown, *Undoing the Demos*, 133.
[12] See chapter 1 for an overview of the contributing factors of marginalization there.
[13] Interview #39, Nairobi, February 2018.
[14] Brown, *In the Ruins of Neoliberalism*. I also discuss this argument in chapter 2.
[15] Focus group with sisters working in the cathedral in Garissa, Kenya, January 2018.

of conversion, rooted in historical memories, and the Christians' commitment to serving this region, despite the threats of terrorism against visibly Christian targets, one sister articulated economic dividends as indicators of why people need to figure out ways to coexist peacefully.[16] The implication here is that nuns channel the neoliberal logic accordingly, creating safe spaces for economic exchanges, and that cooperation constitutes a peacebuilding mechanism, an instrument of responsibilization.

Another sister actively involved in efforts to connect peace with nourishment and food (and thus economic dividends) to enhance its sustainability remarked, "So, we have used the strategy of working with women. And then we also decided to add work with youth. Because we discovered women and youth normally are the ones who are misused when political leaders want to cause chaos. They use youth, they use women, they use children at times to cause chaos. So we use the same group for peace building, so that the women we know, we ask them, 'Where are your sons and daughters so that we can also bring them together through activities to make them work together?'"[17]

Hence, activities enabling income augmentation have become sites for tackling peace and security, tasking mothers with small-scale economic and securitizing responsibilities. To engage the neoliberalization of religion through this kind of peacebuilding praxis, I now examine what it means to theorize religion within the neoliberal frame, shifting the focus from a prosperity gospel to a piety of survival or pious resiliency. The prosperity gospel, as Kate Bowler writes, "inscribes materiality with spiritual meaning," and so worldly displays of wealth, health, and victory come to signify blessedness.[18] If the prosperity gospel preaches wealth, neoliberal "resiliency" links survival with piety and reforming subjectivities to be more conducive to keeping the peace.

Religion within the Neoliberal Frame

The study of neoliberal religious piety exposes what Osella and Rudnyckj call "economies of morality," which are the product of "economic and religious

---

[16] Ibid.
[17] Interview #33, Nairobi, January 2018.
[18] Kate Bowler, *Blessed: A History of the American Gospel* (Oxford: Oxford University Press, 2018), 8. Bowler traces how Americans came to see wealth and health as signifying a divine chosenness that transformed the values of the supposed Protestant ethic of asceticism and likewise consolidated a sense of triumphalism.

practice under regimes of neoliberal reform."[19] The emergent focus on "neoliberal piety," however, is more consistent with an aspiration for assuaging the consciences of those enriched by capitalism in the face of the apparent inconsistency between wealth disparities and religious values. The humanitarian and charity fields provide effective rerouting for greed without reshaping any underpinning inequalities. Racialized religion has always animated colonial difference. Now, transposable conceptions of "good" religiosity generate neoliberal subjectivities. They draw upon the bounded and hermeneutically closed definitions of religious and cultural traditions as resources for pious resiliency, as we saw in the Maguindanaoan women's assessment of the link between their pious religiosity and their capacity to survive.

Their pious survival instantiates the neoliberalization of piety.[20] The moralization of the economic sphere as well as increasing wealth disparity contrasts with the apparent immorality and ethical shortcomings of capitalism and represents itself as a totalizing solution to such failures.[21] Accordingly, those who engage in charitable giving translate their economic success into a religious obligation to invest in the spiritual and economic renewal of the community, whereas recipients of assistance are required to transform themselves economically and spiritually into self-sustaining, pious, "responsible," and "productive" members of society. Charity therefore became a vehicle for transforming the dispositions of recipients, cultivating their entrepreneurial drive as well as their religious piety.[22] This signals the convergence of economic and spiritual virtuosity. Or, more accurately for the cases I examined, it signals the alignment of survivalist piety with a prophetic lite and hermeneutically closed account of tradition. Of course, the onus on the intrapersonal transformative capacity to create self-sustainability *qua* resiliency conceals, through the paradigm of charity and development partnership, the possibility of a more reparative approach to enduring systemic forms of violence, historical injustices, and other forms of marginalization.

---

[19] Filippo Osella and Daromir Rudnyckyj, "Introduction: Assembling Market and Religious Moralities," in *Religion and the Morality of the Market*, ed. Daromir Rudnyckyj and Filippo Osella (Cambridge: Cambridge University Press, 2017), 1–28, 12.

[20] Mona Atia, *Building a House in Heaven: Pious Neoliberalism and Islamic Charity in Egypt* (Minneapolis: University of Minnesota Press, 2013), xix.

[21] Filippo Osella, "'A Poor Muslim Cannot Be a Good Muslim': Islam, Charitable Giving, and Market Logic in Sri Lanka," in *Religion and the Morality of the Market*, ed. Daromir Rudnyckyj and Filippo Osella (Cambridge: Cambridge University Press), 217–39, 218. doi:10.1017/9781316888704.011. Here, Osella develops a textured account of the cultivation of neoliberal subjectivities and forms of piety within Muslim contexts.

[22] Ibid., 233. See also Atia, *Building a House*.

The neoliberal view of the relations between personal and societal transformations resonates strongly with the theory of change informing interreligious peacebuilding engagements facilitated through the work of CRS and its local partners in the Philippines and Kenya. In those places, to reiterate, there is an assumption that investing in a welfare project leads to the cultivation of new dispositions more open to pluralistic coexistence, or "social cohesion," and vice versa. Earlier, I interpreted "social cohesion" as demand for homogeneity and unitary conceptions of community, constitutive of and indexed to religiocultural hermeneutical closures upon which "effective" intergroup bridging activities thrive. Engaging in solidarity projects across communal divides necessitates intrapersonal work and de-othering. The successful project, in turn, reinforces a novel disposition toward intercommunal cohabitation, which is itself dependent upon "individual and collective responsibilization" and the flourishing of "the entrepreneurial self."[23] Pious neoliberalism is a form of self-disciplining of economic and religious subjectivities.[24] Accordingly, as Atia writes, it "generates self-regulating and ethical subjects as faith and the market discipline them simultaneously."[25] A more apt description of subjectivization, in the cases I explored, is that of "pious survival." Pious survival exposes the very spirituality of survival and peace practices as well as how they unfold within a neoliberal frame that depoliticizes religion/culture through a reductive analysis of the causes of conflict (and poverty) and singles out the religious as key to unlocking local buy-in. This unlocking effectively enhances resiliency, which further entrenches the neoliberal frame—an entrenchment generative of and reliant upon forging neoliberal subjectivities.[26] Cultivating neoliberal survival piety, within the intersecting discourses of capital and security, is interpreted as a resilience mechanism, where resiliency becomes a site of piety and spiritual formation.

---

[23] Osella, "'A Poor Muslim,'" 228–29. See also Lazzarato, trans. by Joshua David Jordan *The Making of the Indebted Man* (Cambridge: MIT Press, 2012).

[24] Osella, "'A Poor Muslim,'" 229.

[25] Atia, *Building a House*, xviii.

[26] It is important to draw distinctions between the neoliberalization and commodification of religion in the Global North, but also in other contexts where one can observe the consolidation of pious consumerism. For instance, on the expansion of halal markets and fashionable pious wear, see Elizabeth Bucar, *Pious Fashion: How Muslim Women Dress* (Cambridge, MA: Harvard University Press, 2019); Marie Juul Petersen, *For Humanity or for the Umma? Aid and Islam in Transnational Muslim NGOs* (London: Hurst, 2015).

Interfaith Income-Generating Activities

This resilience-enhancing rationale, consistent with the liberal framework that links peace with economic self-interest, for example, informs the work of the women's groups that have been organized via the cathedral in Garissa and with the assistance of multiple donors and organizations inhabiting the "religiocratic" class I examined in the previous chapter. Despite the resonances with the anticolonial practice of *harambee*, or self-help community organizing in Kenya,[27] programs such as a women's co-op depoliticizes even as it empowers women as "change agents." Unlike mutual aid principles of political transformation, the co-op targets women for their economic and securitizing potential. The security and charity discourses are interwoven. But after talking to the women and hearing their stories of change, survival, and forming friendships across ethnic and religious boundaries, it is difficult to subsume such stories into neoliberal schemes simply. The composition of the women's co-ops is always characterized as "interfaith" because all economic initiatives and projects involve Muslims, Christians, and non-Christianized and non-Islamized African traditionalists. The stories that participants told me fell into one overarching psychologizing narrative about how economic self-empowerment through interreligious (but also intertribal and interclan) collaboration facilitates the overcoming of fear of one another and benefits everyone in tangible economic ways. Because of the extreme poverty, the economic benefit was noted repeatedly as the primary motivation for partaking in such interfaith programmatic spaces.

In chapter 1, I examined some of the historical underpinnings and colonial afterlives of the lines of divisions and sources of conflict among communities

---

[27] See chapter 1 for an examination of *harambee* as a state-making mechanism initially articulated by Jomo Kenyatta, for whom *harambee* was ideologically resignified, denoting the collective effort to transform supposedly traditional (precolonial) attitudes into a specifically Kenyan state-building ideology. A focus on Kenyan motifs such as the traditional *harambee* was supposed to generate unity and commitment in the early anticolonial struggle and postcolonial era as well as community-based incentives to encourage people to participate in projects of community development in the 1950s and 1960s. This was carried out under the colonial framing of the Department for Community Development, which actively retrieved and resignified *harambee* to challenge schemes of colonial land consolidation. These are the community development schemes that were disrupted after independence only to be metamorphosed into clientelism. See, for example, Njuguna Ng'ethe, "Underprivileged: The Origins and Nature of the Harambee Phenomenon in Kenya," *Journal of Eastern African Research & Development* 13 (1983): 150–70, esp. 159–60, https://www.jstor.org/stable/24325584. For an analysis that connects the late colonial and early postcolonial eras and that challenges and decenters conventional narratives of the Kenyan period of decolonization and development, see Kara Moskowitz, *Seeing Like a Citizen: Decolonization, Development, and the Making of Kenya, 1945–1980* (Athens: Ohio University Press, 2019).

in the marginalized regions of Kenya. While a historical analysis rejects any reductive culturalist explanations, divisions along religious and ethnic lines and clannism were often articulated as one of the main challenges facing the communities I interfaced with during my fieldwork. One Christian woman told me, "In the beginning, when Christians and Muslims interacted, there were many problems and clear separation. The Christians stayed together and the Muslims the same because of these tensions, because of religion but also ethnic [tribal] tensions. Those two things are our key challenges, but the formation of the groups has helped reduce this."[28] The Muslim women also expressed their fear of conversion and the stigma that others in the community associate with mingling with Christians. One woman, for example, talked about her initial hesitation to join a co-op, after she was introduced to the concept at the market where she sold produce. She explained, "I feared that there would be a lot of rumors with regard to me converting to Christianity." The co-op recruiter contacted the woman's spouse to ask for his permission. This woman shared the following account:

> When I did ask him, he went on to say that everyone has his or her own religion, but what matters is what is in your heart. He encouraged me to join and even provided the first three hundred shillings that I needed to contribute. He told me about his sister who was also part of a group and was benefiting from it, that recently she was able to purchase a goat. I was still hesitant, but I chose to stay calm. When I went to my first meeting, I was relieved to see so many Muslim women there. When we meet we talk about issues, we pool our money together and divide it among ourselves at the end of the year, and now people often ask me, "Why do you spend all your time with the group?"[29]

Others recounted variations of this story. One woman spoke about access to banking and, concurrently, improved intercommunal relationships afforded through the groups:

> The relations among Christians and Muslims in Garissa before, and those we have now, are vastly different; we are now bonded with love. There was initially a lot of disrespect and suspicion between the two groups, but since

---

[28] Participant in a focus group, Garissa, February 2018.
[29] Ibid.

joining this group, we have grown together and supported each other. Many of us have little access to formal banking, but here we are able to loan each other money to start businesses and educate our children. We have also learned how to be more accepting of our differences, and have built an empathy to better understand other people's experiences.[30]

These quotations convey the peacebuilding concept behind the women's otherwise economic initiative and telegraph how, through a joint economic activity, relationships and mutual trust are formed. But the storyline does posit the economic aspects (or increase the likelihood of having food at the end of the day) as an engine of peace. "Peace" here means resiliency and entails reliance on the double closure of religious and communal hermeneutics in which economic survival becomes the engine of intercommunal coexistence and collaboration. Being able to buy a goat (or generate a small income otherwise) is the genuine objective of interreligious engagement—and it is crucial for the survival of the women involved. This stresses, on a very local and tangible level, the necessity of an integrated approach to peacebuilding/development. An integrated lens responds to the interlinking of the issues in people's daily struggles.

Another participant in my focus group with the women's co-op stressed the issue of intra-ethnic tensions, for example, between the Somali and Warde Muslims who quarrel over the use of Somali land and the tree-cutting therein for charcoal. But the prevailing narrative they tell conveys how increased contact, collaboration on livelihood projects, and relationship building over time facilitate both overcoming mutual suspicion and economic empowerment. One woman said, "In the beginning, we were ignorant as Muslims, but since we joined Wendo[31] we have come to see that there is no real difference in the religion, we have learned from both traditions, and we have found similarities, especially in terms of lifestyle teachings. We have studied together and received training and now view each other as family. Forming this group has also empowered and uplifted us as women."[32] The women learned buzzwords to echo back to donors: they have been "empowered," and there is an allusion to how bridging activities enhance their capacity to reduce

---

[30] Ibid.
[31] Wendo is the largest such interfaith women's group in the Garissa region.
[32] Participant in the focus group conducted with representatives of the women's co-ops, Garissa, February 2018.

intergroup violence, especially when economically incentivized, even if only at the level of survival.

Still, the primary motivation for partaking in collaborative ventures boils down to economics, specifically to survival, through the generation of a small income. This is not a prosperity gospel type of triumphalism but rather imbuing the interfaith space as causally generative of income and a threshold for survival. One woman shared:

> I was in another group in Mororo, and one woman advised me to join. Previously my community mainly engaged in farming, and sometimes cutting grass to sell. This woman told me about the monthly contributions and how the women here support each other. I then decided that it was better for me to join this group as opposed to trying to find grass to cut or burning charcoal. We later started making mats and carpets that we first traded within ourselves and later began to sell. . . . We initially started as a group of ten women and increased until we were twenty-two. We also diversified the things we made and began to make small purses that took less time than the mats and that allowed us to make money quicker.[33]

An older woman who identified herself as traditionalist likewise underscored the economic incentive: "Initially I thought it was too much effort to go there, but now I see how I can also obtain my livelihood from here. On my part I see the fruits of this interaction."[34] Yet another focus group's participant added her story, which also contextualizes the conflictual and tense landscape of Garissa:

> When we were approached . . . to start this group in the beginning, there was a lot of tension in Garissa, we were very afraid of interacting with each other as Christians and Muslims. There was also a lot of animosity following attacks on the Christians by the Muslims, which made it difficult to reconcile. Even so, the sister [who coordinates the co-ops] taught us that unity is strength and used an analogy of firewood. A lone stick will easily break but a bundle tied together will not. And so, we began to have the courage to interact and see how we could support each other. We also feel protected because if there were ever any rumors of a threat, our sisters would tell us. We

[33] Ibid.
[34] Ibid.

also feel comfortable being together in public places; for example, when we go to the market we greet each other, whereas earlier we would be afraid of being seen together and would be scolded and accused of interacting with heathens. We have seen that there are many different ways we can help each other, and we are happy together now and we thank God for that.[35]

This is a nutshell description of the bridging between the integrated approach and peacebuilding/development where the women harmoniously, as the narrative goes, interact with one another in the market, regardless of their different backgrounds, while their crosscutting socioeconomic condition remains survivable and thus sustainable, thereby revealing the operative logic of a depoliticizing neoliberal resiliency discourse.

This neoliberal outlook, of course, includes the internalization of the burden not only of intrasubjective transformation but also of the role of change agent or seed of peace, which I have argued may traffic in the rhetoric of scaling up while, in actuality, deflating any such possibility. This deflation is enhanced through the patterns of double closures. Indeed, another interlocutor spoke about the responsibility of the women who benefited from the interfaith co-op groups to disseminate "their learning" to others in their community, so that they might effect broader change: "As women in the group, we should organize outreach programs at a grassroots level to educate other women about the benefits of pooling our resources together. Among us we have started businesses, we have paid school fees for our children, and this is how we build the future generation. We hope that they will follow our example and continue to preach peace through the Peace Clubs and other related sports activities."[36] In these words, I heard a sense of pride about their self-sufficiency. But I ask questions about the causes of marginalization and poverty. They challenge constructing poverty as a "natural given" and deemphasize reductive culturalist frames that seek to explain away why specific communities are starving, blocked from banking, hampered in their ability to obtain identification cards and running water, and mired in ethnic/religious conflicts. These issues are partly an outcome of the devastating effects of global warming (e.g., long droughts, aridity, and a lack of access to water), of which communities in the Global South often bear the brunt, even though

---

[35] Ibid.
[36] Ibid. Organizing communal sporting events is something I observed in both the Kenyan and Mindanaoan contexts, where such events are viewed as community-building mechanisms. See the discussion of PeaceConnect in chapters 2 and 3.

they are not the drivers of it. The women have an analysis around these issues, but they inhabit a pious survivalist agency, directing their actions to the tasks of survival.

Indeed, as with the women I spoke to in Maguindanao, the stories of responsibilization as self-remaking abound. These stories link the capacity to engage with the "other" and augment one's income to enhanced religious piety. In other words, survival as minimal nourishment and peace/security depends on reshaped subjectivity. Another Muslim woman from the group at Ngamia spoke about her self-transformation and understanding of the interfaith space as generative of improved relations with other communities:

> I have seen a lot of growth in myself over the years; I have educated all my children, and even have a grandchild in baby class here now. Recently, I came to visit my grandchild and was brought here [to the Catholic Cathedral compound] on a *tuktuk* owned by a Somali; when I came back to the gate, I found another *tuktuk* parked there as well. The *tuktuk* driver asked the person who had dropped me earlier why he was waiting outside the church. This was a Somali asking another Somali. My initial *tuktuk* driver responded by asking him in what world he still lived, and went on to sing praises to the school run by the church... and that him stopping outside the church does not mean that he will be converted to Christianity.[37]

These stories demonstrate that the women's main motivation for partaking in interfaith activities is economic, driven by the need for income augmentation (survival!). However, the participants also recognize how collaborative projects can facilitate the potential for conflict resolution in the communities, greater mutual understanding of one another, and overcoming fear and hostility through the cultivation of pluralistic ethics of survival.

A focus on livelihood in this interfaith collaborative space is designed to keep the peace rather than transform the underlying conditions and causes of marginality. On this point, another female participant told me that the dividend of participating in this intercommunal venture attracts male participants—which, in her view, gives the co-op a bit more communal legitimacy—and also youth, who may otherwise be vulnerable to financial

---

[37] Participant in the focus group with the representatives from the women co-ops, Garissa, February 2018.

manipulation by violent groups in the region of Garissa.[38] Another woman spoke about the interfaith women's groups as emboldening the training of women in conflict resolution techniques: "You find that women are peacemakers in the household, that it is mainly the men and youth who fight, isn't it? If you think about the conflict that occurs, it's the youth and men who are fighting. But if we recruit more women, and they study peacebuilding, they will be able to share these teachings with their husbands and the violence will [be] reduce[d]. The problems will be taken care of before, while it is still in a matchstick phase as opposed to a full flaming fire."[39] Conveyed in these words is an understanding of how her social reproductive location as a woman (one who is also more empowered economically) can contribute to devolutionary communal peacebuilding. Her words echo, from the ground, the top-down responsibilizing logic underpinning the theory of change that targets the "women sector." Economic "empowerment" translates into an enhanced capacity to play their gendered and scripted roles within the household and the community as those most responsible for ("securitizing") the children and for "keeping the peace." The programmatic space of the co-op offers these women opportunities to gain "literacy" in conflict resolution, the success of which is measured in actual instances of conflict mediation and de-escalation. Nevertheless, this success depends on accepting traditional hierarchies, even if the women interpret their new capacity as a form of empowerment.

Another woman told me about youth-related violence that erupted in the town of Madogo, across the Tana River. She said it "was quickly resolved because the youth spoke to their counterparts [from the other community] to manage the conflict in line with the teachings on conflict resolution. It is important to follow up with the youth every month because it is possible that there are people who may be interested and didn't previously get the information, and in that way it's helpful."[40] Another focus group participant indicated that the problem with the youth is their "idleness," a sentiment echoed by others. This claim again exemplifies the internalization of a culturalist explanation that attributes the blame for violence and marginalization to the personal failures of individuals. This is an explanation that, as noted above, neglects a deeper grappling with the root causes of poverty and the ongoing

---

[38] A consensus that emerged among the women (and the few participating men) during the focus group, Garissa, February 2018.
[39] Participant in the focus group with representatives of the women co-ops, Garissa, February 2018.
[40] Ibid.

legacies of land grabs, illiteracy, and lack of education. Further questioning did not lead the women I interviewed to bring up these other explanations. A historical lens and narratives about the root causes of contemporary marginalization, poverty, and exploitative practices are not present in the day-to-day struggles of the people who are simply trying to survive economically and obtain minimal nourishment. These are the struggles and realities that the decolonial lens obscures, as I analyze in the concluding chapters.

Similar issues emerged in my focus group with representatives from an interfaith youth club from Garissa County and the town of Madogo, in Tana River County. The activities of the club reflect an elicitive process whereby the youth decide on a collective project, such as building a public toilet in a town where there was none, and thus address, through the method of collective problem-solving, a public health issue, while at the same time generating a small income by charging people for the use of the toilet, a public shower, and drinking water.[41] One participant explained the process: "We approached it from a need-based perspective, realizing that one problem in Madogo is a lack of water. There are also no toilets and you often find people helping themselves out in the open, which isn't decent. So we asked ourselves how we can have a project that benefits the community and also allows us to advance and make some income. It is then that we began to figure out ways to build toilets."[42] The project's success, with the help of external investment from interested foundations and organizations, encourages the youth to seek other income-generating opportunities. Another participant proclaimed, "Most of the people around come here for the toilets, and it has changed us and made us responsible."[43] The word "responsible" resonates with my discussion of neoliberalism and its dissemination through responsibilization. Responsibilization requires those who are already most burdened and marginalized to take up additional labor.

Indeed, the business model of the youth club, which perceives self-transformation as integral to producing public goods and which displays coexistence or a coming together through the interreligious frame for problem-solving, attracts donors who wish to be able to measure the success and effectiveness of involving religion in development/peacebuilding projects. The recurring narratives about overcoming animosities associated

---

[41] For a twenty-liter gallon of water, they charge ten shillings; showering costs twenty shillings; and using the toilet costs ten shillings.
[42] Participant in a focus group with youth in Madogo, February 2018.
[43] Ibid.

with identity-based boundaries, however, reveal how constructing new interreligious or intergroup social spaces—whether in the youth clubs or the women's co-ops—is driven by economic incentives that reduce civic participation to buy-in, thereby entrenching and interweaving neoliberal rationality and survival piety. The generation of meager income by the youth embodies survivalist piety, which, in turn, reinforces a thin ethics of plurality. This ethics enhances the capacity of the community along the Tana River to de-escalate overt eruptions of violence so that they will be able to survive. This is peace as stability.

More pronounced than in the case of the women's co-op, the reasons the youth provided for participating in the club included their aspiration to create a meeting space that transcended religious, ethnic, and tribal divisions and that allowed them to help one another by identifying common issues they could work on together to "problem-solve." One of the participants identified water shortage as an issue that transcended identity-based divisions and that needed to be tackled through an intercommunal process: "*Kama hakuna maji*, [meaning] there is no water in Madogo. If there is water, there is water. If there is no water, everybody is crying water. Which is life."[44] Still, the number one challenge, according to participants, is land and the fact that, due to poverty and marginalization, people were tricked out of their land for a low price and now they have been turned into renters with no capacity to grow their food and provide for their families. What the youth perceive as an exploitative practice of land grabbing is a critical source of their anger and makes them susceptible to recruitment into violent extremism. Other challenges articulated include unemployment; food insecurity for a vast majority of the population due to climate change, droughts, and conflicts; low levels of education due to a long history of marginalization, including low levels of girls' education, in particular; the apparent lack of political will to prioritize and improve education; and the poor quality of public health. Unlike the women, who did not mention their sense of belonging (or not) to Kenya as a factor in their daily struggles, the youth stressed their experiences of marginalization. One young man even joked, "We are fifth-class citizens of Kenya."[45] Strengthening intergroup relationships through economic incentives, however, depoliticizes people's ability to see how systemic power structures their marginality beyond the logic of double closures.

---

[44] Ibid.
[45] Ibid.

Instead of such an intersectional prism, they are told to overcome their cultural obstacles and focus on their self-actualization/transformation *qua* survivalist economic productivity.

The youth, like the women, need to tackle deep-seated fears and stereotypes, a process that requires self-interrogation. Alluding to how the broader context of marginalization may underpin local conflicts and how identities are employed in such contexts, one youth said, "Marginalized people are marginalizing others."[46] Another youth mentioned the opportunity that the shared space affords to transform gender relations, at least within the club: "In this community women are said to be behind, or hidden in a corner, but in this group they believe in the power of a woman, that they have the ability. That is why in their group they have women in the leadership. . . . That is how they are overcoming that stereotype in the community."[47] One young woman confirmed this point: "Before joining the group, I was very conservative and introverted. I would not speak to other people. However, after joining the group and attending the meetings I became more assertive and would contribute to the discussions freely. I also didn't travel much before and kept to myself, but since joining the group I am more involved in community activities; for example, we farm together. I have learned so much by being here."[48] When I asked how they moved away from the normative segregation of women, one participant attributed the move to an intergenerational disjuncture and to the societal interactions among young people in multiple spaces, such as schools. These, the participants suggested, broke the taboo. Still, the women who participated in the focus group were hesitant to talk as the young men dominated the conversation.

Echoing the co-op women's concern with the problem of idleness among the youth, some young men told me about their previous behavior, such as chewing *khat* (a stimulant made out of twigs), a time-consuming and unproductive activity. One participant explained, "It is culture, you know, there is a society around chewing those twigs. Even the grownups, the old people, the younger people, they are all chewing the stuff. So they consume a lot of time, it makes them idle, and at the same time it affects their health, both mentally and physically. When somebody chews the whole day and night, the next morning they cannot do any work. So you see it affects them."[49] Joining the

[46] Ibid.
[47] Ibid.
[48] Ibid.
[49] Ibid.

youth club and participating in its income-generating activities, which help to solve public issues, is then highlighted as transformative of such idle and uneconomic behavior. This narrative about laziness and personal failings shows the internalization of a broader Kenyan narrative that interprets the supposed "underdevelopment" of the Coast and the North Eastern provinces as an outcome of culturalist causes. When I interviewed a Nairobi-based man centrally involved in the private sector, he spoke about the people of these regions as if they inhabited a different kind of humanity. "They are lazy," he said, and "they do not value education."[50] The idleness/laziness storyline was repeated even by much more empathetic actors, such as Sister Clarisse, who is trained as a social worker and who has devoted her life to the region. In explaining the focus on youth, she stresses, "An idle mind is the devil's workshop. When they are busy, they do not have a lot of time to think of the chaos they have to cause."[51]

Therefore, the Garissa women's and youth groups exemplify how processes of responsibilization can veil root causes. These processes burden those at the lower levels of power and influence with the obligation to overcome their conditions of poverty and food insecurity through self-transformation into economically self-sufficient and resilient individuals whose very resiliency also shapes a pious neoliberal subjectivity. As in the case of the interreligious and multisectoral task of overcoming cultural and religious obstacles, such as the apparent condoning of child marriage in the Malindi region, the Garissa women and youth illuminate how their self-transformation involves overcoming ethnic and religious antagonisms. In both instances, religion appears as if it were an obstacle for human security, covering up, it seems, multiple layers of historical violence.

What makes the women's and youth groups of the Garissa and Tana regions an interfaith undertaking is much less clear than the interfaith dimensions of the multisectoral effort to reduce child marriage and sexual abuse in Malindi, even though, for the participants themselves, it is "interfaith" just by virtue of the intentionality of their composition and the challenges and fears that the participants face. Unlike the proof-texting of the clerics in Malindi, faith and tradition come through for the youth and the women in the form of prayer. Prayers bookmark and punctuate all interreligious peacebuilding activities there. Each meeting begins and ends in alternating Muslim, Christian,

---

[50] Interview #47, Nairobi, November 2018.
[51] Interview #39, Nairobi, February 2018.

Figure 4.2 Prayer to commence the meeting of the women's co-op in the Garissa region, Kenya.

and traditionalist prayers, a practice interpreted and experienced as causal, not just performative.[52] Prayers temporally, but also normatively, frame the space and practice of economic collaboration for mutual survival and infuse the mundanity of such activities with sacredness (see Figure 4.2).

But besides how the participants identify themselves and use prayers to open and close meetings, what makes these income-generating activities "interfaith" or "interreligious"? With what conception of tradition do they operate? As in the case of the women's co-ops, prayer in the meetings becomes the primary mechanism through which faith seems to appear. The practice of alternating Muslim, Christian, and traditionalist prayers is meaning-making and perceived as having the capacity to construct the normative interfaith space and influence what happens in the meetings. Praying is a causal mechanism and a spiritual practice ensuring that what transpires will be good. One participant in the focus group in Garissa commented, "If we start with [Muslim] prayer, everyone respects that, and after that is done we will also

---

[52] The causality of prayers is a site of an important scholarly intervention that interrogates the secularist assumptions that render prayer a noncausal practice. For an example, see Tanya B. Schwarz, *Faith-Based Organizations in Transnational Peacebuilding* (New York: Rowman & Littlefield, 2018). See also Andrew Prevot, *Thinking Prayer: Theology and Spirituality amid the Crises of Modernity* (Notre Dame, IN: University of Notre Dame Press, 2015); Robert Orsi, "The Higher Power," in *Reverberations: New Directions in the Study of Prayer*, March 2, 2013, http://forums.ssrc.org/ndsp/2013/03/02/the-higher-power/. This intervention is one among others within the *Reverberations: New Directions in the Study of Prayer*, sponsored by the Social Science Research Council, which seeks to broaden, through an interdisciplinary study, an understanding of the anthropological and spiritual meanings of prayer as practice.

have a Christian pray for us. That has caused us to be more tolerant and receptive to each other's religions."[53] In participants' experiences, the very performance of alternating prayers produces tolerance, mutual trust, and respect. The conception of tradition that emerges from this practice operationalizes the notion of belief as universal and generic to establish commonalities, a key factor for engaging in income-generating endeavors. One man who participated in the women's co-ops remarked, "When a person prays, they are praying to God, and I doubt anyone ever prays for something evil or malicious. So, when we hear Christians pray we invite the prayer, and when a Muslim prays we do the same because we are praying to the same God. We are all praying for each other's needs; therefore, there is no difference."[54]

A sanctifying conduit for economically productive activities, this performance of neoliberal survival piety demonstrates how depoliticizing bridging activities that produce perceptions of interreligious harmony (here represented in the practices of prayers to frame livelihood projects) depends on individual self-transformation into a change agent. A woman's motivation for constructing an ethics of plurality is ultimately tied to economic incentives and neoliberal survivalist piety or subjectivity. It also reveals that what amounts to "interfaith" within this framework thrives on a generic religiosity and unitary conceptions of communal belonging as the constitutive ingredient of an ethics of the common good.

Mere survival does not need more substantive, historically embedded, or critical forms of religious literacy or *knowing*. It needs *doing*. The above stories show how economic incentives can strengthen interreligious/intercommunal ties, thereby turning "religion" into a relevant form of social capital for peacebuilding and conflict resolution. This process also produces and is produced by neoliberal subjectivities, which further infuse a sacred logic into the task of keeping the peace that is placed on those in the margins.

Surviving around the Tana River

After a long morning talking to representatives from the women's groups, I went with Sister Genevieve, a young man from Nairobi who worked with the sisters, and my host from CRS to visit one of the villages where the women

---

[53] Focus group with representatives of the women's co-ops, Garissa, February 2018.
[54] Ibid.

I met just that morning had come from. Sister Genevieve drove us in one of the Church's vehicles. It was a bumpy ride that turned, at one point, from the main, roughly paved road onto an unpaved, steep path leading into the village. At that moment, I understood why the sisters in the cathedral's compound insisted on taking Father Samuel's truck. I was barely keeping my motion sickness under control when I saw some of the women I spoke to earlier walking up the path and jumping happily into the back of the truck, thankful to be driven the rest of the way. When my host took me to town to eat lunch, walk around a bit, and retrieve some cash from a heavily guarded ATM, these women were walking back home, first on the paved road and then up the unpaved path. The sun was burning, and the air was dusty and dry. Having been driven to the village but still recognizing the long time it took since we ended our session until we reunited with the women, I began to grasp what it means in terms of time for these women to participate in meetings in the cathedral. Sister Genevieve and the other sisters visit them at home as well, of course. This is how meaningful relationships are built over time. However, the distances are long, the paths are arduous, and the climate is harsh.

When we finally reached the hill, we saw a few children crossing the Tana River in a small boat. They were returning from school. The adults were watching them fearfully, thinking of the hippopotamus that had been haunting them. The kids were in danger there in the water. Sister Genevieve turned to me and told me that often when the kids returned home, there was no guarantee that there would be food waiting for them. The women and a few men showed me the pump they had been given to get water from the river to take care of their crops. Installing the pump was one of the projects in which CRS and other organizations had invested. It looked promising, except for the hippopotamus problem they were trying to solve. As we were walking to the pump, a group of pastoralists appeared from behind the trees, which resulted in an altercation that my host said could have easily escalated into violence. The pastoralists came with their animals to graze, and the farmers' crops were in danger. These kinds of conflicts are routine and are only exacerbated by global warming.[55] In this episode, the pastoralist clarified that they were moving into this territory in search of food.

---

[55] For further exposition of the underlying causes of pastoralist-farmer conflicts in African contexts, see M. C. Rufino, P. K. Thornton, S. K. Ng'ang'a, I. Mutie, P. G. Jones, M. T. van Wijk, and M. Herrero, "Transitions in Agro-Pastoralist Systems of East Africa: Impacts on Food Security and Poverty," *Agriculture, Ecosystems and Environment* 179 (2013): 215–30, https://doi.org/10.1016/j.agee.2013.08.019.

As I walked through the village, I was struck by the poverty; the lack of resources, running water, and proper sanitation, and the sights of makeshift homes that I knew were subject to occasional floods. When the floods come, Sister Genevieve told me, the people fold their houses up on the tops of trees and move to evacuation centers. Not all of the women participating in the co-ops experience such serious precarity, but many do. It is in this context of poverty and marginalization (Nairobi appeared very far from the daily life of this region) that responsibilization happens and that the burden of change is exerted upon those at the lower end of the power structure. Labeling this responsibilization "interfaith" enhances the formation of a survivalist neoliberal piety as a peace/security mechanism.[56] This is not the ostentatious, magical, philanthropic richness to which the concept of "neoliberal piety" points in the academic literature. The stories of the women's groups in Garissa bring into sharp relief how a focus on a religious sector or on interfaith engagement as a change mechanism at the local level reflects the neoliberalization of religion. IRD/A as a mechanism for responsibilization, through the formation of neoliberal survival piety and myopic accounts of suffering as the outcome of intercommunal discord and personal shortcomings, is effective in many respects because it channels the "remainders" of the technocratic model. I borrow the concept of "remainders" from China Scherz, who interprets religion as "the raw material necessary to craft a moral salve that some see as capable of healing the wounds precipitated by neoliberal markets."[57]

Indeed, in addition to the functionalist capacity of religious leaders, institutions, and networks to reach and mobilize the local, unlocking the transformative power of religion within a neoliberal paradigm entails investing responsibilization with spiritual and religious dimensions and reshaping subjectivities through an ethics of labor productivity. Neoliberal survival piety exposes the connections between food and peace. Hunger often results from war and other less overt forms of violence rather than being its cause. The problem is that mere survival became imbued with sacredness, enhancing the neoliberal devolutionary model.

---

[56] For an analysis of neoliberal spirituality that likewise highlights the burdening of the individual over and against an analysis of structural/cultural violence, see Andrea Jain, *Peace Love Yoga: The Politics of Global Spirituality* (New York: Oxford University Press, 2020).

[57] China Scherz, "Persistent Forms: Catholic Charity Homes and the Limits of Neoliberal Morality," in *Religion and the Morality of the Market*, ed. Daromir Rudnyckyj and Filippo Osella (Cambridge: Cambridge University Press, 2017), 177–95, 179.

A Multidirectional Street

My findings show how the postsecular turn to access the local and affect bottom-up responsibilization entrenches top-down neoliberal rationality as it infuses it in survival piety and Sisyphean patience. However, the neoliberalization of tradition as part and parcel of a broader process of responsibilization and trauma healing does not account for the multidirectionality and agency of those involved. Nor does it account for how friendships exceed neoliberal projects' always limited span. Even if the friendships formed are not political, their realness is agentic and long-lasting. For example, CRS's report "Getting Their Act Together: The Clean-up of Saniag River"[58] describes how, in June 2018, CRS—along with USAID—focused its Binding, Bonding, and Bridging activities for peace on mobilizing the communities in a remote village in the Ampatuan municipality of the Maguindanao province to clean up the river. This river used to be a source of income and the center of the village's life, but it had become polluted due to encroachment by logging companies and decades of neglect. The brochure designed to report to funding agencies and promote further fundraising describes the underlying conditions of marginality and extractive capitalism, but only as background to an otherwise successful event, due to its sustainability. Evidence for this sustainability is that, following June 2018 and the formal conclusion of the project, the communities (Christians, Muslims, and Lumads) showed up to clean the river anyway. Additionally, efforts to change garbage practices among the village's inhabitants included signage in strategic locations along the river and internal work on hygienic norms. The latter again exerts pressure on people to transform themselves and assumes that their "failings" are the primary source of their misery.

While this cleanup project is particular, the second iteration (2015–18)[59] of the 3Bs worked in twenty-five barangays to improve relationships between identity groups locked in conflict. The intention was to train targeted traditional religious leaders, women leaders, and youth leaders to enhance their capacity for conflict resolution. Here, success was indicated in the fact that 846 people were trained, which exceeded the initial target of 500. The training involved developing skills necessary to facilitate peace and conflict mapping and culture of peace seminars, among other proficiencies. The

---

[58] A brochure was shared with me during a visit to the CRS office in Davao.
[59] The first, which I discuss in chapter 2, was implemented between 2012 and 2015.

project also included a concentrated effort to strengthen local conflict resolution mechanisms. Accordingly, project facilitators worked with 135 traditional religious leaders to enhance their conflict resolution skills and with 79 Lupong Tagapamayapa, or localized reconciliatory peace committees, and 43 Baranagay Peace and Order Council members. All of these numbers signify success from an organizational perspective. This training resulted in 134 inter-identity-bridging events and 32 community action projects, such as the aforementioned cleanups.[60] IRD/A thus enhances this conceit of neoliberalism. Problem-solving, which Wendy Brown analyzes as an outcome of neoliberal governance's de-democratizing effect, nevertheless becomes a mechanism for deepening relationships and thus contributes to an apparent resilience against violent modes of conflict resolution. These are the remainders that exceed the neoliberal business model.

The subfield of religion, conflict, and peacebuilding does not often situate its analysis of religion in conversation with a critique of neoliberal rationality and neoliberal peacebuilding. Nor is the subfield conversant with scholarship on religion and neoliberalism and the insights it offers concerning the tasks of self-empowerment and the formation of neoliberal piety.[61] Exposing this oversight, as I have done, shows how the business of religion and peacebuilding, or neoliberal religious peacebuilding through IRD/A, dilutes the prophetic resources previously associated with religion and struggles for peace and justice and renders religious virtuosity in terms of one's capacity to master the religiocratic playing field. At this juncture, I circle back to the operative concept of partnership underpinning the "global engagement with religion."

The Limits of "Partnership"

Perhaps the most striking example of the postsecular turn in development policy is the gradual embrace of the "religion factor" by the World Bank. This institution embodies secularist and Euro-Atlantic political and economic power. The World Bank has transitioned from an uncomfortable (or

---

[60] This information is provided in an internal document shared with me: CRS, "Applying Binding, Bonding and Bridging for Peace: Applying the 3Bs for Peace in Mindanao, Philippines," December 2018.

[61] Cecelia Lynch's work is a notable exception. See, for example, her "Local and Global Influences on Islamic NGOs in Kenya," *Journal of Peacebuilding & Development* 6, no. 1 (2012): 21–34. See also my discussion in chapter 3, where I map the Religion, Conflict, and Peacebuilding field.

indifferent) relationship with religious actors, institutions, and networks during the first few decades following World War II to a full-fledged embrace of religion by the early decades of the twenty-first century. It now works with religious actors as "partners" in implementing sustainable development programs. The establishment of the World Faiths Development Dialogue by James D. Wolfensohn, then president of the World Bank, and Lord George Carey, then archbishop of Canterbury, intended "to facilitate dialogue and partnership" already in 1988.[62] It offered a designated institutional frame, which, under the leadership of Katherine Marshall, could aid in creating partnerships with "faith actors." The World Bank's focus on partnerships betrays an assumption about what religion is and who the religious actors are, as well as what it means to be "developed."[63]

In portraying the tension between the World Bank approach to development and faith-inspired actors, Marshall highlights, for instance, the issue of water privatization. The World Bank promotes privatization as a commonsense approach to attract investment in clean water. It does so without an interrogation of the underlying ideological neoliberal frameworks. Such narratives about partnerships, however, often also involve examining apparent tensions between faith and development by positing faith as a driver for resolving financial stress faced by developing countries, as exemplified by the earlier global Christian campaign known as the Jubilee 2000 movement for debt forgiveness or the Micah Challenge as part of the UN Millennium Goals. Bringing religion into the conversation allows one to make moral arguments against requiring poor countries to repay debts.[64] Such a narrative assumes that religious actors are always on the side of the poor and marginalized[65] but says nothing about religion's relation to racial capitalism, colonialism, neoliberalism, political and environmental violence, and, of course, gender-based violence. A generic understanding of religion depoliticizes and disentangles religion from the conditions of people's

---

[62] Katherine Marshall, "Development and Faith Institutions: Gulfs and Bridges," in *Religion and Development: Ways of Transforming the World,* ed. Gerrie ter Haar (London: Hurst and Company, 2011), 27–56, 34.

[63] Some of these questions are internally debated, as in the subfield of development ethics, which I examined in the previous chapter.

[64] For an example of this trajectory, see Katherine Marshall and Marisa Van Saanen, *Development and Faith: Where Mind, Heart, and Soul Work Together* (Washington, DC: World Bank, 2007), especially part 1.

[65] This argument is also reinforced by a flood of postsecular literature focusing on poor people's religiosity. For example, see Deepa Narayan, Robert Chambers, Meera K. Shah, and Patti Petesch, *Voices of the Poor: Crying Out for Change* (New York: Oxford University Press, 2000).

suffering and allows organizations like the World Bank to fall back on a thin morality to enact their myopic problem-solving policies as if poverty and hunger were natural predicaments.

It is not surprising, then, that, since the 1990s, pursuing dialogue and creating partnerships has not involved engagement with the complex legacies of colonialism and modernity. The focus on partnerships (even when it is framed in terms of an "engagement with religion") entails subcontracting problem-solving—via grants and other instruments—to more localized, manageable, and specific actors.

To the degree that such partnerships or outsourcing involve expanding religious literacy, it is to instrumentalize "good" religion to create better "outcomes." One high-profile example is the Ethics in Action forum convened by the American economist Jeffrey Sachs shortly after ratifying the SDGs. The purpose of this forum was to generate conversations regarding implementing the seventeen SDGs. The SDGs capture an admirable intention to end poverty, protect the planet, and ensure conditions of prosperity for all. They do so with an understanding that achieving each goal requires multisectoral cooperation. In the postsecular moment, this kind of cooperation also includes ensuring buy-in from the religious sector. Meeting at the Vatican, with the expected pomp and circumstance, Sachs's initiative sanctioned, at the highest levels, the instrumentalization of certain religiocrats and other experts to promote the SDGs. The initiative illuminated the many ways in which religious actors can harmonize their religious traditions with the ethical framework of the SDGs. In various statements, which were shaped through the rubrics of "ethics in action," Sachs, with the help of his religious actors and experts, sought to articulate a certain shared "generic" moral and ethical consensus on an array of SDG-related issues, including modern slavery, human trafficking, and justice for the poor and vulnerable. The apparent moral clarity here reflects proof-texting logic yet again. The same logic underpins the theological labor of the clerics in Malindi who want to show consistency between the UN Convention on the Rights of the Child and their traditions.

During the meetings at the Vatican, religious credentials were also deployed to sanction the SDGs as highly consistent with the teachings of religious traditions. The sanctioning, however, was multidirectional. This is because the very "prophetic" authority of the religious actors undertaking the synchronization between the SDGs and all ethical and religious traditions is sanctioned by the very neoliberal framework that shapes them into experts on religion and technocratic religious actors. This approach can be contrasted with an intersectional praxis and analysis that exposes and seeks to transform the interlocking structures of power and domination. Such a praxis relies on robustly situated ethical horizons.[66] In contrast, the religious sector, or the aggregate of those deemed religious actors, relies on thin morality and technocratic tools.

This thin secular morality permeates the multiple levels of *doing* religion in the peacebuilding/development business. Hence, the heads of transnational, global organizations focused on religion gain stature as religious authorities (in the name of "religion in general"), while religious authorities who provide local access gain the bureaucratic and neoliberal capacity to ensure their own organizational "sustainability" (another neoliberal buzzword). Ironically, this postsecular turn bills itself as unlocking the prophetic capacities of religious traditions. Often heralded are the prophetic commitments of religious actors to the poor and marginal. Yet, under the neoliberal paradigm, religion is what I have called the "prophetic lite" and is understood in terms of its effectiveness and "prosociality,"[67] or as having cohesive, rather than disruptive, force. Evidence-based research on religion is marshaled to shore up the validity of this social scientific concept of prosociality. At most, grandiose interfaith statements and other declarations constitute a "prophetic lite" intervention, which is carried out by signing interfaith or faith-based declarations, offering symbolic gestures in fancy hotels, and bringing in more local religious leaders to engage in interfaith trickle-down performativity.[68] The misrepresentation of the bureaucratic, priestly, and conservative as charismatic, prophetic, and disruptive of the status quo is especially exemplified in the virtuoso case of *Laudato Si'* (2015), the second encyclical of Pope Francis, subtitled "On Care for Our Common Home."

---

[66] Jakeet Singh, "Religious Agency and the Limits of Intersectionality," *Hypatia* 30, no. 4 (2015): 657–74.

[67] A wave of scholarship examining the prosocial dimensions of religion relates to the broader postsecular turn and tries to decipher, or rather demonstrate, how being religious makes people more generous, adaptable, resilient, and/or willing to participate in social life. See, for an example in psychology, Olga Stravrora and Pascal Siegers, "Religious Prosociality and Morality across Cultures: How Social Enforcement of Religion Shapes the Effects of Personal Religiosity on Prosocial and Moral Attitudes and Behaviors," *Personality and Social Psychology Bulletin* 40, no. 3 (2014): 315–33, https://doi.org/10.1177/0146167213510951. See also Christian Smith and Hilary Davidson, *The Paradox of Generosity: Giving We Receive, Grasping We Lose* (Oxford: Oxford University Press, 2014). Such research happens at the intersections of biology, psychology, and even neuroscience, while other scholarship permeates the social sciences and is often deployed to enhance religiocratic investment in various religion-related projects, agencies, offices, and initiatives.

[68] See also Atalia Omer, "Beyond the Performance of Interfaith Solidarity," *Contending Modernities*, June 11, 2019, https://contendingmodernities.nd.edu/global-currents/beyondinterfaith/.

As a faith-based *doing, Laudato Si'* indeed typifies an effort at mobilizing an interfaith coalition of actors. Pope Francis implored religious leaders to tap into their traditions' ethical and prophetic resources to devise ways of redressing the global predicament of poverty and inequality. The encyclical reflects Pope Francis's roots in liberation theology. With the gravitas of the institution of the Church and the office of the papacy, it constitutes an impactful act of public diplomacy. It also indicates a willingness to partner with multiple actors (including self-described "secular" Jews such as Naomi Klein) to work together to fight against the destruction of the climate in ways that involve a radical critique of exploitative capitalism and global structural and historical violence.[69]

This kind of dialogue approximates the one between Father Gustavo Gutiérrez, one of the foundational thinkers of liberation theology in Latin America, and the late Paul Farmer, a renowned Harvard public health scholar and practitioner. Both engage in penetrating analyses of the global dimensions of poverty, which include, notably, rendering the histories of colonial and capitalist exploitation as sinful. The theological reflections of Gutiérrez influenced Farmer's own approach to the "preferential option for the poor." He does not simply want to distribute philanthropic crumbs to the people of Haiti. Instead, his approach has been explicitly nondevelopmentalist. It challenges the development paradigm for failing to redress root causes. Only by prioritizing the perspectives and needs of the poor, Farmer and Gutiérrez thought, could such root causes be alleviated. Instead of arguing for partnership and investment through water privatization, the operative logic for the Farmer-Gutiérrez convergence is driven by solidarity and accompaniment. Rather than denoting a normative orientation to redress the historical outcomes of colonial exploitation, or what Freire called "false generosity,"[70] the inclusion of religion in governmental, intergovernmental, and local peacebuilding efforts is more often connected to a preoccupation with making religion "safe" for investment.

Still, (male) liberation theologies, for all their capacity to explicate structural forms of violence, failed initially to recognize the "option for the poor as [an] option for the poor woman" as well.[71] This failure resides in the depth of

---

[69] For the inclusion of Naomi Klein on the pope's climate team, see Inés San Martín, "Pope Francis Adds 'Secular Jewish Feminist' Naomi Klein to Climate Team," *Crux*, July 1, 2015, https://cruxnow.com/church/2015/07/pope-francis-expands-climate-team-with-addition-of-naomi-klein-secular-jewish-feminist/.

[70] Freire, *Pedagogy of the Oppressed*, 44.

[71] Ivone Gebara, "Option for the Poor as Option for the Poor Woman," *Concilium* 194 (1987): 110–17.

entrenchment in heteropatriarchal norms and a gendered dualistic outlook. When feminist liberation theologians illuminated the oversight already in the 1980s, the dominant discussion remained heteropatriarchal.[72] Hence, to the degree that *Laudato Si'* exemplifies a prophetic interruption grounded in a liberation theological scaffolding that confronts rapacity and the global structures of exploitative capitalism, it fails to link the one set of dominating relations (humans to the environment; colonialism to Indigenous peoples; capitalism to labor) to another (gender: the basic binary of domination) in which it is complicit ontologically and materially.

I highlight *Laudato Si'* not because of its prophetic dimensions, however limited, considering the authority of the pope derives from the priestly institution of the Church, but because it invites a set of questions concerning the *doing* of religion and the symbolic force of such interventions as *Laudato Si'*: (1) Why are such disruptions of hegemony often articulated through appeals to religious meanings? and (2) Why is it that, when religious authorities articulate appeals to religious meanings, they can *do* things in the world? It is not that religion monopolizes ethics. Indeed, it does not monopolize ethics, as Farmer, Klein, and many other "secular" humanist interlocutors demonstrate in their critiques and actions. Instead, religion—more often than not—is weaponized by discursive forces and is implicated in their ideological and political violence, which then gains an aura of sacredness and piety. Yet its empirical force in reshaping people's concrete lives (including through food and healthcare services) shows that mere critique is as reductive and unhelpful as unreconstructed celebrations of "good" religion. What is fruitful, however, is to examine the models of secular-religious co-resistance and solidarity rather than "partnerships." The former engage with multiple layers of violence, including colonialism, capitalism, and neoliberalism. This engagement can be seen in the dialogue between Farmer and Gutiérrez. This dialogue contrasts sharply with other forms of partnership that do not employ such levels of critique. Instead, these forms rely on co-opting religion, religious actors, and institutions/networks as subcontractors for peacebuilding/development.

Indeed, the very process of becoming partners necessitates the bureaucratization and neoliberalization of what it means to *do* religion, where *doing religion* does not entail critical religious literacy, hermeneutical depth, or

---

[72] See Elaine Nogueira-Godsey, "A Decolonial Way to Dialogue: Rethinking Ecofeminism and Religion," in *The Routledge Handbook of Religion, Gender and Society*, ed. Caroline Starkey and Emma Tomalin (London: Routledge, 2022), 365–84.

efforts to engage in epistemologies, or people, from the margins, which, as I noted, *Laudato Si'* did in terms of its challenge to anthropocentricity, but not to androcentricity.[73] The overall effect of the language of "partnership" invisibilizes those on the margins by overlooking historical injustices and their long-term impacts. A social justice and solidarity lens, in distinction, prioritizes the margins—or, in the language of liberation theology, it commits to a "preferential option for the poor."

Feminist hermeneutics would take this approach to the levels of feminist emancipatory potentialities and situatedness. Such emancipatory articulations of religious traditions are not essences to be mapped, identified, and partnered with, but rather upshots of embodied feminist and queer hermeneutical labor. Such hermeneutical fluidity works against the utilitarian neoliberal partnership model's reliance on hermeneutically closed definitions of religious and cultural traditions. The partnership approach treats religion as an independent sector (distilling its "ethical teachings" and identifying its helpful institutions and service-providing infrastructures). It distinguishes it from narratives of historical injustice and oppression. Accordingly, its logic works against an intersectional lens by design, not merely due to the pragmatic demands of *realpolitik*. It reveals the transmogrification and redrawing of the colonial zone.

The "poor"—from within a feminist "preferential option for the poor" framework—include, in my view, all those who occupy the epistemic, socioeconomic, and political margins. Treating the poor preferentially means prioritizing their needs, meaning-making agency, and counternarratives. Therefore, the work that is carried out at the margins cannot be accommodated by a partnership model that proceeds from the centers and heights of power in society or one that seeks to operationalize prepackaged sound bites and reified accounts of religious traditions. The partnership model is utilitarian and thus trades in "generic" (or status quo) versions of religious hermeneutics. The preferential option for the poor, conversely, is justice-oriented and thus necessarily has to convey embodied and situated hermeneutics. Theology looks a lot different when you are hungry or when you are counted as less than fully human. Liberal amnesia and a harmonious celebration of diversity cannot cover up this fact. Hence, any deployment of

---

[73] See, for this line of critique, Nicole M. Flores, "'Our Sister, Mother Earth': Solidarity and Familial Ecology in *Laudato Si*," *Journal of Religious Ethics* 46, no. 3 (September 2018): 463–78, https://doi.org/10.1111/jore.12227.

"intersectionality" as a buzzword within a developmentalist frame, which in reality simply means "multisectorality," dulls the critical impact that an intersectional approach can have and constrains its emancipatory potential.

Thus, to make the invisible visible and the thin complex (or queer and feminist) would entail moving from a stated commitment to end poverty through "false generosity" to addressing through reparative practices the root causes of poverty, not as "natural" givens but as consequences of human history. Globally, this would have to take place through an analysis of Euro-Christian complicity with colonialism and the long-term ramifications of land grabs, conversions, slavery, and genocide. Feminist and queer hermeneutics would illuminate the links between colonial exploitation and patterns of racialized dehumanization that are so central to these violent legacies. The links between gender injustice and Indigenous decoloniality, in other words, reveal how the emergence of modernist conceptions of human control over nature relate to and parallel patriarchal normativity.[74]

Moreover, as decolonial and intersectional feminist and queer thinkers have stressed, gender functions as a basic metaphor of control and subordination, shaping the colonized world according to presumably sacred ontologies and totalizing theologies that authorize hierarchization through gendered racialization.[75] This critique points to intersectionality as a necessary analytic vehicle for rearticulating peace and justice, the absence of which reveals the entrenchment of "peace" within unjust structures and cosmologies. Indeed, the concept of "partnership" euphemistically enhances such oppressive structures and transmogrifies their long-term legacies. In this context, religious actors appeal to and speak in generic and androcentric ways, in the name of all religions and none at all.

Within a neoliberal framework of peacebuilding/development, which is also nested within a P/CVE landscape with its own securitizing rationality, religious peacebuilding agency needs to be quiet, compliant, Sisyphean, and content with small connector projects, such as cleaning up polluted rivers, building wells, and creating limited forms of peace within existing structures

---

[74] See, for instance, Teresa Toldy, "Someone Is Missing in the Common House: The Empty Place of Women in the Encyclical Letter 'Laudato Si,'" *Journal of the European Society of Women in Theological Research* 25 (2017): 167–89, https://doi.org/10.2143/ESWTR.25.0.3251310; Rosemary P. Carbine, "Imagining and Incarnating an Integral Ecology: A Critical Ecofeminist Public Theology," in *Planetary Solidarity: Global Women's Voices on Christian Doctrine and Climate Justice*, ed. Grace Ji-Sun Kim and Hilda P. Koster (Minneapolis, MN: Fortress Press, 2017), 47–66.

[75] Maria Lugones, "Heterosexualism and the Colonial/Modern Gender System," *Hypatia* 22, no. 1 (2007): 186–209, https://muse.jhu.edu/article/206329.

of control and domination. This is not an emancipatory and prophetic form of religious agency but rather a compliant and priestly (NGO-ized) form. The mechanisms of interreligious action function as a crutch for coloniality through its patterns of neoliberalization and spiritualizing survival. The next chapter examines more explicitly the securitization of religion and peacebuilding practice.

5
Religion and "Soft" Security
Countermessaging and Surveillance

Containing "Bad" Religion

"I work... within *my* space and what *I* can change. If I reach the women [of] the community... I've achieved my goal, I believe somebody else will do the rest. Do you understand? To answer your question, I'll frustrate myself if I think, 'I can be here, there, and transform everything,' you understand?"[1] This is what a teacher associated with a Nairobi mosque told me when I asked how she sees her role as a trainer and facilitator of workshops intended for various communities (youth, women, imams, and sheikhs) to build their capacity to identify warning signs of radicalization into violence and wrong and violent interpretations of the Qur'an and, in some cases, help recruits reintegrate into society. She rejected any broad structural analysis or comprehensive vision of her work's socioeconomic and political transformation. Like other religious actors positioned to access vulnerable communities, her motivation is to reduce the capacity of wrong or violent interpretations of religion to manipulate and fatalistically direct people, preying on their religious illiteracy and, more critically, on their hopelessness and insecurity. This chapter examines how *knowing religion* or *intrafaith* hermeneutical first-aid becomes a crucial site of peacebuilding and security practice.

To understand this mode of first-aid hermeneutics, we need to return to the concept of "soft power," which reveals the operative force of the securitizing lens and its nonmilitarist complementary work. Further, recent scholarship has expanded the notion of security itself beyond military concerns and realist international relations paradigms to include the provision of human rights and justice.[2] "Human security," James Wellman Jr.

---

[1] Interview #143, Nairobi, July 2019, emphasis mine.
[2] For interventions in the concept of "security," see Barry Buzan, *People, States and Fear: An Agenda for International Security Studies in the Post–Cold War Era* (Boulder, CO: Lynne Rienner, 1991); P. D. Williams, *Security Studies: An Introduction* (Abingdon: Routledge, 2008).

explains, "represents a shift from the 'hard' power of state politics to the 'soft' power of civil societies and community organizations . . . a unit of analysis that is more amorphous and difficult to grasp than hard power, yet critical nonetheless for the well-being—the holistic and sustainable security—of citizens of all states."[3]

Religion emerged explicitly as a security issue for the field of international relations already at the end of the Cold War.[4] It thus became a focus of studies examining its capacity as a force multiplier, accessing nonverbal symbolism and multiple social and political networks, providing resources for reconciliation, and reinterpreting international relations' theoretical paradigms in light of postsecular insights, among other relevant sites of analysis and influence.[5] While conveying one particular mode of security, defending the "political" or "secular nationalism" from religious intrusions, divisiveness, and irrationality, the secularist paradigm was challenged by the empirical realities of the late 1970s and following years and the crumbling binary of peaceful secular liberalism versus violent religion, a hallmark of the myth of modernity.[6] So it is not that international relations discovered religion as a factor in security, but rather that the nature of the engagement with religion shifted, as did the contested and fluid meanings of security.[7]

---

[3] James K. Wellman Jr., "Human Security: A Secularized Social Gospel and the Rediscovery of Religion," in *The Routledge Handbook of Religion and Security*, ed. Chris Seiple, Dennis R. Hoover, and Pauletta Otis (London: Routledge, 2013), 193–203 (194). See also, for the initial conceptualization of "soft power," Joseph Nye, *Soft Power: The Means to Success in World Politics* (New York: Public Affairs, 2005). This shift was consolidated in 1994 with the publication of the UNDP's *Human Development Report: New Dimensions of Human Security*. It conveyed a growing realization of the relations among war, instability, and human insecurity entailing physical safety as well as protection of dignity, welfare, and social and human rights.

[4] Religion is also critical in the very framing of the Cold War. See Jeremy Gunn, *Spiritual Weapons: The Cold War and the Forging of an American National Religion* (Westport, CT: Praeger, 2009).

[5] See, for example, Stacey Gutkoski, "Religion and Security in International Relations Theories," in *The Routledge Handbook of Religion and Security*, ed. Chris Seiple, Dennis R. Hoover, and Pauletta Otis (New York: Routledge, 2013), 125–35; Daniel H. Nexon, "Religion and International Relations: No Leap of Faith Required," in *Religion and International Relations Theory*, ed. Jack Snyder (New York: Columbia University Press, 2011), 141–67; Nukhet Sandal and Patrick James, "Religion and International Relations Theory: Towards a Mutual Understanding," *European Journal of International Relations* 17, no. 1 (2010): 3–25, https://doi.org/10.1177/1354066110364304.

[6] William Cavanaugh, *The Myth of Religious Violence: Secular Ideology and the Roots of Modern Conflict* (Oxford: Oxford University Press, 2009). Philip Gorski and Gülay Türkmen-Dervişoğlu highlight the relations between the myth of religious violence and the myth of secular nationalism as constitutive of one another and stress the importance of meso-level analyses of nationalist discourses; see "Religion, Nationalism, and International Security: Creation Myths and Social Mechanisms," in *The Routledge Handbook of Religion and Security*, ed. Chris Seiple, Dennis R. Hoover, and Pauletta Otis (London: Routledge, 2013), 136–47.

[7] For a critical reassessment of international relations through a neo-Weberian lens, see Cecelia Lynch, "A Neo-Weberian Approach to Religion in International Politics," *International Theory* 1, no. 3 (2009): 381–408; Cecelia Lynch, "A Neo-Weberian Approach to Studying Religion and Violence,"

For those who thrive on simplistic paradigms, the events of September 11, 2001, appeared to verify "clash of civilizations" types of ahistorical reductive arguments.[8] This momentous event also launched the "war on terror" and eventually a network of P/CVE that viewed religion *qua* Islam primarily through a security lens. This prism lacks self-reflexivity in terms of historical, socioeconomic, and cultural contexts; internal plurality of tradition; and Western complicity in contributing to the conditions of violence associated with religion. The fight against so-called religious extremism became multipronged. It involves homeland securitizing of already racialized religious minorities and surveillance of mosques, religious leaders, and messaging, as well as cultivating global networks to combat terrorism through establishing effective intelligence collaboration and infusing aid into military and police forces.[9]

The "soft" security discourse seeks to contain "bad" religion, sometimes by engaging the very same local and global actors and dedicated religiocrats trained to identify and harness "good" religion. The paradigms of securitization/containment and neoliberalization/unlocking work in tandem and thus need to be analyzed together.[10]

"Go Back to Mogadishu"

In the Philippines, the counterterrorism discourse was adopted early on to accommodate the U.S. "war on terror" and to enhance the Philippine government's military capacity and legitimacy in its long-standing efforts to diminish the CPP-NPA, Muslim national resurgence, and Islamist organizations with deepening cross-fertilization with Daʻesh, al-Qaeda, and other

---

Millennium: Journal of International Studies 43 (2014): 273–90, https://doi.org/10.1177/0305829814541506.

[8] For a classic critique of this thesis, see Edward W. Said, "The Clash of Ignorance," *The Nation*, October 4, 2001, https://www.thenation.com/article/archive/clash-ignorance/.

[9] There is much discussion in the literature of biopolitics and necropolitics, the control of life and death. Some signposts in this genealogy include Michel Foucault, *The Birth of Biopolitics: Lectures at the Collège de France 1978–79*, ed. Michael Senellart, trans. Graham Burchell (New York: Palgrave Macmillan, 2008); Mbembe, *Necropolitics*. This policing and securitizing of bodies is also always gendered, as has been the case with the coloniality of power. For this point, see María Lugones, "Heterosexualism and the Colonial/Modern Gender System," *Hypatia* 22, no. 1 (2007): 186–209, https://muse.jhu.edu/article/206329.

[10] For an earlier articulation of this point, see Cecelia Lynch, "Religious Communities and Possibilities for 'Justpeace,'" in *The Oxford Handbook of Religion, Conflict, and Peacebuilding*, ed. Atalia Omer, R. Scott Appleby, and David Little (New York: Oxford University Press, 2015), 597–612.

globally circulating movements. To recall, the militarized Countering Violent Extremism (CVE) approach had gained momentum in the Philippines under President Gloria Macapagal-Arroyo (2002–10), who enabled enhanced surveillance and banking restrictions and mandated the creation of the Anti-Terrorism Council to ensure the implementation of the Antiterrorism Act and to oversee the newly created National Counter-Terrorism Action Group.[11] In Kenya,[12] CVE also meant profiling based on apparent religious identity, which reveals the globalization of anti-Muslim racism. This globalization likewise meant other acute human rights abuses and violations, including extrajudicial killings, kidnappings, and executions.[13]

The profiling mechanism represents a direct importation of Euro-American orientalist outlooks. A Somali Kenyan Muslim man I met in Nairobi, who is immersed in U.S.-funded P/CVE work that aims to mobilize communities to resist violent radicalization, finds himself in this line of work precisely because his daily life has involved people telling him "to go back to Mogadishu."[14] His motivation, furthermore, is to disentangle the association of Islam with violence. Working for a U.S.-based organization is not prohibitive for him and others in the P/CVE space. They insist that their relationships within their communities render them trustworthy and dispel concerns about outside influence.

---

[11] Here I refer to the passing by Congress of the Republic Act No. 9372, the Act to Secure the State and Protect Our People from Terrorism or the Human Security Act of 2007, which I discuss in chapter 1. Further legislation made it even harder to launder money (see Act No. 10365, Anti-Money Laundering, http://www.amlc.gov.ph/laws/money-laundering/2015-10-16-02-50-56/republic-act-10365, and Republic Act No. 10168, the Terrorism Financing Prevention and Suppression Act of 2012, http://www.amlc.gov.ph/laws/terrorism-financing/2015-10-16-02-51-58). See also the antiterrorism law of 2020 in the midst of or under the cover of the COVID-19 pandemic. The bill authorizes the imprisonment of perceived terrorists without charge for weeks: Congress of the Philippines, Republic Act 11479, July 22, 2019, chrome-extension://efaidnbmnnnibpcajpcglclefindmkaj/https://www.officialgazette.gov.ph/downloads/2020/06jun/20200703-RA-11479-RRD.pdf. Please refer to a review of critical reactions to the 2020 bill: Julie McCarthy, "Why Rights Groups Worry about the Philippines' New Anti-Terrorism Law," National Public Radio, July 21, 2020, https://www.npr.org/2020/07/21/893019057/why-rights-groups-worry-about-the-philippines-new-anti-terrorism-law.

[12] The United States invested extensively in Kenyan counterterrorism. See, for example, U.S. Department of State, "Country Reports on Terrorism 2019: Kenya," https://www.state.gov/reports/country-reports-on-terrorism-2019/kenya/ (accessed October 13, 2020); Samuel L. Aronson, "United States Aid to Kenya: A Study on Regional Security and Counterterrorism Assistance before and after 9/11," *African Journal of Criminology and Justice Studies* 5, nos. 1–2 (2012): 119–26.

[13] For this discussion, see Kareen Jayes, "Kenya's War of Terror," *TRTWorld*, September 11, 2017, https://www.trtworld.com/opinion/kenya-s-war-of-terror-10333; Human Rights Watch, "Kenya: Events of 2016," https://www.hrw.org/world-report/2017/country-chapters/kenya (accessed October 12, 2020); Rael Ombuor, "Rights Groups Demand End to Kenyan Police Extrajudicial Killings," *VOA News*, February 14, 2020, https://www.voanews.com/africa/rights-groups-demand-end-kenyan-police-extrajudicial-killings; see also chapter 1.

[14] Interview #62, Nairobi, July 2019.

Suppose attribution to religion as a cause of violence describes realities. In this case, these realities reflect a conflict narrative enhanced by the opportunistic assimilation of governments into the global "war on terror" and its abstracting and orientalist tropes. The religious leaders I encountered interpret such realities as an outcome of manipulation by an array of opportunists such as al-Shabaab due to hopelessness, poverty, and religious illiteracy. To the degree that such religious actors participate in P/CVE efforts, they echo the neoliberal logic of responsibilization through microfinancing and enhancing the capacity of the family unit to monitor radicalization into violence and to equip authority figures within the Muslim educational landscape with skills to respond to violent disruptions. For example, a key leader of the Mosque Family Resource Center in Nairobi underscored that his participation in securitization efforts was intended to redress hopelessness. "So many young people in the slums of Nairobi," he told me, "have nothing to lose. They are hopeless and so are easy targets for recruitment, and so we are trying to empower them economically. For many of them, they can be disappeared in Somalia or be recruited by gangsters in the slum. So why not pursue the promise of Somalia and al-Shabaab, especially since they offer them economic incentives?"[15] This link between hopelessness and violence reinforces the rationale behind the integrated approach to peacebuilding/development, which, when articulated through religious idioms, infuses survival with piety and reduces the meaning of hope to this resiliency.

I heard a lot about hopelessness sitting on a plastic chair at a community center in Majengo, one of Nairobi's marginalized districts, where my interviewees are key organizers. The center focuses on peacebuilding and preventing violent extremism (PVE) in the neighborhood. My interlocutors started working in an organized way in 2014. Still, they registered with the government formally only in 2018, prompted by what they identified as corruption plaguing the many organizations clamoring over P/CVE money. This corruption manifests, according to my interlocutors, in failures to reach the affected communities. Well-funded organizations take the money "but cook the books in falsely reporting engagements with the communities... beyond some cosmetic work."[16] And so, one of the founders remarked, he finally registered the Community Peace Network to enhance its capacity to connect

---

[15] Interview with a key interlocutor in the Mosque Family Resource Center in Nairobi, July 2019.
[16] Participant in a focus group with key people involved with the Majengo community center, Nairobi, July 2019.

investment to the affected communities from where al-Shabaab emerged and where, by his account, there is a high level of recruitment due to poverty, lack of education, and crime. As a result, the network has now become partners with the donor community, including USAID. This means that it combats, on the ground, the logic of a religious war that al-Shabaab is actively promoting. The problem, one of my interlocutors retorted, is that there are not too many options in poverty-inflicted neighborhoods besides al-Shabaab. It is a ripe topography for recruitment to prostitution and extremism, including just "regular" crime and gangs. However, police profiling and brutal cracking down on mosques have generated further division and mistrust.[17] "The terrorists are very smart," they told me, because they capitalize on genuine grievances. This is what they tell the young people they target:

> "This is a government of Christians. It doesn't like Muslims. They kill you. There is extrajudicial killing in this neighborhood because you are Muslims and you cannot fight, you are helpless because you don't have weapons, you are not going through training." And they tell them "The only difference between you and a police officer is the AK-47 and the training [to use it]. So, come to this other side, we will train you, and give you AK[s]." So many of the young people because of abuse of power by law enforcement people, most of our young people have been forced, or pushed towards the wall and crossed the red line and joined terrorist organizations.[18]

Identifying a link between a lack of opportunity or hope and recruitment into violent groups explains why P/CVE has denoted a shift away from an exclusive reliance on militarized responses, supplementing them with development/peacebuilding initiatives, such as the Communal Peace Network in Nairobi.[19] The shift from counterterrorism to P/CVE or development-centric

---

[17] Ibid. For an analysis of the detrimental effects of criminalizing youth and poverty in Kenya as part of the CVE approach, see Melissa Finn, Bessma Momani, Michael Opatowski, and Michael Opondo, "Youth Evaluations of CVE/PVE Programming in Kenya in Context," *Journal for Deradicalization* 7 (2016): 164–224, https://journals.sfu.ca/jd/index.php/jd/article/view/62.

[18] Participant in a focus group with key people involved with the Majengo community center, Nairobi, July 2019.

[19] A similar logic applies within the framework of the Filipino landscape that, like Kenya, is another partner of the U.S.-instigated "war on terror(ism)." Its policies likewise exemplify the incorporation of nonmilitary approaches to supplement the militarization and enhancement of the security apparatuses. The Filipino counterradicalization program is called Payapa at Masaganang Pamayanan (PAMANA), or Resilient Communities in Conflict Affected Communities, which is, in effect, a government program focused on conflict resolution and development in conflict-affected regions. See Office of the Presidential Adviser on Peace, Reconciliation and Unity, Payapa at Masaganang Pamayanan (PAMANA), November 14, 2016, https://peace.gov.ph/2016/11/payapa-masagan

containment is by design, global in reach, and backed by a technocratic community of experts (including religiocrats) whose evidence relies on empirical research often conducted in the NGO spheres and through local informants. Tackling despair through "livelihood" supplemented with "first-aid" hermeneutics may reduce immediate eruptions but contributes to the same patterns of depoliticization that I associated with the neoliberal resilience discourse.

Indeed, this exposition shows that CVE, as it morphed into P/CVE, became an official development-focused framework to confront the phenomenon of ideologically/religiously motivated violent movements during the Obama administration (2008–16). Even if it moved beyond counterterrorism, P/CVE remained beholden to security paradigms.[20] The concern with insecurity due to terrorism associated with religion led the international community to care about the marginalized districts of Nairobi and the coast. The recognition that religion, even if not necessarily a sole driver of conflict, is relevant to understanding the manifestation of overt violence also led to recognition that it could be a resource for combating this violence. In any case, the framework is utilitarian, generating opportunities for neoliberal hope through self-sustainability. Within the neoliberal postsecular frame, scholars increasingly highlight the links between religion and security, like the links between peacebuilding and development (and religious freedoms and peace/stability), in terms of sustainability, building on the

---

ang-pamayanan-pamana/. PAMANA also issued Certificate of Ancestral Domain Titles (CADTs) in support of Indigenous land claims, which signals an effort to redress root causes of marginalization of Indigenous communities. The slow pace and at times uncertain implementation of the Bangsomoro Organic Law strained the capacity of civil society actors to contain the potential eruption or reemergence of violence. This reflects the coordination between a longer-term focus on development and the shorter-term deployment of various actors (including religious or self-defined faith-inspired actors) who can facilitate frustration management. Echoing the line of interventions exhibited by PAMANA, according to *A State of National Security Annual Report* (2016), Kenyan youths' high rate of unemployment and sense of marginality make them, as in other contexts, vulnerable to recruitment by al-Shabaab and other organizations. According to a 2013 Pew Research Center survey, a majority of Kenyans supported military operations against al-Shabaab in Somalia and yet expressed frustration with the government's capacity to deal with terrorism, the increased militarization of the counterterrorism approach directed against Kenyan citizens, and its ramifications in terms of curtailing democratic institutions and violating human rights norms. See Brian J. Grim, "Nairobi Westgate Mall Terrorist Attack is Part of Kenya's Sharp Rise in Religiosu Hostitilities" *Pew Research Center* September 24, 2013 https://www.pewresearch.org/fact-tank/2013/09/24/nairobi-mall-terrorist-attack-is-part-of-kenyas-sharp-rise-in-religious-hostilities/.

[20] See Office of the President, "Strategic Implementation Plan for Empowering Local Partners to Prevent Violent Extremism in the United States" (Washington, DC: Office of the President of the United States, 2011). See also Elizabeth Hume and Laura Strawmyer, "The Evolution of Countering Violent Extremism Policy," in *The Ecology of Violent Extremism: Perspectives on Peacebuilding and Human Security*, ed. Lisa Schirch (New York: Rowman & Littlefield, 2018), 189–209, esp. 190.

concept of human security as denoting correlations between structural violence or a failure to meet basic human needs and the eruption of direct forms of violence.[21]

This linking of religion to security has come under scrutiny. Critiques can be roughly classified into two lines of inquiry: critical human rights and secularism studies.[22] Such critical interrogations elucidate why the postsecular interest in religion for securitization and its coalescing with other sites that underscore religion's relevance for sustainability as peace/development demands an analysis of how they interweave with one another and reinforce neoliberal rationality. What the praxis of religion and security obscures is the global diffusion of anti-Muslim racism.[23]

Reductive explanations that attribute blame for violence and "underdevelopment" monocausally to cultures, religions, and traditions myopically conceal material and historical conditions of dispossession, exploitation, and elimination associated with colonial legacies. Such explanatory frames thrive on invented ontological distinctions generated through epistemic violence, which then inform the reliance of paradigms of peace/development on responsibilization. This paternalistic outlook reverberates through the cases I highlighted in the previous chapters. Regardless of the extended Muslim histories of empire, a contextual analysis of radicalization into "Muslim" violence can be interpreted only through a critical engagement with modernity as coloniality, which, for Muslims' experiences, entails their racialization and reified invention as the "other" of Europe. The recognition of links between

---

[21] James K. Wellman and Clark B. Lombardi, *Religion and Human Security*; Jude Howell and Jeremy Lind, *Counterterrorism, Aid and Civil Society* (Basingstoke: Palgrave Macmillan, 2008); Chris Seiple, Dennis R. Hoover, and Pauletta Otis, "Introduction," in *The Routledge Handbook of Religion and Security*, ed. Chris Seiple, Dennis R. Hoover, and Pauletta Otis (New York: Routledge, 2013), 1–8 (2–3).

[22] These critiques of human rights broadly and the discourse of religious freedoms in particular expose the enduring "liberal grammar" of rights' language when employed in international and global contexts. This is the same grammar that underpins the (neo)liberal peace paradigms examined in chapter 2. The genealogical critiques accordingly challenge this liberal legacy's embeddedness in colonialism and intersections with "culture wars" and currents of exclusionary White Christian nationalisms in the West. See, for example, Saba Mahmood, *Religious Difference in a Secular Age: A Minority Report* (Princeton, NJ: Princeton University Press, 2016); Samuel Moyn, *Christian Human Rights* (Philadelphia: University of Pennsylvania Press, 2015).

[23] The orientalist lens was mainstreamed with the publication of Samuel Huntington's thesis on the presumed "clash of civilizations" that interpreted conflict and violence in the post-Soviet era as raging along civilizational (interchangeable for him with "religious") lines that, in his orientalist fashion, were monolithic, ahistorical, essentialized, and irreconcilable. Huntington was not the first to use the concept of a clash of civilizations, but he certainly popularized it, partly due to the timing of his original article and partly due to its platform in the *Journal of Foreign Affairs*. For Edward Said's important critique of Huntington's thesis, see his "The Clash of Ignorance."

human insecurity and the likelihood of religiously mobilized terrorist actions emboldens religion's roles in peacebuilding/development synergies.[24]

Peacebuilding Co-opted

For many policy-oriented actors and analysts embedded in peacebuilding discourse, the multiple convergences of postsecularism, localism, and neoliberalism has entailed a concentrated effort to reframe the language of P/CVE in ways that nevertheless still utilize a securitizing language to denote the links between underlying conditions and susceptibility to violent extremism. This language includes the proliferation of the operative (and psychologizing) concept of "resilience" and the securitizing concept of "early detection" through funded projects increasing livelihood options, strengthening governance, and responsibilizing key demographics along the lines of the synergies of peacebuilding/development articulated in the SDGs. Through this recalibration, peacebuilding spaces have become assimilated into the securitizing discourse. For example, Search for Common Ground is an organization looking at alleviating and reducing violence through dialogue, media, and community-based conflict transformation.[25] It sought

---

[24] UNDP, *Journey to Extremism in Africa*, 2017, http://journey-to-extremism.undp.org/content/downloads/UNDP-JourneyToExtremism-report-2017-english.pdf conveys the links between underdevelopment and violent extremism. The UNDP already examined the connection between development and security, on the one hand, and underdevelopment and insecurity, on the other, in a 2015 report focused on Africa, *Preventing and Responding to Violent Extremism in Africa: A Development Approach*, which intended to work across and with different sectors and institutions, including faith-based, "to augment PVE interventions." *Journey to Extremism*, however, provides robust evidence based on interviews with former recruits from a variety of violent extremist groups in Africa for drivers of violence and tipping points in the recruitment process. The findings stress that peripheral contexts where multidimensional poverty is high and more intense than national averages, compounded with unemployment and underemployment, are severe drivers of violence. The report also underscores that underlying root causes need to be redressed in order for "radicalization" to diminish. The UNDP report, as well as a slew of supporting research and further policy articulation (e.g., Organization for Security and Cooperation in Europe [2012]; White House [2011]; Norwegian Ministry for Foreign Affairs [2015]; Sara Chayes, "Corruption: Violent Extremism, Kleptocracy and the Dangers of Failing Governance," testimony given to the U.S. Senate Foreign Relations Committee, Carnegie Endowment for International Peace, June 30, 2016), therefore recommends rights-based reassessment of security-driven P/CVE approaches, reinvigorating state legitimacy through improved governance performance and accountability consistent with Goal 16 of the Sustainable Development Goals and connecting P/CVE with peacebuilding and sustainable development policy frameworks articulated in the Transforming Our World: Sustainable Development Agenda 2030 (ratified in 2015) as pathways for cultivating a fabric for resistance to recruitment. See also Omer, "The Intersectional Turn."

[25] Search for Common Ground, "What We Do," March 15, 2020. https://www.sfcg.org/what-we-do/.

to reframe the securitizing tone of P/CVE by drawing on its peacebuilding knowledge and experience and by developing the lens of preventing and *transforming* violent extremism (PTVE), the "transforming" intended to signal an effort to move beyond first-aid hermeneutics to tackle systemic issues.[26] Despite its best intentions, the PTVE lens does not depart from the securitizing logic. Drawing on the development/peacebuilding integrated approach, it travels a binary and utilitarian hermeneutical landscape from configuring mechanisms to accessing "good" religion and containing "bad" potentialities.

In particular, what Lisa Schirch frames as an "ecological" approach to violent extremism[27] requires taking seriously not only the question of the utility of religious actors (i.e., how to engage them effectively to promote various peacebuilding/development agendas) but also what they can contribute through intra- and interfaith engagements in delegitimizing violent readings of religious traditions. This shifts the conversation from function to content, while remaining beholden to an instrumentalist discourse (i.e., how intra- and interfaith work can be utilized to reduce violence). It resonates with Mohammed Abu-Nimer's articulation of an integrational peacebuilding approach to P/CVE that challenges the association of violence with religion, singling out Islam as a target of P/CVE designs. Foregrounding the analysis of root causes and human security paradigm, Abu-Nimer's intervention seeks to identify the appropriate roles for intra- and interreligious dialogue and spiritual and faith languages in devising programs for tackling violence.[28] Even if this means paying greater attention to religious actors and meanings, the hermeneutical turn also denotes the instrumentalization (including of Indigenous conflict resolution mechanisms and even the concept of communal policing) for securitizing as much as for development. Religion is ingrained in nonobvious ways in the very racialized "secular" ideology that undergirds the grammar of the "war on terror" and the opportunistic

---

[26] Search for Common Ground, "Transforming Violent Extremism: A Peacebuilder's Guide," 2017, https://www.sfcg.org/wp-content/uploads/2017/04/SFCG-Peacebuilders-Guide-to-Transforming-VE-final.pdf.

[27] See Lisa Schirch, ed., *The Ecology of Violent Extremism: Perspectives on Peacebuilding and Human Security* (New York: Rowman & Littlefield, 2018).

[28] Mohammed Abu-Nimer, "Alternative Approaches to Transforming Violent Extremism: The Case of Islamic Peace and Interreligious Peacebuilding," in *Transformative Approaches to Violent Extremism*, ed. Beatrix Austin and Hans J. Giessman, Berghof Handbook Dialogue Series No. 13 (Berlin: Berghof Foundation, 2018), 2–21; Mohammed Abu-Nimer, "Islamicization, Securitization, and Peacebuilding Approaches to Preventing and Countering Violent Extremism," in *The Ecology of Violent Extremism: Perspectives on Peacebuilding and Human Security*, ed. Lisa Schirch (New York: Rowman & Littlefield, 2018), 218–25.

abstraction it affords to localized conflict narratives such as in Kenya and the Philippines, simplifying complex colonial afterlives and reducing them to another front in a global war against Muslims.

This issue, however, is further complicated by the fact that local actors, such as the imam from the Family Resource Center in Nairobi, interpret their participation in the PTVE space as empowering and spiritually meaningful. Involved in various PTVE-related activities, including the aforementioned microfinancing but also working within the madrasas' infrastructure, the imam celebrated rather than criticized the Kenyan government's policy on family reporting of "warning signs" in relatives. His only worry was that this policy proposal would not be implemented on the ground.[29] A female trainer in PVE work and a religious teacher likewise endorsed strengthening people's capacity to identify warning signs. For her, this was not a mechanism to enhance state surveillance and violence but a form of communal grassroots agency and ownership. She spoke specifically of how women engage her and partake in the challenge of PVE because it is not difficult for them to imagine their children disappearing, physically and metaphorically. She told me, "So now, every mother doesn't want to lose her son, we don't want to lose our children [because] of terrorism. We can imagine that it is our kids who are killed, imagine that we'll never see our children again ever in life."[30] Mothers, families, teachers, and other actors populating the social reproductive sphere become, therefore, first responders in a securitizing discourse that synergizes development/peacebuilding.[31] They are also, of course, long-term participants in building resilience.

Let Me Teach You to Be My Eyes and Ears

The centralization of development in containing violence blurs the distinctions that peacebuilding practitioners paint between peacebuilding- and development-centric approaches to violent extremism. In the case of the Philippines, experts operating within the P/CVE space view strengthening

---

[29] Interview #80, Nairobi, July 2019.
[30] Interview #49, Nairobi, November 2018.
[31] See also an interview conducted by Shannon N. Green with Mossarat Qadeem, founder and director of PAIMAN Alumni Trust in Pakistan (focused on community-based prevention of violent extremism initially in Pakistan, but influenced by lessons learned through similar initiatives elsewhere). She is also a partner of the Women's Alliance for Security Leadership. *On Violent Extremism*, podcast, July 6, 2016.

"grassroots" civil society as integral to consolidating the security strategy. Accordingly, grassroots empowerment, in one case, takes shape through developing Integrated Community Action against Radicalisation and Extremism, which markets itself as a "people-centric template for intervention that enhances the resilience of local communities in the country against the forces of Islamist and Communist-based violent extremism."[32] This means activating and training the Barangay Information Network, the Barangay Peace and Order Council, and the Barangay Peacekeeping Actions Team to function as "the eyes," "the brain," and "the fist," respectively. Interfaith and faith-based groups and platforms are cited as constitutive of such "people-centric" grassroots approaches to P/CVE.[33] This time, "engagement with religious actors" is not only for their devolutionary functionality as local-access civil society actors, but also for their supposed hermeneutical facility or *knowing* of the "real" teachings of their traditions.

The P/CVE approach therefore promotes itself as a nonmilitary method for reducing recruitment to violent movements by redressing "underdevelopment," focusing on youth, and cultivating grassroots capacities to identify warning signs and to teach "value complexity," or "the ability to think in more complex ways about the issues relevant to extremism," as articulated in the design and implementation of a USAID-funded program targeting former al-Shabaab members and "vulnerable" individuals in Kenya.[34] Indeed, in Kenya, as in the Philippines, a consensus has emerged about the need for grassroots ownership in combating and preventing apparently ideological and religiously motivated violence. Such a shift away from an exclusively militarized approach involves an investment in livelihood (which, in previous chapters, I deemed as projects focused on survival rather than any kind of prosperity and flourishing or future alternatives not already constrained by a realist interpretation of the present) and other related development projects.[35] The devolutionary logic means the family unit nested within other

---

[32] Richard F. De Leon, Marlon V. Rufo, and Mark D. M. Pablo, "Preventing and Countering Violent Extremism in the Philippines: Grassroots Empowerment and Development of Homeland Security Framework," *Counter Terrorist Trends and Analyses* 10, no. 8 (2018): 10–17 (13), https://www.jstor.org/stable/26481829.

[33] Ibid. See also Joseph Franco, "Preventing Other 'Marawis' in the Southern Philippines," *Asia & the Pacific Policy Studies* 5, no. 2 (2018): 362–69, https://doi.org/10.1002/app5.227.

[34] Sara Savage, Anjum Khan, and Jose Liht, "Preventing Violent Extremism in Kenya through Value Complexity: Assessment of Being Kenyan Being Muslim," *Journal of Strategic Security* 7, no. 3 (2014): 1–26, http://dx.doi.org/10.5038/1944-0472.7.3.1.

[35] See, for example, Finn et al., "Youth Evaluations of CVE/PVE Programming"; James Khalil and Martine Zeuthen, "A Case Study of Counter Violent Extremism (CVE) Programming: Lessons from OTI's Kenya Transition Initiative," *Stability: International Journal of Security and Development*

caregivers becomes instrumental to the state's ever-expanding securitizing apparatus.

I heard one of the most explicit accounts of the neoliberal securitizing synergies of peace/development from a young Kenyan researcher working for an international faith-inspired actor. The researcher became entangled with producing research for policymakers both in Kenya and "back home" in the European country where the organization has its headquarters. This local religiocrat spoke of the need to identify "alternative dispute-resolution mechanisms" within violence-prone communities, revealing how the "local turn" can also mean co-opting, domesticating, and responsibilizing people and their traditions for the continuous perpetuation of "peace." Why is it in the interest of the government and the international community to find alternative dispute-resolution mechanisms? His response revealed the operative force of reductive culturalist explanations and their burdening of grassroots efforts to transform the adverse effects of people's supposed captivity within their cultures by locating solutions therein: "Because you want the community to understand that the problem comes *from within themselves*. The solution is *within themselves*, home-grown solutions. They should not wait for external sources to come and find resolutions to their problems."[36] While the apparent allusion to elicitive agency ("Don't wait for external interveners") may sound empowering, the culturalist explanatory frame once again glosses over peace's violent legacy. Not only that, but such reductionism continues to perpetuate this violence while also adding that the "solutions" come not only in the form of technical skills but also in the form of "correct" religious hermeneutics. The researcher added the need for "advocacy for women's involvement in peacebuilding, because studies show that women play a huge role as a catalyst. Maybe also actively advocating for women's involvement in peacebuilding and youth involvement." Such advocacy to unlock soft power comes, once again, in the form of "livelihood projects" and identifying mechanisms for devolution and responsibilizing by locating a "relevant set of actors to work with community members to find alternative dispute-resolution mechanisms."[37] Importantly, the "power" part

---

3, no. 1 (2014): 1–12, http://doi.org/10.5334/sta.ee. For a critique of the "gender neutrality" of P/CVE approaches with a specific emphasis on the case of Kenya, see Uyp Salifu and Irene Ndung'u, "Preventing Violent Extremism in Kenya: Why Women's Needs Matter," East Africa Report 13, Institute for Security Studies, May 2017, http://issafrica.s3.amazonaws.com/site/uploads/ear13.pdf.

[36] Interview #37, Nairobi, November 2018.
[37] Ibid.

of "soft power" does not relate to the potentiality of the women and youth to act politically to transform their conditions through moving power from the ground up and intersectional coalition building, but rather to the capacity of other state and global actors to promote *their* agendas through nonmilitary methods. Hence, the concept of local empowerment is delimited to depoliticized problem-solving and resilience. "Grassroots ownership," in the form the researcher articulates, coheres with responsibilization, which tends to burden those already at the margins and reaffirms an argument threaded throughout this book concerning how the focus on women's livelihood and empowerment is also and perhaps pivotally a security rather than a moral issue concerning androcentric normativity.[38]

The P/CVE space in Kenya has become populated by multiple organizations that generate evidence-based research (beholden to a Eurocentric and orientalist episteme) on paths to radicalization into violence as well as measuring the effectiveness of self-described "holistic" programs for preventing and transforming violent extremism. Seeking to control and standardize the P/CVE industry, the Kenyan government passed a bill in 2019 that would require civic organizations to report to the national intelligence agency, thereby risking their capacity to work transformatively.[39] The bill potentially criminalizes failure to report "warning signs" to radicalization into violence. A similar legislative turn unfolded in the Philippines.[40] This legislative turn entails the securitization of parental and communal caregiving and social reproductive roles performed by teachers, parents, and religious and communal leaders, all of whom are positioned at the grassroots level in potentially devolutionary monitoring capacities vis-à-vis the "at-risk" youth.[41] Securitization of communal relationships builds upon responsibilizing patterns that instrumentalize intra- and interreligious engagements and

---

[38] See, for example, World Bank, *Gender Equality and Development*, World Development Report, 2012, https://openknowledge.worldbank.org/handle/10986/4391. The Moroccan *murshidat* and Turkish *vaize* exemplify governmental recognition of the links between women's empowerment and security. See also al-Jazeera, "Morocco gets First Women Preachers," April 28, 2006 https://www.aljazeera.com/news/2006/4/28/morocco-gets-first-women-preachers; Y. Schleifer, "In Turkey, Muslim Women Gain Expanded Religious Authority," *Christian Science Monitor*, April 27, 2005.

[39] This is in line with a broader assault on civil society and NGOs working to expose human rights violations; see Godfrey Musila, "The Spread of Anti-NGO Measures in Africa: Freedoms under Threat," Freedom House, Special Report, 2019, https://freedomhouse.org/report/special-report/2019/spread-anti-ngo-measures-africa-freedoms-under-threat.

[40] See note 11.

[41] For an example of the criminalization of youth and their labeling as "at risk," which underscores the instrumental role of religious actors and institutions in curtailing violence, see Khalil and Zeuthen, "A Case Study of Counter Violent Extremism."

thus denotes, once again, the utility and convergences of the postsecular and local turns.

Such convergences instrumentalize local or Indigenous conflict-resolution mechanisms to facilitate peacebuilding and securitize religious and traditional meanings and the actors who populate spheres of social reproduction. The responsibilization of women through various livelihood projects involved cultivating, in tandem, their economic productivity and their pious grounding in hermeneutically closed accounts of tradition, as I showed in the previous chapter. The economic survival of the women from the Garissa co-op, recall, also contributed to their capacity to read and to convey, across communal boundaries, "warning signs" in youth and spouses as well as to try to contain their potential disruptive violence. Meanwhile, the CICC's clerics also spoke of the need to educate girls to be more productive members of society, equating their worth with economic productivity. Enhancing women's labor productivity and reducing child marriage and other harmful practices—in conjunction with top-level interreligious dialogues of action—is presumed to contribute to overcoming the cycles of poverty. A focus on girls and women helps tackle human insecurity, hopelessness, and thus a propensity to propel recruitment into fatalistic worldviews. Such is the logic of arguments seeking further investment in projects, like the peace clubs and landing and borrowing accompanying incentives in Malindi and in other marginalized communities.[42]

One of the most significant findings emerging from a plethora of studies produced by organizations populating the robust P/CVE space relates to the matter of religious literacy as contributing to resilience against the path of violent extremism. This now refracts my earlier point about *doing religion* as the practice of double closure over *knowing religion* or a critical hermeneutical depth and openness through a security lens. Because of the urgency presented by violence articulated through religious idioms and claims, the more holistic PTVE involves equally urgent efforts to combat manipulated religion with "correct" religion. This inserts hermeneutics as a mechanism for securitizing religion, but also delimits the hermeneutical horizons for reinterpreting religion (and all religions) as peace and generic morality,

---

[42] See also chapter 2 for a discussion of the move away from the language of "harmful cultural practices" as part of investment in theological/scriptural and public health interventions on the part of faith actors. This move entails an emphasis on structural causes of gender-based violence and yet requires "authentic" cultural and religious responses through scriptural proof-texts.

precluding counterpublics.[43] In the short run, these efforts translate into specific programs designed to mitigate and combat immediate issues surrounding the capacity to resist recruitment to violent organizations or the process of de-radicalization. The next chapter will discuss other longer-term mechanisms for cultivating resilience.

Countermessengers on the Battleground

"My passion comes from my desire to protect my religion. I get affected when my religion has been misunderstood and people think they can use my religion to kill."[44] This is the response to my question about what motivates a female teacher I met in Nairobi to teach and train imams, women, youth, and others in their battle against the manipulation of Islam by groups such as al-Shabaab. "I always say," she continued, "God blessed me with knowledge and so I take it as my responsibility to go out there and try to clear some of these misconceptions. I work to explain exactly to the community what jihad really means. I work to explain to the community what the Qur'an teaches us about the position of everybody. That drives me." It drives her even when confronted by sexist rejections of her authority as a woman standing in front of sheikhs and imams in workshops on countermessaging and P/CVE who occasionally exclaim, she tells me, "Why do we need to listen to a woman?"

An interlocutor from a key Muslim organization in Kenya commented on the problem of reintegrating returnees from Somalia who are mostly confronted by the policy of extrajudicial killing. Reintegration, accordingly, needs to combine countermessaging with income-generating possibilities.[45] The prevailing analysis is that, at core, the problems in Kenya are not religious but rather relate to malfunctioning governance. However, because terrorism feeds not only on hunger and marginalization but also on religion, Muslim actors need to deploy credible and recognized religious authorities to combat religious manipulation. The key, he underscored, "is to push back the toxic and violent message by using religious scholars who can guide the

---

[43] The concept of the "counterpublic" refers to the work of feminist political philosopher Nancy Fraser and her challenge to Jürgen Habermas's conceptualization of a "public" inattentive to margins, exclusions, and subaltern narratives. See Nancy Fraser, "Rethinking the Public Sphere: A Contribution to the Critique of Actually Existing Democracy," in *Habermas and the Public Sphere*, ed. Craig J. Calhoun (Cambridge, MA: MIT Press, 1992): 56–80.

[44] Interview, Nairobi, July 2019.

[45] An interview with two key actors in the PVE space, Nairobi, July 2019.

communities in the right direction."⁴⁶ These interlocutors focus on building communal and individual resistance to manipulation that deploys religious warrants through hermeneutical countermessaging.

Religious knowledge or *knowing* thus becomes a tool for resilience. The resiliency discourse, recall, points to two conflicting yet mutually reinforcing sites. The one relates to neoliberalism's burdening of the individual with the responsibility to overcome her cultural trappings and structural obstacles. The other points to the agency of people themselves and their efforts to reinforce the capacity of their children to resist the forces of hopelessness and despair. This agency becomes especially effective through unlocking people's sense of cultural and religious resources, which reinforces a conflation between survival (or adaptability to worsening conditions) and self-realization, often operative at the spiritual experience of conversion from hate to friendship. This is the intrasubjective engine of neoliberal peacebuilding.

My interlocutor from the leadership team of the Kenyan Muslim Youth Alliance told me how, through the organization's work in Nairobi, he realized the low level of religious literacy and understanding across communities, and that this religious illiteracy needed to be combated through cross-learnings of the basics.⁴⁷ A recovery of a sense of self-worth and religiocultural fundamentals becomes a resiliency practice to combat violent radicalization.

Returning to my plastic chair in Majengo and my conversation with the young men who lead efforts to make the international PVE money work meaningfully for their neighborhood, they described the meanings of intergenerational marginalization and "languishing in poverty." They underscored that their ancestors, in effect, were relocated from the coast by the colonial government. They do not own property, and so they are now targeted for eviction due to gentrification and the building of malls, known conduits to launder money—"blood money," as one of my interviewees remarked, "from the war in Somalia, UN refugees, warlords, black market." He added, "Because the land developers are putting up big malls. They're replacing human beings with shoes and secondhand clothes. They are putting [in] stores. And those are some of the things that are pushing people to [terrorism]." My interlocutors continued speaking about the high level of trauma people in their community experience due to bureaucracies, law enforcement, exclusionary practices, and marginalization, as well as the related

---

⁴⁶ Interview, Nairobi, July 2019.
⁴⁷ Interview with a key representative of the Kenyan Muslim Youth Alliance, Nairobi, 2019.

problem of drugs, prostitution, crime, and a lack of infrastructure to reintegrate formerly incarcerated individuals as well as returnees from Somalia and al-Shabaab. Additionally, so-called sympathizers are harassed by the security apparatus, which works against people's ability to open up about their legitimate grievances.

These so-called sympathizers then become targets for constructive work. The main agenda of the Communal Peace Network is to shrink the capacity of al-Shabaab and others to recruit.[48] The complex issue of sympathizers sheds light on the need for communal interventions and to decrease the fertility of the recruitment ground. As another of my interlocutors in Majengo said, "We are trying very hard to shrink the pool for radicalization and breeding of terrorism. And most of these people [the recruiters], because they also have sympathizers helping in recruitment and radicalizing communities, are not happy because it's like a business, yeah. We are reducing their stocks, we are making it more difficult for them to recruit."[49] Therefore, such recruiters call PVE actors "spies" and "government allies" or "informants." They tell them, "You are selling Muslims to the government and the Americans." "But the good thing," another of my interviewees concluded, "is that the community responds to those people. They are telling them, 'You people, you are the bad element in this neighborhood.'" Further, he said, persisting is a "religious obligation. This is the true jihad." When I prompted him for more, he added that the real jihad is to strive to live in harmony and peace; therefore, it is a religious obligation to fight the terrorists: "Terrorism is not Islam."[50]

For the men I interviewed, this is personal, not business. They are not "instruments" of a global securitizing apparatus, though they did enter into a transactional relationship with this infrastructure. They grew up in Majengo and are "tired of burying friends" and "the traumas." Instead, they tell me, "We want to be resources for peace. We want to make a difference; we want to reduce some of these challenges we are experiencing as a community."

---

[48] This issue of the sympathizers came up repeatedly in interviews that I conducted with people who came to the topic of violent radicalization from a peacebuilding background and thus adamantly reject any connotation of their work in such underprivileged and marginalized neighborhoods that may diminish the reasons behind the sympathizers' tacit support. Hence, any opening toward criminalization of sympathetic proclivities is detrimental from a peacebuilding perspective, which aspires to redress the sources of grievances that condition people's sympathy to begin with. See, for example, Dishani Jayaweera with Nirosha De Silva, "Peacebuilding as 'Countering Violent Extremism,'" in *Making Peace with Faith*, ed. Michelle Garred and Mohammed Abu-Nimer (New York: Rowman & Littlefield, 2018), 167–86.

[49] Participant in a focus group, Nairobi, July 2019.

[50] Ibid.

The Communal Peace Network hosts restorative justice programs, including trauma-healing sessions with law enforcement officers who have directly harassed the community. It also organizes well-attended dialogue forums convening families affected by recruitment into terrorism. These forums help by sharing different profiles of recruits (some are educated, some are not; some are extremely poor, some are not). They seek, as a community, to identify the "pull" and "push" factors, as they are referred to in PVE parlance. Intercommunal forums or dialogues in affected marginalized communities involve retrieving "positive stories" from the past or nostalgia of "how we used to coexist. For example, during Christmas and Eid, Muslims and Christians celebrated together. They shared the feast and the food with one another, even during tough times. When young people were gunned down, people did not ask who they were but stood together against extrajudicial killing,"[51] and thus against state violence that also thrives on divisions along religious lines.

One of my interlocutors recalled how his madrasa teacher encouraged Christians and Muslims to study Islam together to live better together. The interreligious forums also involve "sharing quotes" with one another, positive scriptural quotes that promote humanity and hospitality rather than violence and destruction: "If you look at the Bible, there are several verses just like the Qur'an that promotes living good with your neighbor. Also, in the Qur'an, there is a verse that says if you kill one human being it's like you have eliminated the whole humanity. And if you save a human being, it's like you've saved the whole humanity."[52] Through their reading of the Qur'an, the men are also ready to combat hermeneutically those who would produce violent verses from the Qur'an, arguments that distort the Prophet Muhammad's teaching about the *kafir* (or infidel). The practices of terrorists constitute a departure from how Islamic sources which indicate force should be used ethically. The men I spoke with provide the attack on Westgate Mall in Nairobi in 2013 as an example of a violation of Islam because God forbids suicide and killing women and children.

Their methodology of proof-texting then becomes codified in manuals and other modes of securitizing religious hermeneutics on the recruitment battleground in the same way we encountered in the effort of the clerics of the CICC on the coast to redress child marriage through first-aid hermeneutics.

[51] Ibid.
[52] Ibid.

In both instances, as one of my interlocutors from Majengo underscored, "hungry people are recruitable." Framed differently, human insecurity threatens the eruption of global nonstate terrorism (with an understanding that there is ample evidence for state-sponsored terrorizing) and points to the need to connect the project of peace with food and enhance people's capacity to refuse fatalism.

In the case of Kenya, explicit efforts to counter violent narratives involving misinterpretations and manipulations of religious traditions led to this kind of intrafaith first-aid engagement, focusing on countering narratives about Islam. The case of Building Resilience Against Violent Extremism (BRAVE) exemplifies this intrafaith practice.[53] The countering narrative approach operates within a discourse of authenticity that inverts the claims of authenticity articulated by violent interpreters of the tradition to delineate boundaries of inclusion and exclusion. In both instances, the language of truth and authenticity is employed to make claims about what the tradition is in essence and textual prescriptions. The one intends to escalate fatalism; the other, to de-escalate. Indeed, one endorsement of BRAVE's peacebuilding and conflict prevention training manual by the chairman of the Council of Imams and Preachers in Kenya stresses that the manual functions as "an important tool to educate the Muslim *Ummah* on the true meaning of *Jihad*."[54] Another endorsement congratulates the manual for its potential to reduce and eliminate recruitment to violent extremism and as a resource for madrasa teachers, often viewed, as noted, as located at the frontlines of such an effort in counternarrativity, with the overall effect of securitizing schools.

BRAVE is a systematic program specifically designed to address the problem of violent extremism in Kenya through articulating a counternarrative framework to "reclaim, take charge of, and control advantages of information asymmetries away from violent extremist groups."[55] As Mustafa Ali, one of the conveners of BRAVE, explains, the challenge and hope are to delegitimize violent extremist groups also "through the mobilization of former violent extremists, sympathizers and returnees [to] join in the media campaign against al Shabab and their sympathizers." "The returnees," Ali continues, "are expected to puncture the 'mysteries' of al Shabab and other

---

[53] A manual for internal use by BRAVE was shared with me during a visit to Nairobi in November 2018. The manual is authored by Mustafa Yusuf Ali and Othman Mujahid Bwana, *Peace-Building and Conflict Prevention Training Manual and Resource Guide for Building Resilience against Violent Extremism* (Nairobi: Center for Sustainable Conflict Resolution, 2015).
[54] The endorsement cited in ibid., xi, is by Sheikh Abdalla Ateka.
[55] Ibid., xiii.

violent extremist groups, their lies and dis-information the group thrives on in misleading impressionable youth."[56]

In addition, BRAVE focuses on Community Resilience Against Violent Extremism (CRAVE), which operates on interfaith registers primarily with Christian religious leaders and the broader public to "dampen the possible backlash and reactive effect from aggrieved Christian groups targeted mainly by al Shabab."[57] CRAVE redresses the relation between violent appeals to religious traditions and the deterioration of intercommunal ties by training influencers within religious and spiritual communities in P/CVE through interfaith collaboration. The latter intends to highlight alternative peace narratives in religious scriptures[58] to reduce "extremist intra-faith and interfaith intolerance," "misuse of scriptures," and "negative narratives of hatred of the 'other.'"[59] The interfaith framework also intends to strengthen religious institutions' capacity to "counter" violent misinterpretations, to tackle "ineffective public reactions to incidences of violent extremism," and to devise "effective strategies to positively tap into the youth energies" and channel them toward constructive outcomes.[60] Employing Johan Galtung's analysis of the relations among cultural, structural, and direct forms of violence, an interfaith resource guide to deepen community resilience against violent extremism clarifies the roles of religious actors and the interpretive reclaiming of religious traditions as imperative in challenging and transforming the apparent antagonism of values as they sanction underpinning structural forms of violence. Religious actors, institutions, and meanings therefore become key to tackling "root causes" that move beyond direct manifestations of violence.[61]

[56] Ibid., xiv.
[57] Ibid., xiii. CRAVE is an interfaith tool with a broader Eastern Africa outlook. According to Mustafa Ali, it "aims to enhance the ability of communities to prevent, address and counter violent extremism." Mustafa Ali, "Introduction," in Goldin Institute, the Global Network of Religions for Children and Center for Sustainable Conflict Resolution, *Community Resilience against Violent Extremism: An Interfaith Resource Guide for Preventing and Countering Violent Extremism* (Nairobi: Center for Sustainable Conflict Resolution, 2016) (henceforth *CRAVE*), xi.
[58] For example, the interfaith resource guide *CRAVE* lists the rescue of a Phoenician widow by Prophet Elijah in 1 Kings 17:7–24; the requirement to welcome the stranger (1 Kings 8:41–43); respect for the religious practices of Naaman (2 Kings 5:1–27); the Samaritan woman (John 4:1–42); and Jesus and the Syrophoenician woman (Mark 7:24–30), as well as an assortment of Quranic motifs: the sanctity of all human life (Q 5:32); respect for and safeguarding of property and environment/earth (Q 28:77); prohibition of oppression and promoting compassion and kind relations with all (e.g., Q 42:42, 60:8); ethical conduct in war (Q 5:8); and peaceful coexistence with non-Muslims (Q 2:85, 42:40–43). See *CRAVE*, 35–39.
[59] *CRAVE*, 18.
[60] Ibid., 18–19.
[61] Ibid., 45–59. See also Galtung, "Cultural Violence" *Journal of Peace Research* 17, no. 3 (1990): 291–305. https://doi.org/10.1177/0022343390027003005.

Indeed, the resource guide underscores religion's "moral capital and motivating force in peacebuilding," viewing "faith communities" as possessing "immense potential, structures, social capital, strategic presence, moral authority and spiritual tools that can be used to prevent and counter radicalization into violent extremism."[62] Therefore, CRAVE's emphasis on interfaith mechanisms illuminates the intersection of security and peacebuilding, contra claims of peacebuilding practitioners who seek to distance themselves from security frames associated with PVE. The focus on root causes means a focus on structural violence as an explanation for social agitations, but the deployment of religion as an asset operates through intra- and interfaith mechanisms as well as community development projects to build up resilience rather than to disrupt entrenched violence. Faith actors thus become a form of moral, social, and cultural capital to mobilize, thereby securitizing them and their religious hermeneutics. This maneuver works in concert with the people-to-people bridging mechanisms that likewise depend on hermeneutically flattening and closing the horizons of religious and cultural resources, indexing them to a peace and harmony message.

While the PTVE opens a space for religious hermeneutics and for naming structural and cultural forms of violence, this space is constrained by the demands to reclaim authentic accounts of religious traditions as capturing a counternarrative of peace. For example, CRAVE's interfaith resource guide stresses that "all religions promote universal values of peace, harmony, love, and selflessness,"[63] and it is these resources that an interfaith framework can help unlock and mobilize. Hence, the hermeneutical space remains narrow and stricken by a dualistic assumption regarding bad/good religion, the religion that sanctions violence and the religion that can be mobilized to counter violence and promote prosocial bridging activities essential for resiliency. Both varieties constitute forms of hermeneutically closed religiosity, whose imagining of peace is determined by the constraints of the present and which is thus subordinated to realist logic. Positing religious meanings and actors and institutions as "assets" and "capital" to be mobilized exposes the neoliberal rationality underpinning the securitizing of religion and its reshaping into a multisectoral resilience discourse.

This instrumentalization of intra- and interreligious practices drove away one of my Muslim interlocutors because, in her view, such practices failed

---

[62] Ibid., 57.
[63] Ibid., 67.

to comprehend the depth of social transformation as a holistic process that cannot focus only on tackling one variable while holding everything else constant. In other words, securitizing youth, women, and teachers as a "bottom-up strategy,"[64] without confronting corruption and other contributing (or "push") factors, cannot be labeled "transformative," no matter what constructive, positive, and peaceful narratives about religion are deployed.[65] Another Muslim woman immersed in the peacebuilding field underscored the need for Muslims to engage in an intratradition examination that opens up to critical reflection and change in light of science and shifting historical contexts. In particular, she agonized over her feelings of marginalization within the Muslim community and her dismissal as not "Muslim enough" for wearing colorful rather than black clothes and head coverings and for seeking higher education and professional independence. A long-term participant in interreligious dialogue, she refused to lend legitimacy through her tokenization to intra- and interreligious engagements that are subordinated to the PVE logic and thereby preclude opening up hermeneutical spaces.[66] A Muslim male interlocutor who became involved in interreligious dialogue in his postmilitary career, on the other hand, stressed the centrality of this praxis of interreligious dialogue as a change engine for "finding the humanity of the other," to "empower people to understand they are their own solution," and thus to deepen resilience to radicalization into violence and the possibility for sustainable peace.[67] For him, the mere fact of women's participation in interreligious dialogues is sufficient. For others, mere inclusion without what my female interlocutor referred to as a "serious intrafaith conversation" about patriarchal normativity means participating in harmful erasures. The realist urgency, though, propels one away from critical hermeneutical horizons.

Indeed, the main foci of mobilization revolve around an intrafaith hermeneutical challenge that is both utilitarian and binary. The expectation was for BRAVE's mainstream media broadcasting, social media platforms,

---

[64] For the use of the phrase, see Shannon N. Green, podcast interview with Edit Schlaffer, founder and executive director of Women without Borders and Sisters against Violent Extremism, which trained thousands of women in identifying warning signs. The organization focuses on strengthening families as a mechanism of sustainability to prevent extremism. This reflects the overall identification of women as the missing link in the international security architecture. See "Voice for Sisters against Violent Extremism," in *On Violent Extremism,* podcast, CSIS Commission on Countering Violent Extremism, August 12, 2016.
[65] Interview, Nairobi, July 2019.
[66] Ibid.
[67] Ibid.

and other aspects of its programming to reach approximately twenty million Kenyans.[68] Mustafa Yusuf Ali and curriculum and communication specialists learned in religious education and Islamic law[69] mobilized and trained hundreds of educators. This team and their focus on mobilizing religious leaders and clerics to deploy religious knowledge for de-radicalization points to the importance of emic religious literacy in PVE. The target audience of the BRAVE manual includes anyone who inhabits the various spheres of education and social reproduction, hence opening the door to the aforementioned securitizing of parental and communal relationships.[70] This includes imams, sheikhs, *'alim* (teachers), madrasa teachers, youth leaders, and women (especially mothers) who can effectively participate in resilience against violent extremism and identify people vulnerable to violent extremism and whose social location positions them as potential interveners in preventing radicalization into violent extremism.

This devolution of the state's security infrastructure, once again, illuminates the operative force of neoliberal responsibilization for pacification logic through "cultivating" countermessaging skills (*doing* religion *qua knowing*) and enhancing the willingness and capacity of caregivers, educators, and others to identify and report "warning signs." This literally signals the expansion of the state's security apparatus into people's living rooms under the umbrella of the emergency discourse of hermeneutical and interpersonal first responders. Challenging information asymmetry in favor of violent extremism involves learning to deploy media effectively for positive and counternarrative work. One focus is on devising "strategies to positively tap into the youth energies, and direct them into constructive and non-violent actions."[71]

Teachers, women, *'alim*, imams, and others in regular contact with youth are sensitized to identify early warning signs and to intervene.[72] Indeed, one of the designers of BRAVE explicitly stressed the "targeting" of imams and religious teachers in madrasas as a critical mechanism for combating the perversion of Islamic concepts and Quranic verses. He spoke of the need to capacitate these religious leaders not only with tools to combat misinterpretations but also with a different story to offer instead of al-Shabaab's apocalyptic

---

[68] Ali and Bwana, *Peace-Building and Conflict Prevention Training Manual*, xiii.
[69] The list of contributors is distinguished and includes Dr. Othman Mujahid Bwana, Shaikh Ramadhan Aula Juma, and Sheikh Ibrahim Asmani Lethome.
[70] Ali and Bwana, *Peace-Building and Conflict Prevention Training Manual*, xiii.
[71] Ibid., 19.
[72] Ibid., 57–64.

and Manichaean scenarios—an effort that, as noted, requires more than just telling a story but also working in tandem across multiple fields of action to combat fatalism. Such coordination is difficult, however, given the enduring patterns of corruption and weak governance.

One story that exemplifies the need for coordination is of an imam in Garissa who spoke up against al-Shabaab in a sermon and then, as he was leaving the mosque, received a call from Mogadishu informing him of al-Shabaab's discontent with his approach. This indicates that al-Shabaab activists were in the mosque that day and maintained open lines of communication in Somalia. The imam was threatened in his home at 2:00 a.m. He immediately called the police, but they did not respond until 9:00. The imam survived. However, the delay reveals the persistent corruption of the security sector (often bribed and on al-Shabaab's payroll) and the need to support religious leaders who become mobilized to challenge, from their place of expertise in Islam and their communal authority, the invocation of violence in the name of religion. Often, however, the teachers and religious leaders trained in counternarrativity (*doing* religion *qua knowing*) are not necessarily learned in Islam beyond primary madrasa education, and their leadership status is acquired more by their context and charisma than through religious knowledge.

It is therefore doubly urgent to reach these "influencers" (in the neoliberal jargon) to sensitize and capacitate them as hermeneutical warriors and first responders. Both verbs ("sensitize" and "capacitate") likewise denote the neoliberal rationality informing the postsecular turn to "unlock" good religion through training, this time in religious knowledge itself. Reaching key demographics has therefore become a focus for securitizing religion, marked as Islam. The shift from "religious leaders" to "influencers" signals the increased irrelevance of actual layered religious literacy or knowing. This is characteristic of the religion and peace/development industry. The shift exposes the operative logic whereby everybody is replaceable with everybody else who attended a particular "professional development" program, adding, in this case, religion to an already populated—but now also religiously literate—toolkit. The countermessaging campaigns waged by influencers, actors I refer to as "replaceable" (Twitter) prophets, also need to be broken down into tweetable and quickly digestible messages to be an effective tool in the battleground of religious messaging. Religious virtuosity under these reconfigured development/peacebuilding foci does not require facility with religious traditions. It only needs actors to be effective in ways measured by security and development indicators. Hence, the conventional understanding of the prophet *qua* peacebuilder as uniquely virtuous and knowledgeable of tradition has been replaced with someone who simply has the right training. Such training is usually provided by organizations associated with the centers of global political and economic power and involves neoliberal concepts such as "benchmarking" and "lessons learned," which I interrogate in chapter 2. Like all positions in modern bureaucracies, even the prophets are replaceable.

BRAVE's media campaign and its focus on messaging also illustrates the countermessage as a brand, easily communicable in witty YouTube videos such as "My Jihad," which was launched by BRAVE to reclaim the spiritual meanings of jihad with a reductive outcome, reframing jihad as a form of self-actualization and professional vocation.[73] It reduced "good" jihad to an individual's orienting aspiration (something between a career and a vocation) and her motivation and perseverance in accomplishing it, whether it is about perfecting homemaking or practicing medicine. A similar concept BRAVE sought to reclaim, through high-level commercial production featured on Kenyan national television, is that of the phrase or cry *allahu akbar*, "God is great," which they found out Christians associate with death because of various Da'esh-type videos, populating the imagination with images of beheadings accompanying this cry. Saturating airwaves with this reclaiming/rebranding of Islam serves to de-escalate the potential for intercommunal violence that groups such as al-Shabaab seek to ignite by developing a strategy targeting Christians. Mediating the complexities of reclaimed Muslim values and principles through TV production packages them reductively as "good" and as ethically consistent with democratic norms. This is not to diminish the emic religious literacy of the leaders behind the media campaign, but rather to underscore the neoliberal frame within which the popular association of religious tradition with violence is countered with sound bites and rebranding.

While an apparent departure from mere functionality to content signals an interest in meanings and hermeneutics, religious or cultural traditions are reduced to a "message" that can be promulgated and diffused by religious authorities and other formal and informal transmission belts (such as religious leaders, teachers, and mothers), as well as a new class of messengers,

---

[73] See *The Brave Focus: A Newsletter of the Brave Movement* (July 2018), 6, https://cscrcenter.org/wp-content/uploads/2019/04/Special-Edition-BRAVE-Newsletter-1.pdf.

youth ambassadors, or influencers (the Twitter prophets) who operate on social media and other platforms. Notably, according to one of my interviewees, the turn to the religious literacy of social influencers should also go in a different direction, directed not only at the most vulnerable but also at those whose very privilege becomes a vehicle to transmit belligerence, conspiracy theories, and falsehoods.[74] The fact that highly educated people espouse conspiratorial outlooks and ignorant prejudice highlights the importance of the university setting, as one interlocutor noted in a focus group I conducted in Davao. In a Nairobi university, the curriculum around PVE also shaped up to create both the conditions for intergroup interactions and substantial cross-learning. One pivotal educator affirmed this basic understanding of the mechanism of change: "People who are not exposed to other religions tend to have very strong prejudice, especially in Kenya, where we experience terrorist attacks from Somalia from al-Shabaab."[75] Religious, historical, and cultural illiteracy, in other words, can be promoted by a whole spectrum of actors.

The focus on youth vulnerability and suffering generates appeals to locate the particular ability of "religious actors" to intervene constructively by accessing spiritual and religious traditions' generic moral responsibility and infrastructural capacity to reach communities. The BRAVE manual, for example, highlights Quranic verses such as "O mankind! We have created you from a single (pair) of a male and female, and made you into nations and tribes, that ye may know each other (not that ye may despise each other)" (Surah 49:13). The focus on rapid media response through out-of-context surahs necessarily reduces the complexities of religious traditions to sound bites that, when triangulated with some livelihood incentives, purportedly enhance people's resilience to radicalization. Indeed, the urgencies of the moment and its *realpolitik* confines dictate a focus not only on generic religiosity/morality but also on further "democratizing" or horizontalizing religious authority by identifying and investing in a whole spectrum of

---

[74] Specifically, my interviewee (interview #61, Nairobi, November 2018) spoke of a relatively small but powerful group of educated Christian professionals in Kenya who very aggressively perpetuate a conspiracy theory about a Muslim plan to control Kenya. This young man, an emerging scholar and religious practitioner of interfaith work, said, with alarm, "You do not get medical doctors and lawyers thinking this way and take it lightly.... They are professionals.... They have the time to read and gather information; the data they are gathering is data to prove their case. It is not information they are gathering to balance off the discussion. It is evidence they are gathering to say: Look here. To hear someone say, looking at the Qur'an, and actually to say that Islam is no religion at all, that's the language they are using."

[75] Interview #43, Nairobi, November 2018.

"social influencers" rather than solely religious leaders or authorities. This reveals how the securitization of religion as a soft power concerns itself with strategizing and galvanizing the influence, or the *doing*, of bottom-up players rather than with their *knowing*, or learned engagement, with religious and cultural traditions.

The commitment to script a counternarrative demands intrafaith contestations, as does BRAVE. Indeed, it is not controversial and unsettling to facilitate a first-aid hermeneutical contestation of the deployment of tradition in the service of overt violence, such as the targeted killing of Christians and those Muslims deem "inauthentic," by retrieving peaceful and violence-averse Quranic commands and by reclaiming jihad and *allahu akbar* from their murderous deployment. Such hermeneutical counternarrativity is generic, which means "male-centric" in terms of its theological register, even if those organizations and projects in the PTVE spheres very intentionally involve women as empowered agents in the mechanisms of surveilling, identifying, and reporting warning signs of radicalization. Adding a critical gender lens to this volatile complexity appears both luxurious and explosive, which is often how gender analysis and hermeneutics end up excluded from "real" world engagement with religion.[76]

Hence, the PTVE's hermeneutical turn subordinates the interpretive space to the demands of geopolitics and to realist social mapping, thus reinforcing not only neoliberal rationality but also heteropatriarchal normativity. This dearth of critical hermeneutical horizons shrinks the interpretive opening and plurivocality of religious and cultural traditions, embedded and embodied in historical contexts and elastically debated over centuries rather than contained ahistorically and exclusively in texts or tweets. Once again, the irony presents itself. More religious literacy on the part of epistemic and donor communities does not necessarily mean a literate facility with religion and cultural traditions of the "soldiers" or "influencers" on the battlefields of counternarrativity. Religious literacy, accordingly, means facility on the part of policy and development practitioners to leverage soft power or bottom-up securitizing strategies more effectively, entrenching the top-down neoliberal status quo with its global inequities and structural injustice.

---

[76] Atalia Omer, "Religion, Gender, Justice, Violence, and Peace," in *The Routledge Handbook of Religions, Gender and Society*, ed. Caroline Starkey and Emma Tomalin (London: Routledge, 2022), 51–64. https://doi.org/10.4324/9780429466953.

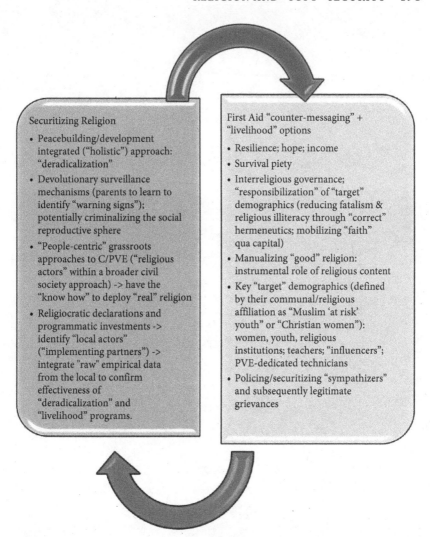

Figure 5.1 First-aid securitizing religion through peacebuilding/development.

To sum up, I have shown in this chapter that P/CVE and PTVE cohabit in one discursive and epistemic space with the synergetic conceptualization of peacebuilding/development (see Figure 5.1). I continue to examine this point in the next chapter by interlinking first-aid hermeneutics with the offline practices of immersion, standardization of religious education, and intrapersonal formation, which all contribute to securitizing religion through neoliberal assemblages.

6
Religious Resiliency and "Soft" Security

Sheikh Google

This chapter shows that the securitizing of religion is not only a function of urgent countermessaging. It also depends on the long-term cultivation of meaningful intercommunal bonds through the mechanism of what I analyzed as interreligious governance and the practices of peace as "getting along." Here, knowledge of the other's tradition is attained through experiential *being* together in various immersive and other activities and trickle-down performativity of intercommunal peace. Religious literacy, or *knowing*, accordingly, is a function of experiential programmatic activities, or *being* together. The underlying theory of change is that knowledge of one another (which also entails an intrasubjective and intrafaith/communal process), plus economic incentives over time, can reduce fatalism and the potential for violence. This security apparatus foregrounds children and youth as target demographics for investment and as a relatively obvious site (like poverty) for "moral" interventions or mobilizations of religious actors.

The focus on "generic" children animates top-level networks of religious leaders and religiocrats interested in harnessing good religion as a moral source for universal ethical rhetoric regarding how to treat the human *qua* human. An emphasis on apparently uncontroversial commitment to the rights of the child signals a convergence rather than a departure of the religious from secular norms and rights and posits religious actors as especially useful mouthpieces affirming ethical commitments.[1] The concern with children, however, is a security rather than a normative matter. The links between instability, underdevelopment, and recruitment of youth—framed as an "at-risk" demographic—to violent organizations inform the

---

[1] For critiques of the underlying assumptions of the UN Convention on the Rights of the Child, see, for example, Priscilla Alderson, "UN Convention on the Rights of the Child: Some Common Criticisms and Suggested Responses," *Child Abuse Review* 9, no. 6 (2000): 439–43. See also Kristina Anne Bentley, "Can There Be Any Universal Children's Rights?," *International Journal of Human Rights* 9, no. 1 (2005): 107–23.

consolidation of broader, child-centric, interfaith efforts that are focused on holistic approaches to reducing violence. Underpinning interfaith partnerships is the apparently self-evident and universal commitment to the health, education, and security of the child.[2] They underscore that the responsibility to care for children is a common ground that assists in building partnerships for interreligious dialogue across multiple divides. They further highlight that the insecurity of children and youth (usually including the teenage years to the late twenties) contributes to their recruitment by violent groups. These violent groups purportedly manipulate religious traditions. This manipulation is possible only due to children's religious illiteracy. To combat religious illiteracy requires reclaiming authority from what many of my interlocutors called "Sheikh Google" (i.e., internet-searchable and potentially false and simplistic religious knowledge). This is achieved partly through the countermessaging of what I have called the "Twitter prophets." They are tasked with promoting a peace-branded version of religion, which often accompanies the promotion of interreligious dialoguing and bridging activities as sacred and spiritual formation practices.

For example, the Mindanao office of Equal Access International (EAI) conducts tech camps targeting youth (as well as Datus, or tribal leaders, teachers, civil society actors, etc.) as "social influencers." The camps equip them with the capacity to intervene in combating violence online through positive messaging, social media, and radio shows, and offline through relationship building. Headquartered in Washington, DC, EAI established a Mindanao office in 2018; it is led by people well versed in the peacebuilding and civil society landscape of the Philippines.[3] The EAI approach grounds itself in "the utilization of social behavior change through communication," which, key facilitators conveyed to me, constitutes "the missing link," moving beyond seminars, workshops, and dialogues.[4] This is especially urgent, my interviewees underscored, as a mechanism to enhance the peaceful

---

[2] See Arigatou International, "What We Do," https://arigatouinternational.org/our-work/promoting-interfaith-and-intercultural-collaboration/ (accessed September 28, 2020). Arigatou has been central in multiple international faith-based forums that have affirmed the commitment and special responsibility of faith actors to end a scandalous reality in which, in 2018, for example, twenty-eight million children were vulnerable and displaced. I analyze this faith-based activism inAtalia Omer, "Domestic Religion: Why Interreligious Dialogue of Action for the Reduction of Child Marriage in the Coast of Kenya Conserves Rather Than Disrupts Power," in *A Requiem for Peacebuilding?*, ed. Tom Sauer, Jorg Kustermans, and Barbara Segaert, Rethinking Peace and Conflict Studies (London: Palgrave Macmillan, 2021), 59–94.

[3] See also chapter 3.

[4] Interview with key interlocutors from Equal Access International, Cagayan de Oro (in Mindanao), July 2019.

consolidation of the BARMM and the implementation of the BOL.[5] The period of transition to implementing the BOL presses the urgency of tackling online in addition to offline the enduring issues of colonialism, historical injustices/grievances, and interreligious perspectives. Tackling these issues exposes both Marcos's era and the internal colonization of Mindanao as a critical disruption of Mindanaoan cohabitation and the region's more organic links to Malaysia and Indonesia. The peace framing in terms of the tri-people harmony formula, or what EAI-Mindanao prefers to call "One Mindanao,"[6] is thus a myopic exercise, caging historical memories in a harmony script. The effectiveness of this process also centrally depends on the narrative of IPs and their land and cultural reclamation.

Offline/Online Youths Renarrating Peace

The Indigenous Peoples Rights Act,[7] designed to reclaim ancestral domains and to signal the government's reckoning with past injustices, proved to be not only dependent on a high level of legal literacy not available to many IPs but also ineffective in reversing the long-term effects of the Regalian Doctrine and the internal Christian colonization processes in Mindanao.[8] The perceptions and experiences of historical injustice, as well as the victimization stories of Christian settlers in Mindanao for holding rights to lands and yet being subjected to harassment, violence, and war with Moro Muslims, are all carried by youth into the EAI's workshops. Therein, they are asked to narrate the stories of their identity groups to one another and to reflect on their own self-perceptions regarding who they are and what traits

---

[5] See chapter 1 for an overview of these critical developments in the chronology of the Moro struggle in Mindanao.
[6] See chapter 1 for an overview of this history.
[7] Philippines Indigenous Peoples Rights Act of 1997, Republic Act No. 8371, An Act to Recognize, Protect, and Promote the Rights of Indigenous Cultural Communities/IPs, Creating a National Commission on Indigenous Peoples, Establishing Implementing Mechanisms, Appropriating Funds Therefor, and for Other Purposes (enacted October 29, 1997). For a contextualizing engagement with the Philippines's recognition of Indigenous peoples' rights, see Cathal Doyle, "The Philippines Indigenous Peoples Rights Act and ILO Convention 169 on Tribal and Indigenous Peoples: Exploring Synergies for Rights Realisation," *International Journal of Human Rights* 24, nos. 2–3 (2020): 170–90, https://doi.org/10.1080/13642987.2019.1679120. See also Renée V. Hagen and Tessa Minter, "Displacement in the Name of Development: How Indigenous Rights Legislation Fails to Protect Philippine Hunter-Gatherers," *Society & Natural Resources* 33, no. 1 (2020): 65–82; Roland G. Simbulan, "Indigenous Communities' Resistance to Corporate Mining in the Philippines," *Peace Review* 28, no. 1 (2016): 29–37, https://doi.org/10.1080/08941920.2019.1677970.
[8] For these processes of dispossession and displacement, see chapter 1.

characterize the "others" in the tripartite Mindanaoan mosaic. This exercise generates a picture that shows there are good and bad elements in each community, a long history of mutual stereotyping, as well as acts of historical erasures of Muslim and IP collaborations and family ties.[9]

The levels of misinformation, patterns of historical erasure, and formulaic neoliberal shaping of intercommunal engagement all facilitate the potential manipulation of narratives and memories of historical injustices, once again exposing the indispensability of narrating (or renarrating) as a site of peacebuilding. As in my discussion of BRAVE in the previous chapter, countering violent interpretations of textual sources means capacitating, during the tech/text camps, "social influencers" to cite in full those verses that groups such as Daʿesh otherwise selectively retrieve and weaponize or to contextualize them within the broader scripture. The assumption is that such hermeneutical skills will reclaim the authentic peaceful meaning of religious traditions. I have already shown how other local access religious actors, such as Pakigdait and UNYPAD, are deployed to ensure resiliency through frustration management in the transition to the BARMM. Their capacity to operate as first-aid responders depends upon their long-term offline resiliency building and their institutional, organizational, and personal credibility, presence, and networking. Their Sisyphean presence enables them to function occasionally as first-aid hermeneutical responders.

My interviewees from EAI underscored, "Where in the world would you see any religion that would tolerate violence?"[10] My answer, of course, is "Everywhere," but they would resist such a response. At the same time reclaiming "good" religion, pursuing a positive "One Mindanao" narrative means revalorizing plurality without historical erasure but through acceptance of the colonial afterlives: "We are all living in one land now, so we must value and respect coexistence. Whoever we are and from whatever tribe and religion, we must live together. We have to live together and protect the land. Protect the land not just from foreign invaders or foreign visitors, but protect its integrity in terms of diversity. We have to value the sense of diversity and find unity in it. This notion of unity in diversity is what we mean in articulating 'Our Mindanao' as a counter- or alternative narrative."[11] The

---

[9] Interview #81 with key interlocutors, Mindanao, June 2019.

[10] Interview with key resource persons associated with EAI in Mindanao, July 2019.

[11] Ibid. Indeed, the erasure of Mindanao history of intercultural and interreligious exchanges becomes another front in the recovery process of counternarrativity. Further, the tri-people narrative of harmony itself invisibilizes diversity among groups (e.g., one Datu can represent only that Datu's specific tribal ways) and the "positive" countermessaging of EAI accordingly emphasizes

point, another of my interlocutors from EAI-Mindanao continued, is that "we all live here at the present moment. Some among us are settlers. Others are not. Take, for example, my wife and me: if I am a native, then perhaps my wife is a settler, right? So, I cannot just easily unpack myself or the identity of my children or disassociate myself [from] the settlers because we are so intertwined."[12] What he expresses here is the utility of a harmony discourse that, rather than abstracting religion as a technology of peace, paves avenues from people's empirical entwining with one another as a matter of course. This intertwining, however, is precisely what the technology of religion and peace erodes through its mechanisms of double closures of religious and communal hermeneutics. I unpack this point further below.

The messaging hubs that EAI-Mindanao underwrites aim to elicit and disseminate positive narratives online, coherent with the "Our Mindanao" frame and designed to shift behavioral norms through social influencers. Underlining this approach is an aspiration for long-term resiliency because of a recognition that many people are entangled, through close family ties, with those whom violent interpretations and radicalization into violence may sway; their transformation needs to unfold through closely interlinked online and offline social networks.

EAI operates in similar ways in Kenya. Targeting mainly Somali youth, who are likewise the target of al-Shabaab's mobile radio and online campaigns, involves developing their media literacy, as in the case of Mindanao, through tech camps, alternative messaging workshops, community reporter training, and peace promotion fellowships. All of these activities teach the youth also to tell their positive transformative stories in pictures and to disseminate them broadly through various social media platforms.[13] The idea is not only to resist bad and manipulative messaging but also to be able to deploy good and constructive messaging as an alternative.

Called Somali Voices–Kenya, this program (launched in December 2018 for an initial sixteen months) explicitly aims to enhance the resilience of youth (fifteen to thirty-five years old) from the Somali-speaking Kenyan communities. The explicit intention is to identify and train "credible, influential voices," which will consolidate "an ecosystem of young leaders

---

"One Mindanao" rather than a tri-people formula, even if IPs are represented generically in the peace framing as IPs.

[12] Interview, Cagayan de Oro, July 2019.
[13] Focus group with key actors within EAI, Nairobi, July 2019.

within religious, cultural, civil society, media, and business communities that have the tools, networks, and information to create powerful alternative narratives and pathways for young people and vulnerable communities."[14] The targeted social influencers, as is evident by now, include "youth, elders, religious leaders, and women leaders," all deemed strategically necessary for ensuring communal resilience to radicalization into violence through "innovative messaging and community mobilization campaigns." Indeed, this is responsibilization par excellence. As in Mindanao, the mechanisms for positive messaging include participatory media (radio, social media, and customized apps) as well as "a regional transmedia network and alternative messaging hub capable of effectively rivaling in size and scope cross-border al-Shabaab communications and overwhelming their influence through powerful meta-narratives that support peace, inclusion, and youth empowerment."[15] Appeals to religion within this context of prophetic lite, hermeneutical first-aid are palpable, generic, and tweetable.

In addition to Somali Voices–Kenya, Somali Voices–Next Generation (also launched in December 2018) focuses on East Africa, specifically on the radicalization into violence occurring in Djibouti, Ethiopia, Somalia, and Kenya. This program targets children ages three to eight and their caregivers and teachers to enhance adults' and children's capacity to articulate and draw upon alternative narratives. This resilience-building mechanism involves a partnership with and content development for Sesame Workshop (*Sesame Street* global outreach, often funded by USAID), where the first fifteen minutes of the program are aimed at children, with a focus on themes such as tolerance, hygiene, and peaceful problem-solving.[16] The next fifteen minutes are dedicated to caregivers, educating them on various issues, from bullying to media exposure of their children to violent ideologies. Somali Voices–Kenya and –Next Generation, therefore, convey the diffusion of media as a mechanism for counternarrativity and cultivating resilience as well as

---

[14] EAI, "Project Overview: Somali Voices–Kenya," n.d., an internal document EAI shared with me.
[15] Ibid.
[16] *Sesame Street* has a long history of trying to promote globally and in conflict zones positive messages regarding common humanity and tolerance. For an example of a critical engagement with the Sesame Workshop and the broader field of peace communication, see Yael Warshel, *Experiencing the Israeli-Palestinian Conflict: Children, Peace Communication and Socialization* (Cambridge: Cambridge University Press, 2021). For analyses of *Sesame Street*'s global work and promotion of tolerance, pluralism, and gender equality through the targeting of children, see Charlotte E. Cole and June H. Lee, *The Sesame Effect: The Global Impact of the Longest Street in the World* (New York: Routledge, 2016). For a critical engagement with this global outreach, see also Naomi A. Moland, *Can Big Bird Fight Terrorism? Children's Television and Globalized Multicultural Education* (Oxford: Oxford University Press, 2019).

the securitizing of parents, caregivers, teachers, religious leaders, scriptural meanings, and women in their social reproductive capacities. The familiar focus on self-transformation and responsibilization as engines of social change persists, even if the tools extend to online and other media outlets.

To reiterate, critics argue that counternarrativity denies the validity of an underlying "sympathy" spanning a whole spectrum of people who identify with the underpinning and legitimate frustration of which violent groups such as al-Shabaab may be symptomatic.[17] This is, however, not the case for people entrenched in this work. One sheikh associated with counternarrativity in Kenya shared with me that he fully understands the grievances that al-Shabaab and comparable organizations exploit in their recruitment process, underscoring especially the problems of corruption and weak governance. These problems amplify the enduring effects of historical injustices, he told me. However, he continued emphatically, "I depart from their position on the question of the use of violence. This is not Islamic and they are not Muslims but terrorists."[18] While transformation can result only from redressing the underlying structures that inform legitimate grievances, this same sheikh stressed that religious leaders are responsible for challenging misinterpretations and reclaiming correct alternatives. This is *knowing* to ensure *doing* religion, which, in this case, means de-escalating violent fatalism.

Consistent with my discussion of the neoliberalization of religion in previous chapters, this Kenyan sheikh views his work on religious literacy (or *knowing* "correct" Islam) as one site among other multisectoral efforts involving the business community, the government, and others. Importantly, it is not enough to offer a positive counternarrative if, for example, Muslims (predominantly ethnically Somali Muslims) struggle to obtain an identification card.[19] Another sheikh likewise explained to me how violent apocalyptic interpretations relate to empirical realities that Muslims endure. He specifically spoke about the challenge of correcting the narrative to which youth are particularly susceptible. This sheikh explained why, in addition to deflating conspiracy-inflected modes of thinking, it is vital to get governmental buy-in for their counternarrative efforts; otherwise, he and colleagues will themselves become suspected of radicalization because they work on correcting

---

[17] An interview with the Office of the Institute of Life & Peace, Nairobi, November 2018. See also Jayaweera and De Silva, "Peacebuilding as 'Countering Violent Extremism,'" 168.
[18] Interview #94, Nairobi, July 2019.
[19] See chapter 1 for this analysis regarding Somali Kenyans.

misperceptions and misinterpretations of concepts and practices such as jihad. The government and the bureaucratic machinery need to be on board for counternarrativity to work, especially since the government's antiterrorism measures have been integrated into the global "war on terror" and its racializing and policing of Muslim communities. Yet focusing on religious literacy and reclaiming Islam has become urgent for him and other religious authorities in the PTVE space. They are fully agentic in this process. Even more so, when I asked another sheikh why he persists, despite threats to his life from al-Shabaab, he replied that it is precisely his religiosity and his *knowing* of Islam as oriented to life in this world rather than some afterlife that nourishes his resolve to partake in *doing* religion.[20]

What I found compelling about talking to religious leaders versed in Islam, and in this way glimpsing their NGO-ization, is precisely how their stories, perspectives, and transformative actions challenge critical accounts that take away their agency by criticizing the religion industry for doing the same thing. And yet their NGO-ization in the PTVE space reinforces the instrumentalization of androcentric or "generic" framing of their religious traditions as "peace," "tolerance," and "coexistence." This closure of hermeneutical horizons has become ever narrower because of a focus on media platforms specializing in branding and sound bites rather than critical depth. This is all the more true when the brand is weaponized to combat al-Shabaab and other negative influencers' branding and facile packaging of religious/communal narratives. Religion, a peace technology thriving on a discourse of authenticity, closes rather than opens communal and political scripts.

One young interviewee associated with the al-Qalam Institute for Islamic Identities and Dialogue in Southeast Asia based in Ateneo de Davao University in Mindanao, stressed his resistance to the language of "countering" and "radicalization": "We don't want to use the word 'countering,' but we want to have positive messaging.... We keep telling our students that... it's not bad to be... radicalized.... Even the Prophet was a radical. They are radical because they don't like the status quo. With what's going on in Bangsamoro right now, so much corruption, so many killings, so many displacements... you can really be radical."[21] This interviewee articulates resistance to the orientalist securitizing discourse that seeks to contain, tame, and instrumentalize religion for managing frustrations. He underscores,

---

[20] Interview #91, Nairobi, July 2019.
[21] Participant in a focus group, Davao City, June 2018.

accordingly, that the prophetic, radical, and disruptive dimensions of religiosity animate its constructive meanings and potential interventionist agency in the world.

This resistance to the orientalist grammar of securitization is familiar in academic settings such as the one al-Qalam inhabits. Likewise, in Kenya at this level of higher learning, a program launched in association with the Hekima Institute of Peace Studies and International Relations in Nairobi for "countering perceptions of extremism" along the coastal region attempted to address complaints raised by Eastern African Muslim interlocutors. Such programs are often driven and funded by U.S. entities. The complaints revolved around Islam being a marked category associated with violence. Hence, the Kenyan Countering Perceptions program, in the words of one interviewee, "targeted both Christians and Muslims together in workshops."[22] Here, however, through the presentation of social scientific evidence-based research, the focus was on encouraging "conversation on the vulnerability of young people who are being radicalized." The intention, not unlike the "My Jihad" media campaign that rebranded jihad as a vocational pursuit of self-actualization,[23] was to dispel misconceptions by pointing to a "few bad [or radical] apples," bypassing the orientalist association of Islam with violence. This approach deflates a prophetic radicalism in favor of a domesticated, depoliticized, and tamed nonradicalism, which the young man from al-Qalam resisted. Here, one identifies resistance to the search for so-called moderate Muslim actors as potential partners in P/CVE or PTVE.[24]

For now, it suffices to highlight, as did my interlocutors with EAI-Mindanao, that the language of "countering" generates discomfort for people who see themselves on the frontline of resisting violent interpretations of Islam. "In our context it's very hard [to employ the label of 'countering'] because you are navigating in society where in one family you have MNLF, MILF, Abu Sayyaf, a Wahhabi and Shi'a. In one family! . . . So, what we do now is we try just to get the positive narrative. Finding all the good things in the Shi'a school of thought, the four Sunni schools of thought. . . . There's a

---

[22] Interview #39, Nairobi, November 2018.
[23] See chapter 5.
[24] For a reflexive analysis of the potential harm of the moderate versus radical binary, see Peter Mandaville and Melissa Nozell, "Engaging Religion and Religious Actors in Countering Violent Extremism," U.S. Institute of Peace, Special Report 413, August 2017, https://www.usip.org/sites/default/files/SR413-Engaging-Religion-and-Religious-Actors-in-Countering-Violent-Extremism.pdf. See also Wilton Park, "Statement: Religion, Radicalization and Countering Violent Extremism," April 29, 2016, https://www.wiltonpark.org.uk/wp-content/uploads/Statement-on-religion-radicalisation-and-countering-violent-extremism.pdf.

level of where we can engage [publicly] . . . certain sensitive matters. . . . That's kind of . . . it's someone from within who can see those things."[25] The discomfort illuminates that "countering" violent manipulation requires *knowing* or a contextual sensitivity and facility with dynamics on the ground that affect families in different ways and thus require equally specialized and historically nuanced engagement with tradition. The hermeneutical task of challenging violent potentialities, in other words, cannot unfold in abstraction from the highly textured and internally contested lived interpretations of religious traditions. However, the NGO-ization and the neoliberal frame of interreligious governance that I have traced in this book push against such nuances to abstract and transposable benchmarking and lessons learned that foreclose hermeneutical futures and subordinate them to the constraints of the present and to unitary conceptions of community and identity.

Further, my focus group in al-Qalam stressed the hermeneutical approach itself as delimiting. One participant said, "We also realized that countering the narratives of the violent extremists, we will use the Qur'an. But they will also use the Qur'an. . . . You could provide ten verses and they will give you a hundred verses justifying their acts. The debate will not end."[26] What this last quotation exposes, once again, is the diminishing scope of religious engagement to the methodology of proof-texting, which, while conducive to translating religious "messages" into tweets, thrives on narrow textuality and disembodied claims of authenticity rather than on contingency, change, and discursive accounts of tradition. Indeed, the urgency of dealing with youth through first-aid and longer offline/online "resiliency" hermeneutical channels remains a priority for al-Qalam in its university setting, as it is for organizations such as EAI. First-aid hermeneutics, offline relationship building, intrapersonal formation, and responsibilization securitize religion and, with it, ensure peace.

Experiential Humanization

Notably, intrafaith engagement does not come only in the form of rapid first-aid hermeneutical response or counter-tweets. It also manifests through educational and curriculum reform intent on building long-term

---

[25] An interview with key actors in EAI in Cagayan de Oro, June 2019.
[26] Participant in a focus group with al-Qalam, Davao City, June 2018.

resiliency against the violent manipulation of religious traditions. This reveals another intersection of development and peacebuilding traversing educational policies and spaces for interrogating internal complexities and divergent histories. For example, one interlocutor from al-Qalam in Ataneo Davao contested the label "Bangsamoro" as lumping together a plurality of Muslim identities and narratives: "For us, it meant an erosion of different moral identities and diminishment of our Southeast Asian Muslim orientation."[27] Beyond the erosion of internal plurality, he voiced a concern I heard in both Kenya and the Philippines about the importation of "foreign Islam" and its connections to money in Saudi Arabia and elsewhere. For example, one Muslim interlocutor active in interreligious work in Zamboanga in Mindanao repeatedly stressed the presence of foreign fighters in Marawi as well as a broader departure from al-Azhar's type of religious training in favor of nonrigorous scholarships to receive religious education in Sudan, Somalia, and Saudi Arabia. Upon their return to the Philippines, those who receive this unorthodox education disrupt the religious authority structures and organically pluralistic outlook of Muslims with foreign puritanical perspectives.[28] Al-Qalam came into being to address some of these issues, with an emphasis on dialogue as a mechanism of resilience and self-interrogation.

Al-Qalam was established in 2011 after the Jesuit president of the Ataneo approached Mussolini Lidasan, a professional facilitator and practitioner of intra- and interfaith dialogue, urging him to create a space within the university dedicated to dialogue. Lidasan, remembering the words of the Prophet Muhammad that the pen is mightier than the sword, named the institute al-Qalam, or "The Pen." Al-Qalam critically engages the employment of Islam in violent actions through discussion sessions, especially after violent attacks such as the one instigated by Abu Sayyaf Group and the Maute, which shook Davao City in 2016. The resulting intra-Muslim conversations on the meanings and practice of jihad and its manipulation navigated a landscape that also involved sympathizers of Abu Sayyaf. Indeed, al-Qalam's leadership does not want to exclude such voices. This engagement also includes bringing speakers and reflections that contextualized the Abu Sayyaf Group.

Al-Qalam thus complicates the Muslim experience in Mindanao and the Philippines more broadly. For example, *Iqra*, the journal of al-Qalam, features peer-reviewed scholarly articles on issues pertaining to the Bangsamoro

---

[27] Ibid.
[28] Participant in a focus group in Zamboanga, June 2018.

struggle as well as the community's internal pluralities and contested identities.[29] Such complexities do not appear in interreligious peacebuilding spaces designed to capitalize on religious resources for peace/development.

Channeling the neoliberal logic of peacebuilding/development/security, a recent graduate of the Ateneo Davao who works with al-Qalam on youth outreach explained her understanding of the need for intrafaith or intra-Muslim reflexivity before intercommunal engagement. Echoing a growing consensus, she stressed the vulnerability of the youth and the need to engage constructively with this demographic to equip it with skills and resources for peacebuilding: "We open opportunities for the youth because . . . [youth] want to act right away. That's what also makes us vulnerable to threats of being negatively radicalized. . . . What we actually do amounts to opening up the doors for the youth . . . for us to use our skills in these kinds of advocacies, peacebuilding activities, workshops on leadership trainings, and so these kinds of . . . they're not very heavy for the younger generations to take. In these kinds of subtle ways we prevent threats to the youth."[30] This al-Qalam activist expresses a familiar PTVE ecological outlook that articulates, through this environmental metaphor, the integrative logic of peacebuilding/development. This perspective contrasts with the al-Qalam facilitator I introduced earlier, who challenged the "radical" versus "moderate" Islam binary, also central to the securitizing discourse. His critical pushback, however, came from personal pain, as he had lost his father to violence authorized through appeals to "authentic" Islam. Coming from a prestigious Muslim family, this young scholar of Islamic studies already had, at the time of my encounter with him, a long history of interfaith engagement that led him to focus his energy on intra-Muslim work, especially during the ascendency of sympathies with Da'esh and other similar groups. Through exchanges with other global and regional Muslim communities, he had begun to design social media campaigns to combat the logic and appeal of violent interpretations of Islam to youth. Like BRAVE in Kenya and other short-term first-aid countermessaging approaches, a sense of urgency securitizes religion through hermeneutical mechanisms and outreach

---

[29] For example, Mary Donna Grace J. Cuenca, review of John Harvey Gamas, Mansoor L. Limba, Anderson V. Villa, Janor C. Balo, Maria Janua P. Cunanan, Heidi K. Gloria, and Ramon Beleno III, *Mindanao Muslim History: Documentary Sources from the Advent of Islam to the 1800s* (Davao City: Ateneo de Davao University, 2017), in *Iqra* 4: 115–19.

[30] Participant in a focus group with al-Qalam, Davao City, June 2018.

technologies that target youth as an "at-risk" demographic with relatively easy and fast access to Sheikh Google and ready-made tweets.

After dealing with the assassination of one of the other leaders of the Southeast Asian youth network focusing on social media activism and countermessaging, of which he had been a member, this young man has found in al-Qalam an opportunity to build offline relationships with Muslim groups and individuals located along a spectrum. Building these relationships transformed him: "What I really realized is that the problem arises when people are coming to conclusions . . . based on what they hear, especially when they hear it from religious authorities. Once you start getting to know them personally . . . personal engagement bypasses all those conclusions and presumptions. Right now, I'm actually a very good friend with all groups."[31] This quotation exposes two critical dimensions of the securitization of religion. The first involves the fragmentation of religious authority, often sanctified unconventionally, not through traditional learning processes and methodologies but through charisma or Sheikh Google. This fragmentation and displacement of religious authority thrive on emic religious illiteracy and other contributing factors, such as poverty, marginalization, and trauma. The second reveals the indispensability of face-to-face relationship building. The practice of relationship building becomes a form of interreligious and intercultural knowledge and practice, as we also saw unfold in the interfaith spaces of women's co-ops. The interpretive practice that countermessaging demands cannot proceed in abstraction from embodied relationship building, which university and high school campuses can facilitate. Indeed, religious literacy as a peacebuilding mechanism becomes a form of *knowing* through relationship building (*doing*) rather than mastery of religious sources, hermeneutical traditions, and learning methodologies. Once again, actual knowing is beside the point.

Relationship building has animated internal and horizontal grassroots peacebuilding efforts in Mindanao for decades, highlighting the mechanisms of people-to-people dialogue through humanization. Humanization thus becomes the sustainable engine of neoliberal peacebuilding. The long-term investment in hermeneutical resiliency does not depend on critical hermeneutical horizons, but rather builds upon and interweaves with the people-to-people, bottom-up dialoguing and bridging approach designed to dissuade individuals from their old prejudices and turn them into "seeds

---

[31] Ibid.

of peace" through intergroup immersion or a programmatic focus on connector "public good" projects. The "public," as noted, is presumed in the designs of such programs to be self-evident and unitary, in line with the generic registers of *doing* religion—registers that always, as feminist political theorists' critiques have exposed, conceal the counterpublics created through the forces of exclusion.[32] I name the existence of counterpublics as a matter of course, but also note that, within the programmatic focus on offline hermeneutics of friendship and relationship building, securitizing religion/people proceeds on the generic registers and through experiential modalities rather than hermeneutical depth and intersectional political consciousness. Youth, of course, present themselves as especially worthy of such long-term investment in love and friendship, translating into the refusal of hate and division. Indeed, this focus on relationships consolidates and spiritualizes, but also exceeds and transgresses, the confines of a neoliberal peace discourse because the relationships' realness does not necessarily dissipate with the drying up of funds or the conclusion of neoliberal time frames.

The volatility, vulnerability, and peace potential of youth have been the focus of activities of al-Qalam dating back to its inception with a series of peace camps, which my interviewees contrasted with the general tenor communicated by the antecedent Ateneo Moro Youth Organization in Ateneo Davao. The latter purportedly advocated radical symbolic violent acts against Christians (e.g., publicly burning the Bible) as solidarity with the Moro struggle. In contrast, the peace camps, which took place in an Indigenous school facility, brought together twenty-five Muslims, twenty-five Christians, and twenty-five IPs from across the country, engaging them in a rigorous education on the historical backgrounds of contemporary tensions and identities. The intensity of the people-to-people experiences and learning led some students to start the Salaam organization back on the Ateneo Davao's campus. Salaam facilitated conversations on international topics such as Palestine, which animated Islamist discourse broadly, but also engaged fully in service within the local communities. Salaam's quiet influence spread beyond Davao to other regions of Mindanao.[33] Through

---

[32] Fraser, "Rethinking the Public Sphere." Fraser's conceptualization of the counterpublic genealogically relates to Spivak, "Can the Subaltern Speak?"; Rita Felski, *Beyond Feminist Aesthetics* (Cambridge, MA: Harvard University Press, 1989).

[33] Focus group with al-Qalam, Davao, June 2018. The Salaam movement, with its focus on youth empowerment for peace, and al-Qalam are intricately linked to one another at Ateneo de Davao University. For a common statement on the Bangsamoro Basic Law and its neglect of some earlier provisions intended to redress grievances of the Bangsamoro people, see "The al-Qalam Institute and Salaam Movement's Statement for the Bicameral Sessions on the Bangsamoro Basic Law," July 9,

the Salaam movement, as it refers to itself, al-Qalam promotes intra- and intercultural conversations, learning spaces, and opportunities for youth to deepen their capacity for peace.[34]

While tech camps for countermessaging capacitate youth with skills to rapidly combat the "information asymmetry" created due to the violent movement's masterful utilization of social media, the long-term investment in youth's resilience entails facilitating immersive intercultural encounters. This slower hermeneutic of friendship as securitization of religion reaches back in the history of grassroots and Astroturf peacebuilding work in Mindanao. Peace Advocates of Zamboanga (PAZ) has also focused on the experiential encounters of youth since the 1990s, with an understanding of the complex background of Mindanao following the end of the Spanish era, the onset of American colonialism, and the systematic marginalization, minoritization, and exploitation of Muslims along with the roles of Christianity and Christians in such processes. PAZ is consequently involved in a secretariat capacity with the Interreligious Solidarity for Peace group consisting of Catholics, Protestants, Muslims, and IPs, which sponsors forums and peace camps for youth to foster solidarity through dispelling stereotypes and building relationships. The camps also focus on leadership skills and vocational training, technical skills, and basic literacy skills to enhance members' chances of eventually gaining a livelihood. Such camps fall into the category of peace education, involving once again an understanding of social change as the aggregate of seed planting, or investment in individuals' self-transformations, positive immersive experiences of intercultural and interreligious humanization, and the capacity to pursue a livelihood, which I have already highlighted as failing, by its depoliticizing design, to scale up or yield full social blooming, regardless of rhetoric.

The testimony of one young female graduate of the youth peace camp's program captures what it is designed to do:

> The impact of this peace camp for the younger generation? . . . Some of them are in the Council for the Youth . . . some are young professionals, like

2018, http://alqalam.addu.edu.ph/news/the-al-qalam-institute-and-salaam-movements-statement-for-the-bicameral-sessions-on-the-bangsamoro-basic-law/.

[34] One example is to intentionally create an opportunity for Muslim Moro Youth to meet and interact with one another; see Kristelle Rizardo, "The MSummit Primer: Social Media Offline Campaigns" November 20, 2018 http://alqalam.addu.edu.ph/uncategorized/the-msummit-primer-social-media-offline-campaigns/.

some now are working in the Office of the Vice President. Some are abroad working, and others are in civil service commission offices—some are lawyers, some are doctors. You can really see the peace camp has broadened their . . . perspectives and their respect [of] other cultures and religious traditions. They can thrive in various communities wherever they are. They are more sensitive. For example, when they graduate the camp, they are very sensitive if they have Muslim colleagues. They are careful not to eat pork or push it on them. They develop cultural sensitivity and they use their skills and talents, because we provide art and music groups in the camps. Journalism too, they articulate their experiences through writing articles and newscasting. The recent output was a video on children's rights. So you can see that these young individuals are much more aware of their rights.[35]

This testimony reveals a recurrent point about the depoliticizing rationality of people-to-people dialoguing and bridging programming. The peace camps conform to the neoliberal logic of peacebuilding/development, where livelihood and even a degree of upward mobility are triangulated with cultivating immersive experiences of intercultural friendship as resilience against stereotyping and other harmful practices and ideas. Such experiences are not designed to generate a critical political consciousness beyond survival and the occasional instance of upward mobility. This is why I interpret such longer-term investment through the same prism as the first-aid hermeneutical work and other peacebuilding/development programming foci. The latter enhances rather than disrupts the neoliberal frame, the logic of responsibilization, and the securitization of all facets of interpersonal and intercommunal engagements. Indeed, an interest in people's hunger is due to the fear of how "their" hunger may affect "my" safety on buses, malls, airplanes, and more.

Hence, an emphasis on peace education does not mean critical peace pedagogies that inculcate tools for resisting social, political, and economic inequalities, but rather a long-term securitizing investment in resiliency against such inequalities.[36] Peace education and religious formation, including spiritualized intercultural encounters (particularly Muslim and Christian) with children, constitute mechanisms for capacitating "subjects" to navigate risks and to embrace coexistence. These connections between

---

[35] Participant in a focus group with people associated with PAZ, Zamboanga, June 2018.
[36] For an analysis of critical peace education, see, for example, Margaret Groarke and Emily Welty, eds., *Peace and Justice Studies: Critical Pedagogy* (London: Routledge, 2019).

religious formation and peace came through in my interview with an interlocutor from World Vision in Mindanao.[37] He remarked that this long-term investment in "resilience" building involves "engaging religious leaders to promote peace in the communities where we work, through culture of peace trainings, interreligious dialogue, and, among Christians, we advocate for ecumenical dialogue. With children, capacity building involves a program called Empowering Children as Peacebuilders, where children are trained as facilitators but also to train their friends on how to cultivate [a] culture of peace."[38] Hence, religious formation is entwined with cultivating peacebuilding spirituality with an overall outcome of building Sisyphean endurance. This captures the formation of survivalist and depoliticized subjectivity well fitted within neoliberal assemblages, which only perpetuate structural forms of violence and continuous exploitation.

Such programming modes, ubiquitous in my case studies, also cultivate resilience to religious manipulation into violence; thus, they become a long-term securitizing investment, always interwoven with vocational training to enhance survivalist piety. Religious formation is indeed central for the work of child-centric organizations such as World Vision that, in the case of Mindanao, links the lack of opportunities, high level of sexual and other abuse, and poverty and food insecurity with recruitment into violent organizations.[39] This apparently more ecological outlook,[40] which has informed the peacebuilding/development synergy, recognizes that peace alone cannot feed people. Thus, a survival threshold can go a long way in ensuring "peace," even if it does not denote the operation of critical pedagogy or a political consciousness that promotes historical and affirmative justice. World Vision works to empower children through religious formation, conflict resolution training, and peace education to become peacebuilders and advocates of peace culture from the grassroots, thus expanding the frustration management that I highlighted earlier. On a different front, the Kenya Muslim Youth Alliance (established in 2002) aspires to capacitate youth by inculcating a culture of civic engagement, holding political representatives accountable, and seeking power themselves to shape their current conditions and their

---

[37] The links between peacebuilding and religious vocations are also articulated by many of the religious actors I introduce in chapter 3 and throughout the book.
[38] Interview #54, Davao, June 2018.
[39] Interview with a key informant with World Vision, June 2018.
[40] See Schirch, *Ecology of Violent Extremism*.

future horizons.[41] However, claiming positions of power that promote unitary and hermeneutically closed group interests is not the same as building critical political consciousness, which requires an intersectional prism and coalition building to move power and to transform systemic violence.

Whether it is tech camps, culture of peace seminars, summer camps, or youth capacity building, all of these activities focus on "planting a seed"—transforming individuals into social influencers or agents/ambassadors of peace and security (always expanding the security apparatus of the state to the level of intrasubjective and spiritual formation) and furnishing them with positive and "authentic" countermessages to combat violence and insecurity. The spiritualization of immersive intercultural relationship building (*doing qua knowing* religion) takes precedence as a peacebuilding and securitizing tool over religious knowledge or critical religious hermeneutical literacy. The Sisyphean capacity of religious leaders is, accordingly, ingrained into youth's self-formation. This contributes to interreligious governance and its depoliticizing effects.

Interfaith Modeling/Performance of Peace

To recall, when I spoke to the board of interfaith religious leaders involved with Pakigdait,[42] my religiously diverse interlocutors underscored their avoidance of theological discourse while sharing the view that "going back to our faiths" is the way to pursue conflict transformation. "We only talk about peace and how can we get there" through listening, diffusing violent escalations, and providing platforms for people to meet, including MNLF and MILF members.[43] Indeed, as I illustrated in earlier chapters, their role entails modeling peaceful coexistence especially between Muslims and Christians and employing their religious authority through the now familiar method of proof-texting to counter violent manipulations of their traditions, and through trickle-down, interfaith performativity. Like the friendships ostensibly formed in peace camps, the religious leaders of Pakigdait getting to know one another and performing an aspired bridging

---

[41] Interview #81, Nairobi, July 2019. See also an interview of representatives of the Kenya Muslim Youth Alliance with Crystal Corman in Berkley Center, "A Discussion with Abdulhamid Sakar, Kenya Muslim Youth Alliance," November 13, 2014, https://berkleycenter.georgetown.edu/interviews/a-discussion-with-abdulhamid-sakar-kenya-muslim-youth-alliance.

[42] See chapter 3 for further discussion of this group.

[43] Participant in a focus group with Pakigdait in Cagayan de Oro, July 2019.

constitute interfaith experiential knowledge, which relies on generic ethical appeals to the common good (Mindanao harmony discourse) and generic humanity consistent with the peace and love basis of all religious and cultural traditions. The emphasis is not on learned mastery but on experiential embodiment—useful for intergroup frustration management and contained in the relationship's very performance (the *doing*).

Pakigdait's many years of grassroots relationship building and modeling of interreligious coexistence persisted despite the hardship and pain that many of its leaders themselves experienced. The late Roman Catholic priest Father Teresito "Chito" Soganub, based in Marawi, was held as a hostage for 116 days by the Da'esh-influenced Maute group during the Siege of Marawi in 2017.[44] This experience tested his faith, but, in the aftermath, he expressed a resolve to continue to embody and model interfaith peacebuilding in Mindanao. He told me that offers came for him to relocate, but he knew he needed to stay in the context where his work was intelligible and meaningful. As someone who experienced violence explicitly motivated by an appeal to religious warrants, Father Chito persisted until his death in his virtuous modeling of peace through his person, interfaith relationships, and programs facilitated by Pakigdait, while nevertheless bracketing theological complexities as irrelevant for the urgency of the peace business. This approach betrays an understanding that all faiths are, in essence, about peace, and the role of religious leaders in war is to model that peace. The problem is that when the prophetic virtuosity of Father Chito is co-opted into a neoliberal securitizing discourse, this virtuosity is diluted into a tweet, brand, or social capital to be mobilized, like currency, in manuals, social media campaigns, and other initiatives that produce "ambassadors," "social influencers," and "Twitter prophets." Rather than denoting a democratic turn, this horizontalization of virtuosity and religious authority depoliticizes and diminishes religious knowledge. This, by design, reinforces neoliberal logic and its assault on a political and democratic consciousness capable of mobilizing coalitions to combat together ("power with") oppressive systems ("power over"). Instead, people perform "getting along" with one another—a spiritualized performance that further entrenches neoliberal logic and its coziness with traditional hierarchies.[45] Still, the performativity of interfaith and intercultural dialogue of action and

---

[44] See chapters 1 and 3.
[45] See, especially, chapter 2 for this analysis regarding the neoliberal logic.

the authenticity of friendships has causal ramifications that exceed this analysis of neoliberal reductionisms.

Indeed, online first-aid hermeneutics and offline relationship building thrive on sound bite accounts of religious traditions and unitary conceptualization of the "public" space, the supposed depository of intercommunal cooperation. The same understanding of relationship and performativity also came through in my focus groups with clerics on the coast of Kenya who spoke about their coming together amid a violent regional crisis between Muslims and Christians in 2004. Unlike the district commissioner, the Muslim and Christian leaders could talk to the parties involved and de-escalate. Their capacity to do so, grounded in their belonging to and credible authority within the communities, prompted their NGO-ization through the formation of the interfaith group that included Muslim, Christian, Hindu, and traditional religious leaders, upon which local authorities then relied for resolving conflicts that usually erupted across tribal lines and around scarce natural resources.

One imam shared with me that his motivation to partake in interfaith peace work involves his understanding of Muslims as committed to doing good in the world, retrieving the story of the Ethiopian Christian king who sheltered Muslims during the time of the Prophet as a peace narrative.[46] Such a retrieval constitutes a familiar *imitatio* Muhammed methodology in interfaith efforts in counternarrativity. This same imam engages in modeling interreligious hospitality because of his understanding that doing so (e.g., inviting Christians into mosques) follows the example of the Prophet. For him, as for other religious actors I encountered during my fieldwork, the "dialogue" is a dialogue of action and of peace, and it reaches its spiritual fruition not on the level of discursivity but in immersive experiences with one another across religious and communal divides. One reverend stressed, "When we go in unity, the people listen to us, and they can restrain from fighting." The performance and modeling of peace shape the contours of the activities framed as intercultural or interreligious. The point is that religion/culture, including religious leaders, enters as a mechanism whose success is measured in terms of "peace" or "development" outcomes.

PAZ's leadership chose the concept of solidarity as most operative in their programming and as deeper than dialoguing, yet this is solidarity not as

---

[46] See chapter 3 for further analysis of this form of retrieval of peace motifs from within Muslim history and sources.

co-resistance but rather as co-survival through rewriting the social script of acceptable pluralistic cohabitation. Co-resistance would require critical pedagogy, while co-survival thrives on aggregating "planting the seed" activities to enhance resilience as ever adaptable to the conditions of mere (and pious) survival. "All of us here," an interlocutor from PAZ underscored, "have been wounded because of the conflict and historical injustices. We have to meet and develop our faith communities into a way of peace."[47] While this statement captures the authenticity of mutual suffering, it nonetheless forecloses the possibility of concrete, historical interrogation of power differentials. For Father Angel, at the helm of PAZ, interreligious dialogue constitutes a complex phenomenon that challenges traditional church teachings about truth and salvation. Thus, he wishes to remain on the level of solidarity based on recognizing a (generic) humanity in all.

Interreligious or intercultural performance of mutual respect, therefore, has become a key focus of religious leaders engaged in modeling social cohesion, often through simply showing up for one another's religious holidays or other rituals. As we saw in previous chapters, a practice of trickle-down, interfaith performativity is complementary to grassroots communal bridging activities and their "planting a seed" peace scaling logic. An *'alim* associated with PAZ reminisced about his involvement organizing the first visit by a bishop to an Eid al-Fitr celebration in the mosque in October 1974. This experiential and symbolic performance permeates peacebuilding practices with interreligious prayers as complex causal factors instrumental in resilience building in contexts shaped by historical injustices and narratives of marginalization ripe for both religious and cultural illiteracy as well as for reductive culturalist/identity-based accounts of the causes of violence. Indeed, such immersive experiences and relationships are not "symbolic" as nonmaterial and/or empty gestures but rather causally transformative in the concrete social worlds that people inhabit.[48]

At the genesis of the dialogue frame in Mindanao and at the helm of the performance of interreligious cohesion is the Bishop-Ulama Conference, whose raison d'être is trickle-down performativity and cyclical horizontal modes of performative interfaith harmony through peace messaging. The Conference

---

[47] Participant in the focus group with Peace Advocates Zamboanga, Zamboanga City, June 2018.
[48] For such a story of in-depth relationship building and religious and peacebuilding virtuosity, see Maria Ida Giguiento with Myla Leguro, "'Dili sayon nang pag sunod kang Kristo' (It is not easy to follow Christ): The Road to Peace Is a Rocky One," in *Making Peace with Faith*, ed. Michelle Garred and Mohammed Abu-Nimer (New York: Rowman & Littlefield, 2018): 111–26.

came on the scene in 1996, around the time of the peace agreement process between the MNLF and the Philippines government, and soon became a key facilitator of peace enculturation, especially noted in the institutionalization of the Mindanao Week of Peace since 1999. The Mindanao Week of Peace amounts to a monumental performance of intercultural and interreligious exchanges and positive messaging, with a focus on youth participation. The intention, one '*alim* associated with the Bishop-Ulama Conference remarked in an interview with me, is to highlight cultural commonalities, while nevertheless learning to appreciate differences as empowering.[49] This mode of appreciation, through experiential dialoguing and actions, contributes to the fabric of intercommunal resilience to violence. In the words of the '*alim*:

> It's fortunate also that during this week, peace comes among the youth—Muslims and Christians can mingle together, especially the youth come together. Then [people] including some of the imams in many locations come together to celebrate the Week of Peace. The Muslims and Christians become open to one another. Christians can come to mosques and Muslims come to churches, and there is a dialogue started. They realize that both religions are open to dialogue. With this dialogue, they're helping each other, if there is a problem in the Muslim community, the Christians come to help and same, likewise—Muslims will help the Christians. That is a result of the dialogue.[50]

This narrative is almost as ubiquitous in Mindanao as interreligious and intercultural dialogue itself, with the cumulative effects that such experiential occasions translate into resilience in the form of mechanisms to manage frustration and enhanced cross-communal networks of relationships further capable of de-escalating violence, should it erupt. Clearly, the *knowing* as *doing* religion has nothing much to do with actual knowledge of one's tradition nor the tradition of another, but rather getting to know one another experientially as people. The '*alim*'s analysis was echoed in my focus groups in the Cotabato region, as with other practitioners of interreligious dialogue and action. And yet others, especially in the peacebuilding field, have grown tired of these practices for their limited impact and apparent ossification of the Bishop-Ulama Conference over time, signaling the erosion of its initial

---

[49] Interview #56, Davao City, June 2018.
[50] Ibid.

symbolic influence.[51] Still, the language of dialogue and the praxis of interfaith modeling and intercultural immersion remain prominent and meaningful on the ground and in people's self-transformations, which are the key change mechanism. Regardless of how far back from the immediate urgency of hermeneutical first-aid we are, the main burden is exerted on the individual to change her own ways and to overcome the violent and inhibiting dimensions of her cultural practices and (mis)perceptions. The hermeneutical battle comes with an infrastructure designed for strengthening the formation of children and youth, where such formation conflates and equates peace with spiritual/religious vocations.

The Mindanao Tri-People Youth Core (MTYC), established as the youth arm of the Bishop-Ulama Conference in 2004, exemplifies the aforementioned links between the focus on youth as an "at-risk" demographic, the need to cultivate interculturality and interreligious dialogue, and the successful implementation of the BOL through bottom-up strategic engagement with influencers and others in a position to join forces to mitigate frustrations and fears. In its years of operation, relying always on volunteers, the MTYC has coordinated experiential learning, peace camps, and immersion programs to facilitate intercultural cross-learning about IPs' practices—experiences that often resulted in sustained friendships *qua* resiliency. The peace camps, key leaders of the organization stress, are designed, as in other educational programs, to be transformational and to appreciate the immense diversity of Mindanao. Attending one another's holiday celebrations was again a profound site of intercultural relationship building. These dialoguing and immersive (bridging) activities unfold in real spaces inhabited by people traumatized by violence. At the time of this writing, the MTYC has been working extensively in the city of Marawi, having attained a competitive bid from the BARMM to promote its implementation of the BOL and thereby join other civil society actors and organizations in managing frustrations and reducing conditions for violent eruptions. They have expanded their work from youth to different demographics, underscoring dialogue as their primary frame for peacebuilding practice; dialogue creates what they call "reflective spaces" for people to reconnect with the "beginning of their faith traditions," by which they mean a process of recovering the supposed peace-and-ethics kernel that all faith traditions purportedly share.

---

[51] According to interviews with key interlocutors who populate the interreligious peacebuilding in Mindanao.

This reductionism reveals the effectiveness of the generic registers and the prophetic lite emblematic of the religiocratic industry guiding local access religious NGO-ized actors tasked with securitizing intercommunal tensions for peace promotion.

Hence, MTYC, as with the other examples, deploys dialogue as *experiential* rather than *theological* or learned in multiple sources of traditions. *Doing* religion, therefore, is not about *knowing* religious traditions but rather about *getting to know one another*. MTYC's activities, familiarly, focus on individual self-transformation and spiritual/peace formation through building friendships, imbuing the intercultural and interfaith immersive engagements with spiritual meanings that link to accounts of religious traditions as essentially and most authentically about peace. This spiritualization of dialogue through trickle-down interfaith modeling and performativity, self-transformation, and experiential humanization (getting to know one another) enhance resilience to violence.

This resilience similarly reflects the broadening of religious leaders' peacebuilding, Sisyphean, virtuoso agency through programmatic spaces of immersive experiences to the communities themselves and to the very relationships that constitute their social ligaments. The virtuosity of religious leaders, in other words, is spread horizontally to all those engaged. Here, virtuosity itself means a capacity to navigate the religiocratic landscape. This outcome does not only mean that the category of religious authority or actor is now reshaped in terms of influencers and their sound bite messaging; it also means that virtuosity itself is reconfigured socially in terms of the securitizing concept and spiritual practice of resilience. The lack of any critical and layered hermeneutical creativity with cultural and religious traditions, however, reinforces the point about how the convergence of religion and peace with the study of violence subordinates the study of religion to *realpolitik* or to the art of the possible. Still, beyond the Twitter conceptions of religion generated by the securitizing neoliberal discourse of the global engagement with religion and concentrated efforts to standardize classical madrasa education and curriculum in both Kenya and the Philippines,[52] on

---

[52] See the Republic of the Philippines's Department of Education, "DO 51, S. 2004—Standards Curriculum for Elementary Public Schools and Private Madaris Amended by DO 40, S. 2011— Amendment to DEPD Order No. 51, S. 2004" (Standard Curriculum for Elementary Public Schools and Private Madaris), August 28, 2004, https://www.deped.gov.ph/2004/08/28/do-51-s-2004-standards-curriculum-for-elementary-public-schools-and-private-madaris-amended-by-do-40-s-2011-amendment-to-deped-order-no-51-s-2004-standard-curriculum-for-elementary-public/ . According to one prominent educator and education policy actor in the Philippines, a thorough comprehension of the Qur'an as a way of life becomes a mode of resilience against manipulation of

the ground, real relationships across religiocultural divides consolidate and exceed their utility because of their genuine empirics. I return to this point in the next chapter. For now, it suffices to highlight that a focus on immersive, intercommunal relationships supplements first-aid hermeneutics as mechanisms for resilience within which the "religion" ingredient plays a key generative role.

One of my interlocutors from the Supreme Council of Kenyan Muslims lamented how the standardization process, which he otherwise embraces, flattens the tradition and learning methodologies. He also underscored that for him the meaning of being Muslim exceeds the Qur'an to include "extracurricular activities such as singing, music, history, languages, literatures, et cetera."[53] Standardization flattens it all into one brand and message. Overall, it reduces "the critical thinking capacity of individuals."[54] Indeed, as I have argued, more religion in peacebuilding does not necessarily denote deeper religious *knowing*, even if it mainstreams *doing* religion. On the contrary, within the neoliberal and securitizing frame, *doing* religion diminishes rather than expands the interpretive scope. This is the case even if the securitizing space illuminates the role of religious education, meanings, and hermeneutical action and thus "content" in addition to "function" or the instrumentality of religious actors as partners in a multisectoral effort to facilitate peace and stability through devolutionary mechanisms and governance.

Religious literacy does not destabilize the discourse of authenticity, especially heteropatriarchal norms that underpin the textual tradition and

---

tradition: "It's the shield that will protect [the children] from joining any of these violent groups." Islam, like other religions, is once again articulated as essentially about peace, which necessarily entails cultivating the capacity to coexist with others. Education reform here too is understood through the familiar metaphor of planting a seed (Skype interview with author, September 2018). Education, especially the madrasa system, has been a strategic security target in the chronicles of P/CVE for a long time, dating back to what Jeffrey Ayala Milligan refers to as the colonial and neocolonial policy of "imperial pedagogy" (see chapter 1). For the history of securitizing Islamic education, see Douglas Johnston, Azhar Hussain, and Rebecca Cataldi, *Madrasa Enhancement and Global Security: A Model for Faith-Based Engagement* (Washington, DC: International Center for Religion & Diplomacy, 2006), 10. They wrote the rationale for securitizing madrasas in simple and striking words: "The best way to fight bad theology is with good theology." A counterexample to the securitizing of madaris approach is the one articulated and implemented by Ebrahim Moosa. See Joan Fallon, "Professor Launches Project to Advance Scientific and Theological Literacy among Madrasa Graduates in India," *Notre Dame News*, April 25, 2016, https://news.nd.edu/news/profes sor-launches-project-to-advance-scientific-and-theological-literacy-among-madrasa-graduates-in-india/. See also Ebrahim Moosa, *What Is Madrasa?* (Chapel Hill: University of North Carolina Press, 2015).

[53] Interview #100, Nairobi, July 2019.
[54] Ibid.

religious praxis. Instead, it circulates within a space that responds to the manipulation of tradition and its mobilization to violence as an authentic expression of faith with countermessages that likewise frame themselves as authentic expressions of the tradition. Indeed, the focus on (immersive) education as a critical mechanism for social change is gendered, as it relies on scripted roles that men and women ought to play as productive members of society, once again channeling what I have termed "survivalist neoliberal piety." It is no wonder that other institutional actors likewise target the household unit as a transformative space with human resources marked either as "at risk" or as useful human capital to tap into, capacitate/sensitize, and mobilize.

Violent, religious, extremist manifestations cannot simply be bombed out of existence, though such militaristic practices persist. Instead, the neoliberal logic facilitates drafting (through various mechanisms, including legal channels) a comprehensive "army" of mothers, caregivers, teachers, and religious leaders to function as the state's eyes and ears and deploy hermeneutical countermessengers. One Filipina educator, a career woman herself, told me about her work with women affected by the violence in Marawi. She related how she, together with other women educators, developed grassroots modules to strengthen the women's capacity to take care of themselves, including their physical appearance, "which women should never neglect because their husbands will start looking elsewhere."[55] She explained that her focus on women reflects her understanding of their key role in the household as wives and mothers. This instrumental approach to the social reproductive sphere works because people do not want their children to disappear and because an entrenched infrastructure that burdens the individual as the engine of change is already in place and itself is imbued with Sisyphean spirituality. The expansion of religion and the practices of peace to the spheres of education and broader work with youth unfolds under the banner of resilience. The securitizing of religion reflects an emphasis on "correct" religious formation for the purpose of ensuring productive and resilient subjectivity. I have shown that, even with a hermeneutical securitizing emphasis on *knowing* (correct) religion, this emphasis is nonetheless utilitarian (see Figure 6.1).

---

[55] Skype interview, September 2018.

Figure 6.1 Securitized religious resiliency through a neoliberal prism.

At this point, it is clear that *doing* more religion does not mean more religious *knowing*. On the contrary, doing more religion entails the neoliberal depoliticization of the discourse on religion and public life. It redraws colonial difference through neoliberal mechanisms. Indeed, doing more religion does not necessarily mean justice or its approximation. However, as I have shown, anyone can be trained to monitor, surveil, and thus enable the harmony and security business. And yet the harmony and security business itself relies on virtuosity. This is because it generates its spirituality and spiritualizing (and resilience-enabling) practices of self-transformation. It also generates interpretations of peace as a religious vocation and vice versa. The empirical evidence shows that many people experience "unwoke" and often unlearned forms of religiosity meaningfully and transformatively. This is where decoloniality's religion problem resides, which is why I have sought to identify where religiosity exceeds the neoliberal frame within the programmatic spaces of the "global engagement with religion."

7
Unrevolutionary Decolonial Love
The Spirituality of Just "Getting Along"

Peace Islands

Pushing against a discursive comparative study that can only see my interlocutors in Kenya and the Philippines as colonized by neoliberal and securitizing logics, I trace religious peacebuilding agency and study it as a religious, social, and spiritual phenomenon, assessing and analyzing its decolonial and emancipatory capacities. One concrete location where this manifests is the "peace island," whether it is an actual geographic territory or an interpersonal and intercommunal network of relationships. The "peace zone" and the "seminar of peace" are prevalent in the peacebuilding landscape of Mindanao, as I have shown throughout the book.[1] The "peace zones" emerged from within the context of the People Power movement against Ferdinand Marcos and the multigroup coalition known as the Coalition for Peace (including church-oriented actors), dating back to the instantiating of peace zones in Hungduan, Ifugao (1986), Naga City (1988), Tabuk (1989), Bituan (1989), and Cantomanyog (1990). This is considered the first wave of peace zones, followed by another wave in the early 2000s. The defining characteristics of these waves include circumscribed geographic parameters and a bottom-up, broad process of communal input in articulating the peacebuilding agenda. Filipino citizens themselves agreed upon the precise parameters. They decided on the peace objectives (a characteristic violated in some instances during the second wave of peace zones under President Joseph Estrada [1998–2001], who declared some areas unilaterally as "peace

---

[1] For further analysis of this phenomenon of peace zones and their unique features and self-understanding as grassroots and bottom-up in Mindanao, see Ed Garcia, "Filipino Zones of Peace," *Peace Review* 9, no. 2 (1997): 221–24, https://doi.org/10.1080/10402659708426054; Soliman Santos, *Peace Zones in the Philippines: Concept, Policy, and Instruments* (Quezon City: Gaston Z. Ortigas Peace Institute and Asia Foundation, 2005); Kevin Avruch and Roberto S. Jose, "Peace Zones in the Philippines," in *Zones of Peace*, ed. Landon E. Hancock and Christopher Roger Mitchell (Bloomfield, CT: Kumarian Press, 2007), 51–70.

zones," thereby essentially occupying them and reflecting an appropriation of the practice of peace zoning).

Policy and development practitioners interpret the maintenance of the peace zones as integral to supporting the national peace process. The apparent success of peace zones attracted positive media coverage and development money, as during the presidency of Fidel Ramos (1992–98). In 1993, Ramos channeled special development funds to seven peace zones (Sagada, Bangilo, Cantomanyog, and four zones in the Tulunan Municipality of North Cotobato), declaring them Special Development Areas. This budgetary decision was part of Ramos's National Unification Commission, which eventually informed the consolidation of his and subsequent administrations' Comprehensive Peace Policy.[2] Though the results varied from one Special Development Area to another, the monetary reward was not necessarily effective over the long term due to mismanagement, suspicion, erosion of bottom-up agency, and co-optation into governmental counterinsurgency policies. The second wave of peace zones, in the early 2000s, changed in character. This model—under variations of the name, such as "peace oasis"—multiplied to over eighty zones, revising their narrative in accordance with the diffusion of the Islamophobic grammar of the global "war on terror," from the communist insurgency conflict narrative to Christian-Muslim animosity. As a result of the global dissemination of the racialized and orientalist anti-Muslim logic of the "war on terror," peace zones now present themselves as an ingredient primarily relevant to the war between the government and the MILF.[3]

Earlier in the book, I showed how CRS and similar project-oriented, faith-inspired actors filled the landscape of Mindanao with examples of solidarity, or connector projects that improved communal life and telegraphed the possibility, even if momentary, of pluralistic cohabitation. Such projects constitute a "dialogue of action." These dialogues of action have also included the creation of Zones of Peace, or *Ginapalad Taka*, which were initially created amid violence and through the initiative of local communal leaders such as Father Bert, whom I introduced in chapter 2 as part of my analysis of interreligious peace governance.

Father Bert experienced his transformation from hatred to an embrace of interreligious peacebuilding through his work in pursuit of the mission

---

[2] See chapter 1 for a historical overview of these events.
[3] See Avruch and Jose, "Peace Zones in the Philippines," 51–63.

of the Church in Mindanao. He tells the story of the Church in the municipality of Pikit as a story of transformation. Multiple wars between the MILF forces and the government resulted in destruction and massive displacement and an enduring "silent war in the hearts of the local inhabitants—Lumads, Muslims, and Christian alike."[4] The Church, as he sees it, was awakened to the suffering of all parties during the war of 2000. "The parish at that time," he continued, "was divided on whether or not to extend humanitarian assistance to Muslim evacuees. It was only after a passionate debate and soul-searching by the members of the parish's Pastoral Council that the parish decided to break [down] the walls of apathy and mediocrity, remembering the command of Jesus in the Gospel that tells them to 'Love your neighbor as yourself,' and the exhortation of Jesus that 'Whatever you do to the least of my brothers, you do it unto me.'"[5]

As a result of this introspection, the parish organized, mostly with young Muslim and Christian volunteers, a Disaster Response Team. Father Bert remarked, "Whether under the scorching heat of the sun or the pouring rain and amidst bullet fire, these young volunteers distributed food to thousands of starving evacuees in various evacuation centers." "We would eat together," he continued, "pray together, and even cry together when we heard that another baby had died in the evacuation center." This initial experience led to the confirmation "that helping the poor is not a matter of choice. For us Christians, it is a duty and a social responsibility." This confirmation required the cultivation of a new inclusive vision for the Church that underscored the centrality of two forms of ongoing and sustainable activity: interreligious dialogue and intercommunal peacebuilding through the mechanism of the culture of peace seminars in multiple barangays and multiple sectors, including youth, women, and teachers. "The main objective," Father Bert writes, "is basically to plant the seed of peace in the heart of every person and to restore the broken relationship of people caused by extreme biases and prejudices."[6] The "planting a seed" thesis reveals the peace mission's reliance on perseverance but also on concrete projects to improve people's material lives. This survival piety and Sisyphean commitment notwithstanding, the peace zones in Mindanao reveal a mixed legacy of grassroots, broad organizing

---

[4] Father Bert Layson, "The Search for the Common Good: Story of the Church in Pikit," presented at the ASEACCU conference, Ateneo de Davao University, August 28–30, 2014. The text of the presentation was shared with me upon my visit to Pikit.
[5] Layson, "The Search for the Common Good."
[6] Ibid and the point was reiterate in interview, June 2018.

that has coalesced to resist the realities of violence, but has also revealed the corrupting dimensions of external development money as well as governmental co-optation and manipulation of the concept of the peace zone.

For Father Bert, however, the "planting a seed" metaphor cannot be critiqued away as a form of co-optation into the neoliberal frame; it defines his work and his spiritualization of intercommunality. Mike (also affectionately called "Papa Mike") from IMAN, who is one of Father Bert's Muslim allies in the region, expressed a similar sense of intercommunal solidarity as he reminisced about how, when he experienced displacement, Father Bert had offered him a place to pray in the church.[7] This is a story that my interlocutors from CRS often repeat. This same Muslim man, who leads a local Mindanaoan organization focused on peace and development, spoke about his process of overcoming hate and the need to get rid of this "baggage" within which he had been incubated. For him, interreligious dialogue (IRD) constitutes a critical practice for reaching a basic threshold for intercommunal action, restoring peaceful relations, and empowering people to achieve minimal economic survival and communal sustainability. Another participant in a focus group I conducted added, "With IRD . . . we are in the process of strengthening the relationship and emphasizing in the community these relationships. We also emphasize the relationship between the creator and man. . . . If you have a relation to God, you can respect the rights of others."[8] Hence, IRD as a peace mechanism is also a spiritual practice affecting an intrapersonal process of strengthening one's religiosity, understood as essentially denoting "love" and "peace."

The Father Berts and Mikes of Mindanao are not the creations of CRS or other international organizations; their agency and aspiration for creating peace through small islands or zones are organically connected to the Mindanaoan landscape. While these cross-communal relationships are deemed useful for devolutionary peace mechanisms, such friendships also exceed the neoliberal frame, as I have highlighted throughout the book. Thus, they illuminate decolonial openings to love as the refusal of hate and division, even if the very assumption of cultural and religious discord as the heart of the violence is a neocolonial narrative or an erasure of historical injustices and power differentials. This echoes my earlier discussion of

---

[7] Focus group in Kidapawan (Mindanao), June 2018.
[8] Ibid.

the spiritualization and convergence of peace and religious vocations and practices, to which I will now return.

Spiritualized Practice

Spiritual virtuosity is not available to everyone. However, I saw throughout my research the cultivation of mechanisms that imitate the virtuous capacity to overcome hate, revenge, and trauma. Such tools and practices depend mainly on training "replaceable prophets" or "Twitter prophets," immersive relationship building, and self-(re)formation designed to strengthen the community's resilience to violent divisiveness. The spiritual and transformative force of such practices thrives on amnesia about how the conditions of people's marginality have informed the religious coloring of violence. One religious peacebuilder who actively participates in facilitating intercommunal dialogue commented, "Those people who are victims of violence, kidnapping, atrocities—it is challenging to preach to them peacebuilding because it is very difficult to forget the cutting [off] of the heads, the killings of their loved ones and members of their family."[9] This man, like other self-defined religious actors I engaged, underwent a transformative process through an experience of loss:

> My brother was killed. He was a soldier. . . . First I was angry. . . . Some cousins of mine were planning revenge, but I told them if you get revenge to get even, it will come back, and there is no peace of mind if we continue to dwell on hatred. I've shared this in one of our IRD forums, [where] I am one of the speakers. I told them I prayed. . . . My brother's body was airlifted here in Zamboanga, so I went here and [when] I was in the boat I saw many Muslims. I prayed a lot, "Lord help me." When I opened my eyes, I saw these were also innocent people—these were not the ones who killed. There are some bad Muslims, just like there are bad Christians. That is the start of healing and moving on.[10]

---

[9] Participant in a focus group with civil society actors and peacebuilders in Zamboanga City, June 2018.
[10] Ibid.

This testimony is consistent with the framing of IRD's concentrated effort to promote visions of harmony to counter an understanding of religiocultural difference as a source of violence. An analysis among committed IRD practitioners in Mindanao of IRD's effectiveness, or lack thereof, suggests the need to access the memories and experiences of friendship among communities, stressing that "friendship transcends . . . theology."[11] But by "theology," I mean that what is conveyed and accessed as a source of peace, love, and friendship is hermeneutically closed. It depends upon proof-texting rather than religious learning methodologies and interpretations or an intersectional structural analysis. Likewise, interreligious and intercommunal harmony discourse is amnesic for its rewriting of the conflict scripts as an outcome of an intercommunal discourse.

Nevertheless, IRD/A, as reflected by religious practitioners populating Mindanaoan civil society, can exemplify healing and restorative justice processes that redress deeply rooted "grievances of the Bangsamoro people, historical injustices, and marginalization through land dispossession."[12] Other civil society actors, some of whom I introduced earlier, highlight IRD/A as a mechanism for effecting a holistic conception of human security, including livelihood projects. Foregrounding value and intrapersonal formation also interlaces with a focus on cultivating a culture of peace. Through peace education, youth receive tools for online and offline resiliency. This peace education diametrically opposes critical peace pedagogies deemed central to articulating an intersectional analysis of the powers structuring people's survival struggles and violent realities. This is a depoliticizing model of peace education, reinforcing the spiritualization of resilience and psychologizing of conflict rather than the possibility of seeing pathways for broad social coalitions. Yet this depoliticizing deployment of religion in and through peace practices and governance exceeds the ideological frame precisely through the relational peace zones they generate.

Indeed, women religious and other female leaders populating civil society spaces involved in intercommunal peacebuilding in Mindanao emphasized love as "the highest value of IRD, especially in the midst of poverty and

---

[11] "A Common Word among Us in Mindanao: Love of God, Love of Neighbor, Love of Earth: A Synthesis of Learnings from the 2016 Mindanao-wide Interreligious Solidarity Conference," September 21–22, 2016, Royal Mandaya Hotel, Davao City, 8. This conference was cosponsored by CRS, the Episcopal Commission on Interreligious Dialogue, and the Tanenbaum Center for Interreligious Understanding. This is an internal document shared with me by CRS actors. See also my discussion of interreligious peace governance in chapter 2.
[12] Ibid., 13.

disempowerment in the local communities," and said that engaging in IRD means "living out love" through compassion and intentional work among and between communities, including with IPs.[13] The employment of the language of love and the sheer enormity of story after story of overcoming hatred, anger, trauma, and pain to participate in dialogue—whether through gathering or action to promote an elicitive conception of the common good—unsettles the totalizing account of the pervasiveness of neoliberal rationality, even if IRD itself has assumed neoliberal characteristics.

A focus on the self-transformative process also features centrally in "universal" metrics for evaluating the effectiveness of interreligious peacebuilding and development projects. In July and August 2015, CRS's measurement of the impact of its 3Bs project in Mindanao involved a systematic collection of the Most Significant Change stories from twenty barangays in Mindanao. Nearly 50% of these stories (out of eighty) highlighted changes in conflict-resolution practices, thereby leading evaluators to conclude that IRD, through the 3Bs method, can facilitate structural change.[14] Change in conflict-resolution processes includes recognizing traditional processes for resolving conflicts. This enhances the role and legitimacy of traditional religious leaders (TRLs) and localized Village Pacification Committees mechanisms (Lupong Tagapamayaoa), including a capacity to issue a certificate of actual occupancy in the land to ensure land security for IPs. One participant in the study underscored that the 3Bs project contributed to the transformation of the TRLs, or the "religious sector," into an organized forum "given legitimate responsibilities" based on their training in land conflict resolution through the program.[15] Another participant echoed, "Because of what has been done through the change of system, especially giving assistance to the tribes, the problems are now settled in the Sitio level (a lover level administrative part of the barangay) rather than in the Barangay level on land conflict issues. Because of what has been done, we already have an organized group of TRLs and [Lupong Tagapamayaoa] wherein they have their role in settling issues."[16] TRLs themselves underscore their appreciation

---

[13] Ibid., 9.
[14] See CRS, "Perceptions of A3B Project Impact among Community Stakeholders in Central Mindanao: Applying Binding Bonding and Bridging to Land Conflict in Mindanao Project," October 15, 2015 (document shared with me). See also Nell Bolton and Myla Leguro, "Local Solutions to Land Conflict in Mindanao: Policy Lessons from Catholic Relief Services' Applying the 3Bs (Binding, Bonding, Bridging) to Land Conflict Project," https://www.crs.org/sites/default/files/tools-research/local-solutions-to-land-conflict-in-mindanao.pdf (accessed on April 16, 2020).
[15] CRS, "Perceptions of A3B," 6.
[16] Ibid., 7.

of the "legal literacy" training, ordinarily unavailable to them.[17] IPs, especially, report enhanced confidence and sense of self-worth relative to other identity groups and dealing with government agencies.[18] Still, other IPs indicate improvement in representation and legal protection at the barangay level and intercommunal relations with Christians or "settlers." In the words of one Christian participant, "I would treat them [IPs] as one of my brothers and sisters."[19] And in the words of an IP, the impact of the 3Bs project also involved a new feeling of belonging within the community and others' recognition of her humanity: "Everyone is treated equally.... I feel that I am really human, which is important as a resident IP or Non-IP."[20] The later iteration of the 3Bs (2016–19), funded by USAID's Office of Conflict Management and Mitigation, further emphasized the importance of transformative personal stories and their causality and power in the aggregate.[21]

During this time frame, CRS worked in partnership with four local NGOs in twenty-five barangays in Ampatuan, Cotabato City, Lamitan City, Marawi, and Zamboanga. Focusing on people-to-people interactions deploying the 3Bs methodology, a sample of 837 recorded stories (60%, or 502, from key leaders across five different intervention areas, and 40%, or 335, from community members in Zamboanga and Cotabato) found that, depending on location, conflicts ranged in terms of the degree to which personal beliefs and group-related issues drove them.[22] Regardless of these variations, years of people-to-people activities suggest a need to invest in strengthening people's commitment to and improvement of local skills and structures of peace and order.

These reflections reveal the neoliberal logic of religiocrats who capitalize on "local" religious and traditional actors, networks, and institutions to ensure the peacebuilding/development agenda while also providing them with other forms of secular literacy, such as facility with legal processes. The

---

[17] Participant in a focus group with TRLs, March 2017.
[18] CRS, "Perceptions of A3B," 8.
[19] Ibid., 10.
[20] Ibid.
[21] The later report, shared with me, was produced by CRS Philippines and is titled "Applying Binding, Bonding and Bridging (3Bs) for Peace in Mindanao (A3B for Peace): Baseline SenseMaker Report February 2017 Version 1.2." A SenseMaker, according to this report, is "a narrative-based methodology that enables the capture and analysis of [a] large quantity of stories to understand complex change. It is a form of meta-analysis of qualitative data that bridges a gap between case studies and large-sample survey data" (iv).
[22] In addition to inter/intragroup conflicts, the study (through the personal narratives) indicated drug-related, political, and resource-based conflicts, though in each category identity plays a role. See ibid.

Indigenous women I met with underscored that gaining such literacy has been empowering, impactful, and beneficial for their survival. This perspective means it is not easy to dismiss such programs as neocolonial, even while their extractive and instrumentalizing underpinnings persist. Still, IPs and other religious and traditional leaders in the contexts of the barangays interpret their peace-promoting roles as beholden to their social locations and their capacity to build relationships through traditional conflict-resolution mechanisms and to ensure intercommunal peace governance. Rather than any kind of theological exchange, the latter depends on ongoing, immersive, and social relationship building, providing continuous horizontal virtuosity. This enables receptiveness to and responsibilizing for "keeping the peace."

In addition to structural change, personal change was ranked as the most significant domain of change by traditional religious leaders, Lupong Tagapamayaoa, and women, including an appreciation of enhanced knowledge about land rights for IPs and the acquisition of skills often not imparted to women. Similarly, in the earlier iteration of the 3Bs, relational change was identified by TRLs from six barangays as the most significant domain of change. By "relational change," they mean the cultivation of better relationships across communities, because they deem "harmony" to be pivotal "in building lasting peace."[23] Women who were generally not participants in the land dispute seminars reported appreciating the community peace projects or connectors as the most significant sphere of change. Such projects included bridge repair to avoid accidents, beds for a local health center to facilitate the safe delivery of babies, and on-site access to drinking water for schoolchildren.[24] Indigenous women, in particular, also reported the unintended impact of projects such as the installation of comfort rooms (bathrooms) on perceptions of the hygiene practices of IPs. Another woman spoke about how installing a water pipeline in Kuden as part of the 3Bs project freed teachers from worrying about the safety of children who previously had to cross busy roads to fetch drinking water.[25] The few women who benefited from the land dispute seminars reported feeling "empowered." Like other women who led nonviolent protests, such as Leymah Gbowee's mobilization of an interreligious coalition of Muslim and Christian women in Liberia, the women's empowerment and agency in forcing substantial peace

---

[23] CRS, "Perceptions of A3B," 4.
[24] Ibid., 11.
[25] Ibid., 11–12.

negotiations did not depend on their feminist rereading of religious texts. Instead, they involved cherry-picking, from the resources of their traditions, narratives about strong women that they cross-referenced with their own experiences.[26] Gbowee talks about the significance of prayer as a practice of peace and protest, which is how the women's mobilization began, with the women gathering for prayer in the fish market in Monrovia.[27]

Indeed, as I show throughout the book, peacebuilding efforts are punctuated with prayers and other methods of spiritualization that sacralize peacebuilding practices, even if they are as basic as earning enough to survive. The practices dubbed "solidarity," where individuals attend one another's religious and traditional holidays and even, in the case of the Philippines, observe certain practices of the other (such as fasting during the month of Ramadan), enhance the social fabric, mutual love, and the practice of peacebuilding as a site of intrasubjective and personal spiritual practice. However, interfaith relationship building that involves observance of others' religious practices requires virtuosity not possible for everyone.

A retired Catholic priest I spoke to told me about his long legacy of substantial engagement with Muslims in Mindanao and his understanding of the observance of Ramadan as a form of solidarity he had practiced for decades: "During Ramadan, we fasted like Muslims for thirty days. It was a way of expressing solidarity with them. But we had to explain also to the Christians in our communities the difference between the Muslim fast and the Christian fast."[28] Such a conversation brings a depth of engagement with theological differences, which, when combined with the urgency to strengthen friendships to enhance human security, reveals a theological and sociological commitment to plurality. This commitment tightens through the spiritualization of such friendships. "The bottom line of interfaith dialogue," he said, "is friendship. And many people forget that when they get involved with interfaith dialogue—they talk too much! But what really counts is friendship, human friendship."[29] However, friendship without knowledge of one's tradition is flawed, in his view. "Dialogue," he continued, "is to understand others as they understand themselves so they can understand us as we understand ourselves. So, the community and the individual person can

---

[26] See also Omer, "Religion, Gender, Justice, Violence, and Peace."
[27] For an interview with Gbowee where she reflects on these questions, see Harvard Divinity School, "Women as Catalysts for Peace," September 29, 2016, https://hds.harvard.edu/news/2016/09/29/women-catalysts-peace.
[28] Interview, Davao City, June 2018.
[29] Ibid.

have dialogue when they know themselves."[30] Reciprocal knowledge of one another is valuable but presumes double closures of communal and theological hermeneutics. My empirical evidence indicates that theological depth diminishes within the immersive experiential camps, the standardization of religious and peace education, interfaith trickle-down performativity, generic articulation of all religions and none at all, Twitter prophets, and first-aid hermeneutical countermessaging.

The same priest also recalled being invited by a Muslim bride, who had lost her father, to be her ceremonial father in her Muslim wedding, a moment he said he would cherish for the rest of his life, self-reflexively analyzing his impetus to engage in interfaith work, but also a life of plurality as grounded in his roots, which he traces to Cordoba, Spain.[31] Cordoba, of course, is a concrete geographic location. Still, it also conjures up the metaphor of *convivencia*, which refers to the history of Spain as a site of Muslim-Jewish-Christian coexistence and is now deployed as a metaphor for harmonious interreligious relations. The priest's acts of solidarity and the many friendships emerging through immersive and other programmatic efforts to bridge conflict-affected communities contribute to and are the outcome of spiritualizing and psychologizing peacebuilding practice. For the religious virtuoso, whose virtuosity also depends on the institutional backing of the Catholic Church—what this priest calls a "dialogue of light"—the very occurrence of friendship among neighbors and the "dialogue of collaboration" where "people get together, helping each other without talking about religion" may be more meaningful than a "dialogue of experts."

Hence, it is vital to listen to these transformative stories and to recognize the depth of the Sisyphean commitment to solidarity and its spiritual dimensions. Solidarity in this context operates through the amnesic conflict narrative and is thus refracted through the partnership model, where different groups are told to overcome their hate and pain. They are propelled to do so to invest in the "common good" or the "city of peace"—interpreted as a space outside their bounded identity threshold, whose supposed "secular" emptiness becomes a location for "interfaith" or intercommunal collaboration. This psychologized understanding of solidarity is different from political views of solidarity as co-resistance across groups based on an

---

[30] Ibid.
[31] Ibid.

intersectional analysis of interlocking forms of power and demands to rectify historical grievances.

The paradoxical outcome is that the religiosity and the spiritual dimensions of intrapersonal transformation from hate to love, solidarity, or relationship building unsettles the stereotypes and othering. This spiritualization makes the IRD an effective tool for rewriting the script of Mindanao as a celebration of harmonious plurality. At the same time, this rescripting unfolds within a neoliberal grammar, further entrenching it as it rhetorically markets itself as seeking to institute mechanisms to scale up interpersonal, intercommunal, and geographic and relational peace islands. Thus, interreligious peacebuilding governance and praxis psychologize and depoliticize peace.

Dan, the virtuoso peacebuilder we encountered in chapter 3, saw joining CRS's peacebuilding team as an opportunity to scale up. He remains committed to this possibility. In correspondence with me, he wrote that he saw his work as a religious and spiritual calling:

> It became an opportunity to serve and contribute on [a] wider scale with poor communities in Mindanao to develop and build [a] culture of peace as an effective response to end the cycle of violence and militarism. Organizing peace and dialogue networks at [the] community level became a great foundation, I believe, in supporting and sustaining peaceful advocacies for both horizontal and vertical peace processes to succeed. Also, engaging with the non-state actors in the peace and conflict transformation training series was very inspiring and encouraging. Learning with them to realize that there is no other means to peace but peace itself. Those were happy experiences with them as the popular support for peacebuilding work and the peace process between the government and Moro rebels was getting wider and scaling up.[32]

The paradox, however, is that the psychologizing (as opposed to political) construction of intercommunality as a form of spiritual practice prevents "scaling up." Scaling up may be the rhetorical output of peacebuilding/development policies that thrive on the "peace island" trope and rely on the "seed of peace" metaphor, burdening people as their autonomous change agents. Reducing individuals and their communities to unitary and homogenizing

---

[32] Follow-up interview via Facebook Messenger, May 2020.

scripts precludes an intersectional mobilization for alternative political futures. This depoliticizing segregationist approach to peacebuilding does not disrupt structures of violence. However, we cannot dismiss the transformative power of intra- and intersubjective change. It paves the way for decolonial love, even if it does not manifest in revolutionary outcomes. The spirituality invested in interculturality constitutes a generative form of religiosity not dependent upon religious learning and methodologies or upon historically and historicist hermeneutics; rather, it is dependent on intercultural immersive experiences, processes of self-formation and responsibilization, and sound bite reclamation of religious and cultural traditions as "good." The spirituality of peacebuilding praxis, even upon its thinness rather than queerness, is a decolonial opening, as I further show in the next section.

Opening from the Underside

The peace island is not a utopia but rather the outcome of relationship building amid hostility, memories of displacement, fear, intergenerational transmission of prejudice and stereotypes, and widespread poverty. The logic of the peace zones as a dimension of a broader understanding of interreligious peacebuilding governance consists, as I demonstrate throughout the book, of depoliticized intercommunal immersion to dispel stereotypes and to develop relationships to counter divisiveness, a focus on personal formation and spiritualization of peace and reconciliatory gestures, and an appreciation of difference as the source of a Mindanaoan plural identity. Intercommunal divisions are thus foregrounded as a source of violence (rather than their outcome), and the construction of peace islands—whether as an upshot of intra- and intersubjective engagements or through the consecration of a circumscribed geography as a peace zone—carves out a moment in time and space of harmony and friendship. This construct is once again a variation of the "planting a seed (of peace)" metaphor that I highlighted as co-opted into neoliberal forces that burdens the individual as an engine of change, as if people's predicaments of marginality, poverty, and discrimination were mere expressions of their cultural baggage.

However, I return to the tension I have sought to capture between the hegemonic logic and its remainders. The friendships born of intercommunal relationship-building and dialogues of action exceed the forces of orientalist securitizing and neoliberalism. This is where Danielle Allen's philosophical account of friendship resonates. For Allen, "friendship is not an emotion, but a practice, a set of hard-won complicated habits that are used to bridge trouble, difficulty, and differences in personality, experience, and aspiration."[33] Like the hard practice of democracy, friendship begins with "the recognition that friends have a *shared* life."[34] Allen's conception of friendship as a pivotal practice for shared, equitable, and democratic public life coalesces with the concepts of justice and agency mediated through ethical and legal reciprocity principles.[35] Unlike Allen's interest in political friendship to enhance an understanding of citizenship, political bonds, and power sharing, friendship as peace islands in Mindanao consolidates within a depoliticizing frame in the form of emotional labor and relational bonds.

Within this Mindanaoan landscape, the deployment of religion as peace and love becomes a mechanism for overcoming hate, fear, and a false sense of superiority through the concretized creation of peace islands. The peace islands, whether in people's hearts or through the formal negotiation of geographic parameters of a ceasefire, become sacred spaces whose maintenance depends on individuals' spiritual formation to resist hate through mutual appreciation and the active promotion of pluralism. The latter operates in tandem with the securitization of religion through the same mechanisms that synergize peacebuilding and development practices. Yet the friendships themselves are interpreted as sacred, pushing the analysis of religion and the practice of peace beyond its neoliberal utilitarian agenda or, at the very least, exposing its boundaries.

Even if the narrative regarding the cultivation of peace commitment exposes the neoliberal rationality of "planting a seed" through piety or self-formation, intra- and intersubjective transformation also depends on being open to decolonial love—a praxis and an instrument of social transformation emerging from the underside of Western modernity or the lived realities of coloniality with an aspiration for imagining ethics of plurality.[36] Imagining pluralistic ethics unfolds through people's scars born of their experiences as well as the legacies and colonial afterlives of the area, which they have no

---

[33] Danielle S. Allen, *Talking to Strangers: Anxieties of Citizenship since Brown v. Board of Education* (Chicago: University of Chicago Press, 2004), xxi. I also allude to Allen's discussion of friendship in chapter 2.
[34] Ibid., italics in original.
[35] Ibid., 130–37.
[36] For an exposition of what it means to think with the "underside of Western modernity," see Nelson Maldonado-Torres, *Against War: Views from the Underside of Modernity* (Durham, NC: Duke University Press, 2008).

choice but to inhabit but which they also subvert through concrete friendship and love. This is not the genocidal, exorcizing, colonial love that seeks to save the colonized from their cultural otherness, but rather a love that persists over, against, and beyond the colonial gaze.[37] This opening to decolonial love through reciprocal friendship shapes liberationist horizons, even if the love emerging from interreligious relationality does not resonate with the revolutionary critique of empire, which also necessitates a critique of heteronormativity and a feminist rereading of religious and cultural authorities.[38] This opening, Joseph Drexler-Dreis explains in his exposition of James Baldwin's notion of decolonial love, reveals itself in the concreteness of a loving relationship "on the exteriority of modernity"[39] and amounts to a form of political praxis of resistance, even if this resistance is mere existence expressed through survivalist piety and survivalist love and friendship.

This survivalist love intersects with but also diverges from neoliberal co-opting mechanisms of resiliency. The resistance to hate constitutes a form of decolonial agency. This is significant even if their nonutopian vision of a future reverberates with the harmony discourse and its depoliticizing contours and even if their narrative about the causes of their disharmony echoes culturalist reductionism that posits intercommunal misperceptions as its source. This constitutes a form of decolonial resistance precisely through the practice of friendship that refuses violence through relational or geographic peace zones. This practice of friendship seeks to manage plurality rather than to agitate a global emancipatory liberation from below. Such emancipatory visions celebrate revolutionary accounts of decolonial love as "a methodology of the oppressed."[40] This methodology draws upon mastery of poststructural, postmodern, feminist, ethnic, and queer theories; for Chela Sandoval, it is

---

[37] For an analysis of decolonial love's revolutionary potential and its place in feminist love studies, see Carolyn Ureña, "Loving from Below: Of (De)colonial Love and Other Demons," *Hypatia* 32, no. 1 (2017): 86–102, https://doi.org/10.1111/hypa.12302.

[38] Joseph Drexler-Dreis, "James Baldwin's Decolonial Love as Religious Orientation," *Journal of Africana Religions* 3, no. 3 (2015): 251–78; Joseph Drexler-Dreis, *Decolonial Love as a Source for Theological Reflection: A Response to Colonial Modernity* (New York: Fordham University Press, 2015). See also Chela Sandoval, *Methodology of the Oppressed* (Minneapolis: University of Minnesota Press, 2000).

[39] Drexler-Dreis, "James Baldwin's Decolonial Love," 255. The articulation of the exteriority of modernity goes back to Enrique Dussel. See his *The Underside of Modernity: Apel, Ricoeur, Rorty, Taylor, and the Philosophy of Liberation*, trans. and ed. Eduardo Medieta (Atlantic Highlands, NJ: Humanities Press, 1996).

[40] This notion of a methodology of the oppressed refers to the important intervention by Chela Sandoval; for the concept of "oppositional consciousness," see her groundbreaking "U.S. Third World Feminism: The Theory and Method of Oppositional Consciousness in the Postmodern World," *Genders* 10 (Spring 1991): 1–24, doi:10.5555/gen.1991.10.1.

fluency in all these critical interventions that constitutes "love," which she understands as "a technology for social transformation."[41] However, these skills require facility with critiques of capitalism and neocolonial globalization as well as a mapping of dissident consciousness produced by Black and Third World feminists.[42] Such conversations appear very far removed from the realities of Mindanao or Malindi. The peace zones, however, aspire to create livable spaces that nonetheless revolve around love as a hermeneutics of social action, even if they do not also decolonize their theological and political imagination.[43]

The culture of peace seminars, the peace zones, and the horizontal foci on intercultural immersion and intrasubjective transformation permeate Mindanao, and their agentic force cannot be simply critiqued away as the transmogrification of colonial domination—even if the scaling-up question persists and indicates how the spiritualization of peace praxis, like the other mechanisms for resiliency building I have traced in this book, depoliticizes, psychologizes, and obscures an intersectional outlook through the double closure of religiocultural hermeneutics indexed to unitary accounts of social identities.

The *Ginapalad Taka* and cultures of peace seminars in the region of Pikit where Father Bert works, similar efforts of peace education in Zamboanga City under the auspices of Father Angel and the Peace Advocates of Zamboanga, interfaith work on peace such as the mandatory annual Mindanao Week of Peace activities—all reveal something that exceeds neoliberal co-optation. These activities generate islands of peace, sustained through openings toward decolonial love, which is a spiritual and political praxis (Figure 7.1).[44] This praxis entails connecting to the core of religious traditions as a resource and a motivation for imagining peaceful cohabitation. It also exposes how imagining a geographic or relational space as a peace island amid suffering is a form of survivalist piety, not a utopian longing.

This particularity confirms why these islands of peace convey authentic relationship building and intercommunal friendships that exceed the developmentalist gaze and persist as channels for conflict resolution. In some instances, they enhance the quality of life, even if this takes the shape

---

[41] Sandoval, *Methodology of the Oppressed*, 2.
[42] Ibid., 3.
[43] Angela Davis, "Foreword," in Sandoval, *Methodology of the Oppressed*, xiii.
[44] See also Leanne Betasamosake Simpson, *Islands of Decolonial Love* (Winnipeg: Arbeiter Ring, 2013).

Figure 7.1 A poster advertising the Mindanao Week of Peace (2018) in Zamboanga. Reproduced with permission by PRO9 Command.

of neoliberal survivalist piety. To be sure, the message of peace, love, forgiveness, harmonious pluralism, and friendship, when it is implemented through summer and peace camps, may need to be subjected to decolonial parsing for all of these concepts' nefarious deployment to enhance hegemonies and maintain the status quo. Still, the friendships, love, care, and aspiration for peace and safety precede and exceed any ideologically inflected critical analysis. But the question regarding scaling remains, even if it does not encompass the critical edges of intersectional critique or subaltern cosmopolitanism.

The issue is not only the challenge of scaling up from peace zones or fleeting moments of friendship cultivated in the culture of peace seminars. Instead, the challenge is identifying how such small-scale peacebuilding praxis is, in effect, highly consistent with neoliberal rationality. Horizontality is all the more enhanced through the religiosity and spirituality invested in interreligious peacebuilding governance and the nonpolitical relationships it builds. Neoliberal rationality and its mechanisms of governance and devolution cohere with religious leaders/actors like Father Bert and their virtuoso commitment to Sisyphean peacebuilding. Father Bert's recovered understanding of his faith as about peace(building) is what he attributes as the source of his refusal to accept the conditions of violence and chaos. Thus his Sisyphean persistence constitutes a transformative plan rather than a faithful resignation to suffering. The aspiration to transform the conditions of suffering opens him up to the routinization of IRD (or his NGO-ization) through the Oblates of Mary Foundation in Pikit, where he oversees cultures of peace seminars and other activities that enable grassroots relationship building and the implementation of peace zones with an expectation that the seed of peace will sprout and even self-sustain.[45]

Yet perseverance, in communal perceptions of the individual (i.e., the "seed") as the engine of broader change, constitutes a form of grassroots psychologizing and depoliticizing praxis that entrenches the devolution of responsibility to those least powerful and capacitates them to sustain—through relationship building, peace zones, and similar bottom-up efforts, such as livelihood initiatives—relative stability and peace while structural and historical forms of violence continue to disadvantage and marginalize. I also have referred to this in terms of the "horizontalization" of religious virtuosity through neoliberal mechanisms and dependency upon hermeneutically foreclosed accounts of religiocultural traditions and depoliticization. The depoliticizing logic thrives upon a non-intersectional approach to intercommunal and interreligious dialogue of action as operative on generic registers intent on maintaining rhetoric about scaling up while actually entrenching a practice of horizontal devolutionary problem-solving, the Sisyphean labor of which continues to burden those at the margins.

Indeed, the peace island trope relies on a modernist logic of closure, which decolonial interjections object to through retrieval of archipelagic social imaginaries. Marcos Cuevas-Hewitt, for example, writes, "The importance of the trope of the archipelago is exactly this: that it shifts attention *away* from compartmentalized island space and redirects our gaze toward the *relational* space of the sea."[46] The island trope relies on hermeneutical religious closure indexed to communal boundedness, which interreligious peacebuilding praxis reinforces. Still, as I have shown, hundreds of intrapersonal and intercommunal transformational narratives attribute causality to participants' regrounding themselves in thin and hermeneutically

---

[45] See also chapter 2.
[46] Marcos Cuevas-Hewitt, "Sketches of an Archipelagic Poetics of Postcolonial Belonging" in *Pangayaw and Decolonizing Resistance: Anarchism in the Philippines*, ed. Bas Umali (Oakland, CA: PM Press, 2020), 24–32 (29).

closed, yet causal, conceptions of their identity (religiosity/culturality) as peace and love.[47]

Tracing the colonial underpinnings of peacebuilding agency grounded in religiosity and culturality, as well as listening to the many people who populate spaces of interreligious action and intercultural engagement in the Global South, also illuminates what Nelson Maldonado-Torres understands as a form of decolonial politics, or "the ethical orientation of the self in conditions of systematic dehumanization."[48] I interacted with communities of peace ("peace constituencies")[49] in the Global South because imprinted in their embodied memories and intergenerational traumas are the violence of coloniality and its construction of "sub ontological difference" among people—violence that relegates them to the "zone of nonbeing," in Sylvia Wynter's formulation.[50] Ethics, in other words, like survivalist decolonial love, does not operate on a different scale in the zone of nonbeing and is not abrogated altogether. Rather, "any act that affirms the potential of ethical orientation of a subject in the zone of nonbeing cannot be taken but as an irruption or violent act. This also points to the inseparability of ethics and politics in decolonization."[51]

This view of ethics from the underside paves the way for an analysis of how IRD has functioned as a vehicle for decolonial ethical relationships among communities divided along communal identities. These are divisions rooted in colonial legacies. These communities' ethical task is to script their "common humanity" through an appreciation of one another's humanity, religiosity, and grievances in the colonial afterlives. Such rescripting from hate to love, even while relying on an anemic conception of the "religious," "justice," and the "secular," nevertheless amounts to a form of decolonial politics. Indeed, the refusal to hate and the construction of peace zones constitute an act of resistance to the divisive colonial logic and to its differentiated abyssal

---

[47] CRS shared with me multiple evidence-based studies and evaluations of programs that present stories of change. The findings are corroborated by multiple studies within the religion, conflict, and peacebuilding subfield.

[48] Nelson Maldonado-Torres, "Race, Religion, and Ethics in the Modern/Colonial World," *Journal of Religious Ethics* 42, no. 4 (2014): 691–711 (706), https://onlinelibrary.wiley.com/doi/10.1111/jore.12078.

[49] The concept of a "peace constituency" was developed by John Paul Lederach; see, for example, his "Sustainable Reconciliation in Divided Societies," in *Building Peace*, ed. U.S. Institute of Peace (Washington, DC: UCIP Press, 1998), 87–97.

[50] Sylvia Wynter, "Unsettling the Coloniality of Being/Power/Truth/Freedom: Towards the Human, after Man, Its Overrepresentation—An Argument," *New Centennial Review* 3, no. 3 (2003): 257–337. See also Maldonado-Torres, "Race, Religion, and Ethics," 706.

[51] Maldonado-Torres, "Race, Religion, and Ethics," 707.

geography. If the invisible lines persist in reconstituting abyssal thinking and zones of disposability, as they do through the neoliberal securitizing interreligious harmony discourse, so will the conundrum of scaling continue in its depolitical technocratic register whose sustainability depends upon the impossibility of scaling up.[52]

The concept of scaling, in other words, does not own up to the violent legacies of peace and therefore participates in further enhancing the neoliberal frame. Similarly, the peace island trope occludes archipelagic sociopolitical imaginaries. Still, one cannot discount the meaningful relationships, which constitute and sustain peace islands, whether geographically or relationally. This is where decolonial ethics reveals itself in the form of humanity and love from the underside of a persistently colonial entrenchment. Some[53] have illuminated such love as the embrace of one another outside and from the underside of the racialized and heteropatriarchal colonial gaze. It is the realness of the experiences and friendships formed in the context of programmatic peacebuilding that speaks back to the utopian expectation of anticolonial and decolonial scholarship to disrupt everything and cultivate a comprehensive analysis of the intersections of oppressive systems and ideologies as a way out of such oppressions.

The communities involved in constructing peace islands of various forms do not subscribe to the normative scope of decolonial love as a praxis centered on a comprehensive decolonial critique of the matrices of oppression and domination or of their underpinning and intersecting gendered and racialized economic logics. Nevertheless, their relationships of love and friendship illumine decolonial openings. And so the issue is not how to shift from horizontal to vertical change but rather how the capacity of the horizontal virtuosity to work depends upon both the vertical perpetuation of neoliberal rationality and decolonial disruptions. The latter themselves depend upon the spiritualization of peace practices whose effectiveness thrives on hermeneutically closed religiosity and unitary conceptions of the community that equate people's traditions with generic appeals to peace, love, and an ethics of plurality.

Intrasubjective transformation from hate to love, which means speaking across cultural and religious thresholds as if the threshold itself is the source of

---

[52] For an exposition of this question of scaling from horizontal to vertical peace in John Paul Lederach's articulation, see Michele Maiese, "Levels of Action" July 2003 *Beyond Intractability* https://www.beyondintractability.org/essay/hierarchical_intervention_levels.

[53] For example, Simpson, *Islands of Decolonial Love*. I also discuss her work in chapter 8.

discord, becomes a form of spiritual practice that sustains this devolutionary neoliberal logic of peace. This logic myopically conceals the underlying afterlife of colonial violence and the possibility of a politicized intersectional analysis and archipelagic social imaginaries that would otherwise transgress an engineered culturally reductive and ahistorical script about the causes of conflict. Still, the transformative experience itself constitutes a spiritual practice that, like the sacred geography and experiential rationality of the peace zone, exceeds the neoliberal and securitizing logics, as I have shown.

What I have been analyzing as hermeneutically closed religiosity hermetically closes communities to the possibility of a democratic political imagination and cross-group solidarity based on common grievances and power analyses. It is to this degree that nonpolitical and segregationist religion and the business of peace/harmony have been weaponized in the service of "getting along" rather than justice. Indeed, the prophet as a charismatic virtuoso exemplar is replaced with the NGO-ized prophetic lite and religiocratic infrastructures as the focus of the analysis of religion and the practice of peace with their maintenance of hermeneutical closures. Additionally, *realpolitik* renders feminist and queer interpretive horizons of justice as luxurious and irrelevant. Such hermeneutical closure is why social justice movements see political struggles as necessarily feminist and queer.[54] This is not the case within the religion harmony business I portray here, which reveals its embeddedness within a neoliberal discourse that relies upon traditional hierarchies and moral authorities.[55]

Nonrevolutionary Love

While interreligious peacebuilding deploys the language of effectiveness and instrumentality in its descriptions of religious actors, institutions, and

---

[54] There are numerous historical examples of solidarity across secular and religious divides, including the celebrated examples of Poland's Solidarity and the antiapartheid mobilization in South Africa. However, the bracketing in such coalitions of feminist and queer religious interpretations may be detrimental to the aftermath of such momentous political revolutionary moments for the persistence of structural and cultural forms of violence, including explicit attacks on LGBTQI+ communities, rampant violence against girls and women, and, in Poland, a consolidation of a right-wing coalition with conservative religious actors. See Rashied Omar's reflection on such questions regarding the aftermath of the antiapartheid coalitional mobilization in "Global Interreligious Peacebuilding," *Kroc Cast Peace Studies Conversations*, episode 27, recorded November 2019, https://kroc.nd.edu/news-events/podcasts/the-kroc-cast/.

[55] For this point about neoliberalism and its openness to traditional hierarchies and morality, see my discussion of Wendy Brown's critical analysis of neoliberalism, especially in chapter 2.

counternarratives, its actual endurance and success rely on the capacity of people to inhabit the potential for decolonial love. As I have shown, an opening to decolonial love manifests through the concreteness of a loving relationship as the overcoming of hate and divisive outlook. Such relationships permeate the landscape of interreligious and intercultural peacebuilding in the Global South, where religion is deployed in multiple ways to combat hopelessness.

I use the language of "potential" and "opening" because "love" does not demystify the conditions of coloniality. Rather than utopian or revolutionary, it is a survivalist decolonial love, a mechanism against fatalism and despair. Empirically, even if not decolonizing religiosity, elicitive interreligious peacebuilding practices contribute to rescripting the common good and mitigating hopelessness and hatred. Indeed, the elicitive appeal to the "common" good operates with a generic register that presumes a unitary public always invisibilizing counterpublics and the exclusions that generate them. Yet the decolonial openings revealed by relational peace zones force decolonial theory to interrogate its distance from such projects of survival.

On the one hand, the distance between decolonial theory and the authentic spirituality and religious peacebuilding agency that I encountered in Kenya and the Philippines clarifies a gap between decolonial theory and the people whose emancipation it purports to care about. Interreligious peace praxis, on the other hand, engages elicitively, but through myopia and hermeneutical closures that delimit its decolonial horizons. The effort of this book has been to put them into a generative conversation with one another.

I also referred to this gap as a "decolonial opening," a site of love and hope irreducible to empire or neoliberal rationality. Such openings to decolonial love rely more often than not on thin rather than critical hermeneutics, and this is the gap across which the irony resides. This is an opening to survivalist decolonial love, even if it does not tap into love's iconoclastic emancipatory potential that liberationist queer and feminist theologies imagine. To further grasp this opening and to identify alternative ways of thinking about hermeneutically closed religiosity beyond its participation in coloniality, we need to identify gaps where religiosity exceeds its deployment as a technology of empire. Throughout the book, I have oscillated between the discursive force of neoliberalizing and securitizing religion and the agentic persistence and authentic spiritual force of people on the ground whose embodied experiences and survivalist piety cannot simply be assimilated into a broad or abstract critique of hegemony and discursive formations. This is the "So what?" of my comparative work.

In the concluding chapter, I examine decoloniality's religion problem and peace studies' decolonial anxiety. What challenges decolonial theory and praxis is that the people I encountered in the programmatic spaces of peacebuilding/development may ultimately enhance neoliberal logic. Nevertheless, they exceed it through their friendships and love for one another. Still, the spiritual meanings of their practices are all but invisibilized for a purist decolonial theory that appears to require a litmus test of norms' disruption at the nexuses of gender, race, religion, class, and so forth. Can the love and genuine relations built across communal divides, whose divisions reach back to and reveal the long operations of coloniality, be recognized as meaningful decolonial openings, even if/as they unfold within engineered, programmatic, postsecular, neoliberal, peacebuilding/development frames? Might such openings speak back to decolonial theory's purism and challenge decolonial thought to attend to the urgent struggles of survival?

8
Does Justice Have Anything to Do with Religion and the Practice of Peace?

Cohering the Peace

This book's layered examination of intra- and interreligious peacebuilding work in Kenya and the Philippines illuminates both the neoliberalization and the securitization of religion. In interviews with numerous stakeholders, the links are clear between the vulnerability of children and youth and their propensity for recruitment to violent organizations. Thus, a focus on children and youth—as also the focus on women—becomes a security policy issue (as I have shown in previous chapters) as much as a moral imperative. Moral arguments are then articulated through appeals to generic humanity and a unitary conception of the "public good," on the one hand, and generic androcentric religion, on the other, problematizing neither and entrenching both. The analytic prism of coloniality refracts the endurance of the colonial in the postcolonial presence and exposes the postsecular turn as utilitarian and dependent on hermeneutically closed accounts of religious and cultural traditions. This is one of the curious findings of my comparative examination, which asks not only what religion can do for development/peacebuilding but what this constellation of practices does for religion.

The Silsilah Dialogue Movement, founded in Zamboanga City in 1984 by Father Sebastiano d'Ambra, offers a response to the latter question. *Silsilah* means "chain" or "link" in Arabic. The movement sees itself as "a call to live the spirituality of life-in-dialogue and to witness God's presence in the plurality of cultures and religions as a habitat and an experience that leads to dialogue and peace."[1] As a Silsilah coordinator I spoke with in Davao stressed, their approach is not merely about relationships, but is also—perhaps primarily—about self-formation and spiritual reconnection to a holistic

---

[1] Information about Silsilah can be accessed at Silsilah Dialogue Movement, "History of Silsilah," http://www.silsilahdialogue.com/history-of-silsilah/ (accessed June 15, 2018).

approach to intercultural relations and ecology.[2] Its immersive intercultural logic, consistent with neoliberal rationality, locates change in individuals—their formation and eventual capacity to act as change agents. According to the movement's description, the numerous alums of Silsilah Forums are said to be transformed through their exposure to the humanity of others. As a result of this transformation, they become committed to peace.[3] Dialogue here "is not a strategy but a spirituality that is needed in moving together towards peace."[4] Participants in the forums are encouraged to spread their skills and insights through various means: participating in seminars on religious formation, engaging in dialogue, leading conflict resolution workshops, and identifying potential Muslim and Christian communities ripe for consecrating "islands of peace" amid regions affected by violence.[5]

The dialogue itself, as another coordinator of Silsilah remarked, centers on connecting to "common pasts even in the languages and the stories" rather than different pasts and stories.[6] Because Silsilah's approach aligns with the approach of religiocrats, it is not surprising that it has attracted investment from other civil society actors and international entities such as the UN. The UN has facilitated the World Interfaith Harmony Week since 2010 with the support of King Abdullah II of Jordan. This connection illuminates how local and global groups reinforce each other's practices through feedback loops. The framing of the UN observance is theologically consistent with Silsilah's commitment to building dialogue between Muslims and Christians. This commitment is based on the commandments of love of God and neighbor and adds a third: "love of good(will)."[7] Hence, the World Interfaith Harmony Week displays the breadth of interfaith actions and an understanding of the role of interreligious dialogue in cultivating cultures of peace. It relies on *A*

---

[2] Interview in Davao, June 2018. Silsilah intersects and cross-fertilizes with the long-standing Bishop-Ulama Conference.

[3] For a critical analysis of the "planting a seed" logic and its reverberation with the scaling discourse, see chapter 7.

[4] To learn more about Silsilah's forums and approach to dialogue, see Silsilah Dialogue Movement, "Silsilah Forum," http://www.silsilahdialogue.com/silsilah-forum/ (accessed June 15, 2018). The Silsilah Forum spread throughout Mindanao and the Philippines broadly, including violence-affected regions such as Antipolo, Basilan, Bongao-Taw-Tawi, Bukidnon, Cagayan de Oro, Cebu City, Cotabato, Davao, Iligan, Jolo, Kidapawan, Manila, Midsayap, Marawi, Pagadian, Pikit, Cotabato, Siasi, and Zamboanga Sibugay.

[5] I focus on the meaning of Zones of Peace especially in chapter 7.

[6] Focus group at Silsilah office in Davao City, June 2018.

[7] World Interfaith Harmony Week, https://worldinterfaithharmonyweek.com/ (accessed October 8, 2020).

Common Word between Us and You, an open letter signed by Muslim leaders calling for Muslim-Christian dialogue (launched in October 2007).[8]

As in previous examples, a "generic" understanding of dialogue based on the commandments that does not include a rigorous account of religion and violence in all their forms enhances utilitarian and androcentric conceptions of religious traditions.[9] Indeed, the limits of the interfaith dialogue framework come through in Silsilah's nonfeminist appeals to ecological connectivity.[10] Unlike the tradition of ecofeminist theology, this framework never challenges stereotypical accounts of gender roles. Often, these accounts embed such visions of gender into the very ontology of the social world. In contrast, the theological insights of ecofeminism challenge human- or androcentric worldviews. They further show how such ontologization affects colonized and marginalized people, whose subordination was often authorized by feminizing them.[11] These ecofeminist insights notwithstanding, the intra- and interfaith dialogue I analyze here is subordinated to the apparent demands of *realpolitik*. It persists in *doing* religion for problem-solving. Because *realpolitik* governs the way these forms of dialogues are carried out, feminist and other marginal epistemologies appear nonpragmatic, luxurious, and irrelevant to the business of peace.[12] This dismissal, however, may present itself as *realist*, but, as I have demonstrated, its confinement

---

[8] Yazid Said and Lejla Demiri, eds., *The Future of Interfaith Dialogue: Muslim-Christian Encounters through a Common World* (Cambridge: Cambridge University Press, 2018).

[9] A similar interfaith and intercultural logic underpins the harmony business in Kenya, as the example of the Harmony Institute suggests. See Harmony Institute, "Our Philosophy," https://harmonyinstitute.or.ke/about-us/#1561032430839-4935d108-02c4 (accessed September 28, 2020).

[10] See, for example, Silsilah, "Dialogue with Creation," http://www.silsilahdialogue.com/dialogue-with-creation/ (accessed January 12, 2021). There is a growing tradition of interfaith or interreligious just peacemaking theory that involves multiple people articulating another paradigm for thinking of the relation between religion and peace/use of force/violence. Other paradigms include pacifism, just war theory, and the Crusades or holy wars. The "interfaith" aspects of interfaith just peacemaking theory involve showing how resources within the Jewish, Muslim, and Christian traditions are conducive to such a theory and are capable of grappling hermeneutically with textual references that appear to justify violence. This theory is valuable but reflects the broader field's tendency to differentiate the discussion of religion, war, and direct violence from analyses of religion and other forms of violence, including discursive, epistemic, structural, cultural, and symbolic. I address those issues in other works, including Omer, "Religion, Gender, Justice, Violence, and Peace." For a representative articulation of an "Abrahamic" approach to interfaith just peacemaking, see Susan Brooks Thistlethwaite, ed., *Interfaith Just Peacemaking: Jewish, Christian, and Muslim Perspectives on the New Paradigm of Peace and War* (New York: Palgrave Macmillan, 2011). This trend also reverberates at the highest and most symbolic levels with a historic conference on nonviolence and just peace convened at the Vatican in 2016. See Ken Butigan, "Historic Vatican Conference Calls for Nonviolence and 'Just Peace,'" *Waging Nonviolence: People Powered News and Analysis,* April 12, 2016, https://wagingnonviolence.org/2016/04/vatican-conference-calls-for-nonviolence-just-peace-pope-francis/.

[11] For a classical account, see Rosemary Radford Ruether, *Gaia and God: An Ecofeminist Theology of Earth Healing* (New York: HarperCollins, 1992).

[12] See also Omer, "Religion, Gender, Justice, Violence, and Peace."

of "good" religion to the utilitarian logic is normative in heteropatriarchal hardwiring. Interfaith dialogue and intercultural encounter, therefore, become fused with hermeneutically closed approaches to religious and cultural traditions that foreclose the possibility of feminist and queer analyses and further entrench the neoliberal regime, itself a moral political project that, Wendy Brown demonstrates, thrives on reinscribed traditional hierarchical structuring of social life.[13]

Silsilah's consistency with the framing of the UN's World Interfaith Harmony Week reveals the consolidation of high-level, grassroots, and Astroturf interfaith dialogue with appeals to "common humanity," the "public good," and apparently self-evident concerns for children and youth. The latter are framed as morally unambiguous and intuitive. This is another example of a "generic" religion. The effectiveness of religion in imbuing certain actors with the designation "religious," regardless of the modes in which this religiosity or culturality is imagined (and regardless of *knowing* religion at all), can only be measurable within the "generic" sphere of action. Accordingly, interreligious dialogue, driven by the demands for urgent collaborative actions and statements, is not conducive to hermeneutical disruption and innovation.

The case of the CICC in Malindi likewise exemplifies this point. This is because it shows that to change harmful practices seemingly sanctioned by tradition, it is necessary to engage interpretively with that tradition. Yet the hermeneutical work, as I indicated earlier, of the CICC does not involve a theological analysis of the androcentrism of scriptural and other traditions. Thus, its focus on changing sexual and gender norms remains firmly within a heteropatriarchal framework. This framework underpins the norms that the clerics seek to transform as part of their broader concern with individuals to overcome poverty and marginalization cycles.

When asked to reflect on how moral and religious teachings affect questions of poverty, one cleric commented that religion can be a contributing factor when "unauthorized and homegrown" religious leaders misinterpret tradition to devalue education.[14] Other clerics confirmed the problem of the increased presence of "religious leaders who . . . do not work under [institutional] umbrellas."[15] Speaking about the challenge of battling cultural norms conducive to girls' commodification in a dowry-based economy, another

---

[13] See chapter 2 for this discussion.
[14] Focus group with the CICC conducted by Tom Purekal, Malindi, August 2018.
[15] Ibid.

cleric talked about the difficulties of addressing misinterpretations and about the need to engage in men-only or boys-only forums "to sensitize [them] to stop looking at girls as income-generating activity."[16] During a focus group with community clerics in Malindi, another cleric responded to a question that probed whether working on the issue of reducing child marriage led to any theological reflections about the strengths of, and gaps in, religious teachings related to gender roles, marriage, and so forth. He said, "Theology contributed to [the] protection of [the] child" and then referred to a familiar Quranic proof-text.[17] A focus group with male caregivers who participated in the Dialogue of Action Project—reflecting the multisectoral efforts to reduce child marriage and sexual abuse[18]—explained that they wanted to solidify sustainable interreligious governance in tackling child abuse for a variety of reasons. One of these included the financial incentives built into the program that enable parents to generate income. These caregivers conveyed that a departure from authentic religious teachings causes the social ills of their communities. When asked whether they always agree with their religion's views of gender roles, the clerics responded affirmatively, assigning blame to those unauthorized religious leaders who depart from "authentic" interpretations of their tradition in condoning harmful practices.[19] When another focus group was asked about culture and religion pertaining to child marriage and other harmful practices, they responded, "This is cultural. According to religion, all children are equal."[20]

Regardless, efforts to stop harmful practices such as child marriage and incest are not necessarily attentive to the harm that the textual and nontextual traditions themselves have long inflicted on girls and women. The limited roles women can assume—daughters, mothers, whores, widows, nuns, saints—reduce them to supporting (instrumental) actors, at best. The (male) clerics argue that better-educated women can be both economically productive and more capable of fulfilling their scripted obligations. As a result, they can influence broader change. Such an argument reflects neoliberal rationality more than substantive theological intervention. It is essential to zoom

---

[16] Ibid.
[17] Focus group with community clerics conducted by a research team of the University of Notre Dame's International Unit, Malindi, August 2018.
[18] See Grace Ndugu, "Coastal Kenya: United for Children's Rights," in *Interreligious Action for Peace: Studies in Muslim-Christian Cooperation*, ed. Tom Bamat, Myla Leguro, Nell Bolton, and Atalia Omer (Baltimore, MD: Catholic Relief Services, 2017), 59–70.
[19] Focus group with male caregivers, Malindi, August 2018.
[20] Focus group with the Local Area Advisory Council of CICC, Mombasa, April 2018.

out to reflect again on the wider terrain of religion and peace/development within which the CICC operates. Even when religiocrats avoid labeling certain cultural practices as "harmful," they do so because such labeling signals culturally deterministic and reductive explanatory frames, which may be ineffective on the ground. Harnessing "religious actors" through a theological approach to tackle such practices relies, however, on accessing "authentic" and "good" (and thus equally reductive) interpretations of religious and cultural traditions.

The point to stress here is that, even in this instance, when religious leaders were directly asked to reflect on gender norms, their underlying theology remained patriarchal and androcentric. Hence, a human rights lens and a focus on gender is superficial if it does not involve a hermeneutical interrogation that disrupts closures of the interpretive space and essentialized accounts of religion and people's scripted roles.[21]

Indeed, women's scripted roles made them worthy of investment. I showed in the previous chapters that, in the case of the Kenyan antiterrorism bill and a similar one in the Philippines,[22] securitizing religion threatens to criminalize parental relations by underscoring reporting duties of "warning signs" of radicalization. Women's instrumentality and positionality on the communal battleground make them a target demographic for investment. This securitization of the sphere of social reproduction illuminates the relevance of gendered scripts to the neoliberal underpinning of peacebuilding/development, which thrives on traditional hierarchies and depoliticization and people's capacity to form coalitions that transgress unitary accounts of their respective identities to make political claims. The realist argument

---

[21] Some of the ironies about navigating the space of religion, conflict, and peace and gender justice are conveyed in Susan Hayward and Katherine Marshall, eds., *Women, Religion, and Peacebuilding: Illuminating the Unseen* (Washington, DC: U.S. Institute of Peace Press, 2015). Both authors identify a form of agency in women's invisibility and marginalized social location. Yet women and others involved with feminist-oriented movements are often not incorporated into the "global engagement with religion" rubric, even if they are explicitly working from within their religious identity. In such cases, their support comes from global institutions aimed at promoting gender justice and women's rights. One example of such an institution is the Global Fund for Women. Examples of groups working firmly within their traditions to expand the scope of gender justice include Musawa–Global Movement for Equality and Justice in the Muslim Family and the Ecumenical Women's Initiative, which is based in Croatia.

[22] See U.S. Department of State, "Country Reports on Terrorism 2019: Kenya," https://www.state.gov/reports/country-reports-on-terrorism-2019/kenya/ (accessed February 15, 2020); Republic of Kenya, Special Issue: Kenya Gazette Supplement No. 104 (Senate Bills No. 20), Senate Bills, 2018 (Nairobi, July 19, 2018); Human Rights Watch, "Philippines: New Anti-Terrorism Act Endangers Rights," June 5, 2020, https://www.hrw.org/news/2020/06/05/philippines-new-anti-terrorism-act-endangers-rights#.

notwithstanding, gender justice is central for peace that overcomes its legacy of violence. A peace that does not also entail gender justice is no peace at all.[23]

Disrupting the Peace

Justice, I have shown throughout the book, has little to do with the practice of interreligious peace. A justice orientation would require an intersectional hermeneutical disruption of peace. However, the hermeneutically closed approach to religion/culture reveals the extent to which religion's intervention in peacebuilding lacks, by design and as a matter of course, theological disobedience, to play on a key decolonial practice Walter Mignolo calls "epistemic disobedience."[24]

But what does it mean to be epistemologically disobedient? For Boaventura de Sousa Santos, it means epistemologies (or ways of knowing) from the South, which he interprets as an intercultural fluidity grounded in a critique of hegemony.[25] Rather than rendering human rights discourse as colonial discourse, Santos reimagines the possibility of human rights' emancipatory potential through epistemological resistance to neoliberalism and neocolonialism. He interprets the mechanism of such resistance as the post-abyssal hermeneutical practice of intercultural dialogue.[26] This entails an antipurist positionality, which departs "from the modern utopias that are at the foundation of the Eurocentric critical tradition."[27] It is an open-ended utopia rather than a hermetically and hermeneutically closed harmony discourse, and thus it disrupts the logic of interreligious peacebuilding. Accordingly, intercultural dialogue, for Santos, entails that all knowledge is interknowledge[28]—whose incompleteness paves the way, from the ground up, for imagining a radical anticapitalist and anticolonial future.[29] For Santos, political emancipation is bound up with anti-imperial epistemological resistance from the South to

[23] See also Omer, "Religion, Gender, Justice, Violence, and Peace."
[24] Walter D. Mignolo, "Geopolitics of Sensing and Knowing: On (De)Coloniality, Border Thinking and Epistemic Disobedience," *Postcolonial Studies* 14, no. 3 (2011): 273–83, https://doi.org/10.1080/13688790.2011.613105.
[25] See Boaventura de Sousa Santos, *Epistemologies of the South: Justice against Epistemicide* (New York: Routledge, 2014). See also the introduction for further discussion of Santos's concepts.
[26] Boaventura de Sousa Santos, "Human Rights as Emancipatory Script? Post-Abyssal Conception of Rights," in *Another Knowledge Is Possible: Beyond Northern Epistemologies*, ed. Boaventura de Sousa Santos (London: Verso, 2007), 3–40.
[27] Santos, *Epistemologies of the South*, 26.
[28] Santos, "Beyond Abyssal Thinking," 66.
[29] Ibid., 71.

Eurocentric universalism and the pragmatic strengthening of what he calls "a subaltern cosmopolitanism" or counterhegemonic globalization. It is a site of post-abyssal interculturality, the result of translation among critical forms of knowledge[30] underlying exchanges and dialogues among social movements, including those led by Indigenous activists.[31] For Santos, political emancipation and global social justice are possible, but depend on epistemic resistance. This is different from those who claim that a decolonial outcome can only mean, materially and not metaphorically, getting back their land.[32]

For Mignolo, reminiscent of long-established feminist insights, epistemic disobedience entails a border epistemology, or a border thinking/sensing/doing, that captures the experiences and consciousness of dispersion, dispossession, and migration among those classified outside the bounds of the normative human. Border thinking/sensing/doing connects the Third World—the origin points of decoloniality—and (im)migrant consciousness.[33] "Dwelling and thinking in the borders" means living "local histories [and] confronting global designs."[34]

Critical border thinking, or what Ramón Grosfoguel reinterprets as nonfundamentalist, subaltern challenges to Eurocentric modernity,[35]

---

[30] Santos, *Epistemologies of the South*, 42.

[31] Santos, "Beyond Abyssal Thinking," 63–65. See also Boaventura de Sousa Santos, *Toward a New Legal Common Sense: Law, Globalization, and Emancipation* (London: Butterworths, 2002), 459. Therein, he talks about "cosmopolitanism of the oppressed." For the burgeoning literature on subaltern cosmopolitanism, see Shail Mayaram, "Rereading Global Cities: Topographies of an Alternative Cosmopolitanism in Asia," in *The Other Global City*, ed. Sahil Mayaram (New York: Routledge, 2009), 1–32; Sonja Buckel and Jens Wissel, "State Project Europe: The Transformation of the European Border Regime and the Production of Bare Life," *International Political Sociology* 4, no. 1 (2010): 33–49, https://doi.org/10.1111/j.1749-5687.2009.00089.x. For works that examine subaltern cosmopolitanism via a borderland epistemology, see Homi Bhabha, "Unsatisfied: Notes on Vernacular Cosmopolitanism," in *Text and Nation: Cross-Disciplinary Essays on Cultural and National Identities*, ed. L. García-Moreno and P. C. Pfeiffer (Columbia, SC: Camden House, 1996), 191–207; Walter D. Mignolo, "The Many Faces of Cosmo-polis: Border Thinking and Critical Cosmopolitanism," *Public Culture* 12, no. 3 (2000): 721–48, https://doi.org/10.1215/08992363-12-3-721. For the convergences of the epistemological and postcolonial turns with critical geography, see David Harvey, *Cosmopolitanism and the Geographies of Freedom* (New York: Columbia University Press, 2009); Alex Lubin, *Geographies of Liberation: The Making of an Afro-Arab Political Imaginary* (Chapel Hill: University of North Carolina Press, 2014).

[32] Eve Tuck and K. Wayne Yang, "Decolonization Is Not a Metaphor," *Decolonization: Indigeneity, Education & Society* 1, no. 1 (2012): 1–40, https://resolver.scholarsportal.info/resolve/19298692/v01i0001/nfp_dinam.xml.

[33] Mignolo, "Geopolitics of Sensing and Knowing," esp. 274. For a key intervention that conceptualizes the borderland as a constructive location of hybridity rather than a divide, see Gloria Anzaldúa, *Borderlands/La Frontera: The New Mestiza* (San Francisco, CA: Aunt Lute Books, 1987).

[34] Ibid.

[35] See Ramón Grosfoguel, "Decolonizing Post-colonial Studies and Paradigms of Political Economy: Transmodernity, Decolonial Thinking, and Global Coloniality," *Transmodernity: Journal of Peripheral Cultural Production of the Luso-Hispanic World* 1, no. 1 (2011), https://dialogoglobal.com/texts/grosfoguel/Grosfoguel-Decolonizing-Pol-Econ-and-Postcolonial.pdf. Grosfoguel highlights diasporic thought or Pachamama, which is a fertility goddess (Mother Earth) revered

illuminates pathways for reimagining democracy, human rights, and humanity beyond antimodern reactionary modernity or the assumption of "an essentialist 'pure outside space' or 'absolute exteriority' to modernity."[36] Grosfoguel, following Enrique Dussel, encourages an emancipatory decolonial project of transmodernity that would entail a "horizontal dialogue" (similar to Santos's intercultural translation and dialogue) rather than a verticality that pretends "an equal horizontal relationship" while concealing the abyssal line or the "colonial difference."[37]

Transmodernity as the outcome of critical border thinking offers a nonreactionary lens through which to evaluate how the business of religion (regardless of its presumed postsecular critique of modernity) entrenches rather than disrupts coloniality without simply inversing Eurocentric binarism. The decolonial turn seeks "pluriversal *decoloniality* and *decolonial pluriversality*."[38] This does not entail "a rejection or negation of Western thought" because it too is integral to the pluriverse. What pluriversality does entail is a refusal of "North Atlantic fictions" regarding its own universality, linearity, and singularity through *re-existence*, which involves a resignification from "disposability" to dignity of all those dehumanized through the global processes of racialized capitalism.[39]

This deflation of the fantasy of pure exteriority to modernity is fruitful for my efforts to identify the decolonial openings within a neoliberal discourse of interreligious peacebuilding/development. Such openings include the love and friendships generated through relational but also intrasubjective peace islands where people overcome hate, mistrust, and suspicion, even if their scripted "harmony" depends on reified accounts of who they are (the kinds that can be broken down into tweets) rather than border epistemologies, archipelagic social imaginaries, and critical pedagogies.

---

by the Indigenous peoples of the Andes around which Bolivian Indigenous activists mobilize to challenge intersectionally capitalist dehumanizing and nature-destroying legacies and practices. The invocation of Pachamama came under feminist critique, which illuminates how, as a gendered symbol, it became co-opted to state violence under Evo Morales. See, for example, Miriam Tola, "Between Pachamama and Mother Earth: Gender, Political Ontology and the Rights of Nature in Contemporary Bolivia," *Feminist Review* 118, no. 1 (2018): 25–40.

[36] Grosfoguel, "Decolonizing Post-colonial Studies."
[37] Mignolo, "Geopolitics of Sensing and Knowing."
[38] Catherine E. Walsh and Walter D. Mignolo, *On Decoloniality: Concepts, Analytics, Praxis* (Durham, NC: Duke University Press, 2018), 2, italics in original.
[39] Ibid., 3.

Decolonial Demystification

The utilitarian postsecular approach traced in this book depends on leveraging religion and the operative concept of partnership. But toward what? Beyond surveying the religious landscape to identify points of contact, create potential partnerships, and track down possible locations for building (or bridging) trust among communities and between global and state actors, this utilitarian approach seeks to build the capacity of "faith actors" to interpret their respective scriptures' positions, especially on a variety of thorny issues. One example might be how they understand the morality of using contraceptives, which would then have ramifications for how to approach the HIV/AIDS epidemic.[40] In this context, the functionality of actors, institutions, and established intercommunal networks become a currency (or capital) to be accessed and mobilized.[41]

Still, the accusation that the religious actors I have studied, in deeply religious contexts such as Mindanao, are instrumentalizing religion becomes complicated when one analyzes their self-understanding of their peacebuilding agency as *imitatio* Jesus and Muhammad. For example, for Christian peacebuilders I met in Mindanao, journeying with Muslim partners, tangibly working on livelihood projects, and building relational ethics through learning about one another's traditions enact a form of accompaniment, the practice of walking alongside the "poor" as an act of solidarity rather than paternalistically leading them. Accompaniment highlights the intersection of peacebuilding/development once again. And for many actors populating this space in Mindanao and Kenya, such practices are infused with religious conviction and piety.

The integrated approach to religion and development/peacebuilding practices, therefore, capitalizes on both the spiritual force and the institutional capacities of religious actors under the constraints of *realpolitik*. It emphasizes *doing* over *knowing* religion. However, to return to how I opened this book, scholarship on religion needs to go beyond such questions as: What

---

[40] Studies also show that bureaucratized faith actors with international reach and access to centers of powers and donors influence restrictive approaches to reproductive and sexual rights within the development framework. See, for example, Jane H. Bayes and Nayereth Tohidi, eds., *Globalization, Gender, and Religion: The Politics of Women's Rights in Catholic and Muslim Contexts* (New York: Palgrave Macmillan, 2001).

[41] See, for example, Berkley Center for Religion, Peace & World Affairs, "The COVID-19 Crisis: From Past Experience to Present Realities," April 16, 2020, https://berkleycenter.georgetown.edu/events/the-covid-19-crisis-from-past-experience-to-present-realities.

possibilities exist within the world as it is? How can those possibilities be implemented effectively? Who can implement them? These realist questions may imagine a future script. Still, this imagination is accountable to the present and never investigates the wider framework in which they are asked or the underlying epistemological assumptions that prompt them. This line of scholarship for policy "use" simply operates within a status quo that accepts hermeneutical closures. Its prescriptions subsequently contribute to further "empowering" people to problem-solve within their localized field of vision, without also engaging in critical reflections that could expand this field. To do so would require problem-posing critical hermeneutics that demystifies this field of vision and exposes the histories and structures within it that contribute to people's suffering and marginalization.

Decolonial theorists, in their labor of demystifying modernity, analyze religion as a site of imperial design rather than an emancipatory resource.[42] Through this decolonial prism, the UN's SDGs function as contemporary manifestations of the colonial history of peace as a civilizational discourse of progress. This is the case even if UN Agenda 2030 presents itself as a benevolent global agenda and the result of input from civil society, including the "religion sector," through consultation (which is not the same as democratic) processes. The pretense of a global "road map" for human flourishing conceals histories of marginalization, deprivation, dispossession, and other legacies of coloniality that, through various mechanisms contributing to "preservation [of violent structures and ideologies] through [their] transformation,"[43] continue today. Such legacies are ingrained in the experiences of those targeted for "development." Their ancestors were targeted for conversion, the civilizing mission, and other forms of "progress." The extension of the colonial moment driven by the "doctrine of discovery" to a contemporary development paradigm brings "good news" through a partnership paradigm that outsources and devolves responsibility rather than through a social justice lens that redresses centuries of colonial and neocolonial exploitation.[44] A Christian universalizing cosmology is a central culprit in this legacy of

---

[42] For example, Enrique Dussel, "Eurocentrism and Modernity (Introduction to the Frankfurt Lectures)," *Boundary 2* 20, no. 3 (1993): 65–76; McClintock, *Imperial Leather*; Walter D. Mignolo, *The Darker Side of Western Modernity: Global Futures, Decolonial Options* (Durham, NC: Duke University Press, 2011).

[43] The phrase "preservation through transformation" was coined by Reva Siegel in "Why Equal Protection No Longer Protects: The Evolving Forms of Status-Enforcing State Action," *Stanford Law Review* 49 (1997): 1111–48.

[44] See chapter 3 for a specific discussion of the problematic aspects of the partnership model.

"peace" (or development *qua* peace) and thus needs to be interrogated as part of any effort to decolonize religion and the practices of peace. The "global" or "international community" is still, as I note throughout the book, presumed to be secular and in search of religious partners with keys to the local. Why do I single out Christianity? Because European Christian history, philosophy, and theology are intricately interwoven into the epistemic and political projects of modernity/coloniality, including in the construction of religion as a comparative, racializing category upon which any discussion of religion and the practices of peace/development is based.[45] Analyzing religion as, by definition, already a racialized category deployed within Western imperial and colonial control also sheds light on the ongoing operation of the double closures of religion and the practices of peace, where religious and communal boundaries are collapsed into one another and imagined only through closed and unitary hermeneutical terrains.

Undoing the link of religion to empire becomes, indeed, a site of intersectional decoloniality that is of immense relevance to religion and the practices of peace with justice. It calls for theological disobedience. Queer theologies, in particular, subvert Christianity's cosmological imperialism and homogenizing impulses, positing such theological praxes as politically critical for decoloniality. In this reading, to decolonize entails delinking religion and empire through queering.[46] Unsurprisingly, emancipatory theological reflections are often intersectional, queer, and ecofeminist, drawing upon, but also pushing beyond, liberation theology's heteropatriarchal normativity.[47] These emancipatory approaches take this form partly because gender and racial capitalism are integral to coloniality and partly because of an aspiration to imagine otherwise and from the margins (including the religious and cultural margins). Foregrounding empire and then whiteness as a key analytic space, postcolonial theological analyses challenge some of the modernist and totalizing underpinnings of liberation theologies[48] where

---

[45] For example, David Chidester, *Empire of Religion: Imperialism and Comparative Religion* (Chicago: University of Chicago Press, 2014). See also Masuzawa, *The Invention of World Religions*; Wenger, *Religious Freedom*; Nelson Maldonado-Torres, "AAR Centennial Roundtable: Religion, Conquest, and Race in the Foundations of the Modern/Colonial World," *Journal of the American Academy of Religion* 82, no. 3 (2014): 636–65, https://doi.org/10.1093/jaarel/lfu054.

[46] For example, Marcella Althaus-Reid, *Indecent Theology: Theological Perversions in Sex, Gender and Politics* (New York: Routledge, 2000); Marcella Althaus-Reid, *The Queer God* (New York: Routledge, 2003).

[47] See chapter 3 for a discussion of feminist critiques of (male) liberation theology.

[48] R. S. Sugirtharajah, *Postcolonial Criticism and Biblical Interpretation* (Oxford: Oxford University Press, 2002), 103–23.

the Bible is read as "unequivocally, unvaryingly, and intrinsically emancipatory," which has the effect of bracketing "postcolonial attunement to ambivalence . . . and hence the necessity of incessant critique."[49] However, the boundaries between liberation theologies and postcolonial, feminist, and queer theological sensibilities are not rigid and even converge for some scholars. Indeed, if liberation theology is also to be decolonial and emancipatory, it necessarily becomes feminist, queer, relational, and embodied.[50] Queering liberation theology emboldens the meanings of the prophetic through the iconoclastic (rather than the survivalist) mechanisms of unrevolutionary decolonial love.

It is through this gendered attunement to coloniality that decolonial or postcolonial theologies are transformational theologies and are thus thoroughly contextual.[51] They require reapproaching tradition, from and as if from the margins, with a fresh and critical perspective. This intersectional, hermeneutical disruption is not what I saw in the programmatic spaces of interreligious peacebuilding in Kenya and the Philippines. The hermeneutical closures therein exemplify the endurance of the colonial legacy of comparative religion and the underlying logic of classifying/defining and conquering. The overall outcome of this legacy in its contemporary manifestation is the emergence of a thin pluralism, which denotes the abstraction of "religious traditions" from the racialized dynamics of controlling and policing the religious communities that inhabit those traditions. This abstraction undergirds a segregationist peace logic and prevents an intercommunal praxis of hermeneutical disobedience against injustice and oppression. This segregationist logic is telegraphed through various tropes such as the "seed" or "island" of peace, breaking sociopolitical complexity and the potential for archipelagic social imaginaries into seemingly autonomous and unitary actors and change agents.

Hence, to imagine religion or religious and cultural traditions through a decolonial lens means disrupting their closed and bounded self-understandings. As Monica A. Coleman argues, insights from womanist

---

[49] Stephen Moore and Mayra Rivera, "A Tentative Topography of Postcolonial Theology," in *Planetary Loves: Spivak, Postcoloniality, and Theology*, ed. Stephen Moore and Mayra Rivera (New York: Fordham University Press, 2010), 3–14 (8).

[50] Mayra Rivera, "Thinking Bodies: The Spirit of a Latina Incarnational Imagination," in *Decolonizing Epistemologies: Latina/o Theology and Philosophy*, ed. Ada Maria Isasi-Diaz and Eduardo Mandieta (New York: Fordham University Press, 2011), 1–21, esp. 6.

[51] Every decolonial theological reflection is embodied and contextual. However, the inverse is not necessarily true: not every contextual theology (responding to particularities of historical contexts) is decolonial and/or intersectional.

postmodern theologies illuminate openings, polydoxy, and relationality that inscribe in such theologies the historical experiences of coloniality: slavery, conversion to Christianity, and syncretic rearticulation of traditional African spiritual practices.[52] This is what is meant by the intersectional articulation of decolonial theology and what is immediately germane to post-abyssal interculturality, which introduces a social justice that subverts segregationist peace scripts.

However, such an approach to just peace as also entailing a queering of religion does not necessarily tally with the empirics I encountered. Indeed, my findings show that it does not compute with practitioners' sense of their religious peace agency. Not only that, this discrepancy renders such queering discourse as itself colonial and presumptuous of the universality of the meanings of freedom and emancipation. This clarifies decoloniality's religion problem. Decolonial critics tend to interpret religion reductively as an instrument of empire and neocolonialism. For all their critiques of modernity, they revert to Marxist and other modernist accounts of religion and ideology.[53] These critics accept only queer, feminist, and otherwise "woke" religious actors as allies in their struggle for an alternative (pluriversal) future. This is because "woke" accounts of religiosity reflect decolonial processes of unlearning and forming critical consciousness. This reductive account invisibilizes how people's often "unwoke" religiosity contributes to the tasks of pious daily survival. It limits how one might imagine an ethics of plurality in a context in which divided colonial taxonomies and state-sanctioned violence dominate. Many in such contexts rely on religion as an ethnic classification. Thus, a decolonial prism reveals the first closure where communal and religious belongings constitute one and the same and the basic level through which people can articulate their interests (rather than intersectionally through building a coalition of co-resistance and political friendships). Still, this prism invisibilizes how, within this closure, religion also constitutes a form of self-empowerment, even if this agentic aspect also relies on a hermeneutical closure of what precisely is meant by the "religion" that is a source of empowerment. The religiocrats see only this empowerment and how to leverage it, while the critics see only the patterns of disempowerment.

---

[52] Monica A. Coleman, "Invoking Oya: Practicing a Polydox Soteriology through a Postmodern Womanist Reading of Tananarive Due's *The Living Blood*," in *Polydoxy: Theology of Multiplicity and Relation*, ed. Catherine Keller and Laurel C. Schneider (New York: Routledge, 2011), 186–202.

[53] See, for example, Santos, *Epistemologies of the South*, 77–78.

This point takes us to finally examine the reactionary decolonial stance that can also be read into apparently conservative and hermeneutically closed conceptions of cultural and religious traditions. In my case studies, conservative androcentric accounts demonstrated utility for the religion business as an instrument of neoliberalism. However, the conservative modality cannot simply be reduced to its use-value for the "global engagement" with religion, especially when conservatism interprets itself, in some instances, as anti- and decolonial.[54] Positing heteropatriarchal and homophobic tradition, therefore, as both an instrument of the "West" (as my case studies suggest) and as its resistance reveals the limits of both accounts.[55]

It is crucial, in light of the above discussion, to underscore that "anticolonial" and "decolonial" are not interchangeable and are not necessarily synonymous with feminist and queer religiosity or with an Indigenous resurgence that most explicitly can be labeled "decolonial." Decolonizing religion, which is what the book analytically brings to bear, entails religion's disentanglement from empire and from Eurocentricity.[56] This disentanglement requires an intersectional approach to religion that refuses its abstraction from race, gender, class, nationalist ideologies, and more.[57] Emancipatory pathways within a decolonial framework entail relationality because "justice" is not self-referential and the resources for a more just cohabitation of space and time require norms beyond singular religious traditions and historical narratives.[58] Hence, scrutinizing the distinction between reactionary and intersectional, decolonial hermeneutics stresses why conservative and androcentric, hermeneutically closed religiosity and its constitutive closures of social boundaries are good for peace business but bad for justice. Hence, the praxis of intercultural translation and dialogue, as in Santos, when oriented

---

[54] Cultural anthropologist Saba Mahmood exemplifies this anticolonial epistemology through her ethnography of the docile agency of pious Muslim women in Egypt. See Mahmood, *Politics of Piety: The Islamic Revival and the Feminist Subject* (Princeton, NJ: Princeton University Press, 2004).

[55] For an analysis that challenges the essentialism that goes into narratives of African homophobia and/or LGBTQI's emancipatory struggle as dependent exclusively on secular rather than also religious resources, see Adriaan Van Klinken, *Kenyan Christian Queer: Religion, LGBT Activism, and Arts of Resistance in Africa* (University Park: Pennsylvania State University Press, 2019).

[56] For works that reflect centrally on such interpretations of modernity, see Santiago Slabodsky, *Decolonial Judaism: Triumphal Failures of Barbaric Thinking* (New York: Palgrave Macmillan, 2014); Atalia Omer, *Days of Awe: Reimagining Jewishness in Solidarity with Palestinians* (Chicago: University of Chicago Press, 2019); Houria Bouteldja, *Whites, Jews, and Us: Toward a Politics of Revolutionary Love*, trans. Rachel Valinsky (South Pasadena, CA: Semiotext(e), MIT Press, 2016).

[57] For example, Pui Lan Kwok, *Globalization, Gender, and Peacebuilding: The Future of Interfaith Dialogue* (Notre Dame, IN: Paulist Press, 2012), 69–92.

[58] One articulation of this argument can be found in Judith Butler, *Parting Ways: Jewishness and the Critique of Zionism* (New York: Columbia University Press, 2012).

not by a presumption of a "culture" or "theology" as a closed system but rather to protest injustice and imagine the world otherwise stands in striking contrast to the harmony discourse's logic of closures.

Santiago Slabodsky helpfully challenges liberation theology's desire to undo the system from within. Instead of such solipsism, he proposes a method of "double critique," one critique directed externally at coloniality and the other directed internally against reactionary elements within the traditions themselves.[59] Doing so expands the scope of dialogue partners beyond one's borders/boundaries and paves the way for intersecting broad-based solidarity and coalition building. Unlike the "harmony" model, this relational approach to solidarity opens itself to critical political consciousness. It is also distinct from reactionary theological analyses of modernity as a declension narrative[60] and from genealogical critiques, which—unlike intersectional theory—refuse to explicate positive ethical and political visions for fear of coming across as "activist" and thus less "scientific."[61] The relational approach also, certainly, diffuses a conception of religion as a hermeneutically and hermetically closed system upon which the neoliberal reconfiguration of coloniality and the interreligious peacebuilding programming spaces I depict in this book operate. The hermeneutical closure also, in other words, corresponds with what I have called "segregationist" (and thus non-intersectional) peace scripts. This is because these double hermeneutical closures conceal the operation of race, ethnicity, and nation (all related to perceptions of blood or inherited relationship) in the abstract production of "tradition" as a standalone historical constant.

While the critical study of religion refuses an "activist" stance, the field of peace studies forces a normative intervention. At the same time, if peace

---

[59] See Santiago Slabodsky, "Not Every Radical Philosophy Is Decolonial" *Contending Modernities. Project-Decoloniality and Philosophy of Religion Series*—University of Notre Dame (June 2020) https://contendingmodernities.nd.edu/decoloniality/not-every-radical-philosophy-is-decolonial/ and Slabodsky, "Christian Hegemonies: Evolutionism, Analectics, and the Question of Interreligiosity in a Decolonial Philosophy of Religion," unpublished. This is reminiscent of Santos's concept of "cross-cultural dialogue" in "Human Rights as Emancipatory Script?," 23.

[60] For an example of this line and its employment of the genealogical turn in the study of secularism, see William Cavanaugh, *The Myth of Religious Violence: Secular Ideology and the Roots of Modern Conflict* (New York: Oxford University Press, 2009). To understand the theological underpinnings that are suppressed in this book, one would have to read it in conjunction with the rest of his theological oeuvre. Otherwise, one might not recognize the persistent theological (and thus also political) agenda informing this scholarship.

[61] I address this tension between critique and constructive engagement in many other places, including Atalia Omer, "Can a Critic Be a Caretaker Too? Religion, Conflict, and Conflict Transformation," *Journal of the American Academy of Religion* 79, no. 2 (2011): 459–96, https://doi.org/10.1093/jaarel/lfq076.

praxis would decolonize its approach to religion through cross-fertilizing with the critical study of religion, its capacity to overcome peace's violent legacies and religion's persistent co-optation therein would be generative. This would open up discursive investigations of how the abstraction and confinement of the "religious" itself domesticates, co-opts, and thereby authorizes the ideological underpinnings of the religious sector's own confinement and disarticulation from an intersectional political consciousness. I now turn to examine the decolonial paralysis within the marginal edges of peace research.

Decolonial Paralysis?

Resurgent currents within the field of peace studies have become immobilized by the field's complicity with peace's violent legacy, which is a familiar trajectory for many modern disciplines. Recent writings in peace and justice studies joined a decolonial trend that imports Frantz Fanon, Sylvia Wynter, Maria Lugones, Gloria Anzaldúa, and a host of Black American intersectionality theorists, such as Patricia Hill Collins, bell hooks, and Indigenous queer theorists,[62] to challenge peace's violent legacy and to imagine, through critical pedagogy, "an/other peace," in the words of Sara Shroff.[63] This an/other peace is imagined in the forms of decolonial, feminist, and queer futurities, but tends to reflect more the authors' grappling with their own epistemic inheritances and situatedness[64] in the Global North(s), and thus with discussions around White (and other) privileges, than with the empirical realities and challenges of survival in the South(s). Moreover, decolonial, queer, and feminist futurities do not organically link with

---

[62] Patricia Hill Collins, *Black Feminist Thought: Knowledge, Consciousness, and the Politics of Empowerment* (Boston: Unwin Hyman, 1990); bell hooks, *Teaching to Transgress* (New York: Routledge, 1994); Maria Lugones, "The Coloniality of Gender," *Worlds & Knowledges Otherwise* 2 (2008): 1–17, doi:10.1007/978-1-137-38273-3_2; Andrea Lee Smith, "Heteropatriarchy and the Three Pillars of Settler Colonialism," in *The Color of Violence: The INCITE! Anthology*, ed. Andrea Lee Smith, Ben E. Richie, Julian Sudbury, and Janelle White (Cambridge, MA: South End Press, 2006), 68–73; Wynter, "Unsettling the Coloniality of Being/Power/Truth/Freedom"; Linda Tuhiwai-Smith, *Decolonizing Methodologies: Research and Indigenous Peoples* (London: Zed Books, 1999).

[63] See Sara Shroff, "The Peace Professor: Decolonial, Feminist, and Queer Futurities," in *Peace and Justice Studies: Critical Pedagogy*, ed. Margaret Groarke and Emily Welty (London: Routledge, 2019), 146–62.

[64] Donna Haraway, "Situated Knowledges: The Science Question in Feminism and the Privilege of Partial Perspective," *Feminist Studies* 14, no. 3 (1988): 575–99, https://doi.org/10.2307/3178066.

people's religious imaginations and empirically inhabited practices, unless they are likewise open to feminist, queer, and decolonial hermeneutics. But what if they are not? What if their interpretation as decolonial or anticolonial means the rejection of freedom as universal objectives? What does it reveal about the decolonial, queer, and feminist "religion problem" in addition to peace's "complicit[y] in white logic,"[65] around which Shroff articulates their critique? I also think of my conversation with a civil society actor in Basilan, Mindanao, who told me about her work with marginalized IPs for whom participation in intercultural peacebuilding programs appears alien as they instead focus on "What are they going to eat tonight?"[66] They certainly do not have the luxury to think of an/other peace. Whether queering hermeneutics constitutes an incomprehensible luxury entirely outside the horizons of one's imagination or whether it is rejected as a colonial epistemic imposition, the religious and peacebuilding agency of the people's inhabiting hermeneutically closed religiosity and their "peace islands" cannot simply be dismissed as a manifestation of colonized consciousness.

Post-abyssal thinking, with its emphasis on the co-presence (as opposed to the colonial difference) of epistemologies and receptivity to intercultural learning and unlearning, may be an exercise of privilege not available to hungry people. Therefore, "I cannot eat peace"—an often heard phrase in the programmatic spaces I visited in the Philippines and Kenya—is an empirical reality that any epistemological critique of peace as violence needs to contend with concretely. We must grapple with it because of the moral imperatives such a statement imposes on us. To the degree that scholarship in peace studies wrestles with its Eurocentricity, it fails to engage with religion as a critical category in the construction of a subontology or nonbeing—in other words, religion as a racialized construct. This oversight may occur, as noted, due to the often Marxist logic informing coloniality scholarship and its interweaving with feminist theory's religion problem.[67] This religion problem points to the persistence of a modernist account of religion, regardless of an otherwise critique of modernity. Religion, religiosity, and decolonial (queering) theologies, therefore, do not appear, to peace studies scholars, as potential emancipatory resources. Decolonial interventions in

---

[65] Shroff, "The Peace Professor," 149.

[66] Participant in a focus group, Zamboanga City, June 2018.

[67] Jakeet Singh, "Religious Agency and the Limits of Intersectionality," *Hypatia* 30, no. 4 (2015): 657–74, https://doi.org/10.1111/hypa.12182; Mahmood, *Politics of Piety*; Elizabeth Bucar, "Dianomy: Understanding Religious Women's Moral Agency as Creative Conformity," *Journal of the American Academy of Religion* 78, no. 3 (2010): 662–86, https://www.jstor.org/stable/27919232.

peace studies remain beholden to a liberal normativity in their accounts of religion. We can see this in how these interventions segregate religion as a distinct field of praxis or a "sector."[68] The differentiation between race, an analysis of which is factored into critical accounts of peace research, and religion—whose inclusion in peace studies remains beholden to its modernist construction as faith, spirituality, institutions, networks, and prescriptive intrasubjective blueprints for formation—is detrimental. In contrast, a foundational understanding of "race as the primary ontology of the social"[69] in modernity exposes religion as a racialized category and vice versa; race/ethnicity is refracted and reproduced, often within the framework of modern nationalism, through (gendered) religious discourses. Understanding contemporary Muslim communities, therefore, cannot proceed in abstraction from the logic of racialization. The same goes for religion in general.

At the same time, because the epistemological scrutiny is so comprehensive, decolonial scholarly interventions in religious studies and other disciplinary spaces tend to bracket a consideration of religion's participation in anticolonial forces[70] and mass social mobilizations generally. Further, such interventions, operating on a purist register, invisibilize and render inaudible the needs for survival of actual people inhabiting the Global South. Therefore, if decoloniality is to become a (queering) peace praxis focused on archipelagic sociopolitical imaginations, it needs to grapple not only with the legacies of *orbis christianus* as an episteme[71] but also with the real marginalized people whose religiosity (or reclaimed culture) functions transformatively (as decolonial openings) to alleviate suffering and reduce violence in empirically measurable ways. This is the case even if transformation unfolds on hermeneutically uncritical channels and sealed in prepackaged containers in ways constitutive of modernist discourse.

Even the centralization of IP grievances does not necessarily denote critical religiosity. Appeals to Indigenous practices without a critical account of

---

[68] For example, see Meera Sabaratnam, "Avatars of Eurocentrism in the Critique of the Liberal Peace," *Security Dialogue* 44, no. 3 (2013): 259–78, https://www.jstor.org/stable/26302249.

[69] Sayyid, "Empire, Islam and the Postcolonial," 12.

[70] Yountae An, "A Decolonial Theory of Religion: Race, Coloniality, and Secularity in the Americas," *Journal of the American Academy of Religion* 88, no. 4 (2020): 947–980, https://doi.org/10.1093/jaarel/lfaa057. For a general discussion from a social movement perspective of religion and social movement mobilization, see Sharon Erickson Nepstad and Rhys H. Williams, "Religion in Rebellion, Resistance, and Social Movements," in *The Sage Handbook of the Sociology of Religion*, ed. James A. Beckford and N. J. Demerath III (London: Sage, 2007), 419–37.

[71] Walter D. Mignolo, "Coloniality: The Darker Side of Modernity," in *Modernologies: Contemporary Artists Researching Modernity and Modernism: Catalog of the Exhibit at the Museum of Modern Art, Barcelona, Spain*, ed. C. S. Breitwisser (Barcelona: MACBA, 2009), 39–41, esp. 41.

epistemic, structural, cultural, and symbolic forms of violence may result in co-opting Indigenous conflict-resolution mechanisms into the neoliberal frame as an expression of devoluntary logic. In multiple locations in Mindanao, for example, Indigenous peacebuilding practices are employed in ways that relieve the government of responsibility for its roles in historical injustice, as in the delegation to Datus (tribal leaders) of the tasks of resolving land and other disputes. This move usually means instituting animal offerings and restorative justice practices.[72] Such practices may be Indigenous, but could also contradict feminist sensibilities and concerns with equality as the resolution of disputes regarding intimate partner violence or adultery unfold as a family honor issue.[73] Hence, what is Indigenous is not necessarily feminist or decolonial, if by those we mean disruption and unsettling of neoliberal devoluntary rationality and heteropatriarchal norms.

While the analytic reveals the intersectional dynamics of racialization as an enduring logic in the postcolonies, people's empirical perception of the religious as a distinct sphere is a social fact, whereas "race" often appears irrelevant to people's experiences of marginality in my two case studies. This is even as religion increasingly, through the parochial but globalizing racializing orientalist discourse of the "war on terror," has become foregrounded as an explanatory frame for various conflict narratives and the predicament of "underdevelopment." Hence, even if the people I met did not talk about race, the degree to which they have been co-opted into such conflict narratives still conveys the relevance of racialization to their empirical postcolonial realities. I mean this by positing religion as a racialized category. These are distinct characteristics of modernity and reflect on questions about religion and peace practices and theory, with a recognition that the two sites of theory and practice may be in tension with one another. This tension became clear during my conversations with Indigenous communities in Mindanao.

---

[72] This is a synthetic reflection based on my focus groups with different tribal leaders in June 2019 and June 2018 in multiple locations in Mindanao.

[73] Focus groups (June 2019) with Indigenous tribal leaders in the Davao region in Mindanao did not reflect any feminist sensibilities, even though they did reflect on the ongoing colonization of IPs. Likewise, in an earlier focus group in northern Mindanao with another grassroots organization of IPs, a similar approach to dealing with interpersonal conflicts came through, underscoring that issues such as adultery are dealt with using traditional conventions and conflict resolution practices. Clearly, Indigenous foci do not at all entail also feminist and LGBTQI sensibilities.

Existence, Not Resistance

The Lumad communities in Mindanao became incorporated into the barangay administrative formation and the land-titling Regalian discourse only during the time of American colonization and the subsequent domination from Manila.[74] This resulted in an erosion of the traditional Lumad forms of government and eliminating traditional authority figures and offices. This encroachment punctured the Lumad legal system and diminished the scope of customary law. This situation also allowed capitalist logic to take hold, together with the increased presence of extractive and trading industries. Karl Gaspar refers to this as the process of the "colonization of the Lumad's lifeworld," but his ethnographic research also illuminates that this process was never complete because of persistent resistance. Nevertheless, the IPs mostly "were forced to coexist with the settlers, accepting the reality that they would have less land and forests."[75] Gaspar's ethnographic engagement with the Lumads (especially with the Arakan Manobo) has demonstrated the endurance of a warrior tradition, the *pangayaw*, even if nonviolent responses also emerged alongside NGOs' and church groups' involvement in various programmatic efforts around education and health.[76]

Facing legacies of continuous marginalization, military repression, and displacement by logging companies, ranchers, and landless settlers, *pangayaw* remains an option for resistance, though many Lumads accommodated the forces enacting their colonization. The land struggles of the Lumads only intensified until an amendment to the 1987 Constitution (during the time of President Corazon Aquino) that stressed an obligation "to protect the rights of the indigenous cultural communities to their ancestral lands to ensure their economic, social, and cultural being."[77] However, it was not until the administration of Fidel Ramos that the issue of ancestral domain, with the passing of the Indigenous Peoples Rights Act (1997), became a focus of policy and an embryonic effort to issue Certificates of Ancestral Domains, meaning a legal linking of IPs to their ancestral lands. This was an outcome of organizing during the Marcos regime, including vibrant legal discussions around pathways to neutralize and reverse the

---

[74] See chapter 1 for an overview.
[75] Karl M. Gaspar, *Manobo Dreams in Arakan: A People's Struggle to Keep Their Homeland* (Quezon City: Ateneo de Manila University Press, 2011), 193.
[76] Ibid., 3.
[77] Ibid., 6.

Regalian Doctrine, UN-focused deliberations on Indigenous rights globally, and the consolidation of the links between ecological disasters and the predicament of IPs.[78] At this moment, cultural forms of activism have emerged to mobilize and facilitate the implementation of claims to obtain Certificates of Ancestral Domains.[79] These certificates enable IPs to reclaim some of the vast lands they had lost. This reclamation of land also entails the reclamation and codification of Indigenous culture. As I noted in chapter 2, the struggle to survive on the land consolidates Indigenous traditions in a shape congruent with "religion" as the other reductive communal definition so pivotal for devolutionary interreligious governance.

My conversations with tribal leaders in 2018–19 revealed their continuous communal survival efforts through navigating the legal framework on ancestral domains, recovering and transmitting intergenerationally cultural practices, and reclaiming their right to educate their children on their ancestral lands, the topography of which is imbued with sacredness and the presence of ancestors. This multifaceted effort signals neither a revolutionary outlook nor an intersectional analysis of interlocking oppressions and violent ideologies. At stake, however, is an interwoven cultural and material survival amid overwhelming forces of exploitative and extractive capitalism and a long history of marginalization imprinted on the community. According to my interlocutors, this marginalization manifests today in persistent conflicts between traditional and settler legal approaches with Indigenous communities living in greater proximity to settlers who do not always embrace Indigenous legal methodologies and with traditional authorities who are forced into barangay-centric legal frameworks. These tensions further complicate the task of adjudicating land conflicts between settlers and IPs because using either legal framework generates grievances on all fronts.[80] This multilayered map of grievances can be detrimental to implementing the peace process in Mindanao; thus, the CRS's intercommunal peacebuilding measures, which I have discussed in this book, focused on strengthening Indigenous peacebuilding mechanisms. Such efforts were also designed to enhance hermeneutically uncritical and hermetically closed group identities through neoliberal technologies of Binding, Bonding, and Bridging, plotting them onto a tripartite (and thus segregationist) harmony and peace

---

[78] Ibid., 194. See also chapter 1.
[79] Gaspar, *Manobo Dreams in Arakan*, 195.
[80] Focus group with a representative cross-section of Indigenous actors in Mindanaon civil society, June 2018.

script. The emphasis on restorative and relational conflict-resolution practices emerged from recognizing that these are key to implementing the peace agreement. Hence, Indigenous autonomy and cultural reclaiming do not depart from the neoliberal frame but rather are appropriated into it. It is also, however, a form of Indigenous cultural empowerment, as per the testimonies of traditional leaders who partook in the interreligious/cultural peacebuilding programming engineered by CRS.[81]

The ironic interlinking of cultural and material survival promotes cultural codification and standardization, often through the (colonial) tyranny of committing elastic oral traditions into written texts, which closes the hermeneutical horizons, consistent with the neoliberal peacebuilding regime. Indeed, not only are cultural festivals and sacred arts and memories codified, but also, as another focus group with an IP organization in northern Mindanao celebrated, a list of punishments for offenses, leaving little room for interpretive elasticity.[82]

Cultural reification authorizes material claims and indeed survival. Gaspar writes to this effect, "They [Manobo] were em*powered* during the advocacy campaigns upon perceiving that it was also through the cultural expressions of their Manobo identity (prayers, epic chants, dances, music, and the like) that they could assert their demands."[83] This interlacing of cultural survival and land reclamation—with the land embodying sacredness (not merely a place), but also with the navigation of a human rights discourse—shows the complex terrains of Indigenous activism and practices of survival and gestures toward fruitful contradictions.

Indeed, elicitive methodologies of peacebuilding (those that the people themselves articulate through conflict mapping and problem-solving) are decisively not decolonial, if we agree with Eve Tuck and Wayne Yang's extension of Aimé Césaire's pronouncement[84] that decoloniality does not amount to "converting Indigenous politics to a Western doctrine of liberation; it is not a philanthropic process of 'helping' the at-risk and alleviating suffering; it is not a generic term for struggle against oppressive conditions and outcomes." Decolonization is "a repatriation of Indigenous land and life . . . not a metonym for social justice,"[85] and thus not necessarily also a

---

[81] Focus group with traditional leaders, March 2017.
[82] Focus group, June 2018.
[83] Gaspar, *Manobo Dreams in Arakan*, 198.
[84] Aimé Césaire, *Discourse on Colonialism* (New York: Monthly Review Press, 2000), 32. See also Tuck and Yang, "Decolonization Is Not a Metaphor."
[85] Césaire, *Discourse on Colonialism*, 21.

feminist emancipatory process. It should not be hijacked by a foreign social justice agenda that all too easily can facilitate settler moves to innocence.[86]

At the same time, elicitive peacebuilding practices challenge this purist and totalizing articulation of decolonial theory by pointing us to a nonfundamentalist critical engagement with modernity's legacies. Tuck and Yang want to redirect us to "the real," away from the metaphorical, but, once again, what if the empirical does not cohere with radical unsettling? The postcolonial Philippines presents a case different from the settler colonial context that dominates the decolonial turn and its antimodern reactionary modernity. Therefore, I trace how IP experiences in Mindanao can reflect on religion and decolonial peace praxis and the decolonial theory that invisibilizes them. This is even if people's resilience may be a testament to the enormity of neoliberalism's grip on imaginable reality.

Decolonial praxis, of course, is not constitutionally disconnected from survival tasks. On the contrary, decolonial praxis concerns itself with what Martin Savransky calls "alter realism," which "seeks not to represent reality but to set realities in motion."[87] An explicitly decolonial approach certainly challenges the realist/utilitarian approach to religion and peace praxis. It likewise refuses to remain merely at the level of critique or the more implicit decoloniality of the reactionary antimodern modernists who may articulate an alter-reality by reclaiming hierarchical ontologies inscribed in an ahistorical and conservative conception of "tradition." An explicitly decolonial stance, however, always also entails an explicit politico-cultural and economic emancipatory project, though not necessarily articulated in feminist or queer registers. Such registers require the prism of double critique. In juxtaposition to the logic of double closures of a peace (and religion) cohering tool such as Silsilah, double critique is alter-realist and does not confine its religiocultural and sociopolitical hermeneutics to the constraints of the present or the ontologies of the past. This means disrupting rather than confirming segregationist peace scripts. Decoloniality, along with emancipatory imaginations, points to double critique, border thinking, and interculturality as pathways for overcoming (Christian/Western) hegemonies and imagined futures, radical or otherwise.[88]

---

[86] On "innocence," see Tuck and Yang, "Decolonization Is Not a Metaphor," 35.

[87] Martin Savransky, "A Decolonial Imagination: Sociology, Anthropology, and the Politics of Reality," *Sociology* 51, no. 1 (2017): 11–26, https://doi.org/10.1177/0038038516656983.

[88] Ibid. Other scholars have also identified problems with this influential thesis, which rejects the supposed metaphorization of Indigenous struggles viewed as somehow diluted if linked to other sites of oppression. In particular, this argument is problematized as overlooking the concreteness of the

But what does it mean to decolonize the harmony discourse and desegregate its peace scripts? Indeed, one limitation of the explosion of decolonial unsettling of Eurocentric epistemology and cosmology resides precisely in this scholarly trend's undertheorization of the concept of the "common good." Claire Gallien asks, "How is the common good created and sustained under conditions of pluriversality, if the languages, concepts, methodologies are all different, and if the starting point is the recognition that what counts as beneficial to one may very well be detrimental to the other? In other words, how does one relate in the pluriverse?"[89] In between the pragmatism of the harmony business and the totality of decolonial imaginaries, however, I met people whose religiosity and spirituality offered a resource for peacebuilding, an ethics of the common good, and openings to survivalist decolonial love that resist the forces of despair and division. Neither religion/culture nor peace/harmony, in those contexts, are decolonized, intersectional, woke, or feminist. Yet they work (albeit not systemically or revolutionarily, nor necessarily with a concrete path to effect structural transformation)[90] to reduce people's precarity. "Existence is resistance," as the Palestinian cry of *sumud* or "steadfastness" captures. This existence as resistance does not mean relinquishing political and cultural claims. Still, it does reveal that the refusal to disappear also constitutes an agentic challenge to the neoliberal concept of resiliency as depoliticized adaptability to ever-worsening conditions.

Resistance as Cultural Lifelines

The question of cultural excavation and the celebration of Indigenous cultures was foregrounded by representatives of the BARMM I met in the

---

legacies of slavery and reducing them to the logic of settler colonialism. See Tapji Garba and Sara-Maria Sorentino, "Slavery Is a Metaphor: A Critical Commentary on Eve Tuck and K. Wayne Yang's 'Decolonization Is Not a Metaphor,'" *Antipode* 52, no. 3 (2020): 764–82, https://doi.org/10.1111/anti.12615 or https://onlinelibrary.wiley.com/doi/10.1111/anti.12615.

Border thinking is, of course, a concept first associated with the work of Gloria Anzaldúa. It finds resonances in the work of decolonial theorists who identify border thinking as "the epistemology of the exteriority; that is, of the outside created from the inside." See Walter D. Mignolo and Madina V. Tlostanova, "Theorizing from Borders: Shifting to Geo- and Body-Politics of Knowledge," *European Journal of Social Theory* 9, no. 6 (2006): 205–221 (206).

[89] Claire Gallien, "A Decolonial Turn in the Humanities," *Alif: Journal of Comparative Poetics* 40 (2020): 28–58 (29), https://www.jstor.org/stable/26924865.

[90] See my analysis in chapter 7 of the discourse of scaling up and its inherent limits regardless of its rhetorical pretenses.

summer of 2018. We met in the autonomous Muslim region near the official buildings of the BARMM in a large outdoor exhibit involving the reconstruction of various Indigenous legacies that looked like a cross between a museum and Disneyland. Visitors could purchase Indigenous crafts, fabrics, and baked goods. In the words of one BARMM official, "This 'Indigenous village' is meant to be a showcase of cultural diversity, every year." Visitors could enjoy dressing up like sultans, sitting on their thrones, and learning about their dynasties, peace treaties, and ways of life. This amalgam village of fossilized pasts indeed celebrates Indigenous presences and knowledges in Mindanao, but it was not a form of the Indigenous resurgence exemplifying decolonial praxis in settler colonial contexts such as Turtle Island (the Indigenous name referring to North America) where theorists interpret any use of settlers' justice discourse as colonialism by other means.

For example, for Leanne Simpson of the Nishnaabeg Nation in Canada, the purpose of recovering "Indigenous theory, thought, and processes" is "to rebuild Indigenous conceptualizations of nationhood."[91] It is for this reason that they underscore "resurgence and movement building," refusing to be co-opted into settlers' justice discourse.[92] Simpson's movement-building resurgence amounted to a "grounded normativity," entailing "the systems of ethics that are continuously generated by a relationship with a particular place, with land, through the Indigenous processes and knowledges that make up Indigenous life."[93] "Decolonizing" thus involves "centering grounded normativity in my life and in the life of my community, while critically analyzing and critiquing the ways in which I'm replicating white supremacy, antiblackness, heteropatriarchy, and capitalisms—structures that are ethically horrific and profoundly unjust within Nishnaabeg grounded normativity. Indigenous resurgence, in its most radical form, is nation building, not nation-state building, but nation building, again, in the context of grounded normativity by centering, amplifying, animating, and actualizing the processes of grounded normativity as flight paths or fugitive escapes from the violences of settler colonialism."[94]

---

[91] Leanne Betasamosake Simpson, "Indigenous Resurgence and Co-resistance," *Critical Ethnic Studies* 2, no. 2 (2016): 19–34 (20), https://doi.org/10.5749/jcritethnstud.2.2.0019.

[92] Ibid., 21.

[93] Ibid., 22. The concept of "grounded normativity" is attributed to the Dene Nation's scholar Glen Sean Coulthard. See his *Red Skin, White Masks: Rejecting the Colonial Politics of Recognition* (Minneapolis: University of Minnesota Press, 2014).

[94] Simpson, "Indigenous Resurgence," 22.

This approach to indigeneity resonates with Filipina ethnomusicologist Grace Nono's critical rejection of cultural archiving and ossifying.[95] Simpson's rejection of settlers' justice discourse also would reject the incorporation of Indigenous narratives into nation-state building processes of the BARMM, which is embedded in neoliberal peace/development discourse and is subsequently reliant on hermeneutical double closures. Indigenous resurgence of grounded normativity or a "fugitive escape" is nothing like the peace zones I encountered throughout Mindanao or their grounding in a discourse of a common good based in generic religiosity's appeals to generic humanity. Of course, what is "generic" always reinscribes certain dominant normativities. Likewise, the Mindanaoan context is different from the settler colonial terrain in Turtle Island because its colonial patterns are distinct and mostly attributed to domestic forms of Christian colonization from Manila, a postcolonial extension of the centuries of Spanish, Japanese, and American colonization of the Philippines. Hence, Indigenous resurgence may have different interpretations and involve different critical modes of analysis in Mindanao, especially since many IPs are Islamicized and Christianized. As Gaspar observes, IPs "have discarded the looms on which they weave patterns of their landscapes. If they still do this, it would primarily be for the tourist trade; and their weavers now use threads from the markets of lowland capitalists."[96]

Yet, as I have suggested, "peace zones" should not be dismissed as insignificant in their glimpses of friendship, love, and decolonial futures because they embody alternatives to the realities of violence. To quote Simpson once more, "creating the alternatives" is often overlooked in social justice organizing and struggles concentrating on "pressuring the state to make the changes for us." Simpson refers to this oversight as the mechanism for state co-optation of First Nations, arguing that a focus on recognition rights has been useful for neoliberal state instruments to co-opt rather than for the enhancement of Indigenous knowledges and communities.[97] Such co-optation

---

[95] Interview June 2019, Agusan del Sur, Mindanao. See also Grace Nono, "Listen to Voices: The Tao Foundation Experience," in *Intangible Cultural Heritage NGOs' Strategy in Achieving Sustainable Development: The Relationship between Safeguarding ICH and Education* (Jeon Ju, Korea: International Information and Networking Centre for Intangible Cultural Heritage in the Asia-Pacific Religion under the Auspices of UNESCO, 2018), 199–224.

[96] Gaspar, *Manobo Dreams in Arakan*, 191.

[97] Simpson, "Indigenous Resurgence," 24. For a critical engagement with the question of communal rights recognition from within the sources of the Eurocentric philosophical canon, see Nancy Fraser and Axel Honneth, *Redistribution or Recognition? A Political-Philosophical Exchange*, trans. Joel Golb, James Ingram, and Christiane Wilke (London: Verso, 2003).

"guts our resistance movements."[98] The BARMM's backing of the archiving of Indigenous histories, cultures, and knowledges entails, on an institutional level, a focus on education and curriculum, along with a sensitivity to ancestral domains and land rights central to the peacebuilding framework, although so many IPs simply cannot hold on to their lands, even if secured via certificates, because they need to sell it for food.

IP survival therefore involves efforts to reclaim cultural practices and their reshaping into a resource and curriculum. Lilian, a Christian woman, still profoundly influenced by her early formation as a layperson working with the Maryknoll Sisters, told me how her later commitment as an educator to reconfiguring IP education related to the relationships she developed during Marcos's martial law era as a peace and justice worker with specific tribes in the Davao region. She was aware of how the Church was complicit with the erasure of Indigenous knowledges, how children were taken away to boarding schools populated by settler teachers, and how the educational system did not "incorporate the culture and traditions of the Indigenous children. They were learning the dominant culture and adapting to the dominant culture and being—in a way—absorbed by the dominant culture. They were losing their languages and cultural identities."[99] This familiar story of the erasure of cultural and linguistic knowledges ("epistemicide," in the language of decolonial scholarship) also coincided with bullying that further pushed IPs to repress their cultural identities and thus accelerated the processes of colonial erasure.

Cultural reclamation then becomes a resource to counter the pain of cultural bullying. Indeed, this reclamation is far from the intention that Indigenous resurgence scholars like Simpson articulate. For them, resurgence amounts to the centering of gender, queerness, and the creation of "constellations of connections with . . . radical communities of color."[100] Nevertheless, cultural reclamation reconnects Indigenous communities with their ancestors and their practices. While this grounded normativity may not also include "Indigenous criticality," involving a cross-cutting analysis of neocolonialism, it does offer "a different way of living in the world," which amounts to "an emergent and generative process."[101] Certainly, learning how

---

[98] Simpson, "Indigenous Resurgence," 24. For a critique of the recognition discourse, see also Coulhard, "Red Skin."
[99] Interview #93, Davao, June 2019.
[100] Simpson, "Indigenous Resurgence," 30–31.
[101] Ibid., 27.

to access and commune with ancestral knowledges as resources for physical/cultural survival is not what Simpson expects in terms of an ultimate mass resurgence (or a place-based Indigenous internationalism), but it is still generative, especially in a context that cannot be defined through the binaries of settler colonialism. The "settlers" are not White and they carry traces of their own colonization. The violence they inhabit relates in particular to their Christianity and to Manila's underpinning policies of Christianizing Mindanao and minoritizing Muslims.[102]

Lilian, carrying with her a self-reflexivity regarding the legacies of Christian settlers in Mindanao and the violence endured by Indigenous communities, told me that "Vatican II really helped [her and her associates] realize that there is another model of church [informing] a theology of struggle."[103] With the consolidation of a legal basis after passing the Indigenous Peoples Rights Act, which eventually offered an opening for tribal culture bearers to shape their curriculum, Lilian felt compelled to work, together with Datus, on reshaping and reimagining tribal education. Because of its elicitive nature working closely with tribal leaders who are holders of Certificates of Ancestral Domains, this process is dialogical. The legal framework underpinning Davao's Department of Education's 2011 policy (adopting the national IP education policy framework) conveyed the familiar neoliberal language: "This policy framework is intended to be an instrument to promote shared accountability, continuous dialogue, engagement and partnership among government, IP communities, civil society and other education stakeholders."[104] In responding to my question about her facilitation of the process as a Christian, non-Indigenous settler, Lilian underscored that, even if the Church failed to take into account its own violent history against IPs, the tribal leaders welcomed "whatever could help their children."[105] This line, echoed in my focus groups and interviews with tribal leaders, deflates radical purism once again in the face of complex historical contingencies. Instead, my interviewees told me about their concrete dialogical efforts to create developmentally and culturally appropriate educational materials, a continuing parent and community education program, the piloting of culturally appropriate education, and the building up of tribal resource centers as a result

---

[102] See chapter 1 for an overview of this point.
[103] Interview #93.
[104] See Mark Anthony Llego, "National Indigenous Peoples Education Policy Framework," DepEd Order No. 62, s. 2011, August 8, 2011, https://www.teacherph.com/national-indigenous-peoples-education-policy-framework/.
[105] Interview #93.

of ongoing research and the documentation of tribal history and its cultural legacy in its varied expressions.

These efforts are evidence of resilience through cultural regeneration and the redressing of systemic obstacles for Indigenous children to gain access to culturally appropriate and empowering education, enhancing their sense of self-worth in the face of bullying and other hardships. Indeed, resilience is often appropriated and deployed as a neoliberal mechanism whereby marginalized communities reveal their capacity to adapt to and persevere in precarious conditions and endure further erosion of their humanity. But resiliency concretely also exceeds its discursive force, if not in the form of Simpson's critical Indigeneity, then in the form of a dialogic engagement that disrupts, however minutely, cultural fossilization and archiving in texts (or the "Indigenous Village" spectacular) and combats the entwined erosions of their health, land, and culture.

Therefore, the curriculum development process navigated legal and policy shifts and involved elicitive and dialogic mechanisms. All decisions, the linguistic reframing of oral languages into scripts by professional linguists, and the stories collected by tribal leaders to enhance communities' historical and cultural memories were likewise subjected to community validation during public sessions with culture bearers. Lilian, who was adopted as a daughter into one of the tribes, came to the initiative with a child-centric approach to education. She explained her elicitive methodology:

> We have asked the tribal elders, "What do you want when you say you want the children to know your culture? What do you want them to know?" And then we ask, "How did you learn when you were a child?" . . . So, we ask the old people how they learned. Even Amo [one of the Datus or tribal leaders involved and whom she introduced to me] said, "You know my father used to bring me to the river and teach me how to get the fish. My father used to bring us to the fields and talk to us about how to do things on the farm and then brought us to the forest [to] look at trees—what were the trees good for? What leaves were medicinal?[106]

The tribal learning center is a pilot for exploring ways of pushing upon the rigid boundaries of a structured educational system and its notions of classrooms and learning spaces. Lilian and the IPs' educational advocates

---

[106] Ibid.

stressed the importance of "an environment outside of the classroom where learning should take place." The questions, then, are:

> How do you design a learning center for the tribe? Will you have the same kind of Department of Education standard classroom? And then second, the designing should be gathered from the community. But even if some things are appropriate to the culture, such as basket weaving, where we come in as educators is by asking, "What is appropriate to the child?" So . . . we are saying that if the curriculum is culturally appropriate, what is our role in helping the IP community and the parents or the leaders make the curriculum child-appropriate. So, for example, the need for the child to be active, that transcends any culture. A child has to be active, that is universal. The challenge therefore is to design [a] culturally appropriate and child-appropriate learning center. So, this process in itself is empowering, it taps on their tribal wisdom.[107]

Lilian interprets the elicitive process as meaningfully dialogical and responsive to the needs of the IPs. Lucia, another active advocate of Indigenous rights and regeneration, likewise underscored the importance of appreciative inquiry, which involves discovery, dreaming, designing, and delivering—an elicitive methodology that recognizes empirical and historical constraints and contexts, but also involves dreaming a future and how such dreaming could be implemented by drawing upon available resources. Appreciative inquiry is also closely linked to another prevalent method that facilitates participants' ability to identify key people, natural processes, and their communal purposes, which, in the words of one organization, help to "manage stress and exhaustion . . . and provide ways for their interventions and engagement to be refueled by more compassion and commitments."[108] These elicitive methodologies for imagining futures once again do not conform to the decolonial register, nor do they constitute Indigenous criticality and grounded normativity or the closely related critical pedagogies and hermeneutic disobedience. However, their dialogic and intercultural forces link cultural reclamation and material empowerment in ways that concretely improve communal life. Like the relational peace islands' opening toward decolonial love, this elicitive imagining constitutes a form of alter-realism,

---

[107] Ibid.
[108] iEmergence, Facebook post, April 16, 2020.

conceptualizing alternative realities, despite and through the multiple erasures and dislocations that underpin colonial afterlives.

Lucia, more strongly than Lilian, described how Christianity's logic of conversion destroyed Indigenous ways of life. "Many Indigenous peoples till recently," she said, "when they saw a white person, they still thought of salvation."[109] This is why, consequently, she sees her activist role as working to recover cultural knowledges, focusing on relinking youth to their traditions. "The mainstream education to which Indigenous children are subjected," Lucia stressed, "constitutes a form of ongoing colonization, as does the health system." In reflecting on her own motivation, she tells me about her grandmother's murder during martial law in 1974 and how this loss taught her what it means to lose one's roots in the past. She further reflects on the Catholicism she learned at home, which involved rote memorization and obedience, and how she later discovered that this very tradition participated in the erasure of Indigenous traditions, practices, and their connectivity to their lands. This basic incongruence between professed principles and colonial crimes propels Lucia in her commitment to navigating elicitively pathways for relinking Christianized Indigenous communities to their traditions and lands without relinquishing their Christian particularity.

My earlier analysis of the elicitive method and its employment of interreligious/intercultural peacebuilding practices exposes how merely eliciting Indigenous epistemologies does not go deep enough into people's capacity to imagine decolonial emancipatory alter-realities. This capacity involves border thinking, theological disobedience, Indigenous criticality and interculturality, and a sociology of absences and emergences.[110] However, my empirical findings reveal that the interlinking of Indigenous cultural and material survival constitutes resistance, nonetheless, to the ongoing forces of colonial erasures through cultural reclaiming and physical survival.

Accordingly, the ability to educate the tribal children in the Davao region in traditional knowledges and within their tribal communities illustrates

---

[109] Interview #94, June 2019, Davao.

[110] This refers to Santos's focus on undoing silences as a way of generating the re-existence of marginalized experiences and interlinking suppressed struggles and epistemologies otherwise erased through a global imposition. A sociology of absence, accordingly, endeavors to imagine the global in a nonlinear fashion. See Boaventura de Sousa Santos, "Nuestra America: Reinventing a Subaltern Paradigm of Recognition and Redistribution," *Theory, Culture & Society* 18, nos. 2–3 (2001): 185–217, https://journals.sagepub.com/doi/10.1177/02632760122051706.

a dialogical relation between changing legal terrains around ancestral domains and Indigenous rights. Multiple actors seize upon this opportunity, from Lilian to the Datus. Processes of community validation enhance their agency, even if turning languages into written scripts and assessing "cultural appropriateness" through theories regarding "child-centric education." The outcome, a pilot tribal teaching center, does not redress the long histories of harm, loss of land and culture, and poverty and multidimensional marginalization, but it does offer a cultural lifeline, resources to mobilize for survival (including incentivizing youth to return to the tribal land from their higher learning in Davao City), and teaching centers in the communities themselves.[111] This is at a point in time when Indigenous children still need to travel long distances to schools and are subjected to abuse-prone boarding facilities, often within the Church's institutional network.

When I asked tribal interlocutors in a focus group what their aspirations were, now that their capacity to control their own lives has been enhanced due to the Certificate of Ancestral Domains and the educational reform, one female leader remarked that "her dream" is for women to be able to attain a livelihood and support their families. This response exposes the operative force of the neoliberal discourse and its violent erasures not only of pasts but also of futures (as in appreciative inquiry elicitive exercises); more critical forms of Indigeneity do not cohere with the daily struggles of people of Matigsalog.[112] Yet the very survival of their families depends on "the preservation of [their] culture and identity." For this interlinking to occur, "we all need to be educated and healthy so that we can all develop as a whole, spiritually," underscored another interlocutor.[113] Hence, decoloniality as queer, feminist, and resurgent appears alien to IPs experiencing extreme marginality, violence, and hopelessness. Yet their existence through cultural reclamation constitutes resistance in ways comparable to how the interreligious relational and geographic peace islands offer glimpses of (nonrevolutionary) decolonial love.

---

[111] Focus group with tribal leaders, Davao region, June 2019.
[112] See Bea Bolario, "Bukidnon: The Matigsalug Tribe: March 24, 2018 *Tribes in the Philippines* https://tribesinthephilippines.wordpress.com/2018/03/24/bukidnon-the-matigsalug-tribe/#:~:text=Matigsalug%20are%20the%20original%20inhabitants,to%20constant%20raids%20and%20harassment.
[113] Focus group with tribal leaders, Davao region, June 2019.

Thin, Not Queer, Religion

The operative concept and practice of decolonial pluriversality presupposes theological or religiocultural, in addition to epistemological, disobedience. Recalling an earlier point about the limits of the concept of pluriversality as a concrete framework to sustain the common good, what would it mean to employ theological and hermeneutical disobedience? It would entail delinking and queering, but also grappling with the legacies of violence internal to religious traditions and in their historical manifestations. It suggests that decoloniality cannot simply detach from the "religious" as an intersectional technology of control. People cannot theorize their religiocultural embeddedness out of existence, although they can reimagine its meaning and thresholds of belonging. For others, the decolonial means reclaiming cultural practices, meanings, sounds, and tastes from the jaws of centuries of erasure and calling all of this "culture" and "religion" in order to survive, not only as a community but also as individuals. This amounts to an intersectional approach to religion/culture and the practices of peacebuilding that interrogates the sites of overlapping oppressions and the sources of emancipatory ethicopolitical imaginations, including friendships or relational peace islands. Sometimes the horizons of the future, as I have shown, confine themselves to physical and cultural survival; this survival in and of itself is radical, even if co-opted into a depoliticizing neoliberal discourse of peace/development (and nation-state building) through the empowerment and essentialization of local traditions, conflict-resolution mechanisms, and deputizing social responsibilities.

Decoloniality for IPs aims at a regeneration of intangible cultural heritage and empowerment of culture bearers, along with their theoretical and practical knowledges. It follows that decolonizing religious peacebuilding among religious traditions implicated with coloniality requires broadening the interpretive space through theological or hermeneutical disobedience. Without such disobedience, the decolonial provincializing of Eurocentricity becomes reactionary and complicit in erasures. A refusal to link the one critique of colonialism to the other of religion and the practices of peacebuilding elevates patriarchal "literal" religious epistemology and devalues feminist religious epistemologies as somehow not authentic and thus colonized by "foreign" ideas.[114] This is what the nonhermetic double critique challenges and why

---

[114] Feminist work within the sources of tradition (in this case, Islam) is as authentic as supposed originalist or literal readings, though it recognizes the hermeneutical process as nonhermetic but in

I suggest that a decolonial approach to religion and the practice of peace is, indeed, decolonial if it is also intersectional. This does not mean adding "religion" to an already crowded field of oppressions, but rather exposing how it intersects and is entangled with all the other categories and praxes designed to establish a colonial difference but which cannot be undone simply as a matter of epistemic or theological fiat.[115] Indeed, an intersectional *doing of religion* would entail hermeneutical disobedience. What does such disobedience mean?

To respond to this question, I began by examining decoloniality as an epistemological demystification of religion's midwifery to imperial violence, but also as a theological and hermeneutical praxis that recovers resources within traditions that are emancipatory rather than oppressive and imperial. This labor matters to people who cannot theorize their embeddedness in religiosity out of existence and become abstracted from such "trappings." This recovery of the emancipatory (which in itself can be an upshot of intercultural translation) is a decolonial opening because it reveals what the colonial gaze has previously obscured. The hermeneutical act of subverting totality, of course, is not only one of retrieval but also one that is historically located and reimaginative, allowing multidirectional innovative exchanges. However, not everybody can attain such level of fluidity and hermeneutical double critique, especially not when struggling for survival—an expectation that reeks of privilege.[116] Further, basic survival is hardly enough for an elicitive imagination to disrupt the rationality that has colonized it.

The religious peacebuilders and "beneficiaries" of interreligious peacebuilding I met in Mindanao and Kenya did not engage in decolonial theological disobedience as border thinking. Instead, as the case of Silsilah exemplifies, segregationist peace and harmony scripts center religion and culture. These people simply strove to exist, and peacebuilding practices themselves came to be imbued in sacredness. The conceptions of tradition that emerged from these practices tended to be thin rather than queer or

---

exchanges with other sources of knowledge and experiences and their contextuality. See, for example, Aysha A. Hidayatullah, *Feminist Edges of the Quran* (Oxford: Oxford University Press, 2014); Zahra Ayubi, *Gendered Morality: Classical Islamic Ethics of the Self, Family, and Society* (New York: Columbia University Press, 2019).

[115] Sayyid, "Empire, Islam and the Postcolonial," 17.
[116] See Atalia Omer, "Decolonizing Religion and the Practice of Peace: Two Case Studies from the Postcolonial World," *Critical Research on Religion* 30, no. 3 (2020): 273–96, https://journals.sagepub.com/doi/10.1177/2050303220924111.

abstract and reified rather than historical and internally fluid, dynamic, and contested. The emphasis on religion as a distinct site of peace programming prevents an intersectional, hermeneutical disruption of peace. Such an intersectional approach decolonizes the very disarticulation of religion from its racialized, patriarchal, gendered, imperial, colonial, and heteronormative historical embeddedness.

In the preceding pages, I have pondered what the consolidation of religion as an instrument for promoting various agendas around peacebuilding/development does to people's accounts of their religious and cultural traditions. This flips the question "What can religion do for development and peace policy actors?" by asking "What do their programmatic footprints do to religious and cultural traditions?" They are resignified as yet another form of capital to mobilize or contain.

I consequently navigated and exposed the discursive and semiotic landscapes within which the praxis of religious peacebuilding and intra- and interreligious and intercultural dialogue (of action) unfolds and coheres with Twitter prophets rather than learned or queer religious literacies. This is not critique for critique's sake but rather an attempt to articulate an intersectional and decolonial approach to analyzing religion and the practices of peace, one that assumes survival and peace are concrete, not abstract, objectives to be debated in academic seminar rooms. The decolonial and intersectional lens cannot obscure the existence of the multiple religious actors in the Global South and their participation in survival projects, which includes investing in interreligious and intercultural peacebuilding actions in ways deeply rooted in their identities or in survival. They should not be theorized away. Analyzing their work and its spiritual dimensions offers an opportunity to rethink the study of religion, violence, and peace, their relevance to theory, and theory's relevance to them.

Why did I bring a decolonial lens to an analysis of interreligious and intercultural peacebuilding praxis focusing on the Global South? I introduced this lens because it illuminates the complicity of interreligious peacebuilding in coloniality. At the same time, I showed the constructive and life-affirming decolonial potentialities of religion and peace praxis—where the experiences exceed the ideologies. Such experiences reside precisely in the capacity to construct relational and concrete (even if non-utopian) peace islands and to imagine new intercommunal scripts, despite the forces of division, fragmentation, and poverty present in global and local histories of deprivation, exploitation, dispossession, and other modes of enduring colonial experiences.

Ironically, this decolonial possibility relies on thin conceptions of "the secular" and "the religious," which makes them still beholden to colonial pasts and the neo-imperial presences. Deciphering this irony creates productive tensions among decolonial theory, religious studies, and peace research and practice. These tensions mediate between a critique that seeks a horizon of revolutionary justice and the empirical realities and spiritualized practices of peace, Sisyphean perseverance, survival, and glimpses of decolonial love.

Index

For the benefit of digital users, indexed terms that span two pages (e.g., 52–53) may, on occasion, appear on only one of those pages.

Figures are indicated by *f* following the page number

Abu-Nimer, Mohammed, 172–73
Abu Sayyaf Group, 42–43, 45, 76, 203
Abushiri Revolt, 26–27
abyssal thinking, 5–6, 9–10, 84, 239–40, 252–53
    See also post-abyssal thinking
Adilao, Aleem Mahmod Mala (The Philippines), 77
African Instituted Churches, 36
African Union Mission, 35–36
Aga Khan Development Network (Kenya), 31
Ali, Mustafa (Kenya), 182–83, 185–86
Allen, Danielle S., 85, 233–34
al-Qaeda, 42–43, 165–66
al-Qalam Institute for Islamic Identities and Dialogue in Southeast Asia, 201, 202–7
al-Shabaab
    recruitment tools, 32–34, 167–68, 199
    targeting of imams, 186–87
American-Philippine War, 42
Anzaldúa, Gloria, 261–62
Appleby, R. Scott, 91
Arakan Manobo peoples. *See under* Lumad peoples
archbishop of Canterbury, 153–54
archbishop of Cebu, 21–22
archbishop of Manila, 21–22
archipelagic social imaginaries, 238–39, 240–41, 253, 257, 263
ARMM. *See under* Bangsamoro Autonomous Region in Muslim Mindanao
Ashafa, Muhammad (*The Imam and the Pastor*), 73

Athens Declaration United Against Violence in the Name of Religion, 100–1
Atia, Mona, 136
Autonomous Region in Muslim Mindanao. *See under* Bangsamoro Autonomous Region in Muslim Mindanao

Baldwin, James, 234–35
Bangsamoro Autonomous Region in Muslim Mindanao (BARMM), 43–44, 47–48
    Autonomous Region in Muslim Mindanao (ARMM), 42–43
    celebration of Indigenous cultures, 269–70, 271–72
    transition to, 67–68, 194–95, 196, 215–16
Bangsamoro Basic Law. *See* Bangsamoro Organic Law
Bangsamoro Organic Law (BOL)
    attitudes toward, 105–7, 120
    implementation, 45, 67–69, 194–95, 215–16
Barangay Information Network (the Philippines), 173–74
Barangay Peace and Order Council (the Philippines), 173–74
Barangay Peacekeeping Actions Team (the Philippines, 173–74
BARMM. *See* Bangsamoro Autonomous Region in Muslim Mindanao
Battle of Marawi. *See* Siege of Marawi
BBL. *See* Bangsamoro Organic Law
benchmarking. *See under* utilitarian peacebuilding

best practices. *See under* utilitarian peacebuilding
bias, anti-Muslim, 22–23, 30–33, 48, 116, 168, 170
   individuals overcoming, 111–12, 222–23, 225
   minoritization, 23, 39–41, 207, 272–73
   negative perceptions of Muslims, 35–36, 165–66, 222
   racialization, 23, 27–28, 37–38, 39–40, 170–71, 262–63
Binding, Bonding, and Bridging (3Bs), 58–59, 152–53, 227–28, 229–30
   implementation, 59–62, 82–83, 130–32, 227–28
bin Laden, Osama, 42–43
Birth of Biopolitics, The (Foucault), 53, 165n.9
Bishop-Ulama Conference (the Philippines)
   experiential relationship building, 213–15
   Mindanao Week of Peace, 25, 77, 213–14, 237*f*
BOL. *See* Bangsamoro Organic Law
border thinking, 252–53, 268, 276, 279–80
Bowler, Kate, 134
BRAVE. *See* Building Resilience Against Violent Extremism
British colonialism. *See* colonialism, British
Brown, Wendy, 53–55, 64, 84–85, 152–53, 247–48
Building Bridges Initiative Taskforce (Kenya), 96–97
Building Resilience Against Violent Extremism (BRAVE, Kenya), 182–83, 185–86, 188–90
   Community Resilience Against Violent Extremism (CRAVE), 183–84

Cadorna, Joaquin Y. (The Philippines), 22
Calvo, Father Angel (The Philippines), 212–13, 236
Canoy, Easter Luna S. (The Philippines), 75–76
Capalla, Archbishop (The Philippines), 77
Carey, Lord George, 153–54
Catholic Bishops' Conference of the Philippines (CBCP), 48–49

Catholic Relief Services (CRS), 13–17
   Catholic Integral Human Development (IHD), 14–16
   individuals within, 111–12, 113–16, 118
   partnerships, 70–71, 87–88, 109, 118, 130–32, 136, 228
   peacebuilding approaches, 58–59
   projects, 130–32, 131*f*, 150, 152
   See also Binding, Bonding, and Bridging
CBCP, 48–49
Certificates of Ancestral Domains (the Philippines), 168–69n.19, 265–66, 273–74, 277
Césaire, Aimé, 267–68
child marriage, 65–67, 129, 147–48, 177, 181–82, 248–49
children. *See* child marriage; United Youth for Peace and Development in the Philippines; youth
CICC. *See* Coast Interfaith Council of Clerics, Kenya
Coalition for Peace (the Philippines), 221–22
Coastal People's Party (Kenya), 27–28
Coast Interfaith Council of Clerics, Kenya (CICC)
   child marriage prevention, 65–67, 79–80, 177, 248–50
   as local partners, 57, 58*f*, 67, 123–24
Coleman, Monica A., 257–58
Collins, Patricia Hill, 261–62
colonialism, American. *See under* United States
colonialism, British, 22–23, 26–29, 31–34, 47–48
colonialism, Spanish, 39–41
Common Word between Us and You, A (open letter), 246–47, 248
Communal Peace Network (Kenya), 168–69, 180–81
Communist Party of the Philippines and New People's Army (CPP-NPA), 23–25, 46–47, 165–66
Community Peace Network (Kenya), 167–68
Community Resilience Against Violent Extremism. *See under* Building Resilience Against Violent Extremism

Comprehensive Peace Policy (the
    Philippines), 222
conflict mapping. *See under* utilitarian
    peacebuilding
Consortium of Bangsamoro Civil Society
    (the Philippines), 81
Constitution of 2010, Kenyan, 27–28, 31–
    33, 34, 47–48, 97
Constitution of Kenya Review
    Commission, 30–31
convivencia, 231
Cooperation Circles, 105. *See also* United
    Religions Initiative
Corregidor Massacre. *See* Jabidah
    Massacre
COVID-19 pandemic, 12, 24–25
CPP-NPA, 23–25, 46–47, 165–66
CRAVE. *See under* Building Resilience
    Against Violent Extremism
CRS. *See* Catholic Relief Services
culture of peace
    manual, 13–14
    programs, 82–83, 208–9, 223–24, 226,
        232
    "seed of peace" metaphor, 4, 77,
        133, 141–42, 223–24, 232–33,
        237–38
    seminars, 13–14, 70–71, 223–24,
        229–30, 236

Da'esh, 45, 66–67, 165–66, 196, 204–5
Datus (Filipino tribal leaders), 263–64,
    273–74, 276–77
decolonial theory
    decolonial opening/survivalist love,
        224–25, 233–36, 240, 241–43, 253
    disconnect from survival, 7–9, 17, 242,
        243, 280
    intersectional, 256–58, 259–61, 278–79,
        280
    limitations toward spiritualized
        religious praxis, 2–3, 219, 258, 263,
        268, 269, 280–81
    pluriversality, 253, 269, 278
development ethics, 55–56, 90–91
Dialogue of Action Project (Kenya),
    248–49
Dialogue Reference Group (Kenya), 97
"doing religion" (definition), 3, 87–88

"double critique" method, 260, 268,
    278–79
Drexler-Dreis, Joseph, 234–35
Dussel, Enrique, 252–53
Duterte, Rodrigo (Filipino
    administration), 24–25, 43–45,
    48–49, 51

EAI (the Philippines), 194–97
elicitive methods
    compared to decoloniality, 242, 267–68,
        276, 279
    responsibilization of individuals, 62–63,
        68, 73–74, 74f
    projects, 144, 273–76
Empowering Children as Peacebuilders
    (the Philippines), 208–9
Equal Access International (the
    Philippines), 194–97
Estrada, Joseph (Filipino administration),
    24–25, 42–43, 221–22
Ethics in Action forum, 155
evidence-based metrics. *See under*
    utilitarian peacebuilding
extremism, recruitment into
    conditions contributing to, 52, 179–80
    resistance to, 81, 163–71, 180–81, 182–
        84, 197–99, 250–51
        hermeneutical, 181–82, 190
        Preventing and Countering Violent
            Extremism (P/CVE), 171–78

Fanon, Frantz, 5–6, 84, 261–62
Farmer, Paul, 157–58
Father Bert (The Philippines), 82–83, 222–
    25, 237–38
Father Chito (The Philippines), 45–46,
    106–7, 106f, 211–12
feminist theology and theory
    disconnect from survival, 241, 242–43,
        261–62, 277
    ecofeminist, 247–48, 256–57
    intersectional, 259–60, 263–64, 278–79
    and poverty, 157–60
    See also hermeneutics, feminist
First Comity Agreement of 1898 (the
    Philippines), 40–41
Foucault, Michel, 53, 165n.9
Francis, Pope, 157

Freire, Paolo, 62–63, 157
From Enmity to Friendship conference, 80–81

Gallien, Claire, 269
Galtung, Johan, 183
Garissa massacre (Kenya), 34–35
Gaspar, Karl (The Philippines), 21–22, 78, 265, 267, 271
Gbowee, Leymah, 229–30
Ginapalad Taka, 236
Global South (definition), 5–6
Goulet, Denis, 90–91
governance, 55–56
    and hermeneutical closure, 74–76, 85, 101–3, 201–2, 232
    interreligious, 58–69
    neoliberal, 55–58
    See also benchmarking; peace islands; problem-solving
Grosfoguel, Ramón, 252–53
Gutiérrez, Father Gustavo, 157–58

harambee, 36, 50–51, 137
Haraway, Donna, 10–11
harmony business (definition), 1–2
Hayek, Friedrich, 53
    Hayekianism, 54–55
Hekima Institute of Peace Studies and International Relations (Kenya), 201
hermeneutics, Christian, 65–67, 222–24
hermeneutics, feminist, 159–60
hermeneutics, first-aid
    limitations, 168–69, 202
    online, 212
    securitization of religion, 163–64, 191*f*, 196, 197–98, 202, 204–5
    See also BRAVE; religious literacy
hermeneutics, Islamic
    critical, 184–85, 200–4, 217
    generic, 188–90, 195–96, 199–200, 201, 245–48
    Islam as "good" religion, 48, 117, 182, 187–88
hooks, bell, 261–62

Imam and the Pastor, The (film), 73

IMAN. *See* Integrated Mindanao Association of Natives
income augmentation, 129, 134–35, 137–49
Indao, Isidro (The Philippines), 78
Indigenous peoples (IPs)
    ancestral lands, 39, 46–47, 75–76, 265–66
    conflict resolution tools, 16, 109–10, 172–73, 177, 263–64, 266–67
    participation in CRS programs, 227–30
    reclamation of culture, 267, 269–70, 272–74, 275–77
    resurgence, 270–71, 272–73
    youth education, 272–77
    See also Bangsamoro Autonomous Region in Muslim Mindanao; Indigenous Peoples Rights Act; Lumad peoples
Indigenous Peoples Rights Act (the Philippines), 47, 195–96, 265–66, 273–74
Institute of Bangsamoro Studies (the Philippines), 75
Integrated Community Action against Radicalisation and Extremism, 173–74
Integrated Mindanao Association of Natives (IMAN), 118, 129, 130–32, 224
Interfaith Mediation Centre (Nigeria), 73. See also *The Imam and the Pastor*
International Partnership in Religion and Sustainable Development (PaRD), 98–99, 108–9
Interreligious Council, Kenya (IRC), 103–5
interreligious dialogue (IRD), 63–64
    assumptions of religions' goodness, 72, 73
    "generic" religion, 184–85, 193–94, 212–13, 238, 246–48
    proponents of, 77, 111–12, 117, 226–28, 237–38
    responsibilization of individuals, 73, 81, 130–32, 151
    resulting solidarity, 72–73, 152–53, 212–13, 215–16, 223–24

See also interreligious dialogue for action
interreligious dialogue for action (IRD/A), 63–64
　examples of, 77, 130–32, 152–53
　responsibilization of individuals, 71–73, 130–32, 151, 153, 226
　See also interreligious dialogue
Interreligious Solidarity Conference, 81
Interreligious Solidarity for Peace (group), 207
In the Ruins of Neoliberalism (Brown), 53–54
IPs. *See* Indigenous Peoples
IRC (Kenya), 103–5
IRD. *See* interreligious dialogue
IRD/A. *See* interreligious dialogue for action
Islamic Party of Kenya, 31
Islamic State of Lanao, 45, 211–12
Islamophobia. *See* bias, anti-Muslim

Jabidah Massacre (the Philippines), 41–42, 78–79
Jemaah Islamiyah, 42–43
jihad, 178, 180, 182, 190, 199–200, 203
　"My Jihad," 188, 201
Jolo, burning of (the Philippines), 22
Jolo Cathedral bombing (the Philippines), 48–49
Jubilee 2000, 154–55

KAICIID, 95–96, 98–100, 109
Karam, Azza, 102–3, 110–11
Kelamanon Manobo Indigenous People's Unity (the Philippines), 78
Kenya Muslim Youth Alliance, 209–10
Kenya National Dialogue and Reconciliation, 29–30
Kenyan conflicts (overview), 26–38
Kenyan constitution. *See* Constitution of 2010
Kenyan Countering Perceptions program, 201
Kenyatta, Jomo (Kenya), 36
Kenyatta, Uhuru (Kemya), 96–97
Kibaki, Mwai (Kenya), 29
Kikuyu peoples (Kenya), 27–29

King Abdullah bin Abdulaziz International Center for Interreligious and Intercultural Dialogue (KAICIID), 95–96, 98–100, 109
Kiram, Jamalul, II (The Philippines), 42
Kitanglad Integrated NGOs (the Philippines), 75
Klein, Naomi, 157, 158
Kulamanon Manobo Lumadnong Panaghiusa (the Philippines), 78

land disputes, 31–32, 59, 61–62, 229–30, 265–67
Laudato Si', 156–59
Layson, Father Bert (The Philippines), 82–83, 222–25, 237–38
Lederach, John Paul, 14–15n.32, 60n.28, 62–63, 80–81, 239n.49, 240n.52
Leguro, Myla (The Philippines), 14, 115–16
"lessons learned". *See under* utilitarian peacebuilding
liberation theology, 157–58, 256–57, 260
listening sessions. *See under* utilitarian peacebuilding
local faith actors, 94–95
Lugones, Maria, 261–62
Lumad peoples (the Philippines), 39–41, 78–79, 265–66
　Arakan Manobo peoples, 78, 265, 267
　See also Indigenous peoples
Lupong Tagapamayao (the Philippines), 62, 227–28, 229–30
Lynch, Cecilia
　on evangelization, 105n.53
　foundational scholarship of, 1–2
　on international relations through a neoliberal lens, 164–65n.7
　on missionary work, 113n.66
　on neoliberal piety, 153n.61
　on SDGs, 56n.17
　on securitization and neoliberalization, 165n.10

Macapagal-Arroyo, Gloria (Filipino administration), 24–25, 165–66
Maldonado-Torres, Nelson, 40n.59, 234n.36, 239

Malindi District Cultural Association (Kenya), 66
Manili Massacre (the Philippines), 42
Marcos, Ferdinand (Filipino administration)
　brutality of, 22, 24–25, 42
　resistance to, 48–49, 115–16, 221–22, 265–66, 272
Marshall, Katherine, 17, 153–55, 250n.21
martial law
　brutality, 24–25, 43–44, 72
　Catholic Church support of, 21–22
　personal recollections of, 22, 113–14, 115–16, 272, 276
Maryknoll Sisters, 21, 272
Mau Mau movement (Kenya), 27–29
Maute Group, 45, 211–12
Micah Challenge, 154–55
Mignolo, Walter, 251, 252
MILF. *See* Moro Islamic Liberation Front
Milligan, Jeffrey Ayala, 39–40, 216–17n.52
Mindanao Theatre Movement (the Philippines), 78
Mindanao Tri-People Youth Core (MTYC) (the Philippines), 215–16
Misuari, Nur (The Philippines), 41–42
MNLF. *See* Moro National Liberation Front
Mombasa Republican Council (Kenya), 27–28
Moore, Diane L., 10–11, 110n.60
Moosavi, Leon, 5–6
Moral Imagination, The (Lederach), 60n.28
Moro Conflict (overview) (the Philippines), 39–44
Moro Islamic Liberation Front (MILF) (the Philippines)
　Moro conflict, 41–44
　participation in peace efforts, 46, 68, 106–7, 210–11, 222
Moro National Liberation Front (MNLF) (the Philippines), 41–44, 68, 210–11, 213–14
MTYC (the Philippines), 215–16

Nagdilaab Foundation (the Philippines), 76
National Cohesion and Integration Commission (Kenya), 29–30
National Commission on Muslim Filipinos, 49–50
National Council of Churches of Kenya, 31–32
National Democratic Front of the Philippines, 24–25
National Unification Commission (the Philippines), 222
neoliberalism (overview), 53–55
Network for Religious and Traditional Peacemakers, 101–3
New People's Army. *See* Communist Party of the Philippines and New People's Army
Nishnaabeg Nation (Canada), 270
Nono, Grace, 271
Nussbaum, Martha, 16, 91n.16

Oblates of Mary Foundation (the Philippines), 237–38
Odinga, Raila (Kenya), 96–97
Operation Enduring Freedom-Philippines, 43
Osella, Filippo, 134–35

Pakigdait (the Philippines), 46
　interreligious performativity, 107–8, 210–12
　photos, 69f, 70f, 83f, 106f, 107f
　programs, 67–68
　See also URI
PaRD, 98–99, 108–9
partnership model. *See under* utilitarian peacebuilding
PAZ, 207, 212–13, 236
P/CVE. *See* Preventing and Countering Violent Extremism
Peace Advocates of Zamboanga (PAZ) (the Philippines), 207, 212–13, 236
peace camps, 206–8, 215–16, 236–37
Peaceconnect Project (the Philippines), 67–68, 120–22
peace islands, 221–25
　decolonial capacities, 233–41, 242, 253, 261–62
　limitations, 223–24, 226, 232–33, 237–39
　See also peace zones

INDEX 289

Peace Weaver Network (the Philippines), 77
peace zones, 59, 221–22, 226–27
   Ginapalad Taka, 236
   See also peace islands
Pedagogy of the Oppressed (Freire), 62–63
People Power Revolution (the Philippines), 21–22, 221–22
People's Commission (Kenya), 30–31
Pope Francis, 157
post-abyssal thinking, 13–14, 251–52, 257–58, 262–63. *See also* abyssal thinking
postsecularism (definition), 8–9. *See also* World Bank
Preventing and Countering Violent Extremism (P/CVE)
   grassroots, 173–75
   Islam, focus on, 165–67, 172–73
   preventing and transforming violent extremism (PTVE), 171–73, 177–78, 184, 190, 199–200
   responsibilization of individuals, 167, 176–77, 183, 185–87, 201
   security, 168–70, 171–77
preventing and transforming violent extremism. *See under* Preventing and Countering Violent Extremism
problem-solving. *See under* utilitarian peacebuilding
PTVE. *See under* Preventing and Countering Violent Extremism
Putnam, Robert D., 60–61

queer theology and theory
   disconnect from survival, 241, 261–62
   intersectional, 256–58, 261–64, 278

racialization, 37–38
   anti-Muslim, 23, 27–28, 37–38, 39–40, 170–71, 262–63
   gendered, 160
   of religion, 39–40, 134–35, 255–57, 262–63, 264
Ramos, Fidel (Filipino administration), 24–25, 42–43, 222, 265–66
Regalian Doctrine (the Philippines), 40–41, 43, 195–96, 265–66

relationship building
   bridging activities, 85, 96–97, 136, 137–41, 145–46, 148–49
   economic survival, 36–37, 137, 138–41, 142–43
   limitations, 36–37, 205–6, 210, 213, 215–16
   peace camps, 206–8, 215–16, 236–37
   prevention of violence, 60, 194–95, 202, 205–6, 228–29
   solidarity, 120–22, 213, 215–16, 230–31, 254
   transformative friendships, 137–40, 205, 207, 215–16, 236–37
religiocrats, 4–5, 95
   "doing religion," 98–111
   religiocratic feedback loop (figure), 126*f*
Religion and Sustainable Development meeting, 87–88
religion, "prophetic lite"
   reductionism, 3, 88, 156, 197–98, 215–16
   religious virtuosity of, 92–93, 111–12, 116, 241
Religions for Peace, 102–3, 105
religion, virtuosity of, 123–24, 127, 153, 216–17. *See also* virtuosos, religious
religious actors (overview), 119–27
religious literacy, 9–12
   "doing" rather than "knowing," 88–89, 93, 158–59, 177–78, 199–200, 205
   illiteracy, 74–75, 123–24, 179, 188–89, 193–94
   intercommunal development, 187–89, 190, 210 (*see also* hermeneutics, first-aid)
resilience (overview), 3, 219*f*
responsibilization of women, 129–34, 137–43, 175–76, 184–87, 228–30
RfP (Religions for Peace), 102–3, 105
Richmond, Oliver, 55–56, 63–64
Rudnyckyj, Daromir, 134–35

Sachs, Jeffrey, 155
Salaam (organization) (the Philippines), 206–7
Sandoval, Chela, 235–36

Santos, Boaventura de Sousa, 5–6, 251–52
Savransky, Martin, 268
Scherz, China, 151
Schirch, Lisa, 172–73
SDGs. *See* Sustainable Development Goals
Search for Common Ground, 171–72
security (overview), 163–65
seminars, culture of peace, 13–14, 70–71, 223–24, 229–30, 236
Sen, Amartya, 16, 90–91
Shari'a, 47–48, 65–66
Shifta War (Kenya), 34–35
Siege of Marawi (the Philippines), 43–46, 72, 120, 211–12
Silsilah (the Philippines), 245–48, 268, 279–80
Simpson, Leanne, 270–73, 274
Sisyphean persistence (overview), 79–80
Slabodsky, Santiago, 260
social justice
  compared to decoloniality, 267–68
  intersectional, 257–58
  neoliberal barriers to, 50, 62–63, 127, 255–56, 271–72
  prioritization of the marginalized under, 158–59, 257–58
social media, 185–86, 197–98
  Sheikh Google, 193–95, 205
  Twitter prophets, 187–89, 193–94, 211–12, 225
"soft power" of religion, 163–64, 175–76, 189–90
Soganub, Teresito, Father. *See* Father Chito
Somali Kenyans, 26, 31–36
Somaliland National League (pan-Somalia), 33–34
Somali Voices–Kenya, 197–99
Somali Voices–Next Generation, 198–99
Suacito, Miriam "Deddette" (The Philippines), 76–77
Supreme Council of Kenya Muslims, 31, 96–97
Sustainable Development Goals (SDGs), 56
  decolonial criticism of, 255–56
  ethical arguments for, 155–56
  used in partnerships, 91, 94–96, 108–9

Tanenbaum Center for Interreligious Understanding, 70–71
terrorism, nonstate
  committed by Muslims, 30–31, 42–45, 52, 165, 181
  counterterrorism, 165–66, 169–70, 172–74
  rejected by Muslims, 178–79, 180, 186–87, 199, 212
  See also bias, anti-Muslim; extremism, recruitment into; war on terror
theological disobedience, 251–52, 256–57, 275–76, 278–79
3Bs. *See* Binding, Bonding, and Bridging
traditional religious leaders (TRLs), 227–28
Treaty of Paris of 1898 (the Philippines), 42
tripartite harmony, 75–76, 77, 194–96, 266–67
  "one Mindanao," 78–79, 108, 194–95, 196–97
  "our Mindanao," 78–79, 80, 196–97
Tripoli Agreement (the Philippines), 42
TRL (traditional religious leader), 227–28
Truth, Justice, and Reconciliation Commission (Kenya), 31–32, 34–35
Tuck, Eve, 267–68
Turtle Island (North America), 269–70, 271

Ufungamano Initiative (Kenya), 30–31
UN Convention on the Rights of the Child, 155, 193n.1
UN Development Program, 98–99, 101, 102–3, 171n.24
Undoing the Demos (Brown), 53–54
UNDP. *See* UN Development Program
United Against Violence in the Name of Religion conference, 99–100
United Religions Initiative (URI), 105–8
United States
  colonization of the Philippines, 23–24, 25n.11, 39–41, 42, 45–46, 265
  influence in Kenya, 31–32, 166

postsecular foreign policy, 9n.18
    See also U.S. Agency for International Development; war on terror
United Youth for Peace and Development in the Philippines (UNYPAD), 119–24
UN Millennium Goals, 154–55
UNYPAD (the Philippines), 105–8, 119–24
U.S. Agency for International Development (USAID), 67–68, 152, 167–68, 174–75
USAID. *See* U.S. Agency for International Development
utilitarian peacebuilding
    benchmarking, 55–56, 70–73, 77, 79–80, 187–88, 201–2
    best practices, 55–56, 71, 72–73, 79–80, 102–3
    conflict mapping, 14–16, 73–74, 152–53, 267–68
    evidence-based metrics, 88, 98, 109, 156, 176–77, 201
    "lessons learned" (metric), 71, 76, 101, 187–88, 201–2
    listening sessions, 68, 69f, 70f, 106–7, 107f, 108
    partnership model, 57–58, 153–61
    problem-solving, 62–63
        examples of projects, 131f, 144–46, 154–55
        technocratic, 67, 111, 124–25, 175–76, 238, 254–55
    See also elicitive methods

Vendley, William, 102–3
Vidal, Cardinal Ricardo (The Philippines), 21–22
Vienna Declaration, 99–101
violent legacy of peace, 25–26, 77, 175–76, 240, 260–62
virtuosos, religious, 111–18, 211–12, 225, 231. *See also* religion, virtuosity of

Wagalla massacre (Kenya), 34–35
war on terror
    anti-Muslim fearmongering, 48, 165–66, 172–73, 199–200, 222
    integration of Kenya, 22–23, 27–28, 30–31, 35–36, 37–38
    integration of the Philippines, 24–25, 27–28, 37–38, 41–42, 43
Wellman, James, Jr., 163–64
Wolfensohn, James D., 153–54
World Bank, 153–55
World Faiths Development Dialogue, 153–54
World Interfaith Harmony Week, 246–47, 248
World Social Forum, 2
Wuye, James (*The Imam and the Pastor*), 71, 73
Wynter, Sylvia, 239, 261–62

Yang, Wayne, 267–68
youth
    clubs, 144–48
    girls, 66–67, 177, 248–49
    Indigenous youth education, 272–77
    "renarrating peace", 195–202
    rights, 65–66, 193–94, 207–8, 248–49
    security focus on, 193–95, 197–99, 204–10, 214–16
    vulnerability to radicalization, 120, 167–68, 193–94, 201, 204–5, 245
    See also child marriage; United Youth for Peace and Development in the Philippines

zones of being/nonbeing 5–6, 84, See Ayssal thinking,
Zones of Peace. *See* peace zones